On the Fly Guide to™
THE NORTHERN ROCKIES

A Traveler's Guide to the Greatest Flyfishing Destinations in Idaho, Montana & Northern Wyoming

Titles Available in This Series

On the Fly Guide to™

THE NORTHERN ROCKIES

*A Traveler's Guide to the Greatest Flyfishing
Destinations in Idaho, Montana & Northern Wyoming*

Chuck Robbins

Wilderness
Adventures
Press, Inc.™

Belgrade, Montana

Dedication

For Gale and Katie, fellow addicts and the best partners a fellow could ask for.

TABLE OF CONTENTS

Montana's Cabinet Range provides a scenic backdrop for anglers.

Montana *Major Roads and Cities*

© Wilderness Adventures Press, Inc.

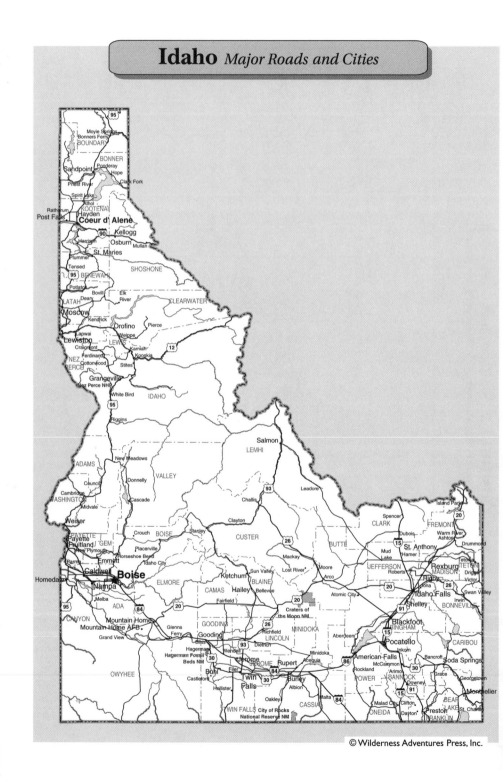

Idaho *Major Roads and Cities*

© Wilderness Adventures Press, Inc.

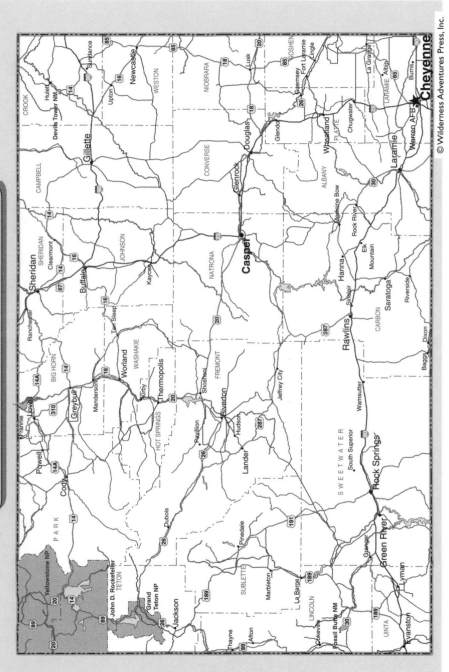

Wyoming *Major Roads and Cities*

© Wilderness Adventures Press, Inc.

The author battles a feisty Kelly Creek cutthroat.

INTRODUCTION

For the purposes of this book, the northern Rockies encompass all of Idaho and Montana and northern Wyoming; not just the vast, timber-clad mountains, but also the endless sagebrush prairie and foothills intertwined with wide, lush river valleys.

It should go without saying that this is major trout country—broad rivers, placid spring creeks, tiny tumbling mountain brooks, prairie potholes, natural lakes, and sprawling reservoirs. But the northern Rockies also play host to bass, bluegill, carp, crappie, perch, pike, steelhead, and salmon, just to name a few of the other species flyfishers might target.

While the waters covered herein are certainly good places to catch big fish, their inclusion has less to do with whether they are "hog factories" and more to do with whether they are fun places to cast a fly. You'll find plenty of famous flyfishing waters, but also a few special fisheries here and there that don't get much attention for one reason or another. Plenty of other worthy candidates didn't make the cut due to the ongoing drought, problems such as whirling disease or overfishing, or space constraints.

I've gathered as much information as possible on all of these amazing waters, focusing not just on flyfishing potential, but on the best places to camp or eat, the most comfortable and friendly motels and lodges, and contacts for additional details.

I hope your flyfishing adventures in the northern Rockies give you as much pleasure as mine have. Maybe this book will help you avoid many of the mistakes traveling anglers new to an area inevitably make.

Chuck Robbins

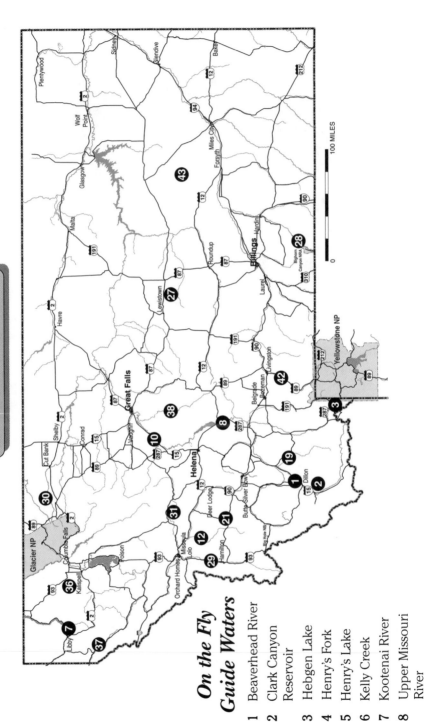

© Wilderness Adventures Press, Inc.

Montana

On the Fly Guide Waters

1 Beaverhead River
2 Clark Canyon Reservoir
3 Hebgen Lake
4 Henry's Fork
5 Henry's Lake
6 Kelly Creek
7 Kootenai River
8 Upper Missouri River
9 Lochsa River

Idaho

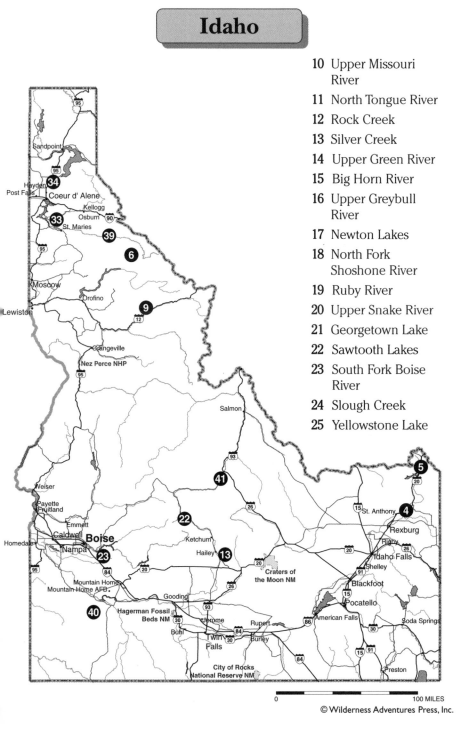

10 Upper Missouri River
11 North Tongue River
12 Rock Creek
13 Silver Creek
14 Upper Green River
15 Big Horn River
16 Upper Greybull River
17 Newton Lakes
18 North Fork Shoshone River
19 Ruby River
20 Upper Snake River
21 Georgetown Lake
22 Sawtooth Lakes
23 South Fork Boise River
24 Slough Creek
25 Yellowstone Lake

0   100 MILES
© Wilderness Adventures Press, Inc.

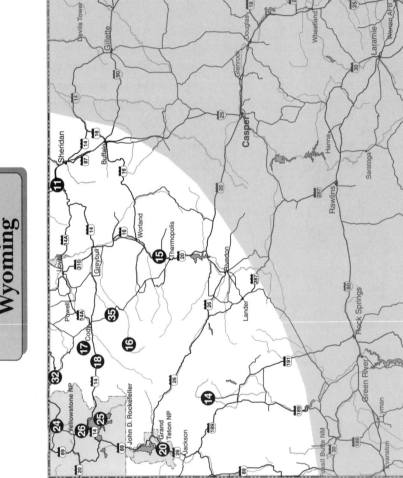

Wyoming

26 Upper Yellowstone River
27 Big Spring Creek
28 Bighorn River
29 Bitterroot River
30 Blackfeet Reservation Lakes
31 Blackfoot River
32 Clark's Fork of the Yellowstone
33 Coeur d'Alene Lakes
34 Hayden Lake
35 Monster Lake
36 Northwest Lakes
37 Noxon Reservoir
38 Smith River
39 St. Joe River
40 Southwest Idaho Bass Lakes
41 Upper Salmon River
42 Yellowstone River
43 Eastern Montana

CHAPTER 1

THE BEAVERHEAD RIVER
Montana's Best Little Big-Trout River

We live about a mile from the Selway Bridge, the nearest public access to the Beaverhead River. Until two years ago we lived on the Wheat Ranch south of Dillon, practically within spitting distance of the river. I point this out in case you detect a hint of bias in my description of this river. The Beav' is our home water, the one to which we compare all others and the one we know best.

Following a hot tip from Dillon outfitter and fishing buddy Shawn Jones (Beaverhead-Big Hole Outfitters) that the PMDs are cooking, it seems prudent to blow off lunch and head for the river. When Shawn says, "Be there around 11:30," I take it as gospel.

Good thing, too. From my parking spot I can see a pack of trout feeding eagerly in the riffle upstream; the predicted hatch is right on time. Watching the trout frolic and listening to the sounds of rushing water and traffic on Dillon's main drag, it occurs to me that this could be as good as it gets on the Beav'.

Time to get on with it. I pull on waders, put together the 9-foot, 5-weight Sage, attach 4 or 5 feet of 4X tippet to my 10-foot tapered leader, and tie on a #16 tan/yellow Comparadun.

Paul and Patti Antolosky release a nice Beaverhead brown.

I wade in at the bottom of the riffle, stopping for a moment to admire the enthusiasm of the mob sipping and splashing in the current. The trout are gorging on the
insects just as they emerge, helpless victims until their wings dry. I tune in to the feeding rhythm of the nearest fish, strip off several feet of line, false cast once, and drop
the Comparadun a foot above where the trout last swirled. It flashes beneath the fly,
but refuses to take, vanishing as quickly as it appeared.

I've grabbed the wrong pattern or the right pattern in the wrong size, or more
likely, I just didn't check the cast abruptly enough, allowing the tippet to straighten
and drag to set in. I shuffle a bit farther upstream to get a better casting angle, launch
a second cast, mend the line in the air, and check the forward progress of the fly a little harder this time. It lands softly, right on the money for a change. The long tippet
falls to the surface in little S-curves, and the fly floats drag-free right down the feeding slot, then disappears.

Trout on!

The rod bucks and jumps as the trout races upstream toward the far bank
before circling back. After a few more surges, I'm able to pull it up for a look before
the release. I estimate it at around 17 inches, which in the real world probably translates to 15 or 16 inches. Hey, I'm a male and a flyfisher, and tend to exaggerate a
little…

Anyway, fooling a trout on the second cast is not a bad way to start the day. I
continue to poke around, hooking a few, missing a few, until a bunch of kids in inner
tubes come yelling and splashing around the bend. But I'm having way too much
fun to quit completely, so I decide to check out one more spot close to town.

Wonder of wonders, Cornell Park is empty. Better yet, I quickly spy two nice-sized
browns working behind a big rock right off the parking lot. The PMD hatch has
waned somewhat. In its place, a swarm of Little Yellow Stoneflies dance over the riffles. I consider switching to a Yellow Sally, but the comparadun dangling from the
end of the tippet has been good to me so far so I stick with it.

In constant motion, the pair of trout dart and weave from one side of the pocket
to the other, every once in a while sliding up to suck a morsel from the surface.
Homing in on the closest fish, I make quick, short casts to land the fly as close as possible to its nose. And eight or ten casts later, I see the fly disappear in a swirl.

I strike hard, hoping the jolt will surprise the trout into turning and rushing
downstream before stopping to slug it out so as not to scare his feeding friend. The
brown puts up a strong fight in the fast current, causing the rod to bend almost double. Finally, the "give and go" turns my way, and I'm able pull it into the slack water
near shore. Before twisting the hook free, I lay the rod alongside to get a true reading
of its length this time. An honest 17-incher this time, a pretty hook-jawed male glow-
ing gold and amber and sporting deep black and red spots.

My tactic has apparently worked, for the other brown is still working along the
far edge of the pocket. I try the same rapid-fire casts and short drifts. Why quit a good

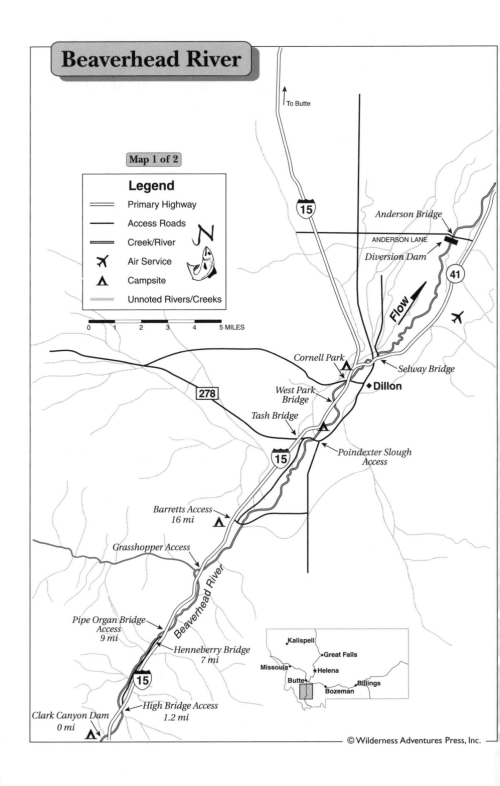

Beaverhead River

To Butte

Map 1 of 2

Legend

— — Primary Highway

——— Access Roads

▬▬▬ Creek/River

✈ Air Service

▲ Campsite

▒▒▒ Unnoted Rivers/Creeks

0 1 2 3 4 5 MILES

15 (interstate)

Anderson Bridge

ANDERSON LANE

Diversion Dam

41

Flow

Cornell Park ▲

Selway Bridge

West Park Bridge

◆ Dillon

278

Tash Bridge

▲

15

Poindexter Slough Access

Barretts Access 16 mi ▲

Grasshopper Access

Beaverhead River

Pipe Organ Bridge Access 9 mi

Beaverhead

Henneberry Bridge 7 mi

15

• Kalispell

• Great Falls

Missoula •

• Helena

Butte •

• Billings

Bozeman

High Bridge Access 1.2 mi

Clark Canyon Dam 0 mi ▲

© Wilderness Adventures Press, Inc.

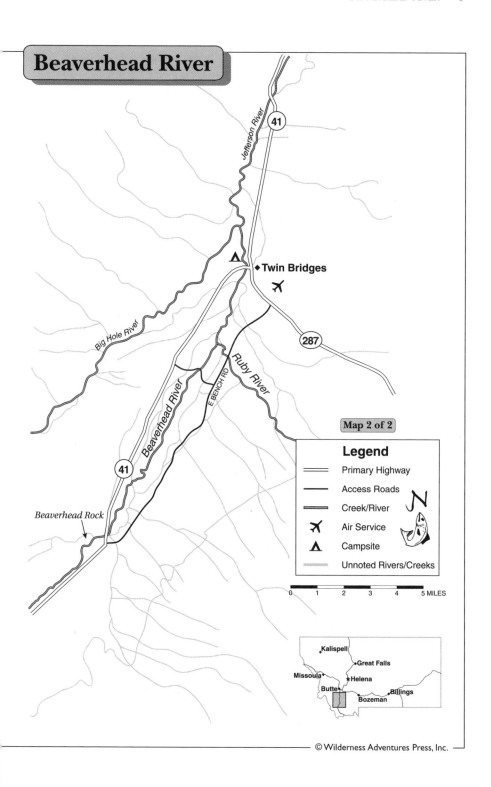

Beaverhead River

Twin Bridges

Map 2 of 2

Legend

	Primary Highway
	Access Roads
	Creek/River
✈	Air Service
⋀	Campsite
	Unnoted Rivers/Creeks

0 1 2 3 4 5 MILES

Beaverhead Rock

Kalispell
Great Falls
Missoula
Helena
Butte
Billings
Bozeman

© Wilderness Adventures Press, Inc.

thing? With twice as many casts as it took to hook the first fish, I finally see this one tilt up, turn downstream, and suck in the fly from behind.

It comes thrashing to the surface, then rips upstream. Once again, the rod bucks and the reel screams—I love that sound. A darker trout than the first, it puts up quite a fight before giving in. I am surprised to find that when measured against the rod he is nearly identical in length to the first, but far heavier.

By Beaverhead standards neither of these trout are monsters. But by my standards they are pretty darn nice trout—and that's good enough for me.

Fishing the Beaverhead

Prior to the construction of Clark Canyon Dam to supply water for irrigation, the Beaverhead was just another small, western trout river—roaring during runoff, withering under the relentless southwest Montana sun until it was often little more than ankle deep by August. Things changed quickly, though, once the dam began regulating flows and releasing water from the bottom of the reservoir. The stabilized flow created nearly ideal habitat for bugs and trout.

What had been a mediocre high-summer trout spot soon turned into a destination hotspot, especially noted for big trout. Body counts supposedly revealed a 20-inch trout for every 40 feet of bank. Such numbers, even if exaggerated, quickly put this little river high in the "hog factory" rankings. Of course, on the days when I've been skunked, such a statistic is quite humbling.

Paul Rebarchak battles a Beaverhead brown.

From Clark Canyon Dam to the town of Twin Bridges—46 miles by highway and roughly 80 by floating—the north-flowing Beaverhead travels a sinuous route. Mid-May through September (irrigation season), the river roars out of the dam gate, rushing pell-mell down a relatively narrow, willow-lined corridor to Barrett's Diversion Dam and the confluence with the water-eating East Bench Irrigation Canal. Along the way it picks up Grasshopper Creek and several strong-flowing springs.

Peak flows in this upper section during irrigation season often exceed 800 cfs. (Outfitters consider it prime somewhere between 400 and 800 cfs.) At these levels, the heavy flow and narrow, winding channel make for arduous rowing that can tax the skills of novice oarsmen.

Just south of Dillon, at Cornell Park, the West Bench Irrigation Canal further reduces the flow. By the time the river reaches Twin Bridges, it's just a shadow of what it was at the dam.

Flyfishing on the Beaverhead is primarily focused on the upper river, from the dam to Barrett's Diversion. In fact, most of the fishing pressure is actually concentrated between the Moose and Pipe Organ bridges. Hardly ever do you hear anyone, with the exception of a few savvy locals or outfitters, talk of fishing the lower river. If you do, it's usually just someone saying, "The biggest trout, you know, are up near the dam; all you catch down below are little ones."

Hogwash, of course.

Our favorite float starts at Tash Bridge just south of town and ends at Cornell Park (locals know the take-out as "Trash," so named for its location on the Dump Road). There are several reasons the float gets such high marks: it's close to home, uncrowded (on the upper river you are almost guaranteed to be part of an armada of drifting watercraft), and the fishing can be as good as it is anywhere on the river.

At normal flows, and with time out for wade fishing, the float takes anywhere from six to eight hours. True to the river's reputation for large numbers of bigger-than-average trout in nearly every pool and run, this stretch holds the potential for hooking a big one.

The fishing gets serious at the confluence of Poindexter Slough, about halfway down the float. From here until the river sweeps under the upper bridge on the Wheat Ranch, there are a series of honey holes and runs. It's from one of these that we usually boat the day's largest trout. On a good day, we expect to hook several 12- to 15-inchers, a few 15- to 17-inchers, and one or two closer to 20 inches. Such a tally keeps the "maybe we really should head upstream next time" thoughts at bay and sends us home with grins on our faces.

"In the good old days, about all you had to do was sling a #2 Yuk Bug up against the willows and hang on for dear life. Hogs were easy and plentiful beyond imagination," a 75-year-old friend likes to reminisce. It's probably something of a stretch to imply really big trout ever came quite that easily; however, even today big trout are boated regularly.

Be that as it may, one thing *has* changed and that's the *modus operandi*—at least for many of us. Most (and often the biggest) trout are hooked on small nymphs like Beadhead Pheasant Tails, Princes, Flashbacks, Copper Johns, Brassies, and various caddis and midge larva imitations in sizes 16-24. The big uglies still take a lot of fish especially during high water and/or low-light conditions, but not like they used to.

The river fishes well below Selway Bridge north of town, and there's even less pressure. This is partly due to the lack of access for long stretches and to the lingering perception that the best fishing is always closer to the dam.

At normal flows, the float from Selway Bridge to Andersen Lane takes around eight to ten hours, depending on how much time you spend out of the boat. This makes for a long day, too long for most anglers (us included), so on the few days we do stick it out we usually have the river to ourselves.

Below Andersen Lane wade access becomes nearly nonexistent unless you know someone. To float from Anderson to Beaverhead Rock, you'll probably need to bring camping gear; ditto for the river's final run between Beaverhead Rock and Twin Bridges. On the upside, your fishing competition will be thin to none. I don't know anyone who floats the river below Andersen, although there are a couple of outfitters and lodges operating there. Be aware that the reduced flow this far down makes floating significantly slower. You can, of course, fish up or downstream from the bridges as long as you remain below the high-water mark, but few anglers do so on the lower river.

Still, the fishing down there can be very good. The same fat browns for which the Beav' is famous live there, and in similar numbers. Twenty-fish days are not out of the question, especially for anglers who know their stuff and are willing to make long hikes.

The best way I know for visiting anglers to learn about the fishing on the Beaverhead is to book at least one day with a guide. The knowledge a guide has on his or her home water is almost always enlightening, though sometimes humbling.

For example, guide Shawn Jones and I fished the lower river together in early April. Spring is one of the best times to fish the Beaverhead if you're looking for some solitude. The river above Pipe Organ Bridge is closed until the third Saturday of May, but the rest of the river is more or less devoid of anglers, despite the impressive Grannom caddis hatch at the start of May.

It was a cool day, even for early April, and the fishing started off slow. But as the sun warmed the water, the fishing took a decided upturn. Through the midday hours we enjoyed plenty of action by dredging the bottom with a variety of nymphs. And not surprisingly, the most productive was a red San Juan Worm.

For me, the day's low point came when it was my turn to fish a particularly good looking run. On the first drift a feisty brown grabbed the SJW, but several subsequent drifts brought no further action. I added split shot, changed position, changed flies— no dice.

Shawn Jones shows off a nice brown.

"Give it whirl," I mumbled to Jones, "just have to be more in here." He proceeded to put on a real clinic, yanking out trout after trout. It didn't really surprise me, as he gets paid good money for knowing how to do just that, but it was still humbling. His rig seemed to be the same as mine, same flies, same indicator, same leader length. Nice guy that he is, Shawn informed me that had I been a paying customer instead of just another freeloading outdoor writer he would gladly have let me in on the secret.

Restaurants and Accommodations

And what will you have? Let me guess, the Teriyaki Chicken and Swiss sandwich and black Americano, right?"

Sara and the waitresses at the Sweetwater Café (26 E. Bannack, 406-683-4141) in downtown Dillon get a big chuckle over my mundane, never-order-anything-different eating habits. If they only knew about our Dillon dinner spot, The Lion's Den (725 North Montana, 406-683-2051), where I stick to the top sirloin. Actually, I *have* tried other items on the menu, although I admit it's been a while.

Since I'm dishing out accolades, I might as well tell you the Longhorn Saloon & Grill (8 N. Montana, 406-683-6839) is the hotspot for local breakfast lovers (not a smoke-free zone in the place). The Longhorn is also Dillon's premier cowboy bar. Until a couple of years ago the doors were open 24 hours a day year-round, but I think now they shut down on Christmas Eve and don't reopen till late Christmas Day! Times, they say, are a changin' and I guess Dillon is no different.

Las Carmelita's (220 S. Montana, 406-683-9368) serves authentic Mexican dishes, and the Blacktail Station (26 South Montana, 406-683-6611) is about as close to fine dining as you'll find in town. During the height of the summer season, reservations are a good idea, especially on weekends.

For a real fine-dining experience, check out the Old Hotel in Twin Bridges (101 E. 5th Street, 406-684-5959) for superb food, a great wine list, and genuine Old West hospitality. Reservations are preferred. Jane Waldie's homemade rolls and avocado soup with tequila and lime are absolutely delicious, as is the Shrimp, Fish, and Calamari entree.

Prime-rib and steak lovers who don't mind a bit of a drive should check out the Buffalo Lodge (Clark Canyon Dam, 406-683-5535) or the Alder Steak House (Alder, 406-842-5159).

Camping beside the Beaverhead is not your usual scenic northern Rockies experience, as I-15 parallels the river through Dillon, and below town the river is flanked by private land. However, within a short drive of the river there are many places to put up a tent.

The Bureau of Reclamation maintains several nice campgrounds around the shores of Clark Canyon Reservoir. Cameahwait, West Cameahwait, and Hap Hawkins on the lake's west side are our favorites. All provide water, toilets, sheltered picnic tables, and fire rings, but no hook-ups. And the KOA in Dillon is popular, providing all the amenities. If you don't mind roughing it, there are thousands of acres of BLM and Beaverhead National Forest land in the surrounding hills where you can pitch camp just about anywhere.

If you're looking for something more comfortable, Dillon is blessed with plenty of motels and lodges. We have friends who stay a week each summer in the Best Western Paradise Inn (660 N. Montana, 406-683-4966) and always make reservations for next year before checking out. The newly refurbished Comfort Inn (450 N. Interchange, 406-683-6831) and the recently built Guest House Inn (580 Sinclair Street, 406-683-3636) just off I-15 are also clean, friendly, and popular.

For a more intimate stay, the Back Country Angler Inn (426 S. Atlantic, 406-683-3462) offers limited lodging, but as a bonus you get Tom Smith, a longtime Montana river rat and first-class guide. And the Goose Down Ranch (Carrigan Lane, 406-683-6704) and The Inn at Pioneer Mountain Farms (3299 Anderson Lane, 888-683-5567) know all about catering to the whims of the traveling fly angler.

Nearby Attractions and Activities

With a population of around five thousand people, Dillon is typical of many small ranching, mining, and tourist towns. One thing is for sure, though. Dillon is one of the few towns left in the New West where real cowboys—authentic right down to the worn chaps and boots sporting real spurs and covered with real range dust—are a familiar sight shopping the aisles at the local Safeway. This is cow country and home base for some of the West's last and largest working cattle ranches (horse and sheep outfits, too).

The Beaverhead-Deerlodge National Forest (Montana's largest at 3.5 million acres) has its headquarters here, and the Bureau of Land Management, Bureau of Reclamation, and Montana Fish, Wildlife, and Parks all maintain field offices. The University of Montana Western campus provides the town a cultural base.

For partygoers, "Montana's Biggest Weekend" heads the year's social calendar; a Labor Day weekend party (held in conjunction with the week-long Beaverhead County fair) features rodeos (pro, amateur, and kids) and a downtown block party–style beer bash.

A big deal of another sort occurs semiannually when the local Patagonia outlet store announces a sale. License plates appear from all over, and parking downtown becomes almost impossible.

Patagonia heads a dwindling list of retail stores, however, and the growing blight of empty storefronts paints a not-so-rosy picture of the town's economic future. On the bright side, all four Dillon fly shops seem to be holding their own, despite the recent prolonged drought that has wreaked havoc with river flows and ushered in late-summer/early-fall fishing restrictions.

Ghost towns like Bannack, the former capital of the Montana territory, and Coolidge, a once-booming mining village located in the Pioneer Mountains, are well preserved and waiting to be explored.

Picking the hot fly on Poindexter Slough.

Near Wisdom in the Big Hole valley you'll find the infamous Big Hole Battlefield, where Chief Joseph and his Nez Perce army engaged in bloody warfare with the U.S. Calvary.

Nearby Fisheries

Poindexter Slough

Perhaps Montana's best-known public spring creek, the Slough actually derives much of its flow from the Beaverhead thanks to an illegal headgate built years ago by an unscrupulous rancher hungry for irrigation water. But, as they say, if it looks like, smells like, and fishes like a spring creek...

Besides, no one I know cares much one way or the other, given the more pressing challenges at hand—like how the heck to convince that trout with the muskrat-sized snout to take a fly.

As spring creeks go, Poindexter is not only challenging, but also unique in that nearly every foot is open to the public. The brown and rainbow trout are wild, free-rising, and of decent size (12- to 18-inchers abound), despite living in the shadow of I-15 and close to downtown Dillon.

Insect hatches seem to occur daily no matter what the season. In winter, midges predominate, Baetis come off heavy in spring and fall (and on almost any cloudy day in between), PMDs start popping in June, and Tricos arrive by the end of July, providing daily action until the first hard frosts of fall kill them off. Caddis and terrestrials are usually around all summer.

Many anglers, myself included, consider hunting snouts at the Slough what fly-fishing is really all about. Just being there during one of the big hatches is a treat. We have friends from trout-rich central Pennsylvania who make a week-long annual pilgrimage to fish the August Trico blitz. And apparently they aren't alone, as just this morning we noticed Pennsylvania, Michigan, Alabama, Arkansas, and Washington plates in the parking lot, in addition to a couple from Montana. Despite its popularity, the Slough is almost never crowded because several miles of equally productive water spread out the overflow.

Big Hole River

Whether or not Montana really is the "Last Best Place" I'll leave for others to ponder. But the upper Big Hole River valley—surrounded as it is by the 10,000-foot peaks of the Beaverhead and Anaconda-Pintlar Ranges—gets my vote as the last best place Montana has to offer. The upper Big Hole hosts some of Montana's oldest and largest ranches.

While the signature haystacks, built using the traditional Beaver Slide mechanism, are declining as more and more ranchers convert to modern technology, there are still plenty to see. And wildlife still abounds, despite the large number of cattle. On any given day you might spot elk, moose, mule and whitetail deer, pronghorn, bighorn sheep, mountain goat, black bear, coyote, bald and golden eagle, or just about any other indigenous critter Montana has to offer.

As if that weren't enough, there is still the river running through it all. The Big Hole truly deserves its great reputation—easy access, scenic floats, a variety of prolific hatches, plenty of big wild trout that like to eat dry flies. Toss in excellent water quality and pretty stable flows (spring runoff and extreme drought years being the exceptions) and you have a special angling experience.

The famous Big Hole Slam consists of four species of trout (brook, cutthroat, rainbow, and brown) plus arctic grayling. The river holds perhaps the last viable fluvial (river dwelling) grayling population in the Lower 48. Some anglers would add mountain whitefish to the list, but that would be the last thing a potential Slammer need fret over, since most days there's a whitey lurking behind just about every rock.

The river runs 114 miles from Skinner Lake to the confluence with the Beaverhead below Twin Bridges (headwaters of the Jefferson River). It is all trout water, but very different in character. Actually, the Big Hole can be broken into three sections: the upper river from Skinner Lake to the confluence of Wise River; the middle river from Wise River downstream to Melrose; and the lower river from Melrose to Twin Bridges.

The upper river, sinuous as a snake, flows gentle and smooth between banks covered with willow, grass, and sagebrush. It runs largely through private ranchland,

Ready to float from Divide Bridge to Melrose, perhaps the Big Hole's most popular section.

but even here a courteous request will often gain access. From Squaw Bridge to Wise River there are numerous public boat accesses, but beware, by August low flows can really put a hurt on the oarsman.

The uppermost reaches play host to brook trout and grayling, while more and more browns start showing up lower down. Some of the brook trout reach a decent size, and downright huge browns are landed on occasion. But the upper river's real appeal lies in the combination of spectacular surroundings, reduced pressure, and trout that gobble dry flies.

The stretch from the confluence with Wise River down to Melrose provides the best overall fishing, with the increased angling pressure to prove it. As summer takes hold and water levels drop, the steeper gradient makes for easier floating. Deeper pools and runs appear, providing more and better holding water and bigger trout— lots of 12- to 16-inchers, with enough bigger fish to keep things interesting.

If the dry fly fishing fizzles, the midsection provides an almost continuous array of good nymphing runs, rocks, and pockets to target with Buggers, Bitch Creeks, and various beadhead nymphs. During all but the wettest years, float fishing becomes an iffy proposition by September.

Below Glen, the number of trout per mile declines, but the average size goes up accordingly. Floats are longer in this stretch, although you'll see fewer anglers. Wading is mostly confined to the fishing accesses and bridge crossings because much of the lower river flows through private lands.

Snowmelt usually peaks in June. In heavy snowpack years, expect flows to top 10,000 cfs, making the river largely unfishable. During the hottest, driest summers, the Big Hole may experience flow and temperature problems, and in the worst drought years it has actually been closed to fishing from late summer into fall. In late summer, algae blooms can become a major hassle, especially for nymph and streamer anglers.

The famous (or infamous) Salmonfly hatch also peaks in June; often corresponding uncannily with runoff. Regardless of the flow, word of the hatch spreads rapidly and anglers and guides show up from far and wide. The ensuing flotilla of driftboats, rafts, pontoon boats creates a circus-like atmosphere and so overwhelms the river that at times it's easy to forget that it was the "fishing" that drew you here.

Other Big Hole hatches occupy my thoughts as winter turns toward spring. The March Browns usually show up toward the end of April, but the big event is the so called Mother's Day caddis hatch. At times, there are so many dancing bugs in the air that seeing through the swarm is difficult and taking a deep breath is a bad idea. Once the hatch has been around for a couple of days, it's not unusual to find trout gobbling caddis emerger patterns all day long.

Tricos appear around the beginning of August. The little white-wing blacks usually provide pretty consistent morning rises into September. During good hopper years, anglers might conceivably tie on a favorite hopper/dropper rig in July and leave it there for the rest of the season, changing patterns only when chewed to unrecognizable. Major ant falls sometimes appear late summer through early fall, and lucky anglers can find themselves suddenly surrounded by rising trout.

After Labor Day the crowds thin and the browns tend to stack up along the banks and at the base of long riffles, gorging on whatever comes along. If you hit it just right it's possible to stand in one spot, cast a short line and big, fluffy dries, and catch fat, butter-yellow browns until your arms ache.

Keep in mind that regulations are currently in place that limit the days on which out-of-state anglers and outfitters may float certain sections of river. Be sure to pick up a regulations booklet when you visit area fly shops.

Author's Tip

The Beaverhead, Big Hole, and Poindexter Slough are popular fisheries, especially on weekends. A good strategy is to fish the less visited sections of river, such as the lower Beaverhead, the upper and lower reaches of the Big Hole, and the pools and runs farthest from the parking lot at Poindexter. Early spring (pre-runoff) and after Labor Day are prime times and relatively crowd-free.

Favorite Fly

Pheasant Tail Nymph

Hook	2X short; 2X strong #16 (Dai-Riki 075), beadhead optional
Tail	Pheasant tail fibers
Body	Abdomen, pheasant tail fibers; thorax, peacock herl
Hackle	Pheasant tail fibers
Wingcase	Pheasant tail fibers

Fast Facts

Beaverhead River

Location	Southwest Montana, Dillon area
Water Type	Narrow, swift tailwater
Primary Gamefish	Brown trout, some rainbows, mountain whitefish
Best Time	Pre-runoff lower river; July upper river
Best Flies	Nymphs (#14-22), San Juan Worms, Woolly Buggers
Equipment	9-foot, 4- to 6-weight rod; floating line; strike indicators
Conditions	Typical Montana; arctic to blistering hot, calm to building-toppling wind; can and often does change fast at any season
Drive Time	From Bozeman: 2 hours
	From Idaho Falls: 2.5 hours
	From Butte: 1 hour
Directions	From Bozeman: I-90 west to Whitehall, MT; 55 & 41 south to Dillon; from Idaho Falls: I-15 north to Clark Canyon Dam; from Butte: I-90 west to I-15 south to Dillon

Local Fly Shops

Back Country Angler
426 S. Atlantic
Dillon, MT 59725
406-683-3462

Frontier Anglers
680 N. Montana
Dillon, MT 59725
1-800-228-5263/406-683-5276

Watershed
11 Pierce Dr.
Dillon, MT 59725
406-683-6660

Harman Fly Shop
310 Main St.
Sheridan, MT 59749
406-842-5868

Hemingway Fly Shop
409 N. Main St.
Twin Bridges, MT 59754
406-684-5648

Uncle Bob's
c/o Rocky Mountain Supply
700 N. Montana, Dillon, MT 59725
406-683-5565

Four Rivers Fishing Company
205 S. Main
Twin Bridges, MT 59754
406-684-5651

Montana Fly Company
150 Hwy 41 S
Melrose, MT 59743
406-835-2621

Troutfitters
Hwy. 43
Wise River, MT 59762
406-832-3212

Big Hole Outfitters
Wise River, MT 59762
406-832-3252

Complete Flyfisher
Hwy. 43
Wise River, MT 59762
406-832-3175

Beaverhead Special
19555 Hwy 91 S
Dillon, MT 59725
406-683-6811

Sunrise Fly Shop
472 Main St.
Melrose, MT 59743
406-835-3474

Guides

Beaverhead-Big Hole Outfitters
406-683-5426

Coyote Outfitters
406-684-5769

Five Rivers
406-683-5000

Diamond Hitch Outfitters
406-683-5494

Crane Meadow
406-684-5773

Flatline Guide Service
406-684-5639

Bloody Dick Outfitters
406-681-3163

Great Divide
406-683-4669

Dave Borjas
406-683-2090

Great Waters Inn
406-835-2024

Broken Arrow Ranch
406-842-5437

Healing Waters Flyfishing Lodge
406-684-5969

Centennial Outfitters
406-276-3463

High Country
406-267-3377

Horse Prairie Outfitters
406-681-3173

Montana High Country Tours
406-683-4920

Lakeview Guide Service
406-494-2585

Pioneer Outfitter
406-832-3128

Last Best Place Tours
406-681-3131

Rainbow Outfitters
406-834-3444

Greg Lilly Flyfishing
406- 684-5960

Stockton Outfitters
406-832-3138

M & M Outfitters
406-683-4579

Upper Canyon Outfitters
406-842-5575

Contacts

Montana Fish, Wildlife, and Parks
406-683-9785

Beaverhead-Deerlodge National Forest
406-683-3900

Scenic, crowd-free fishing on the Upper Big Hole.

CHAPTER 2

CLARK CANYON RESERVOIR
Montana's Best Trophy Stillwater

In mid-July, flyfishing madness peaks on the nearby Beaverhead and Big Hole Rivers. Squadrons of driftboats descend the two rivers on a daily basis, and too many times we find ourselves waiting in line to launch at popular put-ins. Yet nearby lies nearly deserted Clark Canyon Reservoir, a trophy-trout lake that offers respite from the crowds.

Just one other truck is parked near the mouth of the Red Rock River, one of our favorite spots. As we pump up the belly and pontoon boats, midges dance all around, covering nearly everything that isn't moving, including us. Looking over the calm lake surface we can see trout swirling in every direction.

We launch and kick just a few yards from shore to start fishing. For the next hour or so we manage to catch a couple and miss a few others. The hot fly, if you can call it that, is a #14 Halo Emerger. When the action slows we switch to sink-tip lines and strip #10 Sheep Creek Specials—a "never leave home without it" pattern for Clark Canyon—and the strategy runs up the score. By the time the wind forces us off, we've landed enough feisty, fat 16- to 18-inch rainbows to call it a success. Even though no real pigs have come to net you'll never hear me complain.

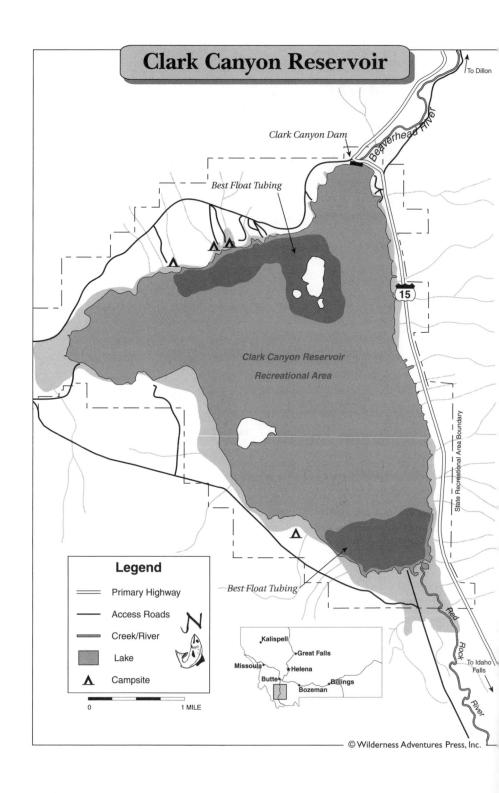

Clark Canyon Reservoir

To Dillon

Beaverhead River

Clark Canyon Dam

Best Float Tubing

Clark Canyon Reservoir
Recreational Area

15

State Recreational Area Boundary

Best Float Tubing

Red Rock River

To Idaho Falls

Legend

═══ Primary Highway

─── Access Roads

═══ Creek/River

▨ Lake

▲ Campsite

N

0   1 MILE

Kalispell
Great Falls
Missoula
Helena
Butte
Billings
Bozeman

© Wilderness Adventures Press, Inc.

If I *were* to file a grievance it would be with the wind gods for kicking us off the lake just as the first Callibaetis started to pop.

Fishing Clark Canyon Reservoir

How big are CCR's rainbows? According to local FWP fisheries biologist Dick Oswald:"The growth rate is exceptional, a (4.5-inch) rainbow stocked in June will be 14 inches the following May. Generally speaking, a three-year-old fish will average 21 inches and range between 5 and 7 pounds at maturity. The biggest run 12 pounds or so. In addition, whopper brown trout reside here and occasionally come to the fly."

Many fly anglers feel Clark Canyon is Montana's best big trout lake. Best is always debatable, but I can certainly testify that the lake's healthy population of fat rainbows are robust enough to keep us smiling.

Flyfishing kicks off when the ice breaks up, typically late March to mid-April. We rig a sparse black marabou leadhead jig under a big strike indicator, toss the mess out next to the ice shelf, and let it sit. My wife Gale refuses to participate, noting that, "It's highly questionable to call that flyfishing." Admittedly hard to disagree, but the rod *is* a fly rod and the line *is* a fly line, and the fly of choice is hand-tied and sports real feathers.

While we're out there kicking around, Gale is likely to be paddling her pontoon boat along the receding ice shelf, playing her favorite ice-out game: toss a weighted streamer up onto the ice, drag it ever so slowly to the brink, and then allow it to fall over and sink. Her theory is that winter-starved trout like to lurk just under the edge waiting to ambush hapless victims. Why this method works is open to debate. Despite close scrutiny, I've noticed very few choice morsels slowly crawling across the ice and falling in, and even fewer trout waiting to pounce. But for whatever reason, it does work.

Once spring actually arrives, we switch to more traditional methods. Using sink-tip or full-sink lines, we strip or slow-troll various nymphs, Sheep Creeks, red or olive Mohair or Rabbit Fur Leeches, or olive, brown, or black Woolly Buggers. Sometimes, we anchor over a promising spot, suspending nymphs and/or midge patterns beneath a strike indicator.

The warming temperatures of May and June trigger the Callibaetis hatch. Assuming the hatch starts before the ever-present wind comes up, pitching emergers and dun patterns in the path of cruising trout works well. A Bubble Top Nymph tossed out among the risers can be effective. Should that fail, we rig three Bubble Tops on a sink-tip line, let the whole rig sink, and then slowly strip it back to the surface.

Damselflies start to show in July and sometimes stay through August. When they are active the trout naturally key on the big nymphs, particularly around submerged

Fishing with an audience at Clark Canyon.

willows at the south end of the reservoir in the Red Rock River channel. Rig your favorite damsel nymph or a Sheep Creek—exact fly pattern isn't nearly as important as using a method that mimics the swimming movement of the active nymphs—and bring it in slowly with long pauses between strips. On the rare day that the rainbows decide to chase airborne adult damsels, a pattern that imitates the adult can be especially dangerous.

By fall, the majority of the locals turn their attention to hunting, and diehard fly-fishers often have the big lake all to themselves, or close to it. As water temperatures cool, the same patterns that worked in spring now come back into play, and midges and Callibaetis hatch throughout September and into October. Be careful early and late in the season, though, as water temperatures can turn deadly cold, and sudden, unexpected swimming is not recommended. Wind in any season is a CCR trademark, so stay alert.

Accommodations and Restaurants

Camp Fortunate, where Lewis and Clark's miraculous meeting with Sacagawea's brother Cameahwait took place, now lies submerged. But weary anglers in need of a campsite need not despair, as several developed campgrounds surround the lake: Lonetree and Hap Hawkins on the south shore; Horse Prairie, Cameahwait, West Cameahwait, and Beaverhead on the west shore and at the dam.

Hap Hawkins, Horse Prairie, and the two Cameahwaits hold the most appeal since they are farther from I-15 and its attendant traffic noise. All are free and offer great views, easy lake access, individual sites suitable for tent, trailer, or RV, sheltered picnic tables and fire rings, water, vault toilets, and garbage collection. There are no hook-ups or dump stations, though. The Beaverhead Marina on the west shore provides gas, groceries, and ice, but due to the extended drought and the resultant limited boating activity, there's some question as to how long it will remain open.

We try to make it a point to plan any fishing excursion to CCR around the dinner hour, so we can head up the hill to the Buffalo Lodge Steakhouse and Saloon just east of the dam. Here, we sip a beverage or two, exchange tall tales, order up a top sirloin or prime rib (depends on the night, as prime rib is usually a weekend special).

If we're feeling up to a longer drive, we might head to the Horse Prairie Hilton in Grant, 12 miles west of the dam on MT 324. The Hilton features a rustic, charming atmosphere and good down-home cooking. Friday and Saturday nights feature prime rib, and the steak is good anytime. Across the road, the one-of-a-kind Canvas Café (really Old West, as meals are served in a wall tent) offers what can only be described as hearty and delicious breakfast, lunch, and dinner specials. There's no bar service here, but I can't imagine anyone leaving hungry or disappointed.

You can, of course, bag camping and stay in Dillon, just 18 miles north via I-15. (For more information on services in Dillon, see chapter 1.)

Author's Tip

The submerged Red Rock River channel, especially near the south end of the reservoir, is almost always a good place to start. Another hotspot is the big island just west of the dam. In spring, the windward shore (normally the marina side) can be good because the wind drives bait close to shore and the trout follow. Bear in mind that the severe drought over the past several years has greatly impacted the reservoir. The current pool size is but a tiny fraction of normal, and while nobody likes to watch a big reservoir slowly dying, it does mean more trout in less water and that should translate into somewhat easier fishing.

Favorite Fly

Sheep Creek Special

Hook	2XL, #6-14
Tail	None
Body	4 or 5 turns of brown hackle at bend, then dark olive chenille
Wing	Small bunch of mallard flank fibers extending over back

Fast Facts

Clark Canyon Reservoir

Location	18 miles south of Dillon, Montana, on I-15
Water Type	Manmade irrigation reservoir, water levels fluctuate according to snowpack and irrigation usage
Primary Gamefish	Eagle-strain rainbow trout; some to 12 pounds
Best Time	Ice-out, later in May and June, and just prior to freeze-up
Best Flies	Midge patterns, flashy nymphs, leeches, and Buggers
Equipment	9-foot, 6-weight rod; floating, sink-tip, and full-sink lines
Conditions	Frigid cold to blistering hot; always expect wind
Drive Time	From Idaho Falls: 2 hours
	From Bozeman: 2.5 hours
	From Salt Lake City: 5.5 hours
Directions	From Idaho Falls, I-15 north to reservoir, 18 miles south of Dillon; from Bozeman, I-90 west to Whitehall, MT 55 & 41 south to Dillon, I-15 south to dam; from Salt Lake City, I-15 north to reservoir, 18 miles south Dillon.

Local Fly Shops

Back Country Angler
426 S. Atlantic
Dillon, MT 59725
406-683-3462

Troutfitters
Hwy. 43
Wise River, MT 59762
406-832-3212

Frontier Anglers
680 N. Montana
Dillon, MT 59725
1-800-228-5263/406-683-5276

Complete Flyfisher
Hwy. 43
Wise River, MT 59762
406-832-3175

Watershed
11 Pierce Dr.
Dillon, MT 59725
406-683-6660

Sunrise Fly Shop
472 Main St.
Melrose, MT 59743
406-835-3474

Harman Fly Shop
310 Main St.
Sheridan, MT 59749
406-842-5868

Montana Fly Company
150 Hwy 41 S
Melrose, MT 59743
406-835-2621

Hemingway Fly Shop
409 N. Main St.
Twin Bridges, MT 59754
406-684-5648

Big Hole Outfitters
Wise River, MT 59762
406-832-3252

Uncle Bob's
c/o Rocky Mountain Supply
700 N. Montana, Dillon, MT 59725
406-683-5565

Beaverhead Special
19555 Hwy 91 S
Dillon, MT 59725
406-683-6811

Four Rivers Fishing Company
205 S. Main
Twin Bridges, MT 59754
406-684-5651

Guides

Beaverhead-Big Hole Outfitters
406-683-5426

Flatline Outfitter and Guide Service
1-800-222-5510

Five Rivers
406-683-5000

Crane Meadow
406-684-5773

Contacts

Montana Fish, Wildlife, and Parks
Dillon Field Office
406-683-9785

Beaverhead-Deerlodge National Forest
406-683-3900

Working the shoreline of Clark Canyon Reservoir.

CHAPTER 3

HEBGEN LAKE

Gulper-Fishing Capital of Montana

In the southwest corner of Montana, just northwest of West Yellowstone and a little west of Yellowstone National Park, lies Hebgen Lake. It's a large lake with a reputation for growing lunker brown and rainbow trout, but a lot of flyfishers are drawn here for its more modest-sized "gulpers."

Early one August morning, by prior arrangement, we met some friends from the East who had never fished Hebgen. Our two-vehicle caravan left from the Madison River Fishing Company in Ennis, heading south on US 287 and then hooking a right toward West Yellowstone on US 191 for about 6 miles to where the highway crosses the Madison River. In short order, we hung another right onto FR 291, which leads to the Madison Arm Resort and Campground. We sped down the dusty dirt track for 5 miles to where it makes a sharp bend to the right; just as it swings left again, a two-track juts off into the lodgepoles, shortly dead-ending. There are a lot of spots to access the Madison Arm of the lake, this just happens to be the one we picked for our morning gulper hunt.

Hebgen's weedy bays produce the thickest swarms of Trico and Callibaetis spinners, thus attracting the biggest pods of marauding gulpers. Gulper fishing on

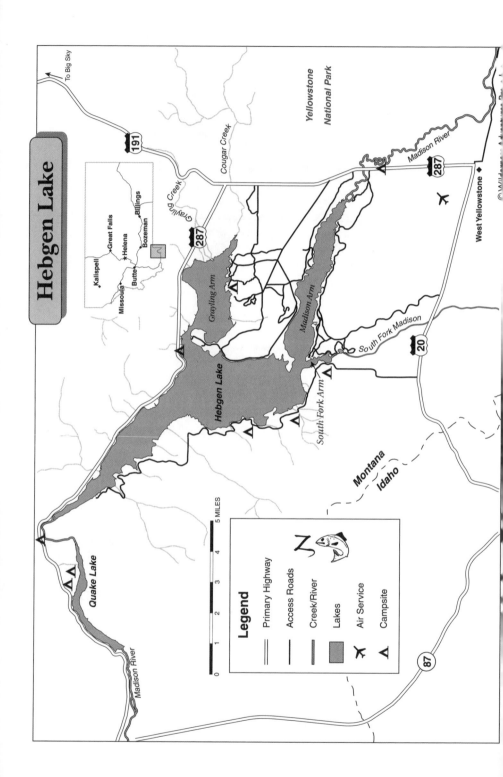

Hebgen's Madison Arm isn't really a secret any more, so despite being a large bay surrounded by national forest, the competition here for the biggest pods often gets intense.

Such was not the case this morning, though, as the crowd was thin—a Boston Whaler, three tubers, a pair of driftboats, a rubber raft, and the four members of our group. So much for the good news.

The flip side was an unusual lack of aggressively feeding fish. There was no wind to speak of and literally millions of flies; the Trico spinners were thick, and the Callibaetis swarm was absolutely unreal. Yet the gulpers never really podded up. Two or three fish would start munching bugs, but before we could manage to kick into range, down they'd go. Several minutes would pass with nary a swirl.

I managed to land two rainbows, just 12-inchers, and I'm chagrined to write that both somehow hooked themselves after grabbing a resting fly while I sat numbly in my tube, anxiously scanning the water farther away for serious gulpers. Our friend Patti finally hooked and netted a single fish that looked like the typical gulper, an 18- or 19-inch, football-shaped rainbow. But that was it for the day, not exactly the type of fishing we'd been bragging about to our friends before the trip.

A week later, Gale and I stopped by again on our way to Yellowstone Park. We launched from the same spot at roughly the same time of day, again on calm, relatively crowd-free water.

The hatch came off as scheduled; clouds of Tricos followed by another unbelievable swarm of Callibaetis, just like the week before. But this time the trout jumped all over the Tricos and stayed on top to gulp Callibaetis until wind killed off the surface action around noon. We landed five or six trout each—fat, healthy rainbows of average size (15 to 18 inches). And I was lucky enough to net a brown that pushed 20 inches. The hot combination was a #16 Red and Black Parachute Ant trailing a #18 Flashback Pheasant Tail Nymph. All but one of my trout ate the nymph, but I like to think the ant drew their attention. Gale landed a couple on the ant, and the rest of her hook-ups came on the trailer.

Fishing Hebgen Lake

I like to rig a long, powerful rod like my 9-foot, 6-weight Sage RPL with floating line, 15 to 20 feet of tapered leader, and 4X or 5X tippet to match the fly.

The term "gulper" presumably describes the sound cruising trout make when sucking floating insects from the surface of a lake. In this case, Trico and Callibaetis spinners get the gulper action going in late July and early August. Mornings are best, but there's no need to launch by dawn's early light. The Trico spinners usually fall by around 10:30 a.m., and the trout pod up and start gulping. The feeding orgy really revs up when Callibaetis spinners hit the surface.

At first glance, solving the gulper riddle seems straightforward: toss a fly that mimics the zillion naturals out into the cruising lane of an oncoming gulper, watch it disappear in a swirl, and then raise the rod and wait for that powerful surge. If only it were that easy.

Forgetting for a moment that the wind can, and often does, kill the whole deal before it ever gets started, the double hatch and incredible number of naturals makes for tough hatch-matching. No matter how lifelike your fraud, having a fish select it from the horde of insects is like hitting the lottery.

Then consider the gulping trout, which don't necessarily gulp in a pattern that you can anticipate. Some do, many more don't. And those that don't can be a royal pain to get a fix on. Meanwhile, you are kicking like hell in a belly boat—surely one of the slowest forms of locomotion yet devised—while the pod gulps randomly here and there, just out of good casting range.

One way to tip the odds in your favor is to use a dropper. A #14-20 Flashback Pheasant Tail, Beadhead Prince, Copper John, or similar fly running 10 to 12 inches below your dry fly will do wonders for your catch rate. Another thing to keep in mind is that when the Callibaetis spinners start to fall, gulpers often key in on the bigger flies. A #14 Spent-Wing or Parachute Adams can be deadly.

Cluster patterns such as LaFontaine's Buzz Ball or even a good-sized Griffith's Gnat often work better than mimicking a single fly. More often than not, though, it's something offbeat that saves my butt—an ant, hopper, cricket, caddis, or attractor dry fly. But even with a dry fly that stands out from the crowd of naturals, I rig a trailing

A typical Hebgen gulper.

nymph. When the trout are keyed on tiny Tricos that cover every square inch of lake surface, there is no doubt the nymph takes the most fish.

Although summertime gulpers get most of the attention, Hebgen actually starts fishing well right after ice-out, usually mid- to late May. We like to set up camp at Lonesomehurst Campground (7 miles west of West Yellowstone, turn right onto FR 1718 from US 20) on the South Arm and target the resident browns or the rainbows staging there prior to the spawning run up the South Fork Madison River.

Prolific midge hatches, and less prolific though still productive mayfly emergences, often bring trout up near the surface, particularly at dawn and dusk. We like to troll or strip a pair of chironomid nymphs tied 18 inches apart on 3X tippet on a full-sink line. If there's a chop on the water, simply hang the pair near the bottom off a strike indicator. The surface action can be awesome early and late in the day. When the trout start swirling it's time to try some sort of cluster fly, like a #14-18 Buzz Ball or Griffith's Gnat. When the action slows on the small stuff, strip #6-10 Conehead Woolly Buggers, Seal Buggers, or Clousers in olive, brown, black, or chartreuse.

Restaurants

The Grizzly Bar and Grill (1409 US 287 in Cameron, 406-682-7118) is a famous watering hole that attracts quite a crowd on most summer evenings. Parched guides and clients, trout bums, cowboys, and other assorted barflies descend upon the rustic log saloon en masse to slake a thirst (full bar, good selection of microbrews, and an extensive wine list), spin yarns, and just have fun. It's a bit of a drive from Hebgen, but the Grizz food groupies rave about the steak, prime rib, and seafood. Having said that, Gale and I usually opt for burgers, which are excellent.

Closer to the lake in West Yellowstone, the Three Bears Restaurant (215 Yellowstone Ave., 406-646-7811) turns out good vittles, and eating there can be quite entertaining. On our way home to Dillon after several days of fishing and camping beside various rivers and lakes within the so-called Golden Triangle, hunger pangs drove us to the Three Bears for dinner. I ordered the usual steak and baked, while Gale opted for the daily dinner special, Pork Prime Rib. I dug in when the food arrived, but stopped when I glanced up to see Gale eyeballing her meal with a peculiar look.

"Something wrong?"

"Look at this meat, it's all fat!" she spat, shoving the plate my way.

"What?"

"You heard me, it's nothing but fat!"

Hoping to avert a scene, I grabbed the plate for closer inspection. It looked to me like the purest white cut of meat I'd ever laid eyes on—every bit as white as uncooked pork fat, but meat just the same. To make sure, I sliced it in half; meat so tender the knife nearly fell through on its own.

"Maybe you should put your glasses on and try this. Sure looks and acts like meat to me, and pretty damn good and tender meat at that!"

After a meal in West Yellowstone, stop in at one of its two excellent bookstores: the Book Worm (14 Canyon) or the Book Peddler and Cappy's Bistro (106 Canyon). Across the street the Arrowleaf Ice Cream Parlor serves, among other chilly delights, the tastiest, coldest frozen yogurt around.

Accommodations

Don't plan on pitching camp beside the Madison Arm, as much of the shoreline is a day- use-only area. The Madison Arm Resort, Campground, and Marina (406-646-9328) is the closest place to camp, but it's way too busy in summer for our taste. Baker's Hole, 3 miles north of West Yellowstone off US 191 (406-646-7637) is a USFS campground offering RV and tent sites, toilets, water, fire rings, grills, picnic tables, and a dump station. It's not too far from the fishing, but also tends to be crowded in summer.

Lonesomehurst Campground, 7 miles west of West Yellowstone off US 20, ranks high on our list of the best USFS campgrounds, but is a bit of a drive. Still, it's generally quiet, well maintained, and to our way of thinking, well worth the driving time. There are 26 sites, grills, fire rings, picnic tables, and water, but no hook-ups or dump station. Within the surrounding national forest, there are many great spots to camp, some developed and some not.

When a warm bed sounds better than the cold ground, we've stayed in West Yellowstone at the Gray Wolf Inn and Suites (250 S. Canyon, 406-646-0000), Fairfield Inn (105 S. Electric, 406-646-4892), Kelly Inn (104 S. Canyon, 406-646-4544), and Three Bear Lodge (217 Yellowstone, 406-646-7353). All have clean, comfortable rooms and friendly service. During the height of the summer season, especially on weekends, make your reservations well in advance.

Nearby Fisheries

Yellowstone National Park

Within Yellowstone National Park lie enough lakes, rivers, and streams to keep a dedicated flyfisher busy for a lifetime. Just the major rivers—the Madison, Firehole, Gibbon, Lamar, Gardner, Yellowstone, Bechler, and Lewis—are enough to keep one hopping all season. While the crowds have spoiled it somewhat, we still suck it up and fish, though blinders and earplugs should probably be de rigueur.

We were fishing the Madison above Nine Mile the other day when dad and mom and the kiddies strolled up beside us and began skipping stones; the same day on the Firehole two anglers did everything but shove Gale out the way to cast where she'd been fishing for some time. Yikes!

In July and August, when the crowds are at their thickest and the roads are clogged with monster RVs, we drive in and out of the park before or after the motor madness begins and hike as far off the beaten path as possible. One nice thing about fishing the Park when the hordes drive you crazy is that there's always somewhere else to go. Bad news at the Firehole? Head for the Madison. Too crowded? Head up to Gibbon Meadows, or over to the Lamar. Keep moving, and sooner or later you'll find a quiet place to cast.

Despite the pitfalls, no matter how often we fish the Park we almost always encounter something new. This past spring we fished the upper Gibbon meadows, a place where we always catch trout, albeit on the smallish side.

Suddenly, tight to the grass, a big snout appeared to suck down a morsel. Then again. On the hunt now, I waded carefully down to where I could execute my best reach cast. Not quite hitting the mark, I made a few quick adjustments to bring the floating fly into position over the target. Wonder of wonders, up came the big snout and down went the floating fly. I reared back and found myself fast to a trout of out-

Float tubes are still one of the best options for fly anglers.

landish proportions. Despite a valiant struggle, the hook held and soon I was able to land the fish on a sand bar—a brown, maybe 18 or 19 inches and very fat.

Pumped up, we went hunting for more big snouts. We actually located and fooled several others of similar heft before the short-lived caddis hatch ran its course. We've caught no more big browns here since, but we know they're in there somewhere, and that's more than enough to keep us coming back.

The Montana Chain of Lakes

Nestled in the foothills west of Hebgen there is a string of aquamarine jewels known as the Montana Chain of Lakes—Cliff, Wade, Hidden, and Elk Lakes. The first two are the more popular among fly anglers, but all four can provide good fishing, especially from ice-out to mid-June and again in the fall prior to freeze-up.

Wade and Cliff are easily accessed via a good gravel road off US 87 just north of the famous Three Dollar Bridge on the Madison River. A reputation for giving up big trout and eye-popping beauty make these lakes tough to resist. In bright sunlight, the lake's light-colored, almost white, mud bottoms and aquamarine water look very much like a Caribbean bonefish flat. And in spring when the rainbows of Cliff Lake come onto those shallow white flats to eat spawning whitefish eggs, the fishing feels a lot like casting to bones.

You can sight fish for cruisers, but you'll need to be persistent and patient. Cliff contains rainbows and cutthroats, and the occasional cutt may push 28 or 30 inches (but don't hold your breath). The most consistent fishing is found near the inlet, where it will cost you five bucks (payable at Cliff Lake Resort) to get access close to the action. Free public access can be had at the other end the lake, but it's a long way to kick in a tube. We pay the five bucks or bring a boat and motor.

Wade also holds rainbows, but outsized browns are the main attraction. The state record, a 29-pounder, was caught here way back in 1966, and one can always hope that her genes are still alive. The lake still gives up some big trout, and 5-pounders are not uncommon, particularly early and late in the season.

Hidden is primarily a rainbow-trout fishery, but it's much more difficult to access. Elk is slightly easier to reach, although you still have to loop around a far corner of the vast Centennial Valley. It contains a mix of cutts, rainbows, and grayling.

Decent fishing can be had on all four lakes morning and evening almost all season long, but early and late in the year is still the best bet. You might find good surface action during hatches, but day in, day out a better plan is to go prepared to "dredge 'em up." These are not particularly large lakes, but all are deep and clear, which means you should use full-sink lines, long leaders, and countdown methods of presentation. Fishing the bays and over weed beds and sunken logs will produce fish, most of which are taken on nymphs and streamers.

Author's Tip

During those times when Hebgen's gulpers don't play fair, try slowly stripping tiny nymphs (red, olive, or black chironomids) using full or sink-tip lines in the channels between the weed beds. If there is a chop on the surface, hang a pair of nymphs near bottom below a strike indicator. A swift kick of the fins every now and then causes the flies to sweep up toward the surface, then settle back. Trout often take just as the flies begin to move up or sink back down.

Favorite Fly

Gulper Special

Hook	TMC 2487 or equivalent sized to naturals
Tail	Grizzly
Body	Tan dubbing
Hackle	Grizzly hen, clipped on top
Wing	Natural deer body hair
Head	Closed-cell, packing foam

Fast Facts

Hebgen Lake

Location	Just north and west of West Yellowstone; accessed from US 20, 191, or 287
Water Type	Large fertile lake known for giving up big trout
Primary Gamefish	Rainbow trout, some browns and cutts
Best Time	Ice-out, just before ice-over, and late July to September

Best Flies	Midge (chironomid) larva, pupa, Buggers and leeches, hatch-matching nymphs, terrestrials, and, of course, your favorite gulper imitations
Equipment	9-foot, 5- to 7-weight rod with floating, sink-tip, and full-sink lines, long tapered leaders for surface fishing, shorter leaders for subsurface; float tubes, pontoon boats, or skiffs make for easier fishing
Conditions	Hebgen is a big lake, and sudden and violent storms are common in any season. Exercise common sense and wear a life jacket.
Drive Time	From Bozeman: 1.75 hours From Idaho Falls: 1.75 hours From Billings: 4 hours
Directions	From Bozeman, take US 191 south; from Idaho Falls, take US 20 to West Yellowstone; from Billings, take I-90 to Bozeman, US 191 south.

Local Fly Shops

Arrick's Fly Shop
37 N. Canyon
West Yellowstone, MT 59758
406-646-7290

Blue Ribbon Flies
315 N. Canyon
West Yellowstone, MT 59758
406-646-7642

Bud Lilly's Trout Shop
39 Madison
West Yellowstone, MT 59758
406-646-7801

Jacklin's Fly Shop
105 Yellowstone
West Yellowstone, MT 59758
406-646-7336

Madison River Outfitters
117 Canyon
West Yellowstone, MT 59758
406-646-9644

The Tackle Shop
P.O. Box 625
127 E. Main
Ennis, MT 59729
406-682-5549

Madison River Fishing Co.
109 E. Main
Ennis, MT 59729
406-682-4293

Guides

Wolfpack Outfitters
406-682-4827

Riverside Motel and Outfitters
406-682-4240/1-800-535-4139

Dream's West
406-682-5261

Eaton Outfitters
1-800-755-3474

Papoose Creek Lodge
406-682-3030

Contacts

West Yellowstone Chamber of
   Commerce
406-646-7701

Yellowstone National Park Information
307-344-7381

Gallatin National Forest
Hebgen Lake Ranger District
406-646-7369

Montana FWP
Region 3, Bozeman
406-994-4042

*Hauling in a Hebgen Lake
gulper.*

Mesa Falls on the Henry's Fork.

CHAPTER 4

THE HENRY'S FORK RIVER
Heaven Sent for Dry Fly Addicts

The Henry's Fork of the Snake River is a dry fly purist's dream. But she's also a temptress who preys on innocent and unsuspecting anglers much the way a female praying mantis treats naive male suitors. One taste and we were hooked deep—catch and release just wasn't an option. Judging by the normal crowds of anglers here, we aren't alone in our addiction.

The most popular stretch is in and around Last Chance, Idaho. This is big-time hallowed water, and anglers flock here from around the world. So don't expect to ever find the river anything like empty; it just doesn't happen. Why this is so remains somewhat of a mystery, as only a few highly skilled anglers come away with much to show for their effort on this technical river full of educated fish. Maybe we flyfishers just like to torture ourselves?

Case in point: Just upstream of Osborne Bridge, inches from the high grass bank, a big trout kept sticking up its snout to suck down about every fifth Flav (*Drunella flavilinea*, stunted cousin of the Western Green Drake) that emerged, while ignoring anything and everything I managed to put near the drift lane. Good shot or not, it made no difference; all were summarily refused.

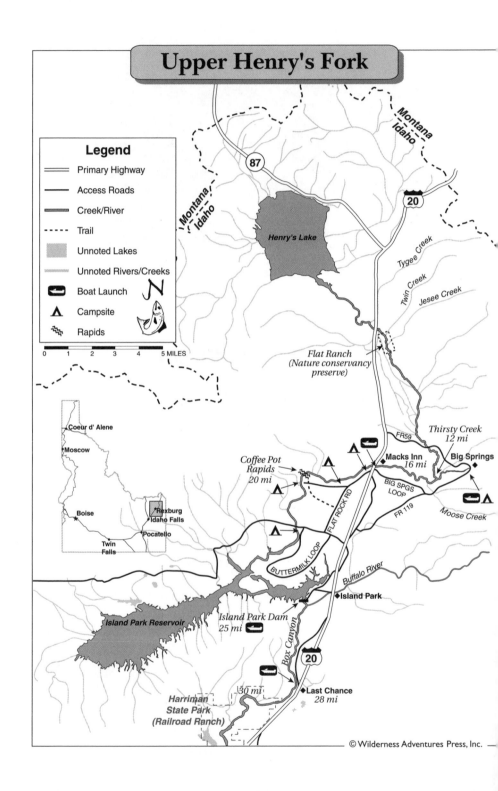

Upper Henry's Fork

Legend

═══	Primary Highway
───	Access Roads
═══	Creek/River
- - - -	Trail
▓	Unnoted Lakes
▒	Unnoted Rivers/Creeks
⬛	Boat Launch
▲	Campsite
〰	Rapids

0 1 2 3 4 5 MILES

Montana / Idaho

87

20

Henry's Lake

Tygee Creek

Twin Creek

Jesee Creek

Flat Ranch
(Nature conservancy
preserve)

Coeur d' Alene

Moscow

Boise

Rexburg
Idaho Falls

Pocatello

Twin
Falls

Coffee Pot
Rapids
20 mi

FR59

Thirsty Creek
12 mi

Macks Inn
16 mi

Big Springs

BIG SPGS
LOOP

FLAT ROCK RD

FR 119

Moose Creek

BUTTERMILK LOOP

Buffalo River

Island Park

Island Park Reservoir

Island Park Dam
25 mi

Box Canyon

20

30 mi

Harriman
State Park
(Railroad Ranch)

Last Chance
28 mi

© Wilderness Adventures Press, Inc.

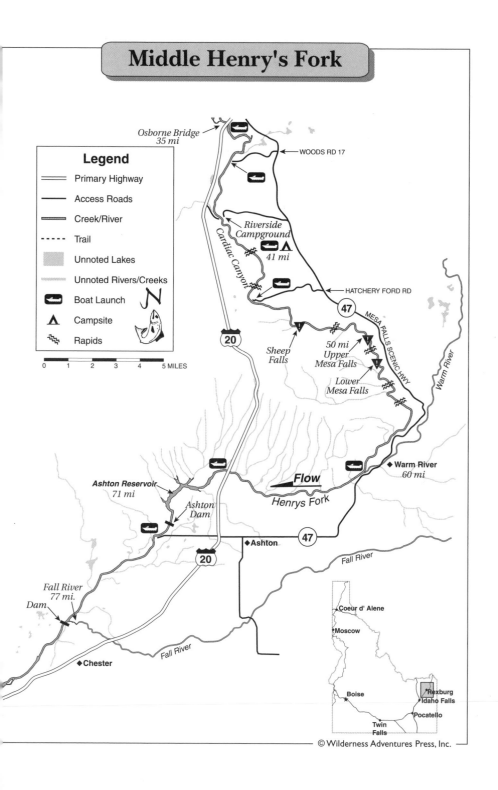

Middle Henry's Fork

Legend

=== Primary Highway

— Access Roads

=== Creek/River

- - - - Trail

    Unnoted Lakes

    Unnoted Rivers/Creeks

🛶 Boat Launch

Λ Campsite

🌊 Rapids

0   1   2   3   4   5 MILES

Osborne Bridge
35 mi

WOODS RD 17

Riverside
Campground
41 mi

Cardiac Canyon

HATCHERY FORD RD

47

20

MESA FALLS SCENIC HWY

Sheep
Falls

50 mi
Upper
Mesa Falls

Lower
Mesa Falls

Warm River

Warm River
60 mi

Ashton Reservoir
71 mi

Ashton
Dam

Flow

Henrys Fork

47

◆Ashton

20

Fall River

Fall River
77 mi.
Dam

Fall River

◆Chester

Coeur d' Alene

Moscow

Boise

Rexburg
Idaho Falls

Pocatello

Twin
Falls

© Wilderness Adventures Press, Inc.

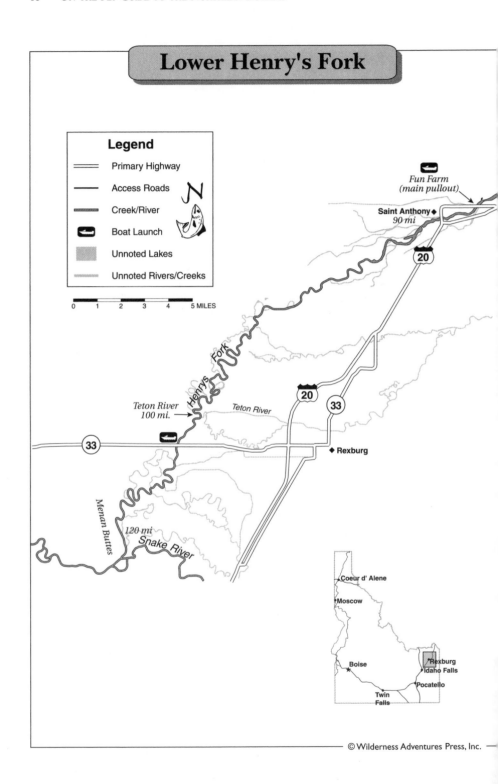

Lower Henry's Fork

Legend

=== Primary Highway

— Access Roads

≋ Creek/River

▱ Boat Launch

▨ Unnoted Lakes

░ Unnoted Rivers/Creeks

0   1   2   3   4   5 MILES

Fun Farm
(main pullout)

Saint Anthony ◆
90 mi

20

20   33

Teton River
100 mi. →   *Teton River*

33   ◆ Rexburg

Menan Buttes

120 mi
Snake River

Coeur d' Alene

Moscow

Boise   Rexburg
             Idaho Falls
             Pocatello
Twin
Falls

© Wilderness Adventures Press, Inc.

First, I fired off several shots from below, the long supple leader and tippet falling in gentle S-curves to allow the perfect-looking #14 No-Hackle Flav to float perfectly. Distraught at my failure, though still a long way from thoroughly defeated, I carefully changed position. Once again, keying into the trout's feeding rhythm, I unleashed a cast, mended the line in the air, and dropped the fly just above the trout's lie. With all the intensity of a feeding heron, I held my breath as it drifted drag-free and ever so slowly into the target zone.

Up came the broad snout. But instead of inhaling the fake, he sucked down the real deal floating right alongside. So close was its take that the wake of the rise actually shoved my fly slightly sideways, leaving it to bob downstream untouched.

Several more refusals made it clear that the trout and I differed in our opinions of the perfect presentation. Deflated, I waded out to the far bank, slumping on the grass just in time to watch my wife Gale hook and release a fat rainbow.

"What are they eatin'?"

" You said Flavs, so that's what I'm feeding them."

"No-Hackle?"

"No what? Oh, you mean does it have prickles, no." Gale is your basic nontechnical fish-catching machine, and doesn't sweat the small stuff.

"Why don't you try that pig I was working on. I can't seem to gain his trust."

"Can't, too deep for me," she said, turning her attention to another riser.

So I stalked back and took up my original position below the fickle trout—a glutton for punishment. As the fish rolled up yet again, I stripped off a few feet of line, false cast away from the lie so the flying line wouldn't spook it, and dropped the fly at least 6 inches to the left and a good foot too far.

"Nice shot, jerk," I mumbled aloud, then stood dumbfounded as a V-shaped wake materialized, charging the fly. Pushing water like a swimming beaver, the trout blasted the poorly aimed fly, sucking it down in an angry boil. By the time my stunned mind told my hand to lift the rod, it was too late.

"Did you miss it?" Gale asked, giggling just loud enough for me to hear.

Fishing the Henry's Fork

From its source at Henry's Lake, the Henry's Fork of the Snake runs 120 miles to join forces with the South Fork a little southwest of Rexburg, Idaho. Together they form the mainstem Snake River. At 1,040 miles long, the Snake is the longest tributary of the still mighty, though tamed, Columbia River.

During its relatively brief run, the Henry's Fork changes character nearly as often as Idaho's fickle high-country weather. At a spot appropriately labeled the Bathtub, the Henry's Lake outflow joins with the nearly half-million gallon a day outflow of Big Springs. The springs (closed to fishing since 1910) boil from the ground at a constant year-round 52 degrees to give birth to a gentle, spring creek–like river for the next 20 miles. The river then constricts suddenly as it plunges through Coffee Pot Rapids for a mile and a half before being abruptly stilled by Island Park Reservoir.

Below the dam, the Buffalo River enters and the flow once again constricts, rushing pell-mell through Box Canyon, though less violently this time. It flattens out just above Last Chance then continues on to the world-renowned Railroad Ranch, once more resembling the giant spring creek many of us picture when we think of this river.

Not yet satisfied, the river once again speeds up, and 4 miles below the Ranch it roars through Cardiac Canyon, a deep, scenic gorge. Then comes Sheep Falls, the 114-foot drop at Upper Mesa Falls, and the 65-foot drop at Lower Mesa Falls farther downstream.

Below the canyon and falls the river mellows somewhat before its junction with Warm River, where it enters yet another canyon. Exiting the canyon, it widens out and tumbles down a series of dancing riffles, minor rapids, and slow, deep pools to eventually dump its flow into Ashton Reservoir.

While cuttbow hybrids (few pure strain rainbows or cutthroats remain) and mountain whitefish dominate the river above the falls, below there browns and a smattering of native Yellowstone cutthroats join the mix. The 7-mile tailwater between Ashton and Chester Reservoirs is a less well-known, though highly productive, big-trout fishery; one that is open year-round and fast becoming a destination hotspot for devotees of cold-weather trouting.

Terrestrials are always a good bet on hot, windy summer afternoons.

Access to the upper river is pretty much unlimited, surrounded as it is by the Targhee National Forest and the extensive public water around Island Park and Harriman State Park (Railroad Ranch). Farther downstream between Ashton and St. Anthony, private lands make access more difficult. Still, there are several public access sites. Below Chester Dam, you'll find a few miles of decent access and good fishing, but then public access wanes. In the final 30 miles, from St. Anthony to the mouth near Mennan Buttes, public access ranges from difficult to impossible.

The upper river (above Vernon Bridge) is further characterized by a complicated set of regulations. Generally speaking, the season is open from the Saturday of Memorial Day weekend to November 30; except Harriman State Park (Railroad Ranch), which is open June 15 to November 30; with exceptions for the Harriman Bird Sanctuary, which is open June 15 to September 30. The river between Warm River and Ashton Reservoir and below Vernon Bridge is open year-round.

Even more complex than the regulations are the river's overlapping insect hatches. It's a rare day, especially on the ever-popular Last Chance to Railroad Ranch section, that you can look upon the coiling currents and say, "Yep, that's it, they're eatin' PMDs." Oh, you can say it all right—it is, after all, our right to free speech—but being right is generally a whole other story. On most days we find ourselves forced to ponder the presence of several aquatic insects that are hatching, mating, egg laying, and/or dying at the same time. As if the aquatics aren't enough to fret about, terrestrials usually enter the mix, as well. And with this much food to choose from, the trout can sometimes be extremely selective.

While I don't really believe Henry's Fork trout hold Ph.D.s in Selective Eating Management, figuring out just what the hell a specific trout is eating at any given time is rarely easy. The simple solution might be to pick another section of river; something with faster, more broken currents, which generally equates to less picky trout. But why would you stoop to something easy when there's all that pain available just for the asking? We usually stick it out, perfectly willing to slink home defeated.

On the other hand, sometimes it's nice to spend a day fishing in the rougher water of the Box or down toward Cardiac Canyon below and around Riverside Campground, or way down around Ashton, where rumors of "less educated" fish fly around like magpies over a dead cow. Henry's Fork trout are definitely easier to fool wherever the water is a bit more ruffled, and for mysterious reasons those areas of the Fork are invariably less crowded. Which of course explains why of late we find ourselves fishing down there more.

The Fork's most famous fly hatches usually begin in May with the eruption of the giant stonefly we've all come to know and love—the Salmonfly. The hatch begins down river around Ashton and works its way slowly upstream, often lingering on the upper river into late June or early July. When the hatch coincides with the opener on

Memorial Day weekend, watch out; an already packed house of anglers can fill to overflowing.

Once the Salmonflies hit town, the rest of the hatches appear in a quick, disorderly procession. These include the Western Green Drake (another popular event that attracts throngs of anglers), the Golden Stone, countless varieties of caddis, lesser Golden Stones (Yellow Sallies), Flavs, PMDs, Brown Drakes, Callibaetis, Speckled Duns, tiny Blue-Winged Olives, and other insects like the Little Blue Dun, Trico, Slate Drake, and Mahogany Dun.

And, of course, there are variations to consider for each mayfly hatch—emergers, cripples, duns, spinners, drowned duns and spinners. When caddis are coming off, you need to consider the larva, pupa, adult, egg-laying adult, drinking adult, skittering adult...I'm sure you get the picture. Solving the Henry's Fork hatch riddle isn't easy, but few things are more interesting or rewarding for a fly angler than to nail one of those 20-inch rainbows on the Railroad Ranch with just the right fly and presentation.

Success on the Henry's Fork usually requires careful attention to hook sizes and colors to match the naturals. So-called "clean patterns" such as "no-hackle" and "thorax" dries, CDC emergers, and sparsely tied, low-floating caddis imitations quite often produce when more traditional imitations fail miserably.

In summer, a good strategy is to ignore the hatches and search for trout with more eclectic tastes. "Serve 'em hoppers, ants, and beetles," a sympathetic local once coached, trying his best to help Gale and me after we had taken a savage beating at the hands of a pack of Railroad Ranch rainbows. It should come as no surprise that we've enjoyed some of our best Henry's fishing in low light and on the worst weather days—conditions more forgiving of poor presentations and fly choices.

Fly sizes run the gamut. Stoneflies are generally #4-10, but as small as #16; Drakes #10-12, some to #14; PMDs start at #16-18, later on #18-20 work better; Baetis can be as large as #16 and as small as #24 or so; Tricos are said to be #22-24, but we've always had better luck with #24-26s; most caddis can be matched with #12-16, but there are a lot of micro caddis more suited to a #20-24 hook size. Grasshoppers generally run #6-10, but #14 or even #16 can be useful at times; ants and beetles around #18-20 are popular, but we like to pound the banks with #10 deer hair patterns. And it seems that on every trip we find a "hot fly of the moment," so be sure to check the local shops before hitting the water.

In addition to just about every dry fly and emerger pattern (and size) known to Man, we also stuff our vests with a wide assortment of nymphs and streamers, such as the Pheasant Tail, Prince, Copper John, Flashback, Disco Midge, RS-2, Brassy, various stoneflies and caddis nymphs, San Juan Worms, Woolly Buggers, leeches, and so on in an equally wide variety of sizes (#2-20). Even then, we often wish we had something else to try when watching one of those super-picky rainbows delicately sipping something invisible from the surface.

Our basic strategy is straightforward: start with whatever looks good, then methodically cycle through our arsenal of flies and methods. Actually, we go at the Henry's Fork just like we go at most big, famous rivers. Whether we hit the hot fly or daylight simply runs out we still have fun.

Restaurants and Accommodations

Back in the dark ages, an old flyfishing buddy forever preached, "It only costs 10 percent more to go first class." Probably a lowball estimate in today's market, but it's still nice to "go first class" once in a while, right? So we pay our plastic debt down to zero before leaving for the Henry's Fork, just in case we decide to treat ourselves to a dining experience at the Henry's Fork Lodge.

Overlooking the river about 3 miles downstream of Osborne Bridge, the lodge is tastefully and masterfully crafted with a highly distinctive wood-and-beam facade. The great room features an exposed-beam ceiling and large stone fireplace, antique furniture and oriental carpets. After a hard day of fishing we take our drinks on the veranda, while the trout still rise in the river below, always teasing us into thinking we quit too early.

Later, seated in the elegantly appointed dining room, the extensive wine list proves too much for me (as usual), but Gale chooses a Cabernet Sauvignon. We

Henry's Fork Anglers is a Last Chance icon.

decide to split an appetizer of Maryland crab cakes—these I remember from previous visits. As usual, trying to choose among the entrees brings us to a second impasse, since we know the choices not only look and sound delicious, but will taste that way, as well.

Once again our waitress comes to the rescue, "Perhaps a second glass of wine might help?"

"Of course, why didn't we think of that?"

Finally Gale settles on the poached salmon with melon salsa, wild rice, and fresh veggies, while I stick with tradition, the Henry's Fork Special: broiled New York strip steak (medium rare) in red wine sauce, baked Idaho potato, and fresh veggies. The cooks manage to outdo even our wildest expectations.

Dessert? Forget it. How much decadence can a person stand in one sitting? And, yes, it costs a little more than an extra 10 percent, but as we overheard the lady at the next table tell the waitress, "My dear, dinner was sublime, as always." Couldn't have put it better myself.

There are also a whole bevy of good restaurants in and around Island Park, such as the Lodgepole Grill (Phillips Lodge, 208-558-9379), which is on par with the best restaurants and not so pricey. Same goes for the newly constructed Riverfront Restaurant, (Last Chance, 208-558-9555) and Ponds Lodge (5 miles north of Last Chance, 208-558-7221), which under new management promises to uphold the long and fine tradition of this venerable eatery. During the height of the season, reservations are always a good idea, especially on weekends.

Gale Robbins fishes the prolific
Flav hatch at Last Chance.

Numerous campgrounds within the nearby Targhee National Forest offer dozens of individual campsites, and farther afield you can camp virtually anywhere you want. Our favorite spot is the newly renovated Forest Service Box Canyon campground, off US 20, a mile south of the Island Park Ranger Station. Nineteen new sites with lots of elbowroom, well-maintained toilets, water (no hook-ups or electricity), fancy concrete and steel picnic tables, grills and fire rings, even a hook to hang the lantern. Better still, it's just a short, steep scramble down to the water.

We've also enjoyed camping at the Riverside Campground off US 20 a couple of miles south of the turn to Harriman State Park. The fishing is pretty good and the river and campground seldom crowded.

We enjoy camping beside the river so much that I must confess to not having tried many lodges and motels in the area. However, we have trusted friends who tell us the Angler's Lodge (Last Chance, 208-558-9555), Henry's Fork Lodge (off US 20 4 miles south of Last Chance, 208-558-7953), and Pond's Lodge (Island Park, 208-558-7221) allow pets and are great places to stay. Phillip's Lodge (Phillips Loop Rd., 208-558-9379) is also popular with visiting anglers, as is Wild Rose Ranch (Henry's Lake, 208-558-7201) and Mack's Inn (on US 20 north of Last Chance, 208-558-7272).

Last Chance, Idaho

Last Chance (Island Park) is your basic northern Rockies' recreational village. Thousands of flyfishers, hunters, and snowmobilers descend on the area at different times of the year. In summer the flyfishers don't just descend, they take over. Sit down in any eatery or look around any of the convenience stores or motel parking lots and the person you see first is almost assuredly a flyfisher.

In a long career of chasing trout on famous rivers I've been to a lot of towns that call themselves the "Trout Capital," but perhaps none have a more valid claim than Last Chance, Idaho. It is difficult to find anyone who doesn't speak at least basic "flyfishingese." Even in the Grub Stake Market and Deli, there is a fly-tying table set up behind the counter and custom flies for sale (pretty spiffy ties too, by the way). Be sure to stop by the GSM&D on the way to the river and order up lunch to go. They manufacture what we believe to be among the best deli sandwiches on the planet.

Other must-sees include Mike Lawson's Henry's Fork Anglers and the Trouthunter Fly Shop right next door. Both shops are justifiably famous among anglers as local outlets for well-thought-out flies designed by long-time veterans specifically for fooling Henry's Fork trout. Renee and Bonnie Harrop at the Trouthunter create a wide variety of beautiful and useful flies, and Mike Lawson, despite selling the shop a few years ago, has probably created as many important patterns as anyone in the West.

Nearby Fisheries

The Fall River

The Fall River gets its start high in a remote corner of Yellowstone National Park. Fifty miles away and over 3,000 feet lower it meets the Henry's Fork, with scenic and productive trout water all the way, although some of the life is sucked from its lower end by increasingly heavy irrigation demands. Cutthroats dominate the upper river, but lower down expect cuttbow hybrids and rainbows. Most of the fish run 10 to 13 inches, with an occasional fish in the 16 to 20 range. Gale once hooked a monster below Cave Falls that broke her off before we got a look, but we came away with a new respect for the size of the fish in this river.

Big trout tales aside, the Fall is a fun river to fish. We've never found it anywhere near as crowded as its famous neighbor, and the trout are far more cooperative, which is handy after a day of getting shut out on the Henry's Fork. And its prolific hatches are much easier to decipher—when tan caddis are hatching, a tan caddis pattern will usually catch fish.

Oh, I almost forgot, the wildlife viewing is excellent. We nearly always spy a moose or two, and the scenery…Well, they don't call it the Fall(s) River for nothing.

Nearby Attractions and Activities

In 1902, several officials of the Oregon Shortline Railroad and other investors purchased what is now Harriman State Park, the place known to anglers far and wide as the Railroad Ranch. Once the private retreat of the Harrimans, of Union Pacific Railroad fame, and the Guggenheims, then prominent in copper, it's now held in public trust by the state of Idaho.

The rich wildlife habitat has been preserved since the turn of the century, when the owners established a private hunting reserve and working cattle ranch. The ranch maintained healthy game, waterfowl, and fish populations, allowing today's park visitors to observe a rare concentration of wildlife in a beautiful setting. Twenty-seven of the original Railroad Ranch buildings, from the cookhouse to the horse barn, are still intact, furnished, and carefully maintained.

Mesa Falls, a spectacular 114-foot drop, makes another nifty side trip (follow the signs off US 20 south of Island Park). The fishing on that part of the river isn't too shabby either, and it's nowhere near as likely to draw a crowd as the more famous water upstream.

Author's Tip

Clean fly patterns, such as the No-Hackle, Comparadun, Sparkle Dun, Crystal Caddis Thorax, and CDC Emerger, seem to dupe the Fork's finicky trout better than conventional, bushy-hackled dries. Long, wispy tippets and long leaders and downstream casts often produce best. And should hatch-matching fail, don't hesitate to "feed 'em something different." A Parachute Ant can be deadly anytime.

Favorite Fly

Flav No-Hackle

Hook	Tiemco 100 #14-18
Tail	Dark dun hackle fibers or Microfibbets, sparse and split
Body	Fine dark olive dubbing
Wing	Gray mallard quill

Fast Facts

Henry's Fork River

Location	Generally follows the US 20 corridor between Rexburg, Idaho, and Henry's Lake
Water Type	Varies from freestone-like, rocky, and broken pocket water to sand-bottomed, weedy, and placid
Primary Gamefish	Cuttbows, with a smattering of browns and pure-strain rainbows and cutthroat
Best Time	Anytime from Memorial Day weekend to the end of the season
Best Flies	Dry flies designed especially for the Henry's Fork

Equipment	9-foot, 3-, 4-, 5-weight rod, floating line, long, light tippet and longer leaders
Conditions	Usually tolerable; can be hot in high summer. Early summer and fall days can be pleasant. Paralleled by a paved road; campgrounds in the area; excellent access.
Drive Time	From Idaho Falls: 2 hours From Salt Lake City: appx. 6 hours From Bozeman: appx. 3 hours
Directions	From Idaho Falls, take US 20 east to Ashton and Last Chance; from Salt Lake City, take I-15 north to Idaho Falls, US 20 east to Ashton and Last Chance; from Bozeman, take US 191 south to West Yellowstone, then US 20 west to Last Chance.

Local Fly Shops

Trouthunter
3427 N. Hwy 20
Island Park, ID 83429
208-558-9900

Fall River Fly and Tackle
221 N. Hwy 20
Ashton, ID 83420
208-652-7646

Henry's Fork Angler
3340 N. Hwy 20
Island Park, ID 83429
208-558-7525

Idaho Irresistibles
268 N. Hwy 20
Ashton, ID 83420
208-652-7269

Three Rivers Ranch
Last Chance, ID
208-558-7501

Guides

Hyde's Last Chance Lodge & Outfitters
208-558-7068, 1-800-428-8338

Wild Rose Ranch
208-558-7021

Contacts

Henry's Fork Foundation
Ashton, ID 83420
208- 652-3567

Targhee National Forest
St. Anthony, ID 83445
208-624-3151

Island Park Area Chamber of
 Commerce
208-558-775

Island Park Ranger Station
208-558-7301

CHAPTER 5

HENRY'S LAKE

Idaho's Best Big-Trout Stillwater

Arriving at Henry's Lake for our first foray years ago, I asked a guy about to launch his float tube, "How big are the trout in this lake?"

"Pretty gawd-awful," was his rather vague reply.

"How big is that?"

"Pretty big," he replied, kicking the tube into gear and making it clear that any further conversation was out of the question.

I might as well tell you that we got shut out that first day. Not long after launching our own float tubes, a big wind roared down from Raynolds Pass, literally blowing us off the water. Since then, though, we've returned every chance we've had. Subsequent journal entries for Henry's Lake run the gamut from great to okay to not so hot. While the word "skunk" doesn't appear often, neither does the word "monster."

My personal best, a hybrid, ate a #4 red and black leech and was recorded as "might have pushed 22 inches." Hardly worth mentioning in comparison to the 30- to 40-inch monsters other anglers often brag about. Still, you'll never hear us complain about the more "average" 18- or 19-inchers that routinely come to net.

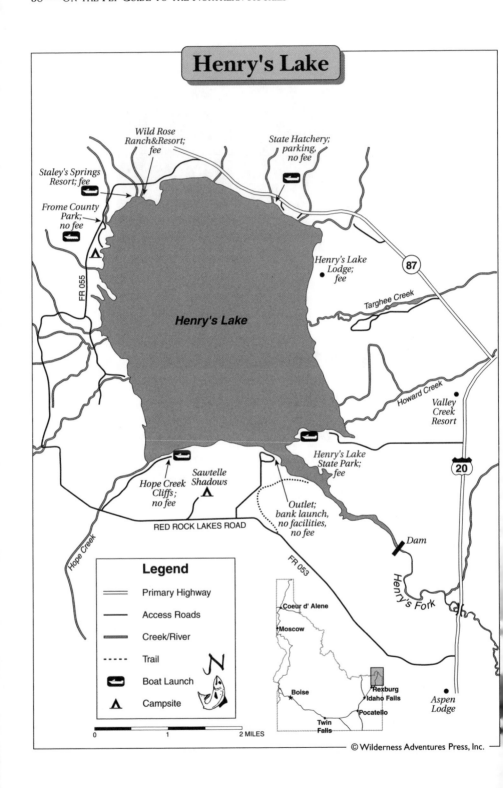

Henry's Lake

Wild Rose
Ranch&Resort;
fee

State Hatchery;
parking,
no fee

Staley's Springs
Resort; fee

Frome County
Park;
no fee

FR 055

Henry's Lake
Lodge;
fee

87

Targhee Creek

Henry's Lake

Howard Creek

Valley
Creek
Resort

Henry's Lake
State Park;
fee

20

Hope Creek
Cliffs;
no fee

Sawtelle
Shadows

Outlet;
bank launch,
no facilities,
no fee

Dam

RED ROCK LAKES ROAD

Hope Creek

FR 053

Henry's Fork

Legend

═══	Primary Highway
────	Access Roads
━━━	Creek/River
- - - -	Trail
🛥	Boat Launch
Λ	Campsite

N

Coeur d' Alene

Moscow

Boise

Rexburg
Idaho Falls

Pocatello

Aspen
Lodge

Twin
Falls

0   1   2 MILES

© Wilderness Adventures Press, Inc.

Thinking that maybe the Hope Creek Cliffs area we usually fish might not be a big-trout hangout, we tried other launch sites, including the famed Staley's Spring Glory Hole. But the trout we caught weren't any different from those we caught at Hope Creek. It wasn't long before we gravitated back to our old familiar haunts along the cliffs, where we were happy to catch fat, healthy cutts, rainbows, and brook trout—even if no monsters.

Typical was a day in late August—sort of an in-between time after the June/July damselfly blitz and before the season's close in October. We kicked around the familiar weed beds, stripping a variety of scuds, Buggers, leeches, and whatnot among the channels and cussing the salad that seemed to spoil nine of every ten casts. The session ended with our usual tally: miss a few, net a few, all modest cutts, rainbows, and hybrids. But nothing close to "pretty gawd-awful," but still pretty darn good fun.

Fishing Henry's Lake

First off, I should probably reveal just how big Henry's Lake fish really are. Bill Schiess, a local lake expert and outfitter, notes that his clients "boated over 600 five-pound trout in one season; 37 of which exceeded 28 inches, including one of 31 inches and the largest a 39-incher." And Idaho fisheries biologists report trout growth rates in the lake as nothing short of phenomenal. For instance, a four-year-old Henry's Lake cutthroat pushes 16 inches, compared to 12 or 13 inches in Yellowstone Lake. Four-year-old cuttbow hybrids averages 18 or 19 inches, and brook trout the same age average 16 inches.

The lake's mud bottom makes wading difficult, so some form of watercraft is necessary for any serious fishing. We use a float tube and a pontoon boat. These crafts obviously limit our mobility on such a big lake, especially when the wind kicks up, but we like to work small pieces of water carefully and with a low profile.

While the lake isn't bashful about serving up big winds, she is surprisingly frugal where fly hatches are concerned. Other than the damsels of June and July, most are not worth mentioning. The most productive fishing methods involve getting the fly down to the trout, rather than trying to entice them to the surface. Sink-tip and full-sink lines are de rigueur, and weighted flies and short leaders help keep the fly in the hot zone.

Olive, black, and brown are good colors to try, whether in the form of Buggers, leeches, scuds, or damsel nymphs. It should be noted, though, that many of the local favorites are much more colorful, with garish reds, purples, and oranges often out-fishing the more subdued patterns. It pays to inquire locally, experiment, and change flies and tactics until you find the magic combination for that particular day. The fly shops in nearby Island Park and West Yellowstone keep close tabs on what is happening at the lake.

Restaurants and Accommodations

We've enjoyed pleasant camps at Frome County Park (northwest side of the lake). There are toilets, running water, and a boat launch. Individual sites provide picnic tables and fire rings, but no electric hook-ups or dump stations. Sawtelle Shadows is a full-service private campground on Red Rock Lakes Road (FR 053). Since it's almost within spitting distance of our favorite Henry's Lake launch it would seem to be the logical campground for us, but it's a little bigger and noisier, and many of the flyfishing campers seem to gather at Frome County Park, which makes for better gossip and fishing tips.

If we happen to be staying on the Henry's Fork, we'll likely set up at the newly renovated USFS Box Canyon campground off US 20 (FR 284) between Mack's Inn and Last Chance. But there are a ton of great camping spots in the area well within reasonable striking distance of Henry's Lake.

Henry's Lake State Park (208-558-7532) has 45 campsites, about half with full hook-ups. It's well maintained, and good fishing can be had right out front in the outlet bay. And since I've strayed somewhat from camping back to fishing, I might as well drop another hot tip: In high water years the outlet stream (headwaters of the Henry's Fork) can be very good when some of the lake's monsters wash over the spillway and end up stacked like cordwood below the dam.

Provided you don't mind driving 8 miles or so west over Targhee Pass into Montana, Lonesomehurst Campground (FR 1718) off US 20 on the south arm of Hebgen Lake is our top camping spot in the West Yellowstone area. It lacks hook-ups, but usually isn't crowded.

If you prefer nicer accommodations, you'll need to head over to West Yellowstone or down to Last Chance, as there aren't many services right on Henry's Lake.

Nearby Fisheries

Island Park Reservoir

According to Idaho Fish and Game biologists, Island Park Reservoir, in years when there is sufficient water, is quite similar to Henry's Lake nutrition-wise. When conditions are right, it grows fat trout fast.

Alas, not all years are sufficient water years. However, given normal water conditions the IPR fishes well, producing trout similar in numbers and size to Henry's Lake. In the highest water years the best flyfishing often occurs in early fall after irrigation demands have drawn the reservoir down somewhat, concentrating trout and making them easier to locate.

High or low, the IPR is big water, and flyfishers tend to congregate in the Fingers/Grizzly Springs area off Green Canyon Road and above McCrea Bridge near the inlet. The usual array of stillwater insects are present: scuds, damsel and dragon-flies, mayflies, and caddis. Buggers, leeches, and Clousers are always a good bet in big lakes. As with Henry's, going low generally pays bigger dividends over the long haul than wiggling surface patterns. Damsels provide the most consistent hatch-matching opportunity starting in late June and extending through July.

Author's Tip

Unless you see rising fish, and the odds are against you, rig a sink-tip or full-sink line and a short leader and plan on getting the fly down to the fish. Weed beds and spring holes are the most consistent producers. Weeds grow thick in summer, so try working the channels in between beds, stripping nymphs, Buggers, leeches, or Clousers until you hit on something that works. A strip-strip-strip-pause cadence often produces better than a steady retrieve. Morning is by far the best time to be on the water, as afternoon winds usually shut things down and make tubing downright dangerous.

Motorized watercraft provide more big-lake mobility.

Favorite Fly

Mohair Leech

Hook	1-3X long nymph hook
Underbody	0.015 to 0.025 lead wire
Tail	Marabou (brown, olive, black, or claret) and Krystal Flash
Body	Mohair yarn, Canadian brown or blood

Fast Facts

Henry's Lake

Location	Just off US 20 between Island Park and West Yellowstone
Water Type	Fertile, coldwater lake
Primary Gamefish	Yellowstone cutthroat, cuttbow hybrids, and brook trout
Best Time	End of May through July
Best Flies	Flashy Woolly Buggers, leeches, and various nymphs
Equipment	9- to 10-foot, 5- to 7-weight rod with sink-tip and full-sink lines
Conditions	Henry's is shallow and sudden storms (wind) can whip it to a dangerous froth in a hurry. Float-tubers and canoeists should head for shore at the first sign of stormy weather.
Drive Time	From Idaho Falls: 2 hours From Salt Lake City: appx. 6 hours From Bozeman: appx. 3 hours
Directions	From Idaho Falls, take US 20 east to Ashton and Last Chance; from Salt Lake City, take I-15 north to Idaho Falls, US 20 east to Ashton and Last Chance; from Bozeman, take US 191 south to West Yellowstone, then US 20 west to Last Chance.

Local Fly Shops

Trouthunter
3427 N. Hwy 20
Island Park, ID 83429
208-558-9900

Blue Ribbon Flies
305 N. Canyon St.
West Yellowstone, MT 59758
406-646-7642

Henry's Fork Angler
3340 N. Hwy 20
Island Park, ID 83429
208-558-7525

Bud Lilly's Trout Shop
39 Madison Avenue
West Yellowstone, MT 59758
406-646-7801

Idaho Irresistibles
268 N. Hwy 20
Ashton, ID 83420
208-652-7269

Eagle's Tackle Shop
9 N. Canyon St.
West Yellowstone, MT 59758
406-646-7521

Fall River Fly and Tackle
221 N. Hwy 20
Ashton, ID 83420
208-652-7646

Jacklin's Fly Shop
105 Yellowstone Avenue
West Yellowstone, MT 59758
406-646-7336

Arrick's Fishing Flies
125 Madison Avenue
West Yellowstone, MT 59758
406-646-7290

Madison River Outfitters
117 Canyon
West Yellowstone, MT 59758
406-646-9644

Three Rivers Ranch
Last Chance, ID
208-558-7501

Guides

Bill Schiess, Henry's Lake specialist
208-652-3669

Wild Rose Ranch
208-558-7021

Hyde's Last Chance Lodge & Outfitters
208-558-7068, 1-800-428-8338

Idaho Irresistibles
208-652-366

Contacts

Targhee National Forest
420 Bridge St.
St. Anthony, ID 83445
208-624-3151

Island Park Ranger Station
208-558-7301

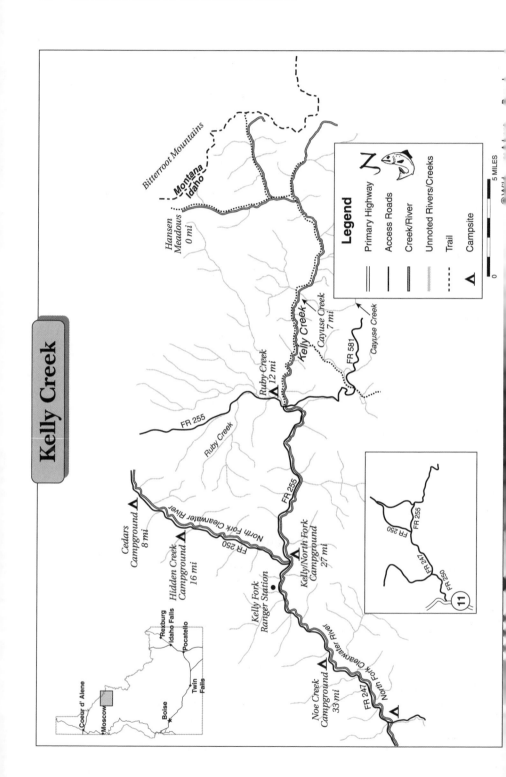

Kelly Creek

Legend

	Primary Highway
	Access Roads
	Creek/River
	Unnoted Rivers/Creeks
	Trail
▲	Campsite

0   5 MILES

Bitterroot Mountains

Montana
Idaho

Hansen
Meadows
0 mi

Kelly Creek

Cayuse Creek
7 mi

FR 581

Cayuse Creek

Ruby Creek
▲ 12 mi

FR 255

Ruby Creek

North Fork Clearwater River

Cedars
Campground ▲
8 mi

Hidden Creek
Campground ▲
16 mi

FR 250

FR 255

Kelly Fork
Ranger Station ●

Kelly/North Fork
Campground ▲
27 mi

FR 255
FR 250
FR 247
FR 250
11

Rexburg
Idaho Falls
Pocatello

Coeur d' Alene
Moscow

Twin
Falls

Boise

Noe Creek
Campground ▲
33 mi

FR 247

North Fork Clearwater River

CHAPTER 6

KELLY CREEK
Idaho's Hidden Gem

The first time we turned the corner at Kelly Forks on the way up Kelly Creek I was rubbernecking so hard I nearly dumped the truck in the creek. That's the sort of siren Kelly is. She doesn't subtly charm her way into your heart, she just flat out sucks you in. In my case, it was love at first sight.

Idaho's Kelly Creek starts its 25-mile tumble to the North Fork Clearwater from high on the western slopes of the Bitterroot Range. The lower 12 miles are paralleled by gravel road, beyond that it's hike or horse only. The surrounding forest supports a lush, green understory—a sea of deciduous fruit-bearing shrubs and ferns, mosses, and mushrooms of every size and description. It's a landscape far different from the dry, lodgepole-dominated woods on the Montana side of the mountains.

The river flows over and around truck-sized boulders that guard deep pools and runs so clear that even 6 feet down the bottom seems close enough to reach out and touch. If there's a trout stream out there with more curb appeal I've yet to find it.

We try hard to include two trips to Kelly each season in our flyfishing itinerary; one in July, the second in September. July's visit is usually short, part of an annual marathon where we try to cram in as many old favorites as possible. We usually just stop for an afternoon, catch the evening rise, and stay for a couple of hours the next morning, then on to somewhere else.

But in September we take our time on Kelly Creek in a last-ditch effort to gaze upon her beauty and see a few of the wild westslope cutthroat trout for which she is famous.

Last year we managed to wiggle free for just three days, including travel. Not much, but I learned a long time ago that in order to maximize time on the water one needs to take it as it comes. As my friend Charlie Meck once succinctly pointed out, "The time to go flyfishing is now."

We arrived late in the afternoon at the Cedars Campground, where the winding road down off Hoodoo Pass bottoms out along the North Fork Clearwater River. Cedars isn't the handiest campground to fishing Kelly Creek. To reach the creek you need to drive another 20 miles down a narrow, bumpy road officially labeled Forest Road 250. We camp there not for convenience, but for the experience of being among the giant trees; trees of such girth that Gale and I, hand-in-hand with arms stretched wide, can't begin to reach halfway around.

After hurriedly setting up camp, we raced hell-bent downriver with fingers crossed that no logging trucks are heading upriver at the same time. Our luck holds, in record time we skid to a halt beside a favorite pool just upstream of Kelly Forks with enough daylight left to at least satisfy our curiosity.

Kelly Creek cutts are suckers for big hopper patterns.

Gale is first to rig up. She slides down the bank, stumbles across boulders to the pool's tail-out, strips off a few yards of line, and drops a #14 Orange Stimulator along the nearest current seam. I hear a whoop, followed quickly by, "Aw shoot! Missed it."

"Was it a cutt?"

"Couldn't tell for sure, but I think so."

That might seem a stupid exchange given Kelly's reputation as a prime cutthroat fishery, but it was getting on toward late September and the cutts have been known to migrate out earlier, especially in low water years. She continues casting and soon hooks another fish. I hurry down and slip the net under this one, a fat 14-incher. It's a pretty cutthroat, and our trepidations are finally laid to rest. No more worries that we might have driven all this way to fish an empty creek. (There are always rainbows, but in this case rainbows don't count.)

In the waning daylight we each manage to net a couple firm, colorful, wild west-slope cutthroats. When the sun drops behind a ridge the air temperature drops dramatically, and like a faucet being turned off, the trout shut down. Nonetheless, we can sleep well knowing cutthroats are indeed waiting in the morning.

There is more than just a slight chill in the air the next day. Overnight our tire tracks in yesterday's mud have frozen solid, and the mud puddles are frozen hard enough not to crack when I stomp on them. Instead of rushing off, we linger in camp over a second and then third cup of coffee, walking along the North Fork to find that real ice has formed overnight in places where the river splashes onto overhanging limbs and roots. It is late morning before the sun finishes its slow crawl to the top of the Bitterroots. The valley warms quickly in the direct sunlight, and by the time we reach Kelly Creek it's Indian summer once again.

Our plan is to park at the trailhead 12 miles upstream of Kelly Forks, hike a few miles up, and then fish our way back down. The fishing really isn't any better upstream than down. We've run up the biggest scores above the trailhead, but caught our biggest fish beside the gravel road.

This time the final decision of where to fish is made easy by a chance meeting at the trailhead with a young man burdened with a heavy backpack and toting a fly rod. He tells us he's just returned from a two-day foray upriver. To our query, "How was the fishing?" he replies, "I'm sort of bummed, the best fishing was from here about a mile upriver; there didn't seem to be any trout farther up, no cutts anyway." Since he seemed about to buckle under the heavy load, we didn't have the heart to fill him in on the wandering ways of Kelly's cutthroats.

I've been around the block too many times to take any fishing reports as gospel, but the young man seemed sincere, so we turned back from the trail and spent a beautiful, sunny afternoon fishing our way down toward Kelly Forks. Except for four trucks—one each from Washington, Oregon, Minnesota, and Montana—bearing six anglers, we had the entire 12 miles to ourselves.

The fishing, like that of the previous evening, turned out fine, although nothing to rave about. Apparently the migration really had begun, or we maybe we just weren't doing something right. Regardless, it was a fun afternoon in a special place, and I really doubt a few more fish would have made a difference. Where fall fishing for wild cutthroat trout is concerned, timing is everything. On this trip, ours could have been a little better.

Fishing Kelly Creek

Seldom do we find ourselves scratching our heads for the "pattern of the day." Most days we just tie on a large (#10-14) Stimulator, Humpy, Royal or Gray Wulff, Elk Hair Caddis, Parachute Adams, or Madam X, switching only when the fly becomes shredded. Kelly's cutts are notoriously unselective, although like trout everywhere, they do become picky at times.

With that in mind we at least carry the full arsenal in the truck, if not the vest. And one July morning it paid off. We were fishing our way up from Kelly Forks, enjoying pretty hot fishing for a couple of hours. Then the action came to an abrupt and unexpected halt. Not really wanting to dredge the bottom, we cycled through our dry fly selection. No dice.

As a final act before nymphing, I rummaged through a seldom-used stock box in the back of the truck, tied on a #18 Elk Hair Caddis with a peacock body and immediately started hooking fish. Gale tied on a larger size of the same pattern and still turned up nothing. Then she dropped down to a #18, and we continued taking fish right until dusk.

The next morning it was once again business as usual. A dark caddis and a bigger dark mayfly were hatching sporadically, and the fish were rising to both. Yet every bushy dry fly we tied on took fish. Go figure.

Restaurants and Accommodations

There aren't any services near Kelly Creek. It is roughly 60 miles of mostly gravel road from Superior, Montana, on Trout Creek Road across Hoodoo Pass and down the North Fork (Forest Road 250), to Kelly Forks. Or if you feel adventurous hook a left onto Forest Road 255, which takes off from Forest Road 250 a few miles below the Cedars Campground. If you're lucky enough to take all the correct forks you'll eventually end up near the trailhead on Kelly Creek. From Pierce, Idaho, it's also a 60-odd mile trip to Kelly Forks over gravel and dirt roads via Forest Roads 247 and 250.

No matter what route you choose, you'll find little in the way of creature comforts. No cafés, no motels, no gas; just rocks, trees, water, and clean air. Trout country as it was meant to be.

Our approach is to toss in the camp outfit, top off the gas tank before hitting the gravel, and stay the night. As mentioned, we like the Cedars Campground, although as campgrounds go it's on the primitive side. There are individual tent or trailer sites, picnic tables, fire rings, and water, but no toilet facilities and no fee. But any lack of amenities are more than made up for by the huge western cedars and the babbling North Fork Clearwater River, which runs right next to camp. And we've never found it busy.

If big trees don't turn you on, there are two developed Forest Service campgrounds nearby: Kelly Forks (where you can stumble right out the door into Kelly Creek) and Hidden Creek (beside the North Fork, roughly halfway between Cedars and Kelly Forks). Both offer tent or trailer sites, picnic tables, fire rings, water, and vault toilets, although there is a fee.

Of course, if you don't want to pay a fee or take the chance of camping next to anyone else, countless undeveloped sites are available within the Clearwater National Forest. For the backpacking angler, the trail that follows the creek offers plenty of spots to pitch a tent, although all campers should remember to set their camps well away from the stream itself.

If you'd rather drive than camp, there are motels available in Superior, Montana, and Pierce, Idaho. In Superior, try the Bellevue (110 E. Mulan Rd., 406-822-4692), Hill Top (201 W. Mulan St., 406-822-4831), or Budget Host Big Sky (103 E. 4th St., 406-822-4831). All are modestly priced and allow pets.

In Pierce, you can stay at the Cedar Inn Miner Shanty and Restaurant (412 S. Main St., 208-464-2704), Three Mountains Retreat (100 Alpine Court, 208-464-2172), or the Pierce Motel (Highway 11 next to the grocery store, 208-464-2324). These are modestly priced and offer RV hook-ups.

Nymphing a typical rock-lined run.

Superior, Montana

Westgate True Value Hardware, located in the basement of Castle's IGA (302 S. River Rd.) is the place to buy a nonresident Idaho fishing license, which will run $74.50 for the season or $10.50 for the first day and $4.00 for each consecutive day after that. The Westgate clerks also hand out free directions to Trout Creek Road, although don't look for anything beyond the basics. On our first trip, the clerk said, "It might be 30 miles to Kelly, though I've never been." To which a customer countered, "Naw, it ain't but about 25 miles, all gravel road and rougher 'n a cob, can't make no time." All well intentioned, but far from accurate.

If you forget to pick up the license, you'll have to turn around or drive roughly 120 miles of mountain road to Pierce, the nearest license vendor on the Idaho side the pass.

There's not a lot else to Superior beyond the grocery/hardware store, a couple of gas stations, the Lolo National Forest Headquarters, a little town park, a handful of rough looking bars, and a giant wood-chip mulch operation. Durango's Restaurant (204 E. 4th Ave., 406-822-4967) is clean and offers "good food at a fair price."

Kelly Creek's westslope cutthroat are wild and beautiful.

When the huge sawmill complex shut down six years ago, the town, while not actually dying, just sort of withered. But like a lot of small, rural towns, it seems to hang in there.

Nearby Fisheries

Kelly Creek feeds the upper North Fork Clearwater River. They're look-a-like streams, and if I were blindfolded and then set down beside one or the other I doubt I could tell the difference—same trees, bushes, humongous rocks, deep, inviting, crystalline pools, and pocket water. The North Fork also hosts westslope cutts and rainbows of similar size; mostly 12-inchers, with a few larger fish and the occasional "tanker." However, there is one major difference: The North Fork lacks Kelly's alluring roadless section.

In our experience the fishing on the North Fork rivals that of Kelly, without the hype. Yet it remains more of a "local" stream, probably because traveling anglers are eager to try their luck on nationally famous Kelly Creek.

Nearby Attractions and Activities

I can't imagine driving to Kelly and not fishing, though I can understand why some do. If we weren't so smitten with the flyfishing bug, I think I'd still come here to just sit in the shade of the big trees and gaze at the towering mountains. It's a rugged landscape, one that nearly killed off the Lewis and Clark expedition in the fall of 1805: "From this mountain I could observe high ruged mountains in every direction...excessively dangerous...thickly stowed with falling timber...steep and stoney...it was almost impracticable to proceed..." Were it not for the roads, the same would be true today.

In spring, the North Fork is just one of many northern Idaho rivers swarming with whitewater enthusiasts who come here to kayak and raft the wild "white horses." Hikers travel the surrounding rugged mountain trails in every season but winter. One September we ran into a group of llama packers about to set out on a week-long backcountry adventure. Needless to say, legions of hunters also visit each fall in search of elk, deer, and black bear.

Author's Tip

After such a long drive, plan on camping out for a few days to explore the pools and runs above and below the trailhead on Kelly Creek and on the nearby North Fork. While the sections of pocket water are hard to pass up, if westslope cutts are your goal concentrate your efforts in the slower runs and deeper pools. Otherwise, you'll run into more rainbows, which isn't necessarily a bad thing, either.

Favorite Fly

Kelly Creek Special

Hook	Tiemco 200R #6-16
Tail	Elk or deer body hair (light or dark to suit)
Rib	Fine gold wire
Body	Fluorescent orange Antron with palmered brown hackle
Wing	Elk or deer body hair (light or dark to match tail) tied half-mast

Fast Facts

Kelly Creek

Location	Northern Idaho, roughly halfway between Superior, Montana, and Pierce, Idaho
Water Type	Picture-perfect, high-gradient freestone; fast flowing, pools, pocket water, riffles
Primary Gamefish	Westslope cutthroat trout, rainbows in faster sections
Best Time	Snow blocking roads and/or runoff can make the creek unfishable into July; August is prime time; low water in September can be iffy
Best Flies	High floating dries, #10-16; Stimulators, Humpies, X-Caddis, Parachute Adams, and Elk Hair Caddis cover most situations; terrestrials in high summer
Equipment	9-foot, 4- to 6-weight rod with floating line; long leaders tapering to 3X or 4X

Conditions   Nights in mountains can be chilly even in summer, but expect hot, sweltering days until mid-September

Drive Time   From Missoula: appx. 2.5 hours
From Lewiston: appx. 4 hours
From Coeur d'Alene: appx. 3.5 hours

Directions   From Missoula, take I-90 north to Superior, follow Trout Creek Rd. across Hoodoo Pass to FR 250 to Kelly Forks; from Lewiston, take ID 12 east to Orofino, ID 11 north to Headquarters, FR 247 to Bungalow Ranger Station, FR 250 to Kelly Forks; from Coeur d'Alene, take I-90 east to Superior, Trout Creek Rd. across Hoodoo Pass, and FR 250 to Kelly Forks.

Local Fly Shops

Clearwater Fishing Co.
P.O. Box 1375
Orofino, ID 83544
208-476-3534

Guide Shop
14010 Hwy 12
Orofino, ID 83544
208-476-3531

Nelson Fly Shop
Pierce, ID
208-464-2777

High Country Sports
Pierce, ID
208-469-2359

Guides

Triple O Outfitters
208-469-2359

Contacts

Clearwater National Forest
12730 Highway 12
Orofino, ID 83544
208-476-4541

Orofino Chamber of Commerce
P.O. Box 2221
Orofino, ID 83544
208-476-4335

Idaho Fish and Game
Panhandle Region
2750 Kathleen Ave.
Coeur d'Alene, ID 83814
208-769-1414

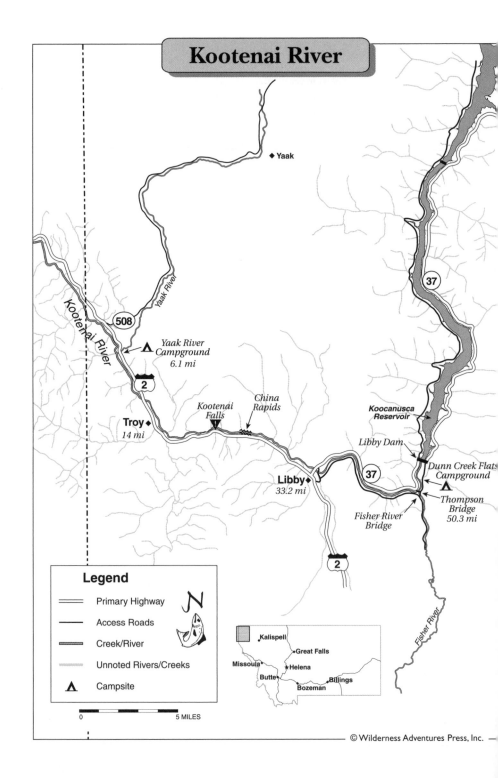

Kootenai River

◆ Yaak

Yaak River

Kootenai River

37

508

Yaak River
Campground
6.1 mi

2

Kootenai
Falls

China
Rapids

Koocanusca
Reservoir

Troy ◆
14 mi

Libby Dam

Dunn Creek Flats
Campground

Libby ◆
33.2 mi

37

Thompson
Bridge
50.3 mi

Fisher River
Bridge

2

Legend

Primary Highway

Access Roads

Creek/River

Unnoted Rivers/Creeks

▲ Campsite

Kalispell

Great Falls

Missoula

Helena

Butte

Billings

Bozeman

Fisher River

0   5 MILES

CHAPTER 7

THE KOOTENAI RIVER
Forgotten Blue-Ribbon Trout River

)ur first trip to the Kootenai wasn't actually about fishing—at first anyway. It was august and we had a new bird dog pup in training, ripe for wild birds. A friend who ·orks for the Forest Service called to say he'd just returned from a work assignment 1 the Yaak Valley and the place was "crawling with ruffed grouse." Sounded too good ɔ pass up, so we dropped everything and headed north. Nearly to our destination, ·e came upon the Kootenai River, and stopped to make camp and wet a line. In the 1orning, Gale heard a ruffed grouse drumming nearby. Naturally, we loosed the og—and somehow, for the moment anyway, the fishing was relegated to the back ·urner.

Late in September, when the gates at Libby Dam typically shut down for the sea-on, we pack up, hitch the tent-trailer to the truck, and head for Yaak River `ampground, located at the confluence of the Yaak and Kootenai just off US 2 eight 1iles west of Troy. We hunt grouse during the cool mornings and spend afternoons nd evenings chasing the Kootenai's wild trout.

Since driving up from Dillon kills most of a day, we fish the runs and pools close ɔ camp the first evening. It's not the most productive portion of the river, but we

usually find enough rising rainbows to at least partially scratch our itch. On our las
time, in the two hours before dark, we each managed six or eight cartwheeling rain
bows, with a couple mellow cutthroats tossed in for good measure.

The evening's blue ribbon went to Gale for netting a feisty 15-inch rainbow tha
gobbled her #14 Orange Stimulator. It was hooked in the curl of current where the
Yaak spills in, jumping two or three times and peeling line from the reel like a run
away freight train. Had I not seen the trout airborne, I would have sworn she had
somehow enticed one of the Koot's big bull trout to the surface. From her whoop a
the take, I think she might have harbored similar thoughts. Wild, Kamloops-strair
rainbows will do that to you.

The next day started out cloudy and cool and remained that way all day—per
fect bird hunting weather. As a result, we didn't get to the river until after dinner. (Thi.
always seems to happen on cast-and-blast trips; no doubt it would be more appropri
ate to rename the operation the Kootenai Cast *or* Blast.) That evening we drove to

Kootenai River rainbows aren't all
large, but they sure are pretty.

Libby to access the Kootenai off River Road. In a single run we got into a whole pasel of hungry 10- to 14-inch rainbows that attacked our dries with reckless abandon. Their lack of size had little bearing on how fun and feisty they were.

In the morning we moved our camp to a nice spot overlooking the river in the spacious Dunn Creek Flats Campground nearer the dam. We spent the rest of the morning chasing ruffs beside the nearby Fisher River. Around noon Katie (the German wire-haired pointer) pronounced it too warm for hunting and went for a swim in the river.

Later, we fished our way downriver from camp to Kootenai Falls, our favorite run for bigger trout. On a whim, I started with a #14 Red and Black Parachute Ant trailing a similar-sized Beadhead Prince Nymph, then switched to stripping a #2 black Conehead Bugger with rubber legs, sort of a cross between a Yuk Bug and a real Woolly Bugger. My plan was to run up the score with the ant/nymph combo and then go after bigger fish with the Bugger.

And it worked, sort of. The nymph provided consistent action, but only a few trout ate the ant. The conehead rolled several hefty trout, but each time I managed to bumble the operation before I could get them to the net. Gale stuck to dry flies in a variety of sizes: Parachute Adams, Stimulators, and Royal, Olive, and Gray Wulffs. The action came in fits and spurts and no one fly seemed to work much better than another, but she managed to land a good number of fish during the afternoon.

In the slower, deeper pools westslope cutthroats outnumbered the rainbows and vice versa in the swifter runs and riffles. Most ran 8 to 12 inches, although Gale once again garnered top honors when she snagged a rainbow of 18 or 19 inches from behind a big boulder. She very nearly scored a double whammy on the next cast to the same spot, but the fish threw the hook.

While this trip we didn't bring our raft, the stretch is an awesome fall float because you can often look down through the clear water into deeper runs and pools and spy log-sized trout. Many are off-limit bull trout, but jumbo-sized rainbows are also present.

Fishing the Kootenai

Whenever I consider the broad and varied landscape of Montana, something about the far northwest corner of the state just doesn't compute. For one thing, the woods resemble a temperate rain forest, dark and wet and lush; quite a contrast to the semiarid sagebrush and lodgepole of southwest Montana. Nothing drives the point home quicker than making a bed beneath giant western red cedar and larch, surrounded by a soft green understory of mosses and mushrooms.

As if the out-of-place landscape weren't enough, there's the huge, brawling river that runs through it. The Kootenai is not your basic spring-runoff-and-low-summer-flow river. Even in late summer this baby is likely to be rocking and rolling, with little sign of let up. In late September or early October the dam gates close, and flows are reduced until spring brings the next flush of Canadian snowmelt.

Born in the high mountains of western British Columbia, a region known for its heavy snowpack, the river's annual surge is slowed by the Koocanusca Reservoir (Libby Dam). From there, the flows often peak somewhere around 25,000 cfs. This is an amazing amount of water to be dumped down one river channel. By comparison, the Big Hole River peaks at around 12,000 cfs in a high water year. And the undammed Yellowstone River has peaked above 25,000 cfs at Livingston just 16 times since 1897.

By almost any standard the Kootenai is a big river. Too big to handle as a whole, so we like to view it in pieces as a bunch of little trout rivers. Before the fall shut down, the huge flow and heavy current are a wade fisher's nightmare. When on foot, we limit our fishing mostly to side channels, in and around boulders. Despite the river's massive current, it's not a difficult place to float, although there are a couple of rough spots, like China Rapids, which can seriously diminish your lifespan (and Kootenai Falls surely will).

There are no official state-maintained fishing accesses, but launch sites are numerous and drifts ranging from a couple hours to all day can easily be orchestrated. The river fishes best from the dam down to Kootenai Falls. Being a tailwater—albeit not with gentle spring creek qualities—the fishing holds up well all summer and into fall. In fact, it may be at its best in October and November, which is a convenient situation for trout addicts, since this coincides with Montana's big game season. If you can tear yourself away from the killing fields, you can expect to find willing trout and few other anglers.

First impressions don't always hold water but in this case the river screamed "pigs," and indeed there are giants. The current state record rainbow, 38 inches and 33.1 pounds, was hauled from under the David Thompson Bridge in 1997, and double-digit bull trout abound. The bulls are supposed to be huge, but get less hype because you can't legally target them and any you catch accidentally must be immediately released unharmed. But it's the Kootenai's 8- to 14-inchers that make it a consistently great fishery.

To have a legitimate shot at the big boys you have to get big, ugly, meaty-looking flies down deep to where these fish hang out. But when it comes to casting dry flies for average-sized trout or dredging bottom for the chance at a monster, we'll stay with dries every time—or almost every time, as visions of super-sized trout occasionally drive me to the depths.

The Kootenai is not really a technical river. Most days, any bushy pattern in size #10-16 will do the trick. Attractors such as the Madam X, #6-16; Olive and Royal Wulff, #10-14; Irresistible, #10-18; and old favorites like the Renegade and Adams will cover most situations. Of course, it also pays to have a few PMD and caddis patterns in case a particularly heavy hatch comes off.

For those odd times when the trout are reluctant to accept surface offerings, nymphs such as the Beadhead Prince, Hare's Ear, Copper John, and Lightning Bug in #10-18 come in handy. Summer through fall, anglers should stock a few #10-18 ants and hoppers in sizes #2-10. Hog hunters might try outsize Buggers, big saltwater-sized Clousers, or Double Bunnies.

In addition to rainbows, westslope cutts, and endangered bull trout, the river holds brown trout, mountain whitefish, and kokanee salmon.

Restaurants and Accommodations

The MK Steakhouse (9948 Hwy. 2 E, 406-293-5686) is open for dinner six nights a week (closed Mondays). This is the place to go in Libby for steak and prime rib. At Beck's Montana Café (2425 Hwy. 2 W, 406-293-6686) the chicken is pretty tasty and the service great, while the Venture Inn (443 Hwy. 2 W) is one of the better family restaurants in northwest Montana.

Our flyfishing excursions usually include camping, but every fourth night or so we spring for a motel room, which has added up to a wide sampling of lodgings over the years. In the Libby area, we've enjoyed brief respites at the Sandman Motel (Hwy. 2 W, 406-293-8831), the Super 8 Motel (448 Hwy. 2 W, 406-293-2771), and the Venture Motor Inn (443 Hwy. 2 W, 406-293-7711). These motels receive additional kudos for allowing dogs.

The Kootenai is a float-fisher's river.

Libby, Montana

Libby (along with Yaak just up the road) is often looked upon by outsiders as somewhat of a mysterious place, inhabited by felons, dope dealers, gun runners, and other shady characters; sort of a Cooke City Northwest. While I don't pretend to know if any of this is true, I can testify that every time we've passed through the folks have been extremely friendly.

For instance, while camped at nearby Bull Trout Lake on our last trip, the lift on the tent-trailer suddenly broke in the middle of the night. The next morning we jacked up the trailer, re-hitched it to the truck, and headed for Libby. As it was a Sunday, we really didn't hold out much hope of finding someone to fix it until the next day. But, low and behold, Twinkle Welding (2337 Hwy. 2 W, 406-293-4576) was not only open, they had the old plate removed and a new one welded in place so fast that we were on our way to the Kootenai River just 30 minutes after walking in the front door. Total cost: $9.82, including parts, new paint, and labor.

Another of Libby's not-so-dark secrets is Rosauer's Food and Drug Store (Hwy. 2 W at 9th St.). If there is a more friendly, well-stocked grocery store than Rosauer's, we've yet to find it; check out the deli and bakery counters.

Nearby Fisheries

The Fisher and Yaak Rivers, farther to the north, are moderate-sized and provide good early season angling. Kokanee salmon run up the Fisher in the fall and can provide a colorful diversion. Both rivers host a fair number of hatches, but selecting flies is usually more a matter of matching the size and silhouette rather than finding an exact copy. Later in the season, low water can make things tough but still interesting.

Several tributaries in the area hold fish, and anyone with a good map and a sense of adventure will find enjoyable fishing.

Nearby Attractions and Activities

Kootenai Falls, just downstream of Libby, is a must-see on any list of attractions in and around town. Only a shadow of its former self since Libby Dam began meting out flows—80,000 to 100,000 cfs dropped to around 25,000 cfs—the roar can still be heard a long way off as the river constricts and drops nearly 300 feet in just a few hundred yards. It's an awesome display.

David Thompson, probably the first white man to see the falls, apparently came away impressed: "The river had steep banks of rock and only 30 yards in width, with violent eddies which threatened us with certain destruction should we misstep; at wherever the river contracted the case was always the same, the current swift; yet to look at the surface the eddies make it appear to move as much backward as forward."

The Kootenai Indians arrived in the region around the 1500s, probably because of the falls, which they considered a sacred site.

The Kootenai River is the third largest tributary to the Columbia River. Seventeen miles upstream from the town of Libby, the 422-foot Libby Dam holds back 90 miles of water in the Lake Koocanusca reservoir. Forty-eight miles of the reservoir lie within the U.S., the other 42 miles are in Canada. Visitors can enjoy boating, fishing, camping, water skiing, family picnics, hiking, cross-country skiing, wildlife viewing, and a host of other outdoor activities.

South of Troy on Highway 56 (known locally as the Bull Lake Road) you'll find the Ross Creek Cedars turnoff a half-mile past the end of the lake. Four miles in you'll come to a grove of giant western red cedar, some of which are more than 8 feet in diameter. The interpretive walking tour, slightly less than a mile in length, explains the ecology and history of the big trees. By the way, the Bull Lake Campground, located just past the entrance to the Ross Cedars, is one of the best in the region.

Author's Tip

Due to the powerful current and rubble bottom, floating in a raft or driftboat is by far the best way to fish the Kootenai. Floating allows access to islands and channels wade fishers can't reach at any river level. If you don't care too much about size, a well-presented dry fly is all you'll need to catch fish; however, if you're after real hogs be prepared to do some major depth probing. This river has some amazingly deep holes.

Although it's a big, powerul river, the Kootenai is easy to navigate—as long as you avoid China Rapids and Kootenai Falls.

Favorite Fly

Marabou Muddler Minnow

Hook	Mustad 9672 or equivalent
Tail	Red hackle fibers
Body	Silver mylar
Underwing	White marabou/peacock herl
Overwing	Deer or Elk body hair, clipped at eye to form a tight round head.

Black Ant (fished as a dropper)

Hook	Tiemco 5212 #10-18
Abdomen	Black fur dubbing
Hackle	Black
Thorax	Black bead head sized to hook

Fast Facts

Kootenai River

Location	Northwest Montana below Libby Dam, near the town of Libby
Water Type	Tailwater with high flows that continue well into summer extremely difficult to wade
Primary Gamefish	Rainbow, brown, bull trout (must be immediately released) kokanee salmon and mountain whitefish
Best Time	September through November

Best Flies	High-floating dries, basic nymph patterns, Buggers, leeches.Check locally to see what's hot.
Equipment	9-foot, 4- to 6-weight rod for dries and lighter nymph work; 6- to 7-weight sink-tip or full-sink lines for dredging deep holes and runs for bigger trout
Conditions	Hot summers, relatively mild falls. Wind can kick up suddenly any afternoon. Respect the powerful current, beware of rapids, and by all means steer clear Kootenai Falls. Good camping on the river and in the surrounding national forest. Libby has all the modern amenities.
Drive Time	From Spokane: 4 hours From Missoula: 5 hours From Bozeman: 8.5 hours
Directions	From Spokane, I-90 east to US 95 south to US 2 east to Libby; from Missoula, I-90 west to US 93 north to Kalispell, US 2 west to Libby; from Bozeman, I-90 west to US 93 north to Kalispell, US west to Libby.

Local Fly Shops

Libby Sport Center
116 E. 9th
Libby, MT 59923
406-293-4351

Kootenai Angler
13546 Hwy. 37 N
Libby, MT 59923
406-293-7578

Guides

Dave Blackburn
Kootenai Angler
406-293-7578

Silver Bow Outfitters
406-293-4868

Linehan Outfitting Co.
406-295-4872

Kootenai River Outfitters
406-295-9056

Contacts

Libby Chamber of Commerce
406-293-4167

Kootenai National Forest
506 US Highway 2 West
Libby, MT 59923
406-293-6211

Montana FWP
Region 1
490 N. Meridian Rd.
Kalispell, MT 59901
406-752-5501

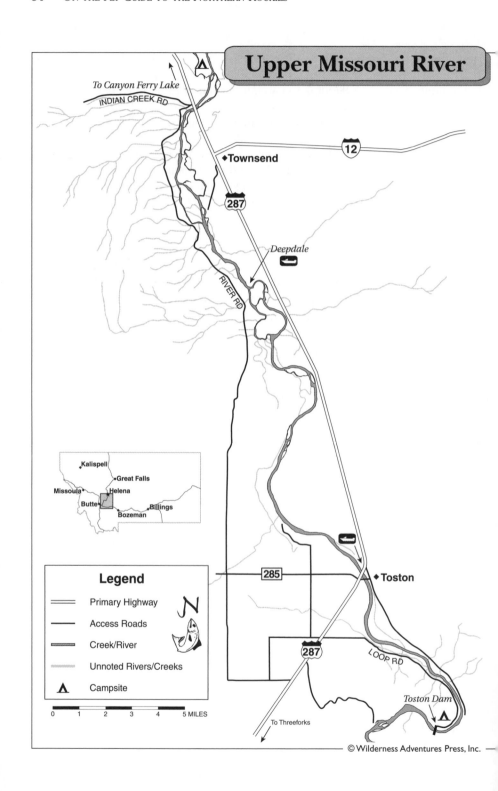

Upper Missouri River

To Canyon Ferry Lake

INDIAN CREEK RD

12

♦Townsend

287

Deepdale

RIVER RD

Kalispell
♦Great Falls
Missoula♦ ♦Helena
Butte♦ ♦Billings
Bozeman

285

♦Toston

Legend

═══ Primary Highway

─── Access Roads

▬▬▬ Creek/River

▬▬▬ Unnoted Rivers/Creeks

▲ Campsite

N

287

LOOP RD

To Threeforks

Toston Dam
▲

0 1 2 3 4 5 MILES

© Wilderness Adventures Press, Inc.

CHAPTER 8

THE UPPER MISSOURI RIVER

Trout Aren't the Only Game in Town

When I signed on to write this book, Chuck Johnson (Publisher, Wilderness Adventures Press) emphasized two things: "This book should not be about trophy trout exclusively or trout exclusively." No argument from me. Even though I'm addicted to trout, variety is the spice of life, and I love catching all kinds of fish.

In Montana trout are king, and other fish rarely come up in conversation. So when I heard that Tom Leeming of Ennis (406-682-4556) was into flyfishing for carp, of all things, I immediately rang him up and set a date to get on the water.

The common carp, though much maligned, is finally starting to garner some attention from flyfishers. If you are among the unenlightened majority, it might surprise you to learn that this fish feeds selectively on aquatic insects and terrestrials; exhibits a high level of intelligence (for fish, anyway); is strong, fast, and nearly invincible to man's most potent pollutants; is spooky beyond belief; never needs to be stocked; and can grow to 50 or more pounds (current world record, 82 pounds).

Leeming not only guides novice carp catchers, he's borderline obsessive about the fishing and the fish: "I'm 52, been fishing since eight years old and carp excite me more than any fish, ever." That says a lot for carp, as Leeming once guided on

Idaho's famed Silver Creek and has cast flies over bonefish and other exotic saltwater denizens.

"Carp fishing is more like bonefishing than bonefishing," he says. And to emphasize the point, he names his favorite carp spots after famous bonefish places: Moxey Creek, Hann's Corner, West of Andros, Double Osprey, Hoverville, Land of Giants, and Last Chance Flat. As the list rolls off his tongue, the gleam in his eye leaves no doubt that the man would rather dupe "kloopers," "mudders," and "tailers" than anything else.

We met on a Saturday morning in mid-August at the York's Islands fishing access on Montana's upper, upper Missouri River, between Toston Dam and Townsend. We were smack in the middle of some of the best trout country in the world, and here we were going after carp. Tom hauled along his driftboat, and the plan was to float the river to the Indian Road take-out just below Townsend. For the most part, he would wield the rod and reel while I manned the camera and pummeled the poor guy with a bunch of stupid questions.

Not long after launching we beached the boat upstream of a big, shallow eddy. Moving as carefully as if he were stalking a trophy brown sipping Tricos in a gin-clear spring creek, he approached a wide tail slicing the thin water—obviously a big carp on the prowl. As if on cue, several more equally wide tails broke the smooth surface; a whole pack of marauding, tailing carp on the prowl.

Camera at the ready, I stalked the action.

Out of the corner of my eye I saw Tom zero in on a target. Ever so slowly the tail moved closer, trailing a muddy plume. As it neared the water's edge he made his play, dropping an imitation crayfish just to the side and slightly behind the tailing carp. He then inched it forward, the fly sending up little puffs of silt to gain the carp's attention. Through the camera lens I saw it turn sharply right, and a wide V-shaped wake appeared as the carp pounced.

Tom reared back on the rod, the line came tight, and all hell broke loose. The water boiled like a small bomb had gone off, and the reel screamed as the carp quickly peeled off all of the fly line and many yards of backing. It was as awesome a run as I'd seen a fish make in a half-century of hooking fish on flies.

A brawl ensued, highlighted by several shorter, though no less powerful, runs. In time, the fight came closer and I found myself silently cheering him on. Finally he was able to back up and winch (literally) the stubborn carp onto the gravel. Before the release, he stretched the tape and found that the carp measured 26 inches long, with a girth of 14 inches. From past weigh-ins Leeming figured it would pull the scales to at least 8 pounds.

"That's probably about average," he shrugged nonchalantly, as he gave the carp a shove back into the river. And, at least for this day, the "average" held true.

Give or take a couple of inches or a couple of pounds, the rest of the fish he caught were mirror images of the first. The fish shared one other trait: Every single

Look at those lips!

hook-up played out exactly the same. Upon feeling the sting of the hook every fish went into the backing and fought like crazy. During that one day I witnessed backing slicing through the water more than I've seen in all my seasons of flyfishing put together. And to actually land a fish was to manhandle it in down-and-dirty, mud-in-your-face, hand-to-hand combat.

Eventually, I could stand on the sidelines no more. I put the camera down, picked up a rod, and on the second or third cast lucked into a carp. It peeled line and was into the backing before I even knew what was happening. It was such a furious run that for a scary few moments I thought I might lose fly, leader, fly line, backing—the whole damn rig. But just as the reel's arbor began to show through, I was able to apply enough pressure to turn it. Next, it ran right at me. Reeling like a maniac, I had just regained all of the backing when it did a 180 and made another wicked run. Pumping and reeling for all I was worth, I finally wrestled it close enough for Tom to hand toss it onto the beach, but we were both thoroughly wet before we managed to subdue the thrashing carp. While I tried to regain my composure and pump life back into my aching wrists and hands, Tom measured and hefted the carp. "This guy's probably closer to 10 pounds, way to go!" Thrilled, all I could think to say in reply was, "What the hell would I do with anything bigger?"

It's difficult to put the unbridled, raw power of a hooked carp into words. So I'll just tell you that Leeming broke three rods in one season before he learned "not to high-stick 'em." I'm not exactly a small man, and I'm used to hauling in all kinds of fish, but at the end of a day of wrestling just a few carp my arms, wrists, and hands felt the workout.

Fishing for Carp on the Upper Missouri

So what are the best conditions for catching carp? Leeming notes that bright sun, a cloudless sky, no wind, clear water, and 90-degree days are ideal. For the upper Missouri, Leeming considers eight to ten fish landed a good day. While that might not sound like a lot, consider that each carp might weigh over 10 pounds, and hooking one requires a great deal of casting skill and stealth.

Then again, a hooked carp and a landed carp are not necessarily one and the same. The actual landing will test your rod-handling and fish-fighting skills. And your knots, leader, rod, reel, and tippet must all do their jobs. Having the hook pull free will likely be the least of your worries, since Leeming has seen very few hooked carp shake loose. The carp's mouth seems to possess ideal hook-holding qualities.

Carp are prolific; a mature female might lay a million or more eggs. They tend to occupy a niche within the habitat where other fish are not in competition, so there's not much to depress a population once it's established. The section of river we fished, for example, becomes too warm during the summer to hold trout. Most just pass through during fall and spring spawning runs. And, so far, the burgeoning small-mouth bass population in Canyon Ferry Reservoir hasn't expanded upriver, although there are apparently a handful of resident northern pike and catfish. But this stretch of the Missouri River harbors few dominant predatory species that eat carp. Except for the occasional bowhunter who comes to shoot carp, Leeming has never seen another carp angler here. If only that were also true on the more famous section of the upper Missouri below Holter Dam!

Upper Missouri River carp average 8 pounds or more.

Carp possess remarkable defenses and are seemingly much more aware of their surroundings than trout, or any freshwater fish I'm familiar with, for that matter. For example, we spotted a pod of surface feeders in a foam-filled back eddy and I wanted photos. I crouched down, camera in hand, and quietly (or so I thought) crept closer. Suddenly all the protruding lips and fins disappeared. I turned sheepishly to Leeming, who stood back grinning.

"Did I spook 'em?"

Tom nodded, "Afraid so."

Incredulous, as I'm not new to stalking fish, I asked the obvious, "How?"

He took a few steps, his sandals making slight crunching noises in the gravel. "They heard that," he said, gesturing toward his feet.

"You gotta be kidding." But I knew he wasn't.

He went on to say that carp possess finely honed senses of sight, smell, hearing, and touch, and are almost impossible to approach from behind. "I find I can approach much closer by standing upright in full view, moving real slow, quiet as possible, until in range." Carp, by the way, hear in three ways: the inner ear, a super-sensitive lateral line, and a web of small bones and ligaments that connect the inner ear to the swim bladder. The combination allows them to hear over a much wider range than trout and bass.

To add to the angler's woes, a frightened or wounded carp emits an odor that alerts other carp in the area. Leeming figures that if he tags anything over one carp per pod he's into bonus territory.

To catch a carp on the fly, the best tactic may be to stay still and let them come to you. This increases your odds, since carp communicate food finds to the rest of the flock. However, one false move, one errant flash of rod or reel, or anything like a noisy approach, and the whole pack will disappear in the blink of an eye.

When a carp does feed into range you must act quickly and make an accurate, unobtrusive presentation. Not exactly your basic chuck-and-chance-it casting program. Leeming coaches anglers to cast slightly beyond and to the side of the target fish, let the fly settle into the silt, then slowly drag it into view, "The fly skittering slowly along the bottom kicks up little puffs, sort of like a big nymph, crayfish, or whatever might come traveling along. The carp are used to seeing this and, provided all else is in order, are quick to pounce. However, a fly sucked in doesn't always mean a carp hooked. Carp are super quick at spitting out something that doesn't taste quite right.

"Casting blind is a waste of time," says Leeming. "You'd be lucky to catch one carp a season; although when the water's murky or in glare or current and I can't see the subtle pick-up, I do sometimes employ small strike indicators. But you'd best be on top of your game. If you think trout sometimes take while barely moving the indicator, try carp. Usually all you see is the slightest hesitation, a wiggle that really isn't, if that."

As carp eat a wide variety of foods, they obviously aren't likely to be particularly fussy when it comes to fly pattern. For example, when cottonwood fluff (seeds) litters the water a small White Wulff apparently passes muster.

Leeming's fly box includes small crayfish imitations, modified saltwater patterns like the Crazy Charlie, small Clouser Minnows. "More important than the pattern, though, is the fact that all of my subsurface patterns are tied to ride point up. In other words, tied with the weight on top of the hook."

Ants, hoppers, mayfly, and caddis imitations all catch carp on top at times. Dave Whitlock even concocted a Popcorn Bug and Mulberry Bug specifically for carp. Leeming finds that certain spots and water types attract surface-feeding carp. Eddies where the surface is thickly foamed are hotspots for surface activity. Throughout my indoctrination float, Leeming pointed out spots where dozens of lips projected through the foam; the noise of their sucking evident even before we spotted them.

It should go without saying, but leave your light rods at home. Carp are tacklebusters of the first order. Leeming recommends rods in the 6- to 8-weight category, and builds custom 7-weights for his own use that are strong in the butt, soft in the tip, and rigged with large-arbor saltwater-type reels capable of holding 200 yards of backing.

Restaurants and Accommodations

Wheat Montana at the intersection of I-15 and US 287 west of Three Forks is a bad place, at least for us. Why? We have an uncontrollable weakness for fresh-baked pastries and hot black coffee, and Wheat Montana has both. Consequently, we rarely pass up the chance to indulge the urge. They also serve good homemade soups, a unique "Wheat Chile" concoction, delicious wheat breads and rolls, and deli sandwiches.

Three Forks and the surrounding area offer a surprising number of dining choices. In addition to Wheat Montana, we can vouch for the food served at Historic Headwaters Restaurant (105 S. Main St., Three Forks, 406-285-9892). A good stop for wine and microbrew connoisseurs, the restaurant prides itself on using locally grown ingredients. The BBQ Pork Spareribs really are finger-lickin' stuff, and the lunch specials, particularly the pasta dishes and the Blackened Prime Sandwich, also make our rave review list.

At Land of Magic (Hwy. 205, six miles east of Three Forks) the catch phrase is "Great Steaks," and we've never found any reason to dispute the claim. The Willow Creek Café and Saloon (6 miles south of Three Forks, follow sign on Main St., 406-285-3698) has an excellent pork chop breakfast special, and great food all day long.

Camping is available at the state-maintained fishing accesses at nearby Headwaters State Park (406-994-4042) three miles east of Three Forks on I-90, then

Landing a carp on a fly rod requires skill, patience, and determination— and the right fly, presented perfectly.

east on Hwy. 205 and north on Hwy. 286. The campground provides 23 sites, vault toilets, RV dump station, grills, fire rings, picnic tables, and drinking water.

If you prefer motel life, the Fort Three Forks Motel (US 287, Three Forks, 1-800-477-5690) and Broken Spur Motel (124 W. Elm, Three Forks, 406-285-3237) are comfortable, clean, reasonably priced, and allows pets.

The Sacajawea Inn

If there's a theme to the fine old inns of the West, it's the front porch, which once provided weary travelers with a bit of relief from their arduous journeys. What better place to sit and rock and relax than a comfy, expansive porch looking out over the region's spectacular open vistas.

The Sacajawea Inn (5 N. Main St., 406-285-6515) has such a porch. It was built in 1910 by the Milwaukee Railroad to serve passengers and crew and was a jump-off point for touring Yellowstone Park. Named for the Shoshone woman who guided Lewis and Clark through the area in 1805, the hotel is situated across from the old railroad depot. The bulk of the hotel was built around the old Madison House, which was dragged to this location by horse teams from its original site in Old Town. Construction was delayed for several months when the contractor lost his horse teams in a poker game. When operations resumed, the old building was split in two, and the main hotel was built between the halves.

The Sac has endured its share of economic misfortune. In 1927 the Milwaukee Railroad extended the line to Gallatin Gateway, which became the final whistle stop for touring Yellowstone, and the hotel lost much of its business. In 1980 its relationship with the railroad finally ended for good when the Three Forks tracks were pulled up.

In its first 80 years the hotel changed hands six times. In 1991 it sold again, and the new owners performed extensive renovations designed to preserve the building's historic character.

In 1998 the hotel changed hands yet again, and the new owners continued the renovation work. Period inlaid wallpaper now adorns the lobby, dinning room, and boardroom, giving them a distinct Victorian flavor. New furniture was installed in the lobby and a 70-year-old mule deer buck hangs prominently just inside the door. A new barroom was built, and the bar itself is a reclaimed trestle. More than a hundred years old, it was once part of a bridge spanning the Great Salt Lake. A stylish new dining room and an extensive outdoor patio were also added.

Amazing as it might seem, in 2002 the old hotel was under new management yet again. Since it reopened Gale and I have dined there twice, once for dinner, once for lunch. For dinner, I had the Chicken Milan served on a bed of Chardonnay sauce with four-blade lettuce salad, salami, and cheese, homemade roll-up breadsticks, pickled beets, sweet potato salad, pasta, and baby red potatoes. Gale opted for Baked Alaska Halibut, which included all of the above extras. Both meals were delightful—and filling.

Nearby Fisheries

Upper Canyon Ferry Lake and Toston Dam hold good carp populations, but you'll need a boat and motor to get at them. It's something like 6 miles from the Missouri River inlet to the first boat access on Canyon Ferry; a hard row or paddle, especially when the lake's infamous wind kicks up. The lower Missouri, from Great Falls to Fort Peck Reservoir, provides adventurous carp seekers boundless opportunities.

And, of course, you can drive an hour in almost any direction and hit a famous trout river.

Nearby Attractions and Activities

Lewis and Clark Caverns, 19 miles east of Three Forks on Highway 2, is one of the West's largest limestone caverns and the site of Montana's first state park.

At the Madison Buffalo Jump state monument, 6 miles south of Logan on Buffalo Jump Road, you can stroll the base of the steep cliffs, admire the bone shards, and imagine the thundering hoof beats as thousands of bison run to meet their maker.

Author's Tip

As flyrodding for carp is such a specialized pursuit, I'd recommend spending a day under Leeming's wing as the best way to start this new addiction.

Favorite Fly

Leeming Crayfish

Hook	2XL saltwater #8
Tail	Orange/black Sili Legs
Body	Root beer Estaz chenille
Eyes	Lead dumb-bells
Head	Elk hair
Claws	Brown bunny strips

Fast Facts

Upper Missouri River

Location	Three Forks to Canyon Ferry Reservoir
Water Type	Broad and flat with a few minor stretches of broken water
Primary Gamefish	Carp
Best Time	July and August, the hotter and brighter the better
Best Flies	Small crayfish, modified saltwater patterns, small Clouser Minnows tied with weight on top to ride point up
Equipment	9-foot for 7-weight, large-arbor saltwater reel with a good disc drag, floating line, minimum 200 yards backing, tapered leader no finer than 3X, preferably stouter

Conditions	Hot, bright sun and low, clear water
Drive Time	From Helena: 1 hour
	From Bozeman: 1 hour
	From Idaho Falls: appx. 4 hours
Directions	From Helena, 12/287 to Townsend, 287 south toward Three Forks, river parallels highway; from Bozeman, I-90 west to Three Forks, 287 north toward Townsend; from Idaho Falls, I-15 north to Dillon, 41/55 to Whitehall, I-90 east to Three Forks, 287 north toward Townsend, river parallels highway.

Local Fly Shops

Bent Willow Bait and Tackle
108 S. Front
Townsend, MT 59644
406-266-4339

Montana Troutfitters
1716 W. Main
Bozeman, MT 59715
406-587-4707

River's Edge
2012 N. 7th
Bozeman, MT 59715
406-586-5373

Bozeman Angler
23 E. Main
Bozeman, MT 59715
406-587-9111

Fins & Feathers
1500 N 19th Ave # B
Bozeman, MT 59715
406-586-2188

Greater Yellowstone Flyfishers
31 Spanish Peak Dr.
Bozeman, MT 59715
406-585-5321

Montana Fly Goods
2125 Euclid Avenue
Helena, MT 59601
406-442-2630

Cross Currents
326 N. Jackson St.
Helena, MT 59601
406-449-2292

Guides

Tom Leeming, C/o Harman's Fly Shop
406-842-5868

When trout get lethargic in the dog days of summer, the carp fishing is just hitting its prime.

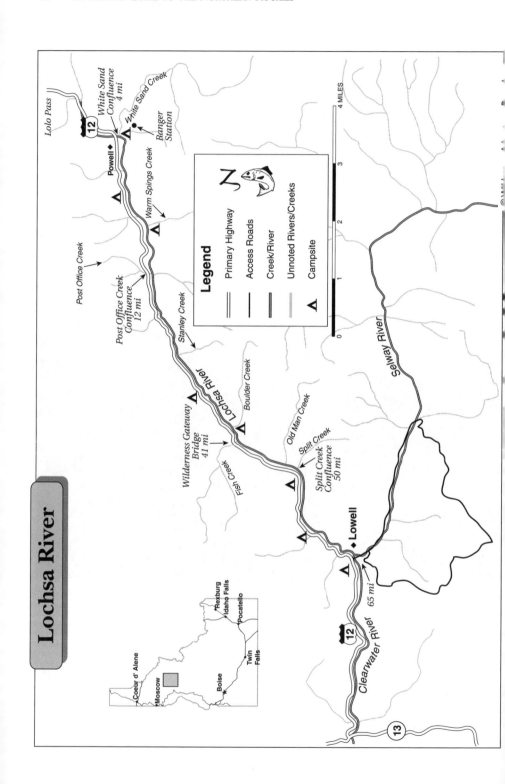

Lochsa River

CHAPTER 9

THE LOCHSA RIVER

Scenic, Accessible, Crowd-Free, and Good Fishing

A few years back, we went over to Montana's Bitterroot River in May, hoping to hit the elusive Salmonflies. Instead, we hit an early thaw and a blown-out river. Finding amusement in Missoula for one day was not a problem, but the prospect of two days in town left me cold.

"Let's head over to Idaho and take a look at the Lochsa," I suggested.

To which Gale, the pragmatist in the family, replied, "What makes you think snow doesn't melt in Idaho the same as it does in Montana?"

"Might have been colder on that side of the Divide. No way to know without looking."

"It sounds like a lame-brained notion, but far be it for me to interfere, though I'm going to have a hard time not saying I told you so."

So we headed west on the Lolo Trail (US 12), climbed Lolo Pass, and dropped into Idaho. While little snow remained on the Montana side, such was not the case in Idaho. The drifts beside the road were level with the truck's windows. I almost blurted out, "See, it *is* colder," but bit my lip just in time. A smart move as it turned out, for when we finally caught sight of the river at the bottom of the steep grade near where

Crooked Fork, Brushy Fork, and Pack Creek come together to form the main Lochsa, the scene was enough to take your breath away. The river was seething, roaring caldron of whitewater for as far downstream as the eye could see.

"Now what, Captain?"

"Let's go home."

Since that trip Gale makes sure I renew my vows annually: "Repeat after me, thou shalt not even think of fishing the Lochsa until at least July, September is even better."

Northern Idaho's Lochsa River is born at around 6,000 feet in the Bitterroot Range hard by the Montana line. It plunges nearly a mile (4,750 feet) in just 65 miles to merge with the Selway River to form the Middle Fork Clearwater River at Lowell. The upper 30 miles are designated Wild and Scenic; the lower 30 are just as wild and scenic but lack the official designation. The entire river, including tributaries, is home to wild and wonderful westslope cutthroat trout, thanks in large part to Idaho's ongoing and progressive wild trout management program.

Once spring runoff abates (after peaking at 10,000 cfs or higher), the Lochsa runs clear and cold, as inviting as any trout river on the planet. Walled in by steep mountainsides cloaked in dark timber, it's a picture-postcard sort of place to wet a line.

I have gotten smarter with age, and these days I usually do wait until September before visiting the Lochsa. The river is still far from a placid meadow stream, but it's sure a lot tamer than it is earlier in the season. Since we've not found much difference in the fishing prospects upriver or down, we usually set up camp at the first available spot beyond the state line and close enough to the river to let its music serenade us to sleep.

The entire river flows through the Clearwater National Forest and is closely paralleled by US 12, making for nearly unlimited access. For obvious reasons, we seek out the pools and runs where the road and river part company. The river harbors cutthroats to 20 inches or more, but the average fish runs more like 10 to 12 inches, with enough 14- or 15-inchers to keep us happy.

Last fall we headed over right after Labor Day. Leaving camp shortly after dawn, we followed the river around a bend or two until the noise of the river drowned out all sounds of civilization. Laying claim to a pair of deep, green pools, we went to it. We both hooked up almost immediately, and that set the tone for the remainder of the morning. As we leapfrogged downstream, the action continued fast and furious. In my case, the catch included a bunch of 10- to 12-inchers and several larger fish; in other words, a pretty good morning.

Because I concentrated mostly on the places cuts tend to hang out—the deep pools and runs and around logjams—I caught more of them than rainbows, although both were in the mix. I fished the same rig throughout, an ugly brown and tan #8 Chernobyl Ant with a #14 Prince Nymph dropper 18 inches behind. The

Chernobyl accounted for nearly all the cutts, while every last one of the rainbows inhaled the nymph.

Gale fished the same bedraggled #14 Stimulator she had tied on upon arrival the evening before. No surprise there, although for a change this Stimi did at least sport a yellow body.

The real news was that the Lochsa trout were, as they say, on the bite big time. And the few anglers we ran into were apparently having a similar good time, although we did meet a pair of whiners: "Nothing but small ones," they cried. "Too much like cookie-cutter stockers." It seemed an odd thing to say about beautiful, wild cutthroats, but to each his own.

The Lochsa, and all the major cutthroat rivers within the Idaho panhandle, including the St. Joe, North Fork Clearwater, and Kelly Creek, are protected, at least in part, by catch-and-release regulations. Collectively, the rivers contain the healthiest populations of westslope cutts anywhere. And for sheer numbers, the Lochsa and nearby Selway are hard to beat. The thing we like best, though, is that they seldom draw a crowd; at least not like the mobs that annually descend on the Henry's Fork, Silver Creek, or South Fork Boise.

Northern Idaho's Lochsa River in fall.

Accommodations

The White Sand Campground, located at the river's confluence with White Sand Creek between Powell and Lolo Pass, is our preferred camping spot. However, with only six sites, the odds are against finding an empty spot during high summer. Rather than fuss about crowding, we just use this as another good excuse not to hit the river until after Labor Day.

In September it's a whole new game, and I can't recall not finding an empty site or two. Last year we shared the campground with a single tent camper; or more to the point, a single tent, since it was never occupied during the two days we camped there. Anyway, the campground is small, usually quiet, and well maintained, with vault toilets and drinking water, but no hook-ups.

If White Sand is full, head down US 12 to Powell Campground or Wendover Campground. With 39 and 22 sites respectively, both are a little large for our tastes, and Powell can get noisy because it offers full hook-ups in addition to the usual stuff.

Lochsa Lodge (208-942-3405) in Powell was highly recommended by friends, but it burned down before we had a chance to give it a try. However, it's since been rebuilt and should be open for business by the time this book hits the streets. The old lodge featured a friendly, comfortable atmosphere, great food, and reasonable rates, and there's no reason to think the new version will be otherwise.

The Lochsa has excellent stonefly hatches.

The Three Rivers Resort & Restaurant (Hwy. 12, Lowell, 208-926-4430) offers full bar service, log cabins, motel, RV and tent sites, and allows pets. Located at the junction of the Lochsa and Selway Rivers, the lodge is popular among anglers.

Nearby Fisheries

The Selway River, also partially protected as a Wild and Scenic river, drains the Selway-Bitterroot Wilderness, one of the wildest corridors left in the Lower 48. The river can only be floated by permit (just 78 are issued each season), and the odds of drawing one are roughly equivalent to winning the lottery. The float season begins May 15, and one can only imagine what it's like to chuck flies from a raft bouncing through flows that might peak in excess of 14,000 cfs. But a lot of anglers do it, and a lot more want to.

The float season ends in July, and flyfishers flock to the upper river on foot or horseback to sample the fast fishing for which the river is famous. Rumors of 30, even 50, fish days crop up everywhere, but any flyfishing excursion into such a wild place is the highlight of the season no matter how many fish are caught.

Almost any mountain rill in the region that still has water flowing in August and September is worth a cast or three. As long as you're looking for solitude instead of huge fish, you won't be disappointed. Watch your step, though, as the area also supports a healthy rattler population.

Nearby Attractions and Activities

All the northern panhandle rivers are well known among whitewater enthusiasts, and any flyfishing trip to the region prior to August will almost assuredly mean sharing the river with kayakers, rafters, and other thrill seekers.

The region is also popular with folks who like to hike and camp. And the possibilities for both are endless, as there are thousands upon thousands of acres to explore.

Author's Tip

While the lower end of the Lochsa gets most of the attention, we like the upper reaches best. Fishing anywhere on the river is by no means technical, and usually just a few basic patterns are all you'll need. Our Lochsa fly box is sparse: Chernobyl Ants, Stimulators, Humpies, Madam X's, Turck's Tarantulas, Royal Wulffs, a few Adams, light and dark Elk Hair Caddis, and a few nymphs and a streamer or two. We bring a variety of sizes, mostly #6-14.

Favorite Fly

Madam X

Hook	Tiemco 5263 #6-10
Tail	Deer hair
Body	Red or yellow poly yarn
Wing/Head	Deer hair tied bullet style, pulled back to form wing
Legs	Round rubber band or variegated Sili Legs

Fast Facts

Lochsa River

Location	Paralleled by US 12 between Lolo, Montana and Lowell, Idaho
Water Type	High-gradient, mountain freestone river
Primary Gamefish	Westslope cutthroat, rainbows, some bull trout
Best Time	August and September; in the worst low water years cutts sometimes begin migration downriver by the end of August
Best Flies	High-floating attractors, terrestrials, and flashy nymphs
Equipment	8- to 9-foot, 3- to 5-weight, floating line, tapered leader, seldom necessary to go finer than 4X tippet
Conditions	Snow can make access difficult well into June; high water often stays through July
Drive Time	From Missoula: 1 hour
	From Lewiston: 2 hours
	From Coeur d'Alene: 4.25 hours

Directions   From Missoula, take US 93 south to US 12 west across
              Lolo Pass; from Lewiston, take US 12 east; from Coeur
              d'Alene, take US 95 south to Lewiston, US 12 east to river.

Local Fly Shops and Guides

Twin River Anglers
534 Thain Road
Lewiston, ID 83501
208-746-8946

Tom Cat & Frank Sporting Goods
618 E Business 12
Kooskia, ID 83539
208-926-4359

Three Rivers Resort, Inc.
HC-75, Box 61
Kooskia at Lowell, ID 83539
208-926-4430

Riverside Sports Shop
P.O. Box 2547, Rt.1 Hwy. 12
Orofino, ID 83544
208-476-5418

Clearwater Fishing Co.
P.O. Box 1375
Orofino, ID 83544
208-476-3534

The Guide Shop
14010 Hwy 12
Orofino, ID 83544
208-476-3531

Contacts

Clearwater National Forest
12730 Highway 12
Orofino, ID 83544
208-476-4541

Idaho Fish and Game
Panhandle Region
2750 Kathleen Ave.
Coeur d'Alene, ID 83814
208-769-1414

Orofino Chamber of Commerce
P.O. Box 2221
Orofino, ID 83544
208-476-4335

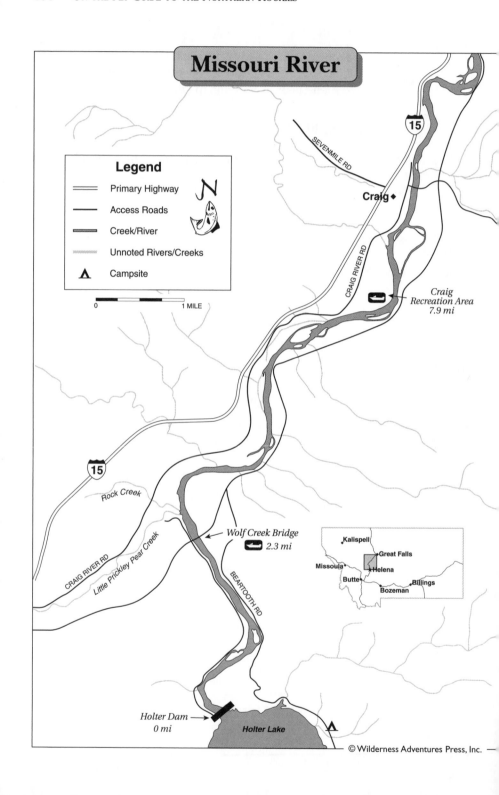

Missouri River

Legend

═══	Primary Highway
───	Access Roads
━━━	Creek/River
⋯⋯⋯	Unnoted Rivers/Creeks
▲	Campsite

0 _____ 1 MILE

SEVENMILE RD

15

Craig ◆

CRAIG RIVER RD

Craig Recreation Area 7.9 mi

15

Rock Creek

CRAIG RIVER RD

Little Prickley Pear Creek

BEARTOOTH RD

Wolf Creek Bridge 2.3 mi

Kalispell
Great Falls
Missoula
Helena
Butte
Bozeman
Billings

Holter Dam 0 mi

Holter Lake

▲

© Wilderness Adventures Press, Inc. —

CHAPTER 10

THE MISSOURI RIVER, HOLTER DAM TO CRAIG

Best of Show Award

The Missouri River between Holter Dam and Craig, Montana, hosts a wide variety of prolific insect hatches, including the mother of all Trico hatches. In mid-July when these little mayflies explode upon the scene, Trico addicts show up from all over the world to sample the action. For such a diminutive insect—#20-26 hooks are the foundation for most patterns—the annual emergence is quite an event. It's a very dependable hatch, and successful Trico anglers usually demonstrate a skill level casual flyfishers can't match.

Tricos definitely aren't for everyone. Unless you enjoy the challenge of fishing nearly invisible patterns to trout dining at a table where every square inch is likely to be covered with real insects; can pull off repetitive, delicate, accurate casts; and handle long leaders with very long, super-thin tippets this might not be your bag. The rewards are big, though, as the Missouri's wild rainbows and browns tend to run larger than average trout on other famous rivers. And there's a special satisfaction in taking fish this way.

A pretty Missouri River rainbow trout.

At dawn on a weekday in early August we meet our friends and fellow Trico addicts Paul and Patti Antolosky, and then we all pile into our 17-foot Old Town canoe. With four adults and fly gear, using one skinny canoe seems odd, but it's only a short paddle downstream from the Wolf Creek Bridge to our destination. The alternative is a long hike on the railroad tracks.

There's nothing particularly special about our chosen stretch of river beyond the fact that the Antoloskys found pod after pod of gulpers here the day before. Even as we beach the canoe, trout are swirling upstream and down.

These trout are picking off emerging Trico duns, a warm-up for the spinner fall later on. Spinners usually start falling sometime around nine, and when they do the trout quickly make the switch from duns to helpless spinners. It's a daily feeding orgy that generally lasts until around noon, although we have fished to trout eating Trico spinners well into afternoon during periods of unusually cool or inclement weather.

For the early fishing to duns we use #20-24 parachutes or Sparkle Duns or a #20-24 CDC emerger trailing a tiny beadhead nymph a foot or so behind. Since these Missouri River trout have seen it all, we concentrate on keeping the float as drag-free as possible.

I man the cameras while the other three begin fishing. Gale casts to a small pod of heads busily working the edge of a current seam, and Paul wades upstream. Meanwhile, Patti spies a wide snout rhythmically poking through the surface just below a big rock that juts out from the bank. "I think I know that guy," she grins, edging her way carefully into casting position.

Patti executes a series of perfect casts, yet not once does the trout show interest. Obviously puzzled by the consistent refusals, she reels up to change patterns. No dice. She reels in again, lengthens the tippet. Still the trout refuses her best shots, and again she reels up and changes patterns. That does it. Patti rears back on the rod. The reel screams as the trout explodes from the shallows. Shattering the river's mirror-like stillness, it tears hell-bent toward the other side. Several minutes later, she is finally able to slip the net under a heavy, 20-inch-plus rainbow, pose it for the camera, and let it go.

Right on schedule, the action changes from casting to a few individual trout eating duns to picking individual trout from large pods now gulping the blanket of spinners that covers the river from bank to bank. This can be tedious, as your single fake fly is floating out there among a zillion or so real insects. It's a crapshoot whether or not a trout will even see your fly, let alone take it.

When the hatch comes off like this, we usually opt for a pattern not at all like the naturals, one we hope might catch a gulper's attention. And one we don't have to squint to see. We try to pinpoint our casts to actually float the fly right into the open maw of the target trout. This still isn't like shooting fish in a barrel, but at least it tips the odds a little bit in our favor.

When casting to pods, try to locate a target and stick with it. Flock shooting generally leads to a long, fruitless casting session. A good strategy is to pick off Tail-End Charlie first, then work your way through the line of feeding fish. I like to stalk as close as possible. Depending on conditions, a hooked trout may spook the entire pod, but if you rest them a bit they should resume feeding. On some days, however, a spooked pod is a spooked pod. On those rare mornings when I'm on top of my game I can sometimes catch two or three trout from a pod before putting down the rest.

I have long since put the camera down and am currently working a trout that leaves a big wake each time it moves to suck in a fly. It has chosen to dine in water barely deep enough to hide its dorsal fin. I am pitching a #20 Foam-Body Red Ant on a long leader that tapers to 6X tippet. The entire leader is 16 to 20 feet long. Even under ideal circumstances such a rig tests my casting skills, but now a gusty breeze has sprung up and pins me on the ropes.

In ten tries, six are stifled by the wind, two are just plain misses, one hits the strike zone and is refused, and one lines the fish's back, spooking the hell out of it. I'm forced to wait several minutes for the frightened trout to resume feeding.

The trout finally starts feeding again, and the scene repeats itself.

After several dismal repetitions, it finally becomes obvious to me that further effort is futile, and I wander off to hunt another target—hopefully one a bit less technical. A few casts later I do find such a fish, but even before I get it in the net I notice out of the corner of my eye that the first bastard is back. And, of course, I can't resist another try.

After what must be at least a thousand refusals, without warning the trout zooms to the fly, eats it, feels the sting of the tiny hook, and breaks off. Just like that. Gone and long gone.

Fishing the Missouri River

These days, it's hard to find a flyfisher who hasn't fished the famous tailwater section of the Missouri River. Crowds during peak season are right up there with other famous western fisheries like the Bighorn or the Henry's Fork. But even with the crowds, an angler can still find ample room to enjoy what I consider one of the best flyfishing rivers around.

Fertile and cold, the tailwater produces blizzard hatches on an almost daily basis, year-round, which help the river's huge wild population of super-charged rainbows grow to a very respectable size. You actually have to work hard to catch a trout less than 17 inches, and most run 19 to 21 inches.

In winter I start out with some sort of two-nymph rig, usually a San Juan Worm with a small, flashy nymph or scud a foot off the hook bend. Whatever the rig, the key in winter is to drift it deep and slow. The cold water slows down trout metabolisms, rendering all but the slowest presentations ineffective. Midge hatches are apt to bring trout to the surface almost any day, but sometimes you'll find a pod working down near Craig with no other sign of surface feeders for several miles upriver. Careful observation and prospecting are key.

In spring the river's trout population falls as many of the rainbows run up tributaries to spawn. Keeping this in mind, we try to cover a maximum amount of water, hunting mostly for browns by stripping big Buggers, leeches, and Clousers. We haul some of the biggest fish from surprisingly shallow lies; it's not uncommon to find a 2-foot trout in 6 inches of water. Early Baetis hatches can also make for hot surface action, particularly on ugly days.

By June, the Mo begins to transform into summer mode. In between hatches, trout hammer San Juan Worms and olive or brown nymphs designed to mimic PMD naturals. Caddis and PMDs are the major June hatches; caddis dominate high water years, while PMDs hold sway during drought years. Mid-July through mid-September expect Trico mornings and caddis evenings. Downstream from Craig, hoppers can provide good afternoon action.

After the Tricos disappear, the river begins to take on its fall dress and tiny Blue-Winged Olives become the primary hatch. Later in October the same Baetis that hatched in spring come back on stage, and some years the giant October Caddis provide a surreal ending to a long season that really never ends.

Restaurants and Accommodations

We took a vote for dinner. Since both Patti and Gale voted for the Dearborn Country Inn (I-15 Exit 240, Cascade, 406-468-2007), it seemed foolish to Paul and me to bother. I presume you married guys get my drift...On the other hand, had we voted it probably would have been unanimous anyway since the DCI just happens to be one of the better eateries in all of Montana.

The excellent soup is made daily on site, and I can think of many restaurants where it would be the highlight of the meal. Not so here. Served with piping hot homemade bread, followed shortly by a fresh tossed salad with your choice of chef-created dressings, who needs an entree? But it would have been a pity to stop since the Chicken Marinara that followed, complete with real mashed potatoes and gravy and perfectly cooked cauliflower in cheese sauce, was delectable.

The Missouri's educated rainbows aren't easily fooled.

While we normally have breakfast in camp and lunch on the river, the Oasis Bar and Café in Wolf Creek serves great oatmeal, while the Frenchman and Me Bar (through the underpass across I-15) serves up tasty burgers, fries, and soup for lunch.

Over the years we've camped beside the river, at convenient pullouts, at the fishing access at Wolf Creek Bridge, in the nearby hills, and at the BLM campground at Holter Dam. Our current favorite is Log Gulch on Holter Lake; 80 sites with picnic tables, fire rings and grills, community water, and vault toilets (no hook-ups). It fills up fast on weekends, but even during the height of the season, there are plenty of empty spots on weekdays.

Frenchy's Motel (Wolf Creek, 406-235-4251) lacks curb appeal, but we've found the rooms clean, comfortable, and modestly priced. Just up the road, Montana River Outfitters (515 Recreation Rd. in Wolf Creek, 406-235-4350) is a full-service fly shop that offers several rental units. It's popular among visiting anglers, so be sure to book early.

Just as popular is the Missouri River Trout Shop & Lodge (110 Bridge Street in Craig, 406-235-4474 or 1-800-337-8528). Also a full-service fly shop, they provide rooms in the lodge and rental cabins. The Missouri Riverside Outfitters & Lodge (3103 Old Hwy. 91, 406-468-9385) offers anglers year-round fishing, guiding, and lodging and is a good place to start for anglers who enjoy one-stop shopping.

With Helena to the south and Great Falls just up the road, it's also easy to stay close to a wider range of services while fishing the Missouri.

Nearby Fisheries

In April we fish #18-20 beadhead nymphs, egg patterns, scuds, or sow bugs 4 or 5 feet below a strike indicator to spawning rainbows in the river between Holter Lake and Hauser Dam. The trout average 3 or 4 pounds, but many run far larger. These days, the trick is getting to the water since the dam was recently closed to visitors (the terrorist threat, you know). No longer can you park at the dam, walk across, and then take the trail downriver. Now you must come upriver by boat from Holter Lake or truck in to the mouth of Beaver Creek and hike upriver. It's no big deal unless there is still snow clogging the mountain roads, which a real possibility in early April.

Despite the access problem, it can get crowded in here. I like to head up the east bank to a mile or so below the dam. There's no need to wade as it's easy to fish from the bank, but if you do choose to wade, please stay off the redds.

A similar fishery is available at the other end of Holter Lake by the dam—same flies, same timing. Any of the Missouri's larger tributaries, such as Beaver and Prickly Pear Creeks or the Dearborn River, can be good early on, but dry summers tend to shorten the season.

Nearby Attractions and Activities

The Lewis and Clark Interpretive Center (4201 Giant Springs Rd. in Great Falls, 406-727-8733) on the banks of the Missouri River at the Giant Springs Heritage State Park is a must stop. Operated by the USFS, the center details the Lewis and Clark expedition through interpretive trails, demonstrations, and an outdoor living history area. The C. M. Russell Museum in Great Falls (400 13th St. N, 406-727-8787) is filled with the artist's famous works and includes Russell's log studio and home as well as memorabilia.

In Helena, the state capital, take a walking tour of the beautifully restored historic buildings. Especially interesting is Last Chance Gulch, the site of one of Montana's biggest gold strikes. The Montana Historical Society Museum across the street from the state capitol provides visitors with a comprehensive overview of the state's rich history.

Author's Tip

The Missouri is one of the best year-round fisheries you'll find anywhere in the country. Summer is by far the most crowded time of year, so if you don't like crowds, try fall or spring. If you live reasonably close by and can pick your days, even the dead of winter can be a good time to fish. While float fishing certainly allows you to cover more water, there is a wealth of fishing available to the wading angler, too.

This is a fertile fishery and what was hot yesterday might not be the best choice today, so check in locally before hitting the water.

Fish on!

Favorite Fly

Loop-Wing Caddis

Hook	TMC 100 #14-18
Shuck	Amber Z-lon
Body	Tan Antron
Underwing	Dirty yellow CDC fibers
Wing	Looped Antron

Fast Facts

Missouri River

Location	13 miles of water between Holter Dam and Craig, Montana
Water Type	Fertile tailwater that looks and fishes like a spring creek
Primary Gamefish	Rainbows, but with whirling disease taking a toll, browns are fast filling the empty niche; some mountain whitefish
Best Time	The crowds are less intense in the spring and fall, but it's hard to beat Trico time—mid-July to mid-August
Best Flies	Season-long opportunities for hatch matching; check local fly shops in Wolf Creek and Craig for what's hot.
Equipment	9-foot, 3- to 5-weight; long leaders and long fine tippets for presenting small flies
Conditions	Typical Montana weather; if you don't like it just wait a minute, it's bound to change; expect wind any day. Plenty of camping spots.
Drive Time	From Helena: appx. 30 minutes
	From Great Falls: appx. 45 minutes
	From Bozeman: appx. 2 hours

Directions

From Helena, take I-15 north to Wolf Creek or Craig exits; from Great Falls, take I-15 south to the Craig or Wolf Creek exits; from Bozeman, take I-90 east to US 287 north to Helena, I-15 north to Wolf Creek or Craig exits.

Local Fly Shops

Missouri River Trout Shop
110 Bridge St.
Craig, MT 59648
406-235-4474, 1-800-337-8528

Cross Currents
326 N. Jackson Ave.
Helena, MT 59601
1-888-434-7468, 406-449-2292

Montana Fly Goods
2125 Euclid
Helena MT 59601
406-442-2630

Dan Kelly's Missouri Angler
280 Recreation Rd
Wolf Creek, MT 59648-8738
406-235-9000

Montana River Outfitters
515 Recreation Rd.
Wolf Creek, MT 59648
406-235-4250/1-800-800-8218

Guides

Missouri Riverside Outfitters
406-468-9385

Paul Roos Outfitters
406-442-5489/1-800-858-3497

Flywater Fishing Company
406-495-0487

Falls Outfitters
406-727-2087

Contacts

Montana Fish, Wildlife, & Parks
1420 East Sixth Avenue
P.O. Box 200701
Helena, MT 59620-0701
406-444-2535

Helena Chamber of Commerce
225 Cruse Avenue
Helena, MT 59601
406-447-1530

Great Falls Area Chamber of
Commerce
P.O. Box 2127
Great Falls, MT 59403
406-761-4434

Montana Fish, Wildlife, and Parks
Great Falls, Giant Springs State Park
4600 Giant Springs Rd.
Great Falls, MT 59406
406-454-5840

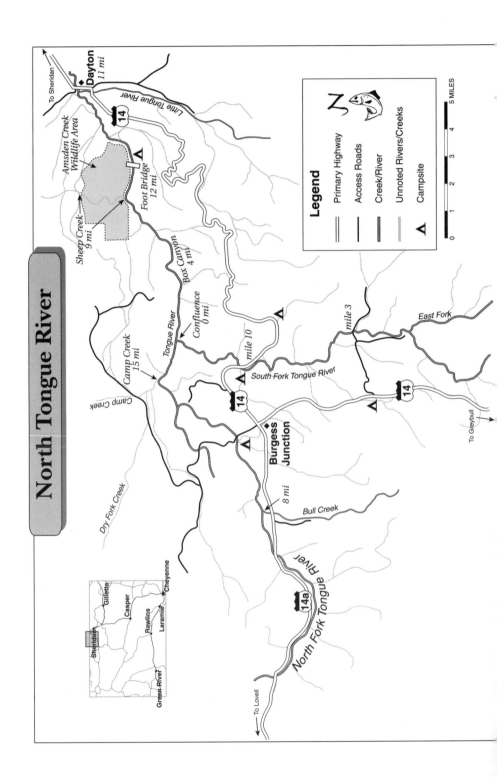

North Tongue River

Legend

——— Primary Highway

——— Access Roads

█ Creek/River

▒ Unnoted Rivers/Creeks

▲ Campsite

0 1 2 3 4 5 MILES

CHAPTER 11

THE NORTH TONGUE RIVER
Flyfishing the Easy Way or the Hard Way

The North Tongue is really two rivers. The one beside US 14-A west of Burgess Junction, Wyoming, courses gently among open meadows and stretches of relatively flat timber; the other plunges wildly down a rugged, rocky canyon until it eventually merges with the South Tongue. From a fishing standpoint, you can go the easy way or the hard way.

Though the fishing near the highway is surprisingly good, thanks in large part to the fact that much of it is protected by catch-and-release regulations, we like the solitude of the boulder-strewn runs and the exquisite wild trout in the canyon. While the canyon is not protected by catch and release, it fishes well because fewer anglers go there. Curious, since the canyon has just about everything a trout stream should: clean, cold, fast-flowing water, solitude, an awesome setting, a bit of adventure, and wild trout of decent size almost always willing to gobble a well-presented dry fly.

Rainbows and cutthroat predominate, with a smattering of brown and brook trout. The fish run 10 to 12 inches on average, with the occasional 14- or 15-incher to keep things interesting. On almost ever trip one of us hooks a real lunker, which in this river is any trout over 16 inches, usually a brown.

To reach the canyon, follow US 14-A just west of Burgess Junction and turn north on FH 15. A mile or so down the road you'll cross the river, turn right, and continue to the end of the dirt track. From there, you'll need to hike into the canyon.

In late August, on a downright cold morning even for 8,000 feet up in Wyoming's Big Horn Mountains, we parked the truck at the end the road and decided to brew a pot of industrial-strength coffee to warm our bones before heading down into the canyon. In deference to Gale's fondness for relatively short, light-line rods and dry flies, I rigged her pet 8-foot, 4-weight Loomis, fiddled with the tapered leader so that a 36-inch, 4X tippet section gave it a total length that matched the rod, and tied on a #14 Royal Stimulator.

As usual the plan was to trade off fishing, with the odd man out running the camera. We make a game of the fishing, and the rules couldn't be simpler: The caster gets one shot, one rise; hook it or miss it. I guess you could call it a competition, but we seldom keep score.

Savoring the hot black coffee to the very last, finally we couldn't stall any longer. We locked the truck and clamored over, around, and between the truck-sized boulders guarding the head of the canyon until we hit water. Gale grabbed the rod and handed me the camera, "Me, first." She then stripped off a few feet of line, false cast twice for good measure, dropped the Stimi beside a half-submerged rock, and in short order yanked a feisty, fat, 10-inch rainbow from the bubbling run. While I did my best to capture the action on film, she admired her prize for a moment then gently let it go.

"My turn."

I flexed the rod, dropped the fly at the edge of a current seam, and watched as it floated barely 6 inches before disappearing in a splashy rise. I missed, but when I tightened the line, up came another rainbow that flopped off the hook. Cheating, I slapped the fly right back down and hooked either the same trout or one very similar. It was every bit as feisty as Gale's and an inch or two longer—honest.

And so it went.

Our progress downstream was painfully slow due to all the bouldering required, but the willing trout made the added effort more than worthwhile. Except for the occasional 6- or 7-incher, the fish were the usual foot-long, fat, and feisty wild rainbows, with a few similar-sized cutthroats.

In early afternoon, after taking a short break for gorp (I seldom go anywhere without an ample supply), we took a vote and decided we'd had enough fun for one day. Gale said, "One more shot and we're outta here." Creeping into position she cast to a deep slot between a big rock on the far side and a fallen log in front of her. To get a proper float required dropping the fly over the log and in front of the rock into a narrow window roughly 18 inches wide.

Her pitch was perfect. The fly no sooner hit the water than *pow*! a heavy trout blasted it. Its acceleration carried it cartwheeling into the air and over the log, where

It landed with a splash. It instantly dove under the log, and just as quickly shot back over the top at the point where the log entered the water. I assumed the fight was over, as the line was now looped around the log.

Gale looked my way and shrugged. I put the camera down, crept carefully out on the log to where I could reach down, and grabbed the line. Out shot the trout.

Again it went over and under the log. The line was still under the log, but it was no longer completely looped, which allowed Gale to get back into the fight. The 4-weight bucked and jumped as the taut line sawed the underside the log. Gale giggled with delight, then suddenly squealed, "Aw shoot, I think he's off!"

And he was. But it reminded us that bigger fish are always a possibility here.

Fishing the North Fork Tongue River

The North Tongue, as it's known locally, is a delightful, little stream. Rather narrow at just 15 to 20 feet wide, it sets a serpentine course through a variety of mountain landscapes—dark timber, swampy stands of dense willows, grass- and wildflower-studded meadows, and finally a dark, boulder-strewn canyon. It meanders along until it reaches the canyon, where it gathers speed for the final 4-mile run to merge with the other fork to form the main Tongue River.

Cutthroats, browns, and rainbows are protected by catch and release from the headwaters down to Bull Creek, although brook trout are fair game for the frying pan. As you might suspect, the easy access and catch-and-release regulations add up

Working a small run on the North Tongue.

to increased pressure. And it should not surprise you to learn that the pushover cut-throats bear the brunt, as evidenced by too many scarred and deformed jaws. Another good reason to stick with small flies and barbless hooks.

This is a typical high country fishery; perhaps a bit more fertile than most, but the short window of opportunity still makes for less than fussy trout. A high-floating #10-16 attractor like a Stimulator, Turck's Tarantula, Elk Hair Caddis, Wulff, Humpy, Madam X, Trude, or Adams will fool all the trout you can handle.

The river does produce a variety of insect hatches, though, including Baetis, caddis, Golden and Little Yellow Stoneflies, Pale Morning Duns, Green and Brown Drakes, even Tricos. Midges hatch sporadically throughout the season, and terrestrials abound through the heat of summer. But even during a hatch, we find that tossing a generic attractor in the right size and silhouette does the job. Should the topside action slow, a nymph tied as a short dropper should do the trick.

Restaurants and Accommodations

If your travel plans take you through Ranchester, Wyoming, at the junction of I-90 and US 14, there's a top-notch campground at the Conner Battlefield just outside of town, which provides tent and RV sites, tables/grills, toilets, and water, but no hook-ups or dump station. And touring the battlefield provides a nice diversion to the flyfishing.

Just up the road in Dayton, the Branding Iron Café and Steakhouse (517 Main St., 307-655-2334) serves the best taco salad and homemade pies in Wyoming. How you manage to eat both at one sitting is not my problem…

The Bear Lodge Resort (307-752-2444) just west of Burgess Junction on US 14-A offers motel rooms, rustic cabins, RV and tent sites, as well as a full bar and restaurant. Pets are allowed, the prices are reasonable, and the river is right around the corner.

One of the things we like best about fishing the North or South Tongue is that it gives us an excuse to return to a favorite camping spot. The well-maintained USFS North Tongue Campground (FH 15 one mile north of Burgess Junction) has 12 sites complete with water, toilets, picnic tables, grills, fire rings, and usually a moose or two hanging around.

The Dead Swede Campground (south of Burgess Junction on US 14, FH 26) has 22 sites, the same amenities, and is just as well maintained, but no resident moose as far as we know. If you plan to fish mostly on the South Tongue, Dead Swede or nearby Tie Flume Campground would be the logical choices since both are right on the river.

The City of Roses

In summer we try hard to include in our North Tongue itinerary an auto tour of tiny Lovell, Wyoming, which is east of Burgess Junction on US 14, to "see the roses," as Gale puts it. A native son, Dr. William Horsley, put Lovell on the map by becoming one of the world's foremost authorities on roses and their cultivation. His enthusiasm spread, and today many of the townfolk continue to carry on the legacy by cramming nearly every square inch of lawn with rose gardens. When the roses stop blooming the huge Mormon Church, which occupies an entire city block, takes over as Lovell's foremost attraction.

The rugged canyon section provides solitude and good fishing.

Nearby Fisheries

South Fork Tongue

Just south of Dead Swede Campground the east and west forks join to form the South Tongue and begin a raucous 15-mile run to the North Tongue, creating the mainstem Tongue River. While there are several short, quiet meadow sections, much of its run is characterized by swift, narrow, rock-strewn pocket water, riffles, and runs. During spring runoff the roar of the South Tongue borders on deafening. Even as late as the end of June we've found it necessary to literally walk away from the river in order to hear ourselves talk. At peak runoff, the fishing is not only difficult, but can be downright dangerous. The river looks like one long set of white horses.

By July, things calm down a bit, and the South Tongue's fishing season begins in earnest. High-floating dry flies, deep-drifted nymphs, and short, stout leaders are good tools for taking the river's mostly 7- to 12-inch rainbow and brook trout. Bigger fish reside here, but getting a fly to them can be difficult. The larger trout tend to hide out on the bottom of the deepest, swiftest runs and around and beneath logjams and undercut banks. Using a dropper nymph will take a few larger fish, but an even better strategy would be to go with standard nymphing tactics to get the fly down quickly and keep it there through the deepest water. If you are lucky enough to hit

A tranquil stretch of the North Tongue runs beside the highway.

the river during a heavy hatch, there's a better than even chance that the big boys will come out to play.

Anglers can access the upper river 5 miles south of Burgess Junction (US 14) off the Red Grade Road at Owen Creek Campground and about 5 miles east of Burgess Junction (US 14-14A) at Prune Creek Campground. We've enjoyed good fishing above the highway, upstream toward the Tie Flume Campground. Especially in fall, the fishing downstream of the Prune Creek Campground can be interesting and quite challenging due to the low, clear water.

Tongue River

The main river plunges approximately 3,400 feet in its first 17 miles down a steep, narrow canyon full of sharp drops, bubbly plunge pools, and rocky riffles, runs, and pocket water. Just above Dayton, it exits the canyon and begins a long meander across the high plains, bound for Montana 60 miles north. This is ranchland that's always hungry for water, and irrigation pumps reduce the river's flow nearly every foot of the way. Yet for the most part it remains a pretty good trout stream, albeit one that's difficult to access.

The Tongue starts on public land where access is free, but hindered by the steep, vertical climb (up to 300 feet) into and out of the canyon. Four miles in, the river enters an impassable canyon bounded by shear rock cliffs where only mountaineers experienced in technical rock climbing can go. Above and below this stretch you can hike along the river, but it's not easy. There is no trail to speak of, and it's often an arduous scramble through brush and over and around boulders. Fly angling enters the realm of real adventure down here, and if you choose to go the best plan might be to stay the night (or several) to get more reward for your effort.

Downstream of the national forest there are just two public access sites, the Dayton Bridge and the Conner Battlefield; the rest is more or less locked up. Much of the lower Tongue is nearly impossible to access, even if you are willing to pay.

The trout—cutthroat, rainbow, and brown at the start, with browns dominating farther downstream—average 8 to 12 inches, with fat 14- to 16-inchers common and bigger specimens not that rare. As with the forks, the trout in the Tongue River canyon are more than willing to grab most any offering that looks remotely edible.

Nearby Attractions and Activities

The Bighorn Canyon National Recreation Area was established by an act of Congress on October 15, 1966, following the construction of the Yellowtail Dam by the Bureau of Reclamation. This dam, named after the famous Crow chairman Robert Yellowtail, harnessed the waters of the Bighorn River and turned this variable stream into a magnificent lake, 55 miles of which are held within spectacular

Bighorn Canyon. The recreation area is composed of over 70,000 acres and straddles the northern Wyoming and southern Montana borders. There are two visitor centers and other developed facilities in Fort Smith, Montana, and near Lovell, Wyoming.

The recreation area itself is a lesser-known treasure waiting to be discovered. It boasts breathtaking scenery, a variety of wildlife (including wild horses), and abundant recreational opportunities, such as boating, fishing, ice fishing, camping, and hiking. Unlike many recreation areas, this one still offers visitors a heavy dose of solitude along with the natural beauty.

Author's Tip

Whether you choose to fish beside the highway or "boulder" your way down into the canyon, the best idea is to keep things simple. It is a rare day when North Tongue trout won't eagerly gobble almost any well-presented dry fly. So you can leave your extra fly boxes and all that gear in the truck and pack light.

Favorite Fly

Humpy

Hook	TMC 100 #10-20
Tail	Elk hair or moose mane
Back	Same as tail
Body	Red Antron
Hackle	Brown and grizzly mixed
Wing	White poly or Z-lon

Fast Facts

North Tongue River

Location	US 14-A between Dayton and Lovell, Wyoming, parallels the stream; public land offers unlimited access
Water Type	Typical mountain freestone trout water, open meadows to rugged canyon
Primary Gamefish	Rainbow, brown, cutthroat, and brook trout
Best Time	July to early fall
Best Flies	High-floating dries, terrestrials, beadhead nymphs
Equipment	7½- to 9-foot, 1- to 4-weight rod, 7½- to 9-foot tapered leader, tippet to suit the fly
Conditions	Cold mornings, hot afternoons; easy access off US 14-A. Lots of camping, and a couple of motels.
Drive Time	From Casper: 3.25 hours
	From Billings: 2.5 hours
	From Cody: 2.25 hours
Directions	From Casper, I-25 north to I-90 west to Ranchester exit, US 14 west to Burgess Junction, US 14-A to river; from Billings, I-90 east to Ranchester exit, US 14 west to Burgess Junction, US 14-A to river; from Cody, take US 14-A to river between Lovell and Burgess Junction.

Local Fly Shops and Guides

Eaton's Ranch
Wolf Creek Fly Shop
Wolf, WY 82844
1-800-210-1049, 307-655-9285

North Fork Angler
1107 Sheridan Ave.
Cody, WY 82414
307-527-7274

Big Horn Mountain Sports
334 N. Main Street
Sheridan, WY 82801
307-672-6866

Fly Shop of the Big Horns
227 North Main Street
Sheridan, WY 82801
1-800-253-5866

The Sports Lure
66 S. Main St.
Buffalo, WY 82834
307-684-7682

Contacts

Bighorn National Forest
1969 S. Sheridan Ave.
Sheridan, WY 82801
307-672-0751

WGFD
Region 3 Fisheries Supervisor
700 Valley View Dr.
Sheridan, WY 82801
1-800-331-9834, 307-672-7418

A fat North Tongue brown ready to be released.

CHAPTER 12

ROCK CREEK
Mountain Freestone Delight

In the midst of a blistering mid-July heat wave, we decided to cool our heels in Rock Creek, and perhaps even catch a few trout. Since the season of famed hatches, or at least the notorious Salmonfly spectacle, was now ancient history, we were hoping to find the Rock relatively deserted for a change. Dream on.

While I wouldn't go so far as to say that the place was overrun, every other pulloff along the dusty, washboarded gravel road held a vehicle. And judging by the license plates many had driven quite a distance—California, Oregon, Washington, Texas, Michigan, Colorado, and Pennsylvania, to name just a few.

Thankfully, Rock Creek is one of those blessed trout rivers where you don't need a lot of elbowroom to have fun; willing trout seem to be scattered everywhere. Rather than aim for a particular favorite series of runs or pools here, we employ a different strategy: Find an empty spot and jump in. Eventually we found one, rigged up, and went for it.

As she so often does, Gale tied on a dry fly, a #14 Elk Hair Caddis, while I rigged a #14 Olive Caddis Emerger with a #16 Beadhead Prince dropper. She headed downstream and I waded in right in front of the truck. I shot a cast toward midstream, and

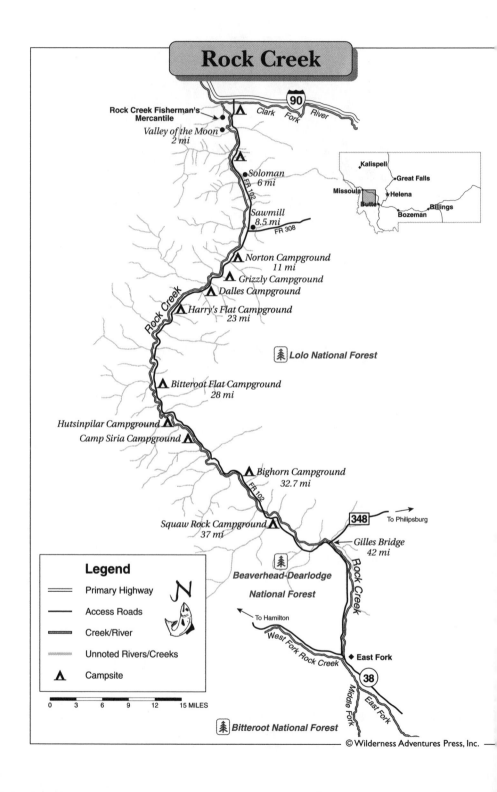

Rock Creek

Rock Creek Fisherman's Mercantile
Clark Fork River
90
Valley of the Moon
2 mi

Kalispell
Great Falls
Missoula
Helena
Butte
Billings
Bozeman

Soloman
6 mi
FR 102

Sawmill
8.5 mi
FR 308

Norton Campground
11 mi

Grizzly Campground

Dalles Campground

Harry's Flat Campground
23 mi

Rock Creek

Lolo National Forest

Bitteroot Flat Campground
28 mi

Hutsinpilar Campground

Camp Siria Campground

Bighorn Campground
32.7 mi
FR 102

Squaw Rock Campground
37 mi

348
To Philipsburg

Gilles Bridge
42 mi

Beaverhead-Dearlodge
National Forest

Rock Creek

To Hamilton

West Fork Rock Creek

East Fork

38

Middle Fork

East Fork

Legend

Primary Highway

N

Access Roads

Creek/River

Unnoted Rivers/Creeks

Campsite

0   3   6   9   12   15 MILES

Bitteroot National Forest

© Wilderness Adventures Press, Inc.

then picked it up and slapped it back down in slack, shallow water tight against the near bank. I watched it sit there for a second, when suddenly a small bubble took its place and a foot-long rainbow somersaulted twice in quick succession out in the heavier midstream current. Just like that, it was gone, and I was left to curse whoever tied that knot—me.

While I rechecked my knots and tied on another fly, I saw Gale hook several fish in a nearby side channel, but noticed that not one found its way into the net. Obviously, we could both use a little help in the landing department. But this was just one of those days, and our landing woes continued. The few fish we were able to release up close were mostly browns about a foot long. Before we quit in early evening I did net a rather robust 16-inch brown that grabbed a #14 Prince Nymph in a deep, swift run below a shady bank.

Despite all our fumbling and the crowd, it was a fun day with plenty of action. After all, we did find enough room to cast our flies, plenty of trout willing to grab them, and even though a bunch got away, we were able to admire a few. On a day this hot, just being immersed in Rock Creek's cold water was enough to satisfy us.

Fishing Rock Creek

Years ago when we lived in Pennsylvania, the first Montana trout stream I recall hearing of was Rock Creek. A fishing buddy returned home with tales of catching "18- to 20-inch trout on dries until my arm ached," and "clouds of insects so thick you could hardly breathe without taking some in." He regaled us with stories of fishing with "one eye on the trout, the other on bighorn rams on the cliffs" and "velvet-antlered bull elk grazing at dawn outside the tent." When he finished, I wanted to head out right that minute.

Alas, "right that minute" stretched into several years, and by then it seemed that every time I thumbed through the pages of an outdoor magazine another story about Rock Creek jumped out. By the time we finally got there to cast our dry flies upon the "hallowed" waters some of the anticipatory edge had worn off; it was just another stop in a long road trip to magical trout waters. As I recall, the scenery and wildlife viewing were as advertised on that trip, but the fishing was just okay. But the crowds! We found it difficult to even find a place to get off the gravel. That was in the 1980s, and I remember thinking as we fled the mob scene, "Enough already, Montana surely can do better."

Despite the letdown, there was something about the Rock that kept calling us back. And since then we've fished it many times. We've had great days and mediocre days, but we've never seen the hordes of anglers we found on that first trip. A lot of that has to do with our strategy of sidestepping around the more popular hatches, which has allowed us to beat the mob scene yet still enjoy good fishing.

Fishing a favorite stretch of Rock Creek.

Looking back over my logbooks, our average trout on Rock Creek hover right around 12 inches, but we almost always manage a couple of 15- or 16-inchers and one a bit larger. Based on our friend's report, Rock Creek is today but a shadow of what it once was. But the really important things—wild trout willing to look up for a fly, a scenic setting, abundant wildlife, cold, clear water, diverse, prolific hatches—are still in place. Maybe things haven't changed that much after all.

Rock Creek epitomizes the Western trout stream. Born high in the Sapphire Mountains, it tumbles for more than 50 miles to merge with the Clark Fork near Clinton on I-90 west of Missoula. The deep pools and runs, fast and slow riffles, pocket water, splits, side channels, and logjams provide a diverse habitat for trout and a wealth of fishing opportunities. Except for a few short stretches of posted private lands, much of Rock Creek and its forks are flanked by gravel road and surrounded by Beaverhead-Deerlodge and Lolo National Forest lands. Access is mostly just a matter of parking the truck and stepping off the bank. Wade fishing is the norm, as the stream is closed to boat traffic from July 1 to November 30.

Fly hatches begin in March or April with the Skwala Stonefly, followed quickly by the March Brown emergence, a hatch many knowledgeable anglers consider the best of the season. The Skwala hatch fizzles as a dry fly event most days, but you can run up big numbers by deep drifting a nymph. The March Browns, however, often provide some of the season's best dry fly action, although the window of opportunity is usually limited to just an hour or two a day. And due to fickle early spring weather and runoff, hitting that tiny window can be difficult.

Just last Sunday (early May), we drove over from Dillon just in time for a downpour; one of those wind, rain, snow, sleet, and hail events that Montana is famous for. The temperature dropped at least 20 degrees, from marginally tolerable to downright cold. In several hours I managed to dredge up a pair of cutts, a brown, a brookie, and several whitefish; not my best day, although I was happy to see the brook trout, which I'd never before caught at Rock Creek.

The March Browns technically made an appearance that day—about six flies came off in as many minutes—but nothing that sparked the fish. When the hatch does make a grand appearance and the fish are rising, a #10 Brown Drake or Parachute Adams works just fine. During non-hatch periods, a similar-sized Beadhead Hare's Ear, Pheasant Tail, or Flashback Nymph will take fish.

As our luck with hitting these early hatches during the hottest dry fly action usually runs on the bad side, I often arrive at the Rock pre-rigged with an indicator, big weighted ugly, and a dropper. I then pinch on two or three BB split shot and dredge the deep runs, current seams, and other fishy spots. Early spring is the one time of year we actually expect to land a few bigger-than-average trout, and the Rock's been good to us; only rarely do we come away disappointed.

Sometime between mid-May and June the annual Salmonfly *blitzkrieg* begins, and for about three weeks Rock Creek is a place we avoid at all costs. Golden Stoneflies follow, but the best summer action begins with the caddis and PMD hatches of early July. A good strategy during the rest of the summer is to fish caddis at dawn, then go find a cool and shady bar or take a midday siesta, and come back later for the PMD spinner fall. For the caddis, try a #14-16 X-Caddis with a LaFontaine Sparkle Pupa as a dropper. The PMD spinners are #16s.

The fall spawning run is probably an even better time than early spring to catch the large brown trout that made Rock Creek famous in the first place. But like many Montanans, we're often hunting and only occasionally able to take advantage. The usual meaty-looking Woolly Buggers, Yuk Bugs, leeches, Clousers, Girdle Bugs, Bitch Creeks, and so on all produce, especially when served up in low light and/or in nasty weather.

After mid-September keep an eye peeled for the emergence of the #6-8 October Caddis. When these big bugs start skimming across the surface some of the biggest trout of the season often come out to play. Hooking one of these slashing bruisers is a ton of fun, although actually landing one is a different story. Use a stout leader and check your knots.

There are other hatches to consider, but Rock Creek trout are seldom fussy and any pattern presented properly will usually fool a fair share of fish. For instance, when #18 Baetis are about, a similar-sized Parachute Adams, soft hackle, or CDC emerger will often work almost as well as the more exact Baetis patterns. Attractors like the Stimulator, Turck's Tarantula, Madam X are also consistent producers. And don't forget terrestrials, which work well most days from summer through fall.

A word of caution to fall flyfishers: Rock Creek is a popular big game hunting spot. It's not a bad idea to at least don a fluorescent orange baseball hat.

Philipsburg

Other roads lead to Rock Creek, but we almost always go via MT 1, the Pintlar Scenic Byway, since it gives us a good excuse to stop in Philipsburg, one of Montana's best little towns. Located in the picturesque Flint Creek valley, with the Flint Range to the east, the Sapphire Mountains to the west, and the Pintlar Range to the south, the town's well-kept, century-old buildings reek of history. The architecture alone makes the visit worthwhile, but as an added bonus there are well-preserved old mines, museums, and ghost towns to explore.

Philipsburg is your typical small western boom-and-bust burg. In the 1860s high grade silver ore was discovered, and by 1867 it was growing at the unheard of rate of "one house per day." By 1869, Philipsburg was dead, with a population of just 36. New mining technology rekindled interest in the area mines and set off a slow recovery, and by 1881 the town was booming once again. The famous Kaiser Palace was built, McDonald's Opera House offered the latest in cultural performance, and Kroeger's Brewery was turning out kegs of the area's most popular beer. However, by the early 1900s the silver mines were all but shut down, and the town, although not quite wiped out, was certainly on its last legs.

Today Philipsburg, while certainly no modern-day boomtown, has undergone a sort of renaissance. In June 2000 it became a finalist in the "Prettiest Painted Places" of America competition. Tourism is big, and vacation homebuyers have discovered the area, an ongoing invasion that shows no sign of letting up.

Gale insists that any expedition to Rock Creek include a stop at the famous Sweet Palace (109 E. Broadway, 1-888-793-3896), perhaps the world's largest collection of very-bad-for-you-yet-impossible-to-refuse candies (750 varieties under one roof and free fudge tasting). The Sapphire Gallery next door is an even more dangerous place to turn her loose—as if I have any say in the matter.

Actually, I don't put up much of an argument because if I time it right the stopover is always a good excuse to lunch at the Rendezvous (204 E. Broadway, 406-859-3529). The homestyle Mexican cuisine and daily soup specials are among the best around, and the espresso bar ranks right up there, too. If we find ourselves in

Philipsburg during the dinner hour we head for the famous Antlers Restaurant and Lounge (128 E. Broadway, 406-859-7000). I make the tough choice between the top sirloin steak and prime rib, while Gale usually opts for shrimp scampi or one of the other seafood dishes.

Accommodations

The Burg Motel (1005 W. Broadway, 406-859-3959) offers clean rooms at a reasonable rate. Twenty minutes closer to the action (you can walk across the road to fish), the Big Horn B&B (33 Lower Rock Creek Rd., 406-859-3388) is a well-appointed, clean, and comfortable place to stay. They serve a great breakfast and the price is quite reasonable, just $69 double occupancy. In season reservations are recommended, but not mandatory.

Most of our visits include at least one night of camping. While there are several USFS campgrounds on the main creek, Rock Creek Road is one of Montana's dusti-

The author releases a nice Rock Creek cutthroat.

est, so we opt first for the East Fork Campground (FR 672), which has 10 sites, each with water and toilets. Our second choice is the Copper Creek Campground on the Middle Fork (FR 5106); seven sites with the same basic amenities as East Fork. Both require a short drive to the creek, but are usually far less dusty and noisy—prime considerations as far as we're concerned.

Nearby Fisheries

The West Fork Rock Creek and Skalkaho Creek across the Divide (toward Hamilton) are both worth a shot. Cutthroat and rainbow, along with brook trout, predominate and some reach a surprisingly hefty size. In the fall, don't be surprised if a larger brown or two shows up. We tend to fish the same patterns and methods that serve us well on Rock Creek. Both creeks run through beautiful country.

Author's Tip

Rock Creek fishes well top to bottom, so instead of losing sleep over the inevitable crowd, we just hunt for an empty spot and go for it. This is one famous stream where you can still drum up business with big attractor dries. Add a trailer nymph and you should be all set for summer fishing.

Favorite Fly

CDC Caddis Emerger

Hook	Mustad 9527 #12-20
Body	Olive Antron (other colors to match naturals)
Underwing	Z-lon to match body
Overwing	Brown CDC feather
Legs	Untrimmed wing butts

Fast Facts

Rock Creek

Location	Western Montana, flows between Sapphire and Garnet Ranges. Headwaters near Philipsburg; flows north to meet the Clark Fork River east of Missoula.
Water Type	Fast-flowing mountain freestone creek, although larger than some so-called "rivers."
Primary Gamefish	Brown and rainbow trout with a mix of brook, cutthroat, even bull trout
Best Time	To beat the crowds try March and April and September to freeze-up.
Best Flies	Match the hatch or go with attractors, dry fly/beadhead dropper rigs, and should all else fail, strip Woolly Buggers.
Equipment	9-foot, 4- to 6-weight rod depending on method and water conditions; floating line and leaders from 7½ to 11 feet
Conditions	Typical Montana, but this is cold country so we never leave home without suitable gear.
Drive Time	From Missoula: 45 minutes From Bozeman: 2.25 hours From Spokane: 3.5 hours
Directions	From Missoula, take I-90 east to the Rock Creek exit; from Bozeman take I-90 east to Anaconda exit, Pintlar Scenic Highway, MT 1 north to Philipsburg, MT 38 west to Rock Creek; from Spokane, take I-90 east to Rock Creek exit in Montana.

Local Fly Shops

Rock Creek Mercantile
15995 Rock Creek Road
Rock Creek, MT 59825
406-825-6440

Riverbend
103 State Street
Hamilton, MT 59840
406-363-4197

Angler's Roost
815 Hwy. 93 S.
Hamilton, MT 59840
406-363-1268

Fishaus Tackle
702 N 1
Hamilton, MT 59840
406-363-6158

Blackbird's Fly Shop and Lodge
1754 Highway 93
Victor, MT 59875
1-800-210-8648

Riverbend Flyfishing
P.O. Box 594
Hamilton, MT, 59840
406-363-4197

Missoulian Angler
420 N. Higgens
Missoula, MT 59801
406-728-7766

Kesel's Four Rivers
501 S. Higgens
Missoula, MT 59801
406-721-4796, 1-888-349-4796

The Kingfisher
926 E. Broadway
Missoula, MT 59801
1-888-542-4911

Grizzly Hackle
215 W. Front St.
Missoula, MT 59801
406-721-8996

Bitterroot Anglers Fly Shop
4039 US 93 N, Ste. B
Stevensville, MT 59870
406-777-5667

Guides

Flyfishing Always
406-363-0943

Lewis and Clark Trail Adventures
406-728-7609, 1-800-366-6246

Foust's Flyfishing
406-363-0936

Montana Flyfishing Co.
406-549-4822

Joe Biner's Rainbow Guide Service
406-821-4643

River Resource Outfitters
406-543-3358

Rocking W Outfitters
406-821-3007

Trouthawk Outfitters
406-721-6121

Thunder Bow Outfitters
406-754-2406

Western Water and Woods
406-251-5212

Backdoor Outfitters
1-888-330-3861

Anglers Afloat
406-777-3421

Five Valley Flyfishing
406-728-9434

Contacts

Philipsburg Ranger District
Beaverhead-Deerlodge National Forest
P.O. Box H
Philipsburg, MT 59858
406-859-3211

Montana FWP
Region 2
3201 Spurgin Rd.
Missoula, MT 59801
406-542-3500

An average Rock Creek brown trout.

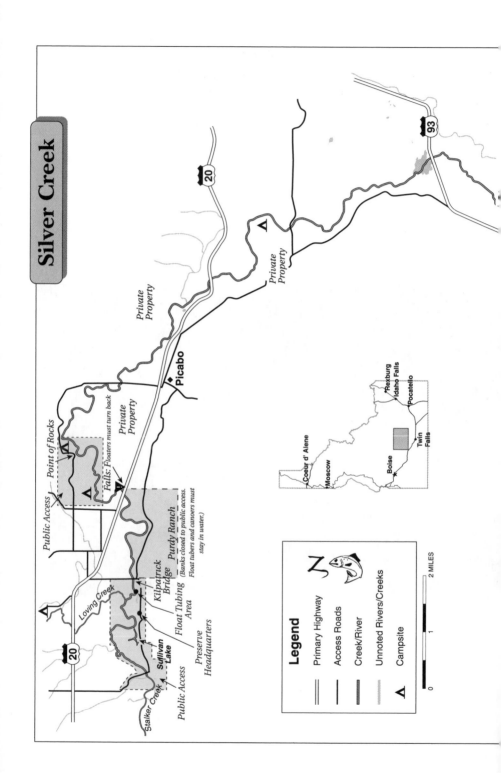

Silver Creek

Legend

Primary Highway
Access Roads
Creek/River
Unnoted Rivers/Creeks
Campsite

0   1   2 MILES

CHAPTER 13

SILVER CREEK
The Final Exam

ıny excuse. That's how easy we are when it comes to Silver Creek. This time a ʋriter's conference in St. George, Utah, provided all the arm-twisting necessary for us ɔ clear the calendar a day early and make the long detour. Some might say that's a ɔt of hassle just for a few hours of fishing, but hey, we're talking Silver Creek here...

We were blasting down US 20 four miles west of Picabo, Idaho, where we turned ɛft onto the gravel road, crossed Kilpatrick Bridge, and pulled into the parking lot at ƕe Silver Creek Preserve headquarters trailing a cloud of dust.

Nasty and raw for early June, it was perfect weather for what we had in mind— ƕe blanket early Baetis hatch. In no time flat we signed in, rigged up, and headed ɫown the well-trodden path toward the creek. We passed several anglers, all but one ƕunkered down on the banks watching and waiting rather than casting, good news ɔr us as the hoped for hatch obviously hadn't yet begun.

Anywhere on the Preserve is okay, but we especially like the water between ʋullivan Lake and the confluence with Loving Creek. It must have been our lucky ɫay, since that was the first stretch we came upon that was devoid of anglers. Better ſill, trout were already breaking the mirror-flat surface, although at first the rises were sporadic and scattered. But the hatch continued to intensify, and we soon found a small pod working steadily below the mouth of Loving Creek. Then, as if someone had thrown a switch, the entire surface became littered with little blue sails. Zillions of tiny Baetis mayflies struggled to dry their wings and lift off before becoming fodder for the dozens of trout now swirling in every direction.

With nervous fingers, I rigged Gale's 8-foot, 4-weight Loomis with a #20 Olive Sparkle Dun and tied a 12-inch 6X dropper to the hook bend with a #20 Beadhead Pheasant Tail Nymph. Handing her the rod, I grabbed the camera and insisted, "You first. Pick an easy target for warm-ups."

"Yeah, right," she said, knowing full well there aren't many easy targets on Silver Creek. She slipped into the creek some distance upstream of the small pod of risers, false cast a few times, checked the forward stroke nicely, and dropped the pair of flies 6 inches or so above the nearest riser…and hooked a trout! First cast. No way, not at Silver Creek, doesn't happen…

The rainbow somersaulted three times and thrashed around the pool before giving up the fight and allowing itself to be lead quietly to net. It was my turn now, but I begged off, "Go for it, dear, you're on a roll. I gladly defer to the lady with the hot hand."

"Thanks, honey, but you know I'm now cursed."

Searching for that perfect pattern.

"Of course, but go for it anyway."

Twenty minutes and several dozen casts later she reeled up, waded ashore, and tossed me the rod. "You and your big mouth."

Now it was my turn. The hatch, if anything, had intensified. The little olive mayflies covered our waders and crawled annoyingly across sunglass lenses and in and out of ears. The trout were in a feeding frenzy. I picked out what appeared to be an exceptional fish that pushed a big wake each time it rolled near the far bank. I dropped the flies into its feeding lane 6, 10, 12, 15 times, and each met with the same flat-out refusal, although twice in quick succession the trout gulped down insects close enough to the Sparkle Dun to shove it sideways. When it happened a third time I started talking to it, "Fussy bastard, aren't you."

"What did you say, my dear? Sounds like frustration setting in."

Desperate times call for desperate measures. I reeled up and switched the Sparkle Dun for a #20 Olive No-Hackle and replaced the #20 nymph with a #22 in the same pattern. A dozen perfect drifts later the trout still continued to pick off real bugs beside my offerings. If it weren't for my own constant grumbling I might have heard it snickering.

For no good reason other than a feeling that I needed to do something different, I waded carefully closer to the bank and took up a position almost, but not quite, directly upstream of the slurping trout. Directing a false cast out toward midstream so as not to splash water or cast shadows, I then dropped the flies 3 feet upriver from the fish's last swirl. Shaking out line to extend the float as far as possible, I almost missed seeing the No-Hackle disappear as the trout nabbed the sunken nymph, although not noticing the bucket-sized boil the sounding trout sent up a nanosecond later would have been difficult.

I reared back, and the rod bowed deeply. The line fairly hummed as the trout zipped to midstream, swapped ends and raced back to the bank, and then turned and pulled hard downstream. Even though rainbows constitute an overwhelming majority on Silver Creek, everything about this fight told me brown trout. So I wasn't really surprised when it turned out to be a brown flopping in the net, although nowhere near the size I would have guessed based on the dogged fight. Still, it was a robust fish, probably close to 19 inches and certainly the biggest brown I'd yet taken at Silver Creek.

Not a bad start to a stolen day of fishing.

Fishing Silver Creek

We are graduates of the School of Upstream Presentation—long leaders and tediously adjusted tippets matched carefully to the fly(s) in order to deliver the package absolutely drag-free. However, Silver Creek is one of the few places where we cast aside our upstream prejudice and turn to chuck our offerings more or less downstream. It still takes me a while. I fiddle and fuss over my leader and tippet and change patterns several times until finally a light comes on, "It's the upstream thing stupid." Then I turn around and invariably catch a couple of trout.

I've also learned, mostly the hard way, that Silver Creek is not the best place to practice my minimalist theory about fly patterns. Take it from me, save yourself a load of grief and bring every fly box you can stuff in your vest pockets. Silver Creek trout are among the fussiest, most fickle feeders anywhere. There really are trout swimming here that might dine only on crippled emergers coming down on the left side; all other offerings, real or fake, are summarily refused.

Of course, the difficulty is no small part of the allure. When you think you finally know it all and really believe you're a master angler, it's time to head for Silver Creek. It won't take long for that old humble feeling to return.

Even Ph.D. trout endure moments of weakness. And there are certain spots (like Sullivan Lake within the Preserve) where stripping Buggers or sculpin and leech imitations can make even Silver Creek sophisticates look like chumps, especially the larger browns. Low light can often make things easier; so can windy summer afternoons when the trout are in a hopper-chomping mood. Often, an odd pattern choice will turn the fishing around just when it seems that nothing will work.

For example, in a fit of frustration one afternoon early last fall I tied on an old Eastern favorite, a Walt's Worm. It's an astonishingly simple, crude-looking imitation of a water worm or cranefly larva. Voila! It so dazzled the Silver Creek mob that I actually had to fight off thoughts that I had unlocked the key to Silver Creek. Of course, I've been down that street before, so when the trout began to refuse the Walt's Worm after their short flurry, I wasn't at all really surprised or disappointed.

Restaurants and Accommodations

One reason we don't camp any more when we come to fish Silver Creek is because Gale found out about all the great Sun Valley eateries and lodgings. Have a hankering for Mexican? Head to the Chapala Mexican Restaurant (502 N Main St., Hailey, 208-788-5065) for great burritos and enchiladas and steak fajitas that are off the charts.

That takes care of one dinner, and the next night it's on to the Red Elephant Saloon (107 S Main St., Hailey, 208-788-6047) where as usual I'm torn between the steak or the steak, while Gale really does agonize over the seafood menu.

Oh, well, there's always Taste of Thai (106 N Main, Hailey, 208-278-2488) just down the road. And if you need a good cup of coffee, you can find it at Java On Main (310 N. Main, Hailey).

We used to camp at Point of Rocks, an okay, though often crowded, campground a few miles northwest of Picabo off Picabo Road. There are also campgrounds near-

>y at Hayspur (N. Picabo Rd. off US 20) and east of Picabo on US 93 at Priest Rapids. ₊ately, however, we've been taking a room in Hailey at the Wood River Inn (603 North ₊Main, Hailey, 1-877-542-0600 or 208-578-0600), one of the newest and nicest motels in ₊he area, or at the Airport Inn (820 S. 4th St., Hailey, 208-788-2477), which offers high-₊peed Internet access and delivers breakfast to your door.

The Nature Conservancy Preserve

₊ilver Creek first gained fame due to a public relations blitz by the staff working to ₊romote summertime traffic to Union Pacific Railroad magnate Averill Harriman's ₊un Valley Resort venture. Such notable figures of the day as Ernest Hemingway, ₊ane Grey, and many Hollywood stars were invited to sample the area's natural treas-₊ures, including the giant rainbows of Silver Creek.

The stream soon gained worldwide recognition, and to well-heeled fly anglers it ₊ecame a sort of mecca. *Field and Stream* magazine labeled it the finest dry fly ₊tream in America. Those were the days of "catch and kill" and "rivers as sewers." ₊etween the horrific catch-and-keep rates and the rapid degradation of water quality ₊ue to harmful agricultural practices, Silver Creek was barely worth fishing by the ₊ate 1960s.

Enter Jack Hemingway, son of Ernest, avid flyfisherman, and lover of Silver ₊reek. Faced with yet another threat, urban sprawl, when the Sun Valley Corporation

Working a pod of risers during a heavy Baetis *hatch.*

put 479 acres up for sale, Jack led a group of like-minded locals to find a buyer who would save their beloved creek. With the help of nationally famous anglers and writers like Ernest Schweibert, the group persuaded the Nature Conservancy to purchase the land and create the Silver Creek Preserve.

The rest is history. Not only was the stream rehabilitated, the Nature Conservancy was able to convince area ranchers and farmers to place their lands in conservation easements to further prevent development and improve the quality of the riparian corridor of the creek and many of its tributaries. Today the protection extends to more than 30 miles of stream that snakes its way through nearly 10,000 acres. With catch and release the rule, the fishery bounced back quickly. Rainbow and brown trout over 20 inches—some as large as 28 inches—show up with regularity, and fish densities approach 3,000 catchables per mile.

Nearby Fisheries

The Big Wood River

Not all flyfishers are enamored of Silver Creek's extreme angling challenge. And one need not travel far to find a pretty good trout river of a far different character, the Big Wood River. On average, Big W trout pale in comparison to the robust specimens haunting Silver Creek, but they aren't nearly as finicky. The stream itself is user-friendly: good wading, classic riffle-and-pool configuration, and easy-to-read currents, which are a welcome change after a day of dealing with the curling, sneaky-smooth flow of Silver Creek.

The Big Wood fishes more like a mountain stream, which it actually is, as its origins are high in the Sawtooth Mountains. Perhaps best of all, the trout seem satisfied to eat whatever comes along. While they don't gobble every fraud that drifts by, they also don't scrutinize bugs through a magnifying glass.

Our favorite stretch is the catch-and-release water above the Ketchum Bridge, but except later in summer when irrigation demands dewater the lower end, the river fishes well throughout. We were once invited by a motel manager in Hailey to "come on over this evening and fish in my backyard." (He's forever numero uno on our motel manager list, by the way.) We did, and had good fishing within sight of our motel.

Nearby Attractions and Activities

The Ketchum and Sun Valley area is tailor-made for the traveling flyfisher who wants to include the whole family in an outdoor adventure—hiking, biking, swimming, shopping, horseback riding, golfing, skiing, ice-skating, roller-skating, skateboarding, star-gazing (the rich and famous discovered Sun Valley long ago), palace-gawking (you can only imagine the homes here, until you see them for yourself), art galleries, fancy dining, and dozens of other activities.

Craters of the Moon National Monument, 18 miles west of Arco on US 20, is a real moonscape that features over 30 lava flows from the Great Rift System, which began erupting 15,000 years ago and ceased just 2,000 years ago.

The Shoshone Indian Ice Caves, midway between Picabo and Shoshone on Hwy. 75 are like a huge natural refrigerator with a constant temperature between 28-33 degrees.

And if you are into majestic mountains, scenic vistas, and knock-your-socks-off natural lakes check out the Sawtooth Scenic Byway (Hwy. 75) between Ketchum and Stanley. By the way, if you find yourself in Stanley in early fall check out the huge chinook salmon finning their last in nearby Valley Creek Salmon Hole. It's an awesome, humbling, and thought-provoking sight, to say the least.

Author's Tip

I don't like to call a trout stream "technical," so let's just say Silver Creek trout can be tough and intimidating. Lofty expectations often lead to big letdowns. The little details often make the difference between okay and not so hot: clean your fly line, build a proper leader, stock up on the current hot patterns, and call the fly shops to ask lots of questions, even silly ones. You'd be surprised at the little tidbits one can pry from the local experts just by playing dumb.

Favorite Fly

Sparkle Dun

Hook	TMC 100 #16-20
Tail	Tan or Amber Z-lon, sparse
Body	Fine dubbing, color to suit naturals
Wing	Deer or elk hair flared to form semicircle on top

Fast Facts

Silver Creek

Location	Off US 20 near Picabo, Idaho
Water Type	Classic spring creek; slow-moving, clear, cold and fertile
Primary Gamefish	Rainbows of larger than average size
Best Time	June, but part of the river remains open through February
Best Flies	A precise match in both pattern and size is necessary during any hatch period. Popular hatches include the Brown Drake (#10), Baetis (#18-22), PMD (#16-20), Callibaetis (#18-20), Trico (#22-24), caddis (#14-22), as well as terrestrials. Check with local fly shops for the current hatch and hot local patterns.
Equipment	9-foot, 1- to 4-weight; floating line; 15-foot-plus leaders; long 5X-8X tippets, downstream presentations
Conditions	Typical mountain valley weather, wind is common. Camping is limited, but other accommodations can be found in Sun Valley.
Drive Time	From Idaho Falls: 2.75 hours
	From Boise: 3 hours
	From Salt Lake City: 5 hours
Directions	From Idaho Falls, take I-15 south to I-86 west to I-84 west to US 93 north to Shoshone, ID 75 north to US 20 east to creek; from Boise, take I-84 east to US 20 to creek near Picabo; from Salt Lake City, take I-15 north to I-86 west to 84 west to US 93 north to Shoshone, 75 north to US 20 east to creek.

Local Fly Shops

Lost River Outfitters
171 N Main St.
Ketchum, ID 83340
208-726-1706

Ultimate Angler
P.O. Box 21
Sun Valley, ID
208-483-2722

Silver Creek Outfitters
500 N. Main St.
Ketchum, ID 83340
208-726-9056

Guides

Middle Fork River Tours
1-800-445-9738

Idaho Angling Services
208-788-9709

Contacts

Idaho Travel Dept.
700 W. State St.
Boise, ID 83720
1-800-VISIT ID, 208-334-2470

Sun Valley Chamber of Commerce
Ketchum, ID 83340
208-726-3423

IDFG, Southwest Region
Magic Valley Region
868 E. Main
Jerome, ID 83338
208-324-4350

A stealthy approach will pay off.

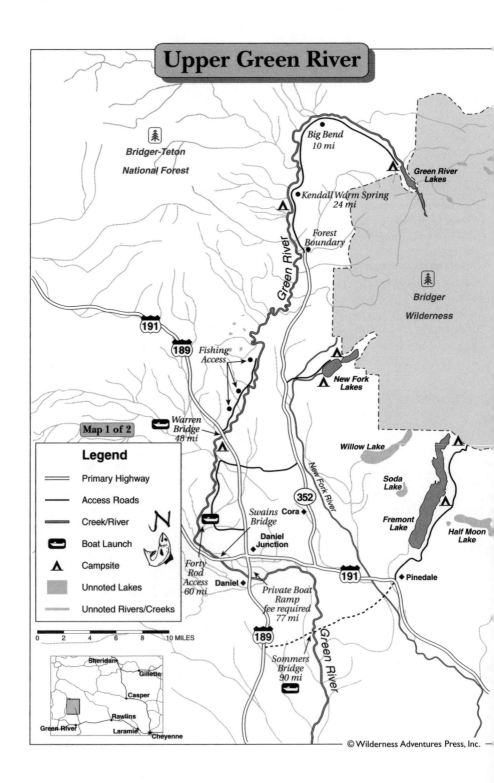

Upper Green River

Bridger-Teton
National Forest

Big Bend
10 mi

Green River
Lakes

Kendall Warm Spring
24 mi

Forest
Boundary

Green River

Bridger
Wilderness

191

189

Fishing
Access

New Fork
Lakes

Warren
Bridge
48 mi

Map 1 of 2

Willow Lake

Legend

Soda
Lake

Primary Highway

Access Roads

Creek/River

New Fork River

Swains   Cora
Bridge

352

Fremont
Lake

Half Moon
Lake

Boat Launch

Daniel
Junction

Campsite

Unnoted Lakes

Forty
Rod
Access   Daniel
60 mi

191

Pinedale

Unnoted Rivers/Creeks

Private Boat
Ramp
fee required
77 mi

0   2   4   6   8   10 MILES

189

Sheridan
Gillette

Sommers
Bridge
90 mi

Green River

Casper

Rawlins

Green River
Laramie   Cheyenne

CHAPTER 14

THE UPPER GREEN RIVER
High Desert Treasure

Timing is everything. And on our first venture to the upper Green we might have done better in that department. It was mid-October, but instead of Indian summer, we were met by a howling wind and a brief, but miserable, snow squall that dropped the season's first 8 inches of new fluff. Nevertheless, when we stopped in to get advice from John Ross at Two Rivers Emporium in Pinedale, Wyoming, he optimistically sent us out into the blow to a favorite stretch of water 25 miles north of town. "There are some good runs up there, and the browns should be stacked prior to the spawn and on the feed with this low front moving through." As we headed out the door, he added, "Strip a Conehead Black Bugger, and you should do okay."

I switched the Ranger into 4-wheel high, pushed the pedal to the floor, and sped to the Warren Bridge turnoff in no time. There were only a couple hours of daylight left, and I didn't want to waste it on a little nuisance like icy roads. Following Ross's advice, I rigged the recommended pattern. Gale, who will risk failure any day to keep from fishing weighted flies, went with her old standby, a #14 Orange Stimulator.

Results: I met the skunk, and Gale hooked and quickly lost the only trout we saw that evening.

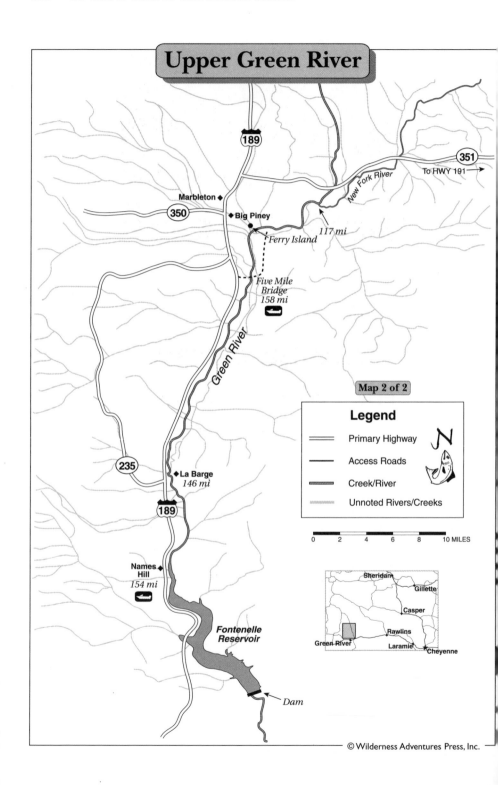

Upper Green River

189

351

To HWY 191 →

New Fork River

Marbleton ◆

350

◆ Big Piney

117 mi

Ferry Island

Five Mile
Bridge
158 mi

Green River

Map 2 of 2

Legend

═══ Primary Highway

─── Access Roads

▬▬▬ Creek/River

▓▓▓ Unnoted Rivers/Creeks

235

◆ La Barge
146 mi

189

0   2   4   6   8   10 MILES

Names ◆
Hill
154 mi

Sheridan

Gillette

Casper

Rawlins

Green River

Laramie

★ Cheyenne

Fontenelle
Reservoir

← Dam

© Wilderness Adventures Press, Inc.

Later, we ran into Ross again and related our dismal performance. He was obviously surprised, but too polite to come right out and say so. "Strange, maybe the browns moved on upstream to better spawning runs."

On the way to a late dinner Gale remarked, "John seems like a pretty nice guy."

"Yeah, and quite the diplomat, too."

The next day dawned on the chilly side (-4 degrees). We pride ourselves on actually being quite fond of polar-bear flyfishing, but everyone has a limit. So we lingered over breakfast at the Wrangler's Café, graciously accepting the offer of a second and then a third refill of our coffee cups.

Meanwhile, the sun started to work on yesterday's snow while warming the landscape a little. Despite leaving the motel room before eight, it was close to eleven by the time we made our way back to Warren Bridge and bounced several miles farther upriver.

With last evening's darkness and frozen fingers, we were way too cold to de-rig the rods. We simply broke them down and tossed them in the back the truck. So rigging up this morning required nothing more than untangling the mess, pulling on waders, and stumbling down the bank to the river to thaw our half-frozen wading boots.

The current coiled around a series of big boulders and spilled into a shallow run, the bottom gravel guarded by several torpedo-like dark shadows. "We ain't gonna have much in the way of excuses today," I announced, pulling on Polaroids for a better look. "The place is crawling with 'em!"

With that, I stripped off several yards of line and shot a short cast toward the base of a big boulder, allowed the Bugger to drift down toward the group of shadows. I stripped it enticingly and—*bam!* Trout on. After a brief struggle I slipped the net under a beautiful black-spotted, butter-yellow brown; a male in his best spawn dress accentuated by a fierce-looking kype.

The brown's struggles scattered the pack, so Gale moved up to a juicy-looking run and covered it bottom to top with the Stimulator but found no takers. Ditto on the next run and the one after that. She finally called a halt to her stubbornness and tied a #14 Prince Nymph 30 inches behind the Stimi. After stalking back down to the starting point, she quickly nailed what would turn out to be the day's biggest brown—a fat female of about 18 inches—on the Prince. I bit my tongue to stop from saying "told you so" in regard to her fierce adherence to dry flies only.

As Ross had said, the browns really were on the prowl, and we probably could have netted a truckload. But we had appointments to keep in other places—doesn't being a working stiff just suck? Anyway, ever since that cold October trip the upper Green holds a high place on our list of favorites. We return every chance we get.

Fishing the Upper Green

"The river fishes well in May prior to runoff and again after, beginning about the first of July and continuing through September. Typically, that means about a hundred days of prime fishing per season," says Ross, who has fished and guided the upper Green since 1979.

The Green gets its start about 50 miles northwest of Pinedale in the Bridger-Teton National Forest at the outlet of Green River Lakes. Twenty miles of rough gravel road parallel the upper portion, giving anglers nearly unlimited access. Below the forest boundary there is private ranchland for several miles and then more public (BLM) land on down to the Warren Bridge on US 191. All the public sections of the river above Warren Bridge can be fished on foot or by canoe, driftboat, or raft, but access through the private ranchland is by water or permission only. Two 8-mile floats between Warren and Daniel Bridge are the most popular, and are best floated when the river runs above 200 cfs. Negotiating the many rock gardens at lower levels becomes difficult.

Wild browns dominate the river, averaging about 14 inches, but with enough bigger specimens to keep things interesting. The stocked rainbows in the river tend to run only around 10 to 12 inches. According to Ross, very few—maybe less than five percent—hold over.

The fishing really picks up in July when the Gray Drakes arrive, and the river's best hatch lasts through August. Other hatches to watch for are various caddis, Little Yellow Stoneflies, PMDs in mid-July, and Tricos in August. While Ross won't divulge his personal secret Green River fly, he flatly states, "You can't go wrong with a Conehead Black Woolly Bugger."

Restaurants and Accommodations

In Pinedale the Wrangler's Café (905 W. Pine St.) serves good hotcakes and omelets and has a good lunch menu.

Coming off the river late one night, we missed last call at our favorite Pinedale-area dinner spot, the Half-Moon Lake Resort and Restaurant (208 FS Road 114, 307-367-6373). By the time we drove back to town it was 10 p.m., on a weekday night, no less.

Sure we'd get tossed out, we headed for an empty table in a far corner of the Stockman's Restaurant (117 W. Pine St., 307-367-4563). Much to our surprise, the waitress greeted us as if we were her first customers of the evening. Then a little gray-haired lady (the owner) came over, sat down, and went over the entire list of specials, making sure we knew the house specialties and rating each personally. We relaxed with a drink and marveled at our luck. The food, including one of the better salad bars we've grazed at anywhere, was excellent. The dilemma these days is choosing between the Stockman's and the Half-Moon.

As for camping, two of the best campgrounds on the river are Whiskey Grove (9 sites) just inside the national forest boundary and the BLM campground at Warren Bridge (17 sites). Both offer the usual picnic tables, fire rings/grills, toilets and water, but no hook-ups.

For those really cold nights, try the Lodge at Pinedale (1054 W. Pine St., 307-367-8800). Pets are allowed, but like the rest of the motels in the area, don't expect cheap rates since the year-round influx of gas-field workers, tourists, hunters, and anglers, make it a seller's market.

Pinedale, Wyoming

At first glance Pinedale comes off as just another withering high-plains community. But we all know first impressions can be deceiving, and the reality is that Pinedale is thriving, with an economy that's on the upswing. There's a steady injection of outside money from vacationers, and business from the recent tapping of a huge natural gas field just south town.

It seems that everywhere you look fancy new homes are sprouting up in the surrounding sagebrush hills. Despite the recent windfall and influx of outsiders, Pinedale remains one of the friendliest towns in the West.

The author hooks up with a big brown in prespawn mode.

Nearby Fisheries

New Fork River

The New Fork is one of those good news, bad news rivers. The good news is that it has great fishing for wild brown trout of good average size (14 inches), with better than average numbers of 16- to 19-inchers and some real lunkers (24-plus inches). The bad news is that it's difficult to impossible to access. In 65 miles it crosses the highway just twice.

Perhaps the best advice I can give for beginner and expert alike is to hire a local guide. If you go it alone, forget wade fishing unless you can wiggle your way onto private property, as the only public wade access is not all that hospitable, and Wyoming has no public access below the high-water mark. Floats, while being the best way to fish, are long and tricky due to the ever-changing character of the river.

For hatches, the New is a twin to the upper Green. And the river's "pigs" require pig tactics: Yuk Bugs, Yellow Yummies, Woolly Buggers, leeches, Clousers. Think big and ugly and you are on the right track. Pound the willow-lined, undercut banks with persistence and reap your rewards.

Several tributaries of the upper Green sport thriving populations of Colorado cutthroat trout, some of surprising size. And a slew of alpine lakes in the nearby Bridger-Teton National Forest, as well as private lakes and ponds, provides plenty of opportunity for the stillwater aficionado. John Ross holds the key to several private fisheries, or you can strap on a pack and hit one of the trails into the Wind River Range for golden trout.

Fremont Lake, Wyoming's second largest natural lake at 12 miles long and up to 600 feet deep, is just 3 miles from town. It's home to giant lake trout (40 pounds), though trying to catch one on the fly might not be worth your time. The only time the big macks are available to fly casters is right after ice-out when they move into the shallows to spawn. There are, however, moderate-sized rainbows and kokanee salmon that provide more consistent angling.

Nearby Attractions and Activities

The Wind River Mountains, spectacular and accessible, provide endless hiking, biking, camping, and angling opportunities. The Museum of the Mountain Man (700 E. Hennick St., 307-367-4101) is a nifty diversion from the angling, with displays, artifacts, and memorabilia from the fur-trapping era, as well as early ranching and tie-hack logging. Gaze upon Jim Bridger's rifle or learn how they trapped beaver and processed hides or how the market for hats helped open the West.

Author's Tip

The upper Green's big browns begin staging for the annual fall spawning run in October. Find the spawning gravel, and you'll likely find browns holding nearby. Try stripping a Conehead Black Woolly Bugger, especially during low-light situations.

Favorite Fly

Conehead Black Woolly Bugger

Hook	Mustad 36890 SF #2-10
Tail	Marabou and Krystal Flash
Body	Chenille, size and color to suit
Hackle	Palmered grizzly or same as body color
Head	Conehead-style brass bead

Fast Facts

Upper Green River

Location	Near Pinedale, Wyoming; starts in the Bridger-Teton National Forest and flows generally southwest until backing up at Fontenelle Reservoir
Water Type	Moderately-sized, meandering freestone river; rocky and faster upstream
Primary Gamefish	Brown trout dominate, with stocked rainbows and mountain whitefish. Browns average 14 inches, with some lunkers over 20 inches.
Best Time	July

Best Flies	Gray Drakes are the best, most prolific hatch; Conehead Black Woolly Bugger is John Ross's pick for day in, day out fishing
Equipment	9-foot, 5-or 6-weight; floating line, tapered leader to suit
Conditions	High-desert winds kick up almost daily; located at 7,000 feet, so expect cool to cold mornings
Drive Time	From Cheyenne: 6.25 hours
	From Casper: 6 hours
	From Salt Lake City: 5 hours
Directions	From Cheyenne, take I-80 west to Rock Springs, US 191 north to Pinedale; from Casper, WY 220 west to Three Forks, US 287 north to WY 28 south to US 191 north to Pinedale; from Salt Lake City, take I-80 east to Rock Springs, US 191 north to Pinedale.

Local Fly Shops

Two Rivers Emporium
211 W. Pine
Pinedale, WY 82941
1-800-329-4353, 307-367-4131

The Great Outdoors Shop
332 W. Pine
Pinedale, WY 82941
307-367-2440

Wind River Sporting Goods
234 E. Pine
Pinedale, WY 82941
307-367-2419

Guides

Big Sandy Lodge, Inc.
307-382-6513 or 307-362-9017
Cell: 307-389-4018

DC Bar Guest Ranch
1-888-803-7316, 307-367-2268

Half Moon Lake Resort
307-367-6373

Green River Outfitters
307-367-2416

The Fishing Guide
307-367-4760

Daniel Float Co.
307-859-8409

Contacts

Pinedale Chamber of Commerce
32 East Pine
Pinedale, WY 82941
307-367-2242

Bridger-Teton National Forest
Box 1888
Jackson, WY 83001
307-739-5500

WGFD
Pinedale Fisheries Supervisor
117 S. Sublette Ave.
Pinedale, WY 82941
1-800-452-9107, 307-367-4353

A beautiful brown heading home.

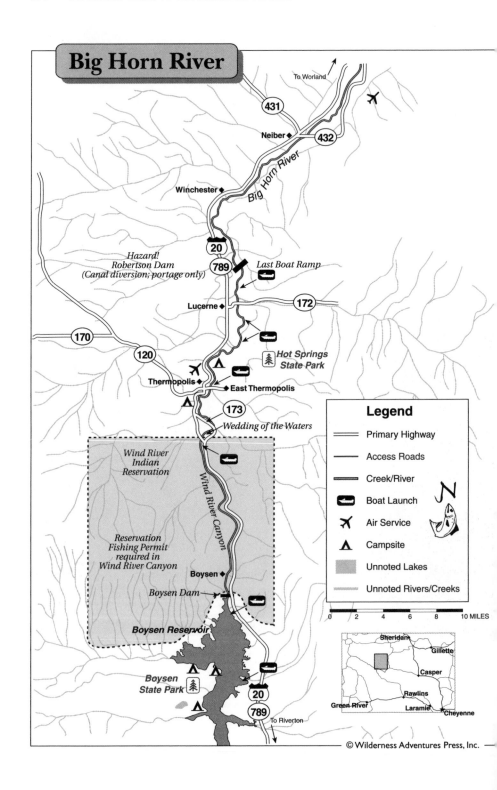

Big Horn River

To Worland

431

Neiber ◆ 432

Big Horn River

Winchester ◆

20

Hazard!
Robertson Dam
(Canal diversion; portage only)

789   Last Boat Ramp

Lucerne ◆

172

170

120

Hot Springs
State Park

Thermopolis ◆   ◆ East Thermopolis

173

Wedding of the Waters

Wind River
Indian
Reservation

Wind River Canyon

Reservation
Fishing Permit
required in
Wind River Canyon

Boysen ◆

Boysen Dam

Boysen Reservoir

Boysen
State Park

20

789

To Riverton

Legend

═══	Primary Highway
——	Access Roads
━━━	Creek/River
🚤	Boat Launch
✈	Air Service
Ⱥ	Campsite
▓	Unnoted Lakes
≈	Unnoted Rivers/Creeks

N

0   2   4   6   8   10 MILES

Sheridan
Gillette
Casper
Rawlins
Green River   Laramie
Cheyenne

© Wilderness Adventures Press, Inc.

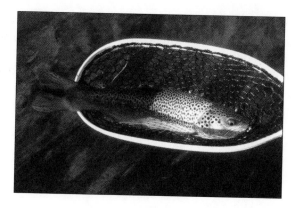

CHAPTER 15

THE BIG HORN RIVER
Wyoming's Version

The Wind River begins as a trickle high in the mountain range of the same name in northwest Wyoming and then cuts an increasingly wide swath southeast for about 75 miles before turning abruptly north. Twenty miles later it spills over Boysen Reservoir Dam and plunges into a deep canyon, the walls of which tower 2,500 feet skyward. (There are some enormous fish in this canyon, but also some hefty rapids.) Upon exiting the canyon the Wind suddenly changes character and…assumes another name.

For this river, born Wind, now called Big Horn, is none other than Montana's famous Bighorn downstream (north) across the state line, but we'll get to that later. First let's deal with Wyoming's version, the Big Horn River. (By tradition, the name is usually spelled differently in each state.)

The river runs a hundred or so miles to the north before crossing into Montana, but only the first 20 miles or so are worth mentioning as a trout fishery. It's admittedly a brief run, although one many anglers believe to be among the West's best. And yes, there are a few spring holes and tributary mouths downriver where big brown trout are known to hang out, but these are too few and far between for the traveling angler to bother with. We usually launch our raft at the Wedding of the Waters a few miles south of Thermopolis on US 20, float down to one of the take-outs in town, and feel we've about covered the best of it.

The first 20 miles are cold enough and fertile enough to produce fast-growing rainbow, brown, and cutthroat trout; fat, healthy fish that average 1 to 3 pounds, with 5-pounders not uncommon. Mountain whitefish and burbot also thrive in the fecund environment.

Despite its fertility, this is one tailwater that doesn't produce heavy daily hatches or trout that swirl at the surface from dawn to dusk. Expect to dredge bottom with subsurface patterns—nymphs, scuds, San Juan Worms, etc.—to have the most success.

For this reason, the Big Horn is not Gale's favorite cup of tea. In fact, as we float today she chooses to sit in the raft shooting photos of me trying to coax the Big Horn's fish into grabbing a red San Juan Worm or tiny hot-pink scud bounced along the bottom beneath a big hot-pink strike indicator (really more of a bobber). I believe a bright red worm (you may also insert the word "aquatic" here if reading the term "red worm" in a flyfishing tome causes your vessels to constrict) and the hot-pink scud suggest…well, isn't it obvious?

The important point is that the trout are gobbling them, and with unusual vigor. In just a mile or two I've boated nearly a dozen fat and feisty trout and lost a couple

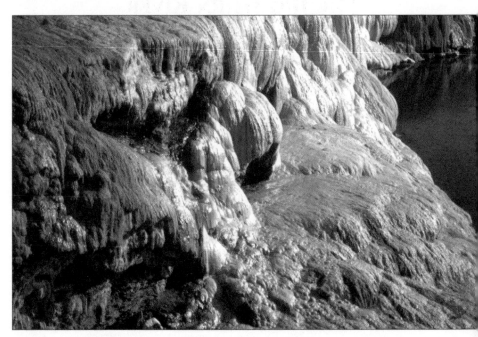

The hot springs at Thermopolis are said to be the world's largest.

of others. It's been an even split between browns and rainbows so far, and all but a couple have taken the worm. Smart money says drop the scud and go with a pair of worms, but why fix something that isn't broken? And besides, it somehow sounds better for a flyfisher to answer the question, "What are you using?" with, "A worm and a scud" rather than just, "Worms."

The Big Horn fishes best at both ends of summer, but it's also one of the West's best and most popular winter trout fisheries, due in large part to relatively mild winters and the "ice free" water meted out by the bottom-release dam at Boysen Reservoir.

Public land and access to private holdings are limited, but several public fishing accesses give wade fishers and floaters plenty of options. Despite a strong current, there are no major rapids to make things rough for amateur oarsmen, but there are diversion dams and other obstacles to look out for, so inquire locally before launching.

Two popular floats, besides the one we're doing, are Wedding of the Waters down to the Hot Springs Park and McCarthy Access, 4.5 miles below the park, to the Black Mountain Road bridge on WY 172 eight miles downstream. Check the local fly shops for hot patterns, directions, and to arrange shuttles. Below the WY 172 bridge, catfish and bass take over, and the trout fishing tapers off rapidly.

By the time we finally reach the Eighth Street bridge take-out, I've had myself quite a time. Lots of trout in the net, and at least half again as many hooked and somehow lost, including two browns that I like to claim topped 20 inches.

Restaurants and Accommodations

If you hanker to dine out in the largest hay bale building in Wyoming, head for the Feed Bag (1025 Shoshone, Thermopolis, 307-864-5177). Not only is the architecture unique, the ranch-style menu eats pretty good also. And it opens early, so you can fill up and still be on the river by sunup.

The Sideboard Restaurant (109 South 6th, Thermopolis, 307-864-5335) serves up great burgers and steaks and puts out a good salad bar, and the pies are on par with my Aunt Pauline's (yummy). A little fancier spread is the Safari Club in the Holiday Inn (Hot Springs State Park, 307-864-3131). Enjoy your favorite beverage from the bar and gawk at the big game trophy display overhead while making up your mind about what to have. Everything looks delicious and, in our experience, actually is.

In nearby Worland, try the Ram's Head Café (629 Bighorn), which serves great New York strip steaks among other delectables.

As for sleeping arrangements, the Plaza Hotel, located within Hot Springs State Park, holds the distinction of being both the oldest and newest hotel in the region. Built in 1918, it was given a $2 million facelift in 1999. Thanks to a team of progressive-thinking renovators, the ambiance of the early 1900s hotel remains intact while still providing all modern conveniences.

The Plaza is the last of 12 such hotel/spa resorts that once graced the park and has been reopened under the management of the Quality Inn and Suites. The hotel features 8 fireplace suites, 10 luxury suites, and 18 deluxe rooms, all furnished with log furniture and adorned with western art. Guests are invited to enjoy a dip in the courtyard pool or a soak in the legendary mineral water, which is pumped directly from the Hot Springs itself.

The Holiday Inn of the Waters (Hot Springs State Park, 307-864-3131) is a more modern venue, with all the modern amenities. And this one allows pets, which is always a bonus. The Cactus Inn Motel (605 S. 6th St., 307-864-3155) is clean, less pricey, and also welcomes pets.

Thermopolis, Wyoming

Located where the high plains meet the Rockies, Thermopolis is sheltered by the high peaks of the Continental Divide and enjoys a relatively mild climate. It is sur-rounded by sagebrush-covered hills and coulees where once dinosaurs roamed and millions of bison grazed. Now it's home to mule and whitetail deer, pronghorn, and even wild horses.

Although the city was not founded until 1897, the brothers Anderson settled across the river near Owl Creek as early as 1870. Originally bean farmers, it wasn't long until they became town fathers to Andersonville, later known as Anderson's Hog Ranch, and, finally, as Old Thermopolis. It was during the "Hog Ranch" years that the Wild Bunch shot up the town in a wild celebration of the infamous robbery of the Union Pacific Overland Flyer and the subsequent dynamiting of the mail car.

Shoshone Indian legend has it that the Thermopolis Hot Springs was discovered when an extraordinary big wind blew through the canyon, loosening an eagle feath-er from a young maiden as she walked the banks of the river with her chieftain boyfriend. The feather floated downstream on the strong current, and when the cou-ple finally caught up to it they found themselves immersed in steam and bubbling hot water. "Magic" water it seemed, since both came away feeling stronger and with far more stamina. Soon the entire tribe was bathing regularly in the hot springs, and the Shoshone became known for their incredible strength and endurance.

Nearby Attractions and Activities

Wedding of the Waters

Early explorers to the territory now known as the state of Montana found bighorn sheep thriving in the river's canyons and named it the Big Horn. Meanwhile, other explorers came upon the same river to the south in what is now the state of Wyoming and named the canyon, and the river that carved through it, the Wind. Thus, one river had two names.

Cartographers eventually discovered the glitch and decided that from a point just beyond the mouth of the Wind River canyon the river would be called the Big Horn River; to the south it would be known as the Wind River. Ever since, the point of change has been known as the Wedding of the Waters, one of the few places where a river changes name midstream, so to speak.

For Indians, mountain men, and early settlers, Wedding of the Waters was a special place, and it remains so today. For wildlife, too, the place holds special merit, as the warmer water released from Boysen Reservoir combines with warmer upwellings of spring water to produce lush stands of aquatic vegetation. This keeps the river open all year and provides an inviting spot for mule deer, bighorn sheep, waterfowl, trout, and other critters, including a large bald eagle population that winters on the river.

Other Area Attractions

The enormous hot springs, reputedly the world's largest, gush hot water and create stunning travertine terraces—and give Thermopolis its name. In addition to soaking in the hot springs, visitors come from far and wide to see the Wyoming Dinosaur Center at the edge of town. Dinosaur lovers get a peek at a real life Jurassic Park.

A remarkable collection of native rock art is located 30 miles northwest of town (arrangements for entry to the site need be made at the Hot Springs State Park office). On a cliff at the site you'll find a series of petroglyphs that represent at least three styles of early Native American art, including those related to the early Hopi.

Author's Tip

Although there isn't much topwater action, the fertile waters of the Big Horn often make the trout fussy. It's better to have one pattern in a wide array of sizes and colors than, say, a dozen different patterns in one size. Hatches are scarce, so I start most Big Horn days with a beadhead nymph, scud, soft-hackle, or San Juan Worm. From mid-summer through fall, pounding the banks with hoppers works, as does stripping Buggers, leeches, or Clousers during low-light periods.

Favorite Fly

Copper John

Hook	TMC 100 #14-20
Bead	Copper or gold
Tail	Pheasant tail fibers
Abdomen	Copper wire, wrapped Brassie style
Thorax	Peacock herl
Wing Case	Pearl Flashabou
Legs	Pheasant tail fibers

Fast Facts

Big Horn River

Location	Just south of Thermopolis, Wyoming, north to the Montana state line; trout fishery confined to first 20 miles or so
Water Type	Strong-flowing, weed-filled tailwater of Boysen Reservoir
Primary Gamefish	Rainbows, browns, and some cutthroat, also whitefish
Best Time	Year-round fishery; one of Wyoming's best and most popular winter trout fisheries
Best Flies	Nymphs, scuds, San Juan Worms, leeches, and Buggers; hoppers, ants, and crickets in season. Mayflies and caddis to match hatch; check local shops for current activity.
Equipment	9-foot, 4- to 6-weight, floating line, tapered leader to suit the fishing method
Conditions	Hot summers, mild winters; Thermopolis has all the amenities; best fishing method is floating, check locally for obstacles and diversion hazards

Drive Time	From Casper: 3 hours
	From Billings: 4 hours
	From Denver: 7 hours
Directions	From Casper, US 20 west to Thermopolis; from Billings, take I-90 west to Exit 434 US 212, go west to US 310, then take MT 72 west to WY 120, continue on to US 20 west and Thermopolis; from Denver, take I-25 north to Exit 189; then US 20/26 west to Thermopolis.

Local Fly Shops and Guides

The Outdoorsman
632 Big Horn Ave.
Worland, WY 82701
307-347-2891

Wyoming Adventures
484 Wakeley Rd
Thermopolis, WY 82443
307-864-2407

Bearlodge Angler
612 Grace Ave.
Worland, WY 82401
307-347-4002

Big Horn River Outfitters
P O Box 1216
Thermopolis WY 82443
307-864-5309

Wind River Canyon Whitewater
210 Hwy. 20 South, Suite 5
Thermopolis WY 82443
307-864-9343

Rainbow Motel (guided float tours)
122 Hwy. 20 South
Thermopolis, WY 82443
307-864-3463

Milliron 2 Outfitters
1513 Culbertson Ave.
Worland, WY 82401
307-347-2574

John Schwalbe
484 Wakeley Rd.
Thermopolis, WY 82433
1-877-837-1064/307-864-2407

Contacts

Wyoming Game and Fish Dept.
Region 6 Fisheries Supervisor
260 Buena Vista Ave.
Lander, WY 82520
1-800-654-7862/307-332-2688

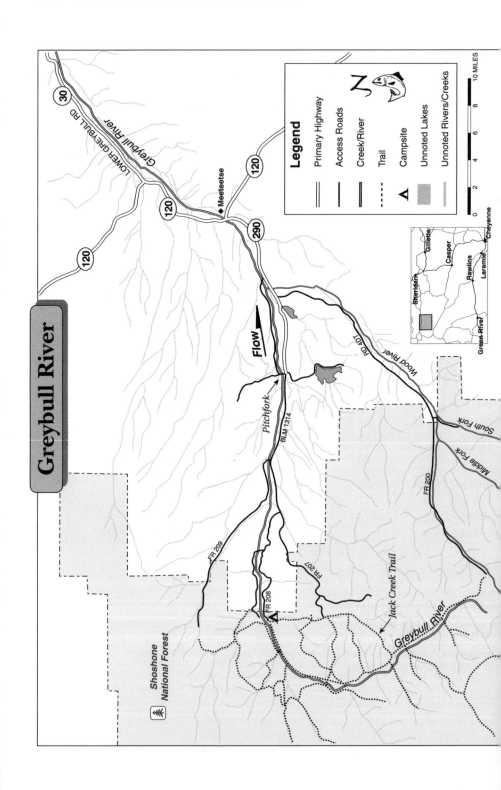

Greybull River

Legend

Primary Highway

Access Roads

Creek/River

Trail

Campsite

Unnoted Lakes

Unnoted Rivers/Creeks

0 2 4 6 8 10 MILES

Sheridan
Gillette
Casper
Rawlins
Laramie
Cheyenne
Green River

30
120
120
120
120
290

LOWER GREYBULL RD
Greybull River
◆ Meeteetse

Flow

Wood River
RD 4DT

Pitchfork
BLM 1314

South Fork
Middle Fork
FR 200

FR 209
FR 207
FR 208

Jack Creek Trail

Greybull River

Shoshone
National Forest

CHAPTER 16

THE UPPER GREYBULL RIVER

Mountain Treasure

Below the Shoshone National Forest boundary the Greybull River runs through a wide valley that was once open, high-desert sagebrush but is now mostly grass and irrigated hayfields. Leaving the privately owned bottomlands to the cows, we point the truck west on WY 290 at Meeteetse, Wyoming, head 20 miles out to where the blacktop ends at Pitchfork, and continue on the rapidly deteriorating gravel road for another 10 miles to the Jack Creek trailhead in the Shoshone National Forest.

Once you reach the upper Greybull, the landscape reverts to mostly sagebrush and limber pine, and the heretofore horizontal landscape becomes abruptly vertical. It's a tilted world of timbered slopes and volcanic rock outcrops set against the spectacular backdrop of high, barren peaks like Francis, Pyramid, and Irish Rock, which soar to heights over 13,000 feet.

Above the trailhead, the bouncing, bubbling river spills like molten silver down through a deep canyon that hosts wild trout. It's a strikingly beautiful and feral place.

In the morning we take the trail toward the canyon, following the river into the Washakie Wilderness. It's difficult to concentrate on the task at hand because we're craning our necks to spot something as exotic as a grazing grizzly or gray wolf, to say nothing of roving bands of elk and mule deer. What we really should be looking fo are the telltale rises of the native Yellowstone cutthroat trout that live here.

Typical of any cool early fall morning, the fishing starts off on the slow side, ther comes alive in fits and spurts as the sun arcs toward high noon. Subtly at first, a few caddis start to pop, and soon the runs and pools become dimpled as if splattered by falling raindrops. All wildlife gazing is put instantly on hold, for nothing improves ou concentration like the spreading rings of rising trout.

As usual, we take turns casting one rod. The action vacillates between hot an just okay. Gale hooks a 12-incher; I hook its twin. Gale nails one a little bigger. Ter casts later I net an 8-incher. A couple of hours later the caddis hatch dwindles, anc the rising trout disappear. Time out for gorp, that wonderful mix of granola, raisins dried fruit, nuts, and whatever else looks good when we're tossing the current batcl together. We spot a sleek cow elk and her no-longer-spotted calf, and then lie back tc gaze at the puffy white clouds wheeling slowly across the impossibly high pale blue sky.

The cutthroats we brought to hand were colorful, firm, and ice-cold. None were wallhangers, of course, but they were beautiful nonetheless. Whatever they lacked ir size was more than made up for with viscous, slashing strikes and scrappy fights.

We continue until late afternoon before calling a halt. But first we each wan one more shot. Gale makes the most of hers, landing a plump 13-incher, while botch mine, executing a long-range release on a scrappy 10-incher.

The upper Greybull is a minimalist's delight. The trout are wild and naive, and it' a good place to leave the bulging vest in the truck. Just tuck a small fly box, extra spool or two of tippet, snips, and floatant in a shirt pocket and go for it. Attractor pat terns such as the Royal Wulff, Stimulator, Humpy, Madam X, Adams, Cahill, Elk Hai Caddis, and terrestrial patterns all produce well. More for comfort than real insur ance, we toss in a few nymphs and small Buggers. We pare the fishing plan down a: well, concentrating on the obvious deep pools and runs and around and beneath logjams, rocks, and undercut banks.

The river and its setting cry out for fishing at a leisurely stroll. Catch a few, miss a few, enjoy the view. About the only improvement I can think of might be to drag the river closer to home—it's a long drive from Dillon to Pitchfork.

Below Pitchfork, the river flows through private ranchlands with limited walk-ir access, and even public access to the river can be a long hike from the fence. From Pitchfork to about 15 miles below Meeteetse, the Greybull remains a nice little cut throat fishery, albeit one with tough access. How nice? Steve Bassett (of Monste Lake fame) tells me he has landed cutts to 26 inches, pretty damn nice in anyone' book and well worth a little knocking and begging for access. Below the 15-mile marker, trout fishing becomes rather iffy as irrigation diversions begin to take a toll

And by the time the river empties into the Big Horn near the town of Greybull, it's just a pathetic shadow of its former self.

Restaurants and Accommodations

While you won't likely find them listed under fine dining destinations (forget extensive wine lists), the Outlaw Parlor Café (1936 State St., 307-868-2585) and Lucille's Café (1906 State St., 307-868-2250) in Meeteetse are surprisingly good eateries. Your basic meat, potatoes, pasta menu; nothing fancy, just good down-home cooking, friendly service, and reasonable prices.

The Vision Quest Motel (WY 120, 307-868-2512) offers suites, kitchenettes, and standard rooms, while the Oasis Motel and RV Park (1702 State St., 307-868-2551) provides cabins, rooms, and RV sites. The Broken Spoke Café and Bed and Breakfast (1947 State St., 307-868-2362) is also quite popular. They are all clean, reasonably priced, and allow pets, but lack just one thing—the outdoors.

Tucked in beside the river at the end of the road, the Jack Creek Campground (30 miles west of town via WY 290 and FR 206) makes a good base camp close to

A fat upper Greybull cutthroat being reeled in.

the action. It's nothing fancy, just seven sites with picnic tables and toilet and corrals and a stock ramp for the horsy set.

The Wood River Lodge (1261 4DT Rd., 307-868-9211) provides a fine alternative to camping. Catering to your every need, the lodge offers individual cabins or bunkhouse living and puts together flyfishing packages to suit.

Meeteetse, Wyoming

In the Shoshone language Meeteetse means, "meeting place." Established in the latter half of the 19th century, the town provided support and services for the surrounding mines and burgeoning cattle industry. The mines are gone now, but the cattle and cowboy flavor remain, evidenced by the wooden boardwalks, watering troughs and hitching rails, and the real cattle drives right down Main Street.

The town's biggest claim to fame remains the infamous outlaw Butch Cassidy who once lived here, no doubt perfecting his particular brand of raising hell. In 1886 his name appeared on a petition for a new bridge, and later, in 1897, court dockets show he was arrested in front of the Cowboy Bar for general rowdiness.

Nearby Fisheries

The Wood River merges with the Greybull 6 miles west of town at the junction with County Road 200. Like its neighbor, the lower Wood runs through private land where access, to put it mildly, is difficult. There isn't much fishing anyway, as severe dewatering and the ongoing drought don't provide much habitat.

But the public water upstream is worth a look. If nothing else, it's certainly breathtaking. Framed by high peaks, the mainstem Wood and its middle and south forks provide anglers with miles and miles of rugged mountain trout water to explore. The Yellowstone cutts found here are just as wild, colorful, and feisty as their Greybull cousins, but in our experience, they run a bit smaller. Still, who wants to quibble about statistics when fishing in such a wonderful place.

Lower and Upper Sunshine Reservoirs are worth checking out if they aren't dried up. Like most western reservoirs, drought can severely impact the fishing here. When there is water, though, the fishing can be excellent for cutthroats of decent size (10 to 15 inches). In 2002 Lower went dry while Upper hung on by a whisker. Another winter with a weak snowpack, and both fisheries could be history. So keep your fingers crossed…

Nearby Attractions and Activities

Pitchfork Ranch

Established in 1879 by Oscar Franc, the Pitchfork was the first cow operation in the Big Horn Basin and soon grew into one of the West's largest cattle empires. The expansive ranch totals many thousands of acres and still shows up on most road maps as if it were just another lonely Wyoming town. A bit of notoriety was added when the first Marlboro Man ads were shot here.

Kirwin, Wyoming

Gold was discovered at Kirwin (9,000 feet elevation) on the upper Wood River in 1885. Eventually, the town grew to 200 people and 38 buildings, but with no cemetery, saloons, or brothels. As the gold and silver were of low quality, no one involved became anything like rich. So when a savage snowstorm struck in 1907 and an avalanche swept down to kill three people, Kirwin residents apparently had enough. When the storm finally abated and crews managed to clear the roads most residents left in a hurry, taking only what they could carry and leaving sheets on the beds and dishes on the tables.

In the early 1930s, one Carl Dunrud purchased the town's remains and the surrounding lands and built the Double D Dude Ranch. Among the first guests were Amelia Earhart and her husband, George Putnam. Later, Earhart asked Dunrud to build a cabin for her, where she planned to come after her flight around the world. When she disappeared in 1937, the cabin was just four logs high. Construction halted, and it was never finished. Later, the Forest Service bought the ranch, and today it's one of the region's more popular historical sites.

Author's Tip

On many mountain rills the fishing gets better the farther you get from the trailhead, and the upper Greybull is no exception. While we have not yet encountered the elusive 20-inchers reputed to live up there somewhere, this is one river where there is a distinct correlation between sweat equity and average catch size. If you decide to check out the uppermost reaches, be forewarned that there are few suitable camping spots in the lower canyon. It takes us (unfettered by camp gear) several hours to hike beyond the canyon's confines.

Favorite Fly

Royal Wulff (variation)

Hook	Orvis 1523 #8-20
Tail	Black moose neck or body hair
Body	Peacock herl, single strand red floss
Hackle	Brown, neck or saddle
Wing	White hen hackle feather

Fast Facts

Upper Greybull River

Location	West of Meeteetse, Wyoming, in the Shoshone National Forest
Water Type	Typical mountain freestone trout water, good pool/riffle configuration
Primary Gamefish	Mix of Yellowstone cutthroat and brook trout in upper river, rainbows and browns below
Best Time	September to early October
Best Flies	High-riding dry flies, attractors, and flashy nymphs
Equipment	7½- to 9-foot, 1- to 4-weight rod, floating line, tapered leader about as long as the rod, long supple 3X to 5X tippet
Conditions	High water early on can make fishing difficult, but by late summer or early fall things settle down. High elevation can make for cool to chilly mornings and evenings, even in midsummer.
Drive Time	From Casper: 5 hours From Cody: 1.75 hours From Billings: 4 hours

Directions   From Casper, US 20 west to Thermopolis, WY 120 north to Meeteetse, WY 290 west to Pitchfork, FR 206 to Jack Creek trailhead; from Cody, WY 120 south to Meeteetse, WY 290 west to Pitchfork, FR 206 to Jack Creek trailhead; from Billings, I-90 east to Ranchester, WY, US 14 west to Greybull, US 16 east to Basin, WY 30 west to Meeteetse, WY 290 west to Pitchfork, FR 206 to Jack Creek trailhead.

Local Fly Shops

Aune's Absaroka Angler
754 Yellowstone Ave.
Cody, WY 82414
307-587-5105

Yellowstone Troutfitters
239 Yellowstone Ave.
Cody, WY 82414
307-587-8240

North Fork Anglers
1438 Sheridan
Cody, WY 82414
307-527-7274

Guides

Wood River Lodge,
307-868-9211

Grub Steak Expeditions
1-800-527-6316/307-527-6316

Bill Cody Ranch
307-587-2097

Dean Johnson Outfitting
1-800-843-7885/307-587-4072

Crescent B Outfitting
307-587-6925

Contacts

Shoshone National Forest
808 Meadow Ln.
Cody, WY 82414-6241
307-527-6241

Wyoming Game and Fish Dept.
Region 2 Fisheries Supervisor
2820 Hwy. 120
Cody, WY 82414
1-800-654-1178/307-527-7125

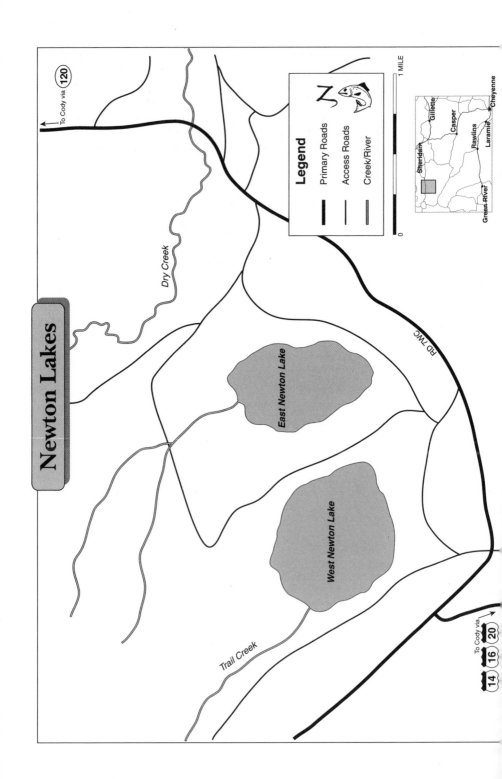

CHAPTER 17

EAST NEWTON LAKE
Big Trout Close to Town

There are two Newton Lakes northwest of Cody, Wyoming, off WY 120. West Newton isn't much, mostly a put-and-take fishery for moderate-sized stockers. East Newton is another story.

Covering just 30 acres, it fishes a lot bigger than it looks. Why, you ask? Well, for starters, East Newton brown trout average about 20 inches and come to net frequently enough that they aren't really a big deal. And there are quite a few larger fish. For proof, just eavesdrop on the local crowd lounging in their float tubes and pontoon boats and casually discussing how yesterday's 2-foot monster "ate this here Callibaetis Comparadun right up next to them weeds over yonder."

While I don't normally listen in on conversations, the way sound travels over water on still, late-summer mornings it's impossible to ignore the 22-, 24-, even 26-inchers that crop up. It's also hard not to marvel at the almost ho-hum attitude the locals exhibit on hooking one of the black-spotted pigs. Apparently, East Newton etiquette requires that you casually haul your 20-inch-plus monster to the side the boat, reach down to twist the hook free, and keep your mouth shut.

You should have seen the cold stares leveled my way when I let fly a few too many hoots and hollers over the capture of a mere 19-incher. Hey, I don't catch that many 19-inchers, and this one just happened to fasten itself to a #14 Callibaetis Sparkle Dun—a dry fly for cripes sake. How could I not celebrate? But then I glanced over at Gale, huffy-looking aboard her cushy pontoon craft and casting that baleful glare, as well. I quickly realized I was severely outnumbered and kept quiet.

Good thing, too, because in the next hour nearly every one of the half-dozen or so tubers and pontooners within earshot, including Gale, had quietly hauled in even bigger trout. Maybe my 19-incher wasn't such a big deal. By the time sunset rolled around I found myself nearly as jaded as the regulars. Even when an unusually fat 22-inch brown came aboard the float tube, I didn't think to call Gale over for the requisite hero shot. Can you imagine? And yes, it did occur to me that a steady diet of East Newton fishing could very well ruin one's outlook on the rest of the flyfishing world.

Fishing East Newton Lake

East Newton is ringed by cattails and assorted brambles, which make it tough to fish from shore, although many anglers do so if the heavily trodden path encircling the lake is any indication. The lake's small stature seems made to order for the small skiff, canoe (no motors allowed), float tube, or personal pontoon craft. It was just a short kick to our favorite spot on the left bank immediately out from the launch site.

Gale, of course, likes to rig a floating line, while I generally start out with a sink-tip unless a rise is in progress. She often casts dries regardless, but lately I've been slowly converting her to the idea of stripping Buggers and small Clousers or nymphs.

Once the weeds bloom, fishing from shore becomes difficult.

from the Sheep Creek Special down to miniscule midges. If those tactics fail, I often tie on a pair of weighted nymphs, let them hang just off the bottom, and sit in the tube while waiting patiently for a trout to cruise by. This method reminds her of watching grass grow, and she wants no part in it, even if I suddenly start hammering fish.

If we are lucky enough to hit a hatch, we both immediately switch to whatever best matches the naturals, although I almost always trail a nymph or emerger behind the dry.

The Newton Lakes are especially popular during spring runoff. But after the area rivers settle down, the pair get surprisingly little attention, even on summer weekends and holidays. We last fished here the Sunday before Labor Day, and shared the water with just six other anglers. They were apparently all locals, because as we kicked by they all seemed anxious to give the "strangers" advice.

"Try a midge larva, did good yesterday," said one. "I like a sink-tip and strip small nymphs. Callibaetis are on now so I got a Flashback and a PT," offered the next. "Doin' okay on a tan Sparkle Dun fished right up against the bank," chimed in a third just before rearing back to set the iron solidly into what looked to be a hefty brown. And, true to form, he quietly and without fanfare slid the pig alongside, twisted the hook free, and continued casting. Just another ho-hum 20-inch-plus East Newton brown.

East Newton holds up well throughout the season, as water is pulled from a nearby irrigation canal to keep it full and fairly cold.

Restaurants and Accommodations

Cody is almost within spitting distance, so there are plenty of choices. Many of the of best are covered with the North Fork Shoshone in the next chapter, but you should also check out Maxwell's (937 Sheridan Ave., 307-527-7749). We usually go for one of the daily Italian and/or pasta specials, and the fresh-baked breads and desserts are worth the price of admission.

We like to set up camp in the parking lot right next to the launch site on East Newton. Not once have we shared space with more than one other trailer. This is just a place to park the camper, so pack your own water and other necessities of life, including firewood if you want a campfire. Toilets are available, however. On the off chance that the parking lot is crowded, the surrounding countryside is mostly BLM land, so finding a quiet place nearby won't be a problem.

If you opt for more cushy living arrangements, Cody has you covered. The Big Bear Motel (139 West Yellowstone, 307-587-3117) is clean, reasonable, and allows pets. The Buffalo Bill Village (1701 Sheridan Ave., 307-587-5555) and Western 6 Gun (423 West Yellowstone, 307-587-4835) cost a bit more, but also allow pets.

Author's Tip

The Cody fly shops keep close tabs on what's happening at East Newton, so stop in for up-to-date information when you hit town. Fishing from shore is a hassle once the weeds bloom, so bring a float tube or boat. Should all else fail, try stripping a #6 Conehead Olive Rubber Legs around the edges and in the seams between weed beds.

Favorite Fly

Conehead Olive Rubber Legs

Hook	Mustad 36890 SF #2-10
Head	Gold conehead bead
Tail	Light olive marabou/Krystal Flash (optional)
Body	Light olive chenille or ice chenille
Hackle	Grizzly palmered over the rear two-thirds; front third black
Legs	Sili Legs

Fast Facts

Newton Lakes

Location	5 miles northwest of Cody, Wyoming, watch for sign off WY 120
Water Type	Small fertile lake
Primary Gamefish	Brown trout averaging 20 inches
Best Time	After runoff when most anglers twitch to river fishing; early fall is especially good.

Best Flies	Match the hatch; otherwise pitch scuds, midge larva, flashy nymphs or big ugly Buggers.
Equipment	9-foot, 5- or 6-weight, floating and sink-tip lines, and float tube, personal pontoon boat or small skiff
Conditions	Hot in summer, chilly spring and fall; small size negates wind problems for the most part; weedy edges
Drive Time	From Casper: 5 hours
	From Billings: 2.25 hours
	From Bozeman: 4 hours
Directions	From Casper, take US 20/26 west to Thermopolis, WY 120 west to Cody to the turnoff to the lakes; from Billings, take I-90 east to Ranchester, WY, US 14 west to Greybull, US 14-16-20 to Cody, WY 120 west to turnoff to lakes; from Bozeman, take I-90 east to Livingston, MT, US 89 south to Gardiner, follow Mammoth Hot Springs-Cooke City road, US 212 east to WY 296 (Chief Joseph Highway) to WY 120 east to turnoff to lakes.

Local Fly Shops

Yellowstone Troutfitters
239 Yellowstone Ave.
Cody, WY 82414
307-587-8240

North Fork Anglers
1438 Sheridan
Cody, WY 82414
307-527-7274

Aune's Absaroka Angler
754 Yellowstone Ave.
Cody, WY 82414
307-587-5105

Guides

Bill Cody Ranch
307-587-2097

Grub Steak Expeditions
1-800-527-6316, 307-527-6316

Crescent B Outfitting,
307-587-6925

Dean Johnson Outfitting
1-800-843-7885, 307-587-4072

Contacts

Clark's Fork Ranger District
203A Yellowstone Highway
Cody, WY 82414
307-527-6921

Wyoming Game and Fish Dept.
Region 2 Fisheries Supervisor
2820 Hwy. 120
Cody, WY 82414
1-800-654-1178/307-527-7125

The Buffalo Bill Museum in nearby Cody, Wyoming.

CHAPTER 18

THE NORTH FORK SHOSHONE RIVER

Great Fishing Beside the Highway

Normally, if I'm standing in a river surrounded by national forest on a cool September morning, the aspens all aflame, while across the way an outfitter packs mules and saddles horses for a trip into the mountains to chase elk, I have trouble concentrating on something as mundane as the mere hooking of a trout on a fly. But this morning, even daydreaming about bugling bulls is not enough to distract me from hooking trout in the North Fork Shoshone River. They are on the bite, big time.

A dozen casts net six or eight rainbows and a couple more long-range releases. A half-dozen drifts down the sweep of a deep, emerald-green pool with a bushy Gray Wulff brings in three cuts and another 'bow. I'm putting on a flyfishing clinic, and there's not a soul around to see it, save the busy outfitter who probably hasn't even noticed that I'm on the water.

And to think, the only reason we stopped here in the first place was so Gale could shoot some photos of the flaming aspen on the hillside across the way. I decided to sneak in a few casts while I waited. After all, how could any flyfisher stand beside the North Fork and not wet a line? Actually, it was the end of a long

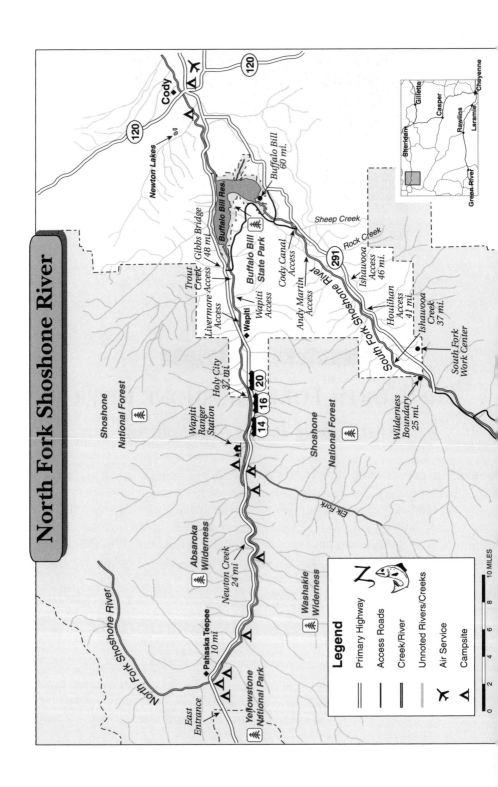

North Fork Shoshone River

Cody

120

120

Newton Lakes

Buffalo Bill Res.

Buffalo Bill
60 mi.

Gibbs Bridge
48 mi.

Trout Creek

Sheep Creek

Rock Creek

291

Buffalo Bill
State Park

Cody Canal
Access

Ishawooa
Access
46 mi.

Livermore Access

Wapiti
Access

Wapiti

Andy Martin
Access

South Fork Shoshone River

Houlihan
Access
41 mi.

Ishawooa
Creek
37 mi.

South Fork
Work Center

Shoshone
National Forest

Holy City
37 mi.

14 16 20

Wapiti
Ranger
Station

Shoshone
National Forest

Wilderness
Boundary
25 mi.

Absaroka
Wilderness

Newton Creek
24 mi.

Washakie
Wilderness

Elk Fork

North Fork Shoshone River

Pahaska Teepee
10 mi.

East
Entrance

Yellowstone
National Park

Sheridan Gillette Casper Cheyenne

Rawlins Laramie

Green River

Legend

N

Primary Highway

Access Roads

Creek/River

Unnoted Rivers/Creeks

Air Service

Campsite

0 2 4 6 8 10 MILES

road trip and I was just about trouted out. Besides, it was September and Montana's archery elk season was already open. Still, this was awfully fun fishing.

A cutt smacks the Wulff in the slick behind a big boulder. After landing him, I decide to add a #14 North Fork Special Nymph to a 30-inch length of 4X tippet as a dropper. I bounce the rig off the same rock, and down goes the Wulff. This is almost too much. I rear back, and a fat 15-inch rainbow cartwheels into the air.

After a time, Gale returns from her photo safari. "How they bitin'?"

As luck would have it, I'm in the midst of a brief lull. "Nothing to write home about," I lie.

"We'd better get on up the road."

"Sounds good to me. Too darn cold for standing in a creek anyway."

Okay, shameful behavior, but like she said it really is too darn cold. And I'm getting an itch for elk hunting.

Fishing the North Fork Shoshone River

The above action took place near Wapiti Ranger Station and the confluence of Elk Fork. From there to where the North Fork takes a hard right into the mountains above Pahaska Teepee you'll find some of the best public access trout water in the northern Rockies.

Despite the fact that US 14-16-20, the main drag from Cody to Yellowstone's East Entrance, closely parallels the river, the North Fork remains a relatively crowd-free, top-notch fishery. Cutthroat, rainbows, and mountain whitefish are present, along with an occasional brown. On average, the trout run 10 to 14 inches, but plenty of bigger trout are in the mix, as well. For some reason, bigger average trout seem to come to net in July and October, rather than August and September.

While the North Fork supports a wide variety of aquatic insects, from the robust drakes and fall caddis to the diminutive Blue-Winged Olives and Micro Caddis, this is a classic "pound 'em up" trout river. You can often forget what's hatching and just put on a favorite attractor pattern with a meaty-looking nymph as a dropper. A good pair of flies to start with would be the locally concocted Double Ugly Tickler (dry) and North Fork Special (nymph), rigged in tandem. (These flies are the creation of Tim Wade at North Fork Anglers in Cody.)

Especially in the upper reaches, where the river comes stairstepping down rock-strewn runs to slick, emerald-green pools, the North Fork is fun rough-and-tumble fishing.

Restaurants and Accommodations

The historic Irma Hotel (1192 Sheridan Ave., Cody, 307-587-4221) was built at a cost of $80,000 by Col. William F. "Buffalo Bill" Cody in 1902 and named for his daughter, Irma. The hotel was soon embellished with a $100,000 cherry wood bar. The magnificent piece was crafted in France and shipped to the east coast, then carried by rail to Red Lodge, Montana, and finally by wagon to Cody. For years, it has been the second most photographed item in Cody, second only to the statue of Buffalo Bill himself.

But the Irma has more going for it than just a historic hunk of furniture; it serves pretty good food, too. The daily breakfast, lunch, and dinner buffets are the chowhound's delight. The Sunday lunch buffet is particularly good, as the chefs seem to go all out to make sure the crowd goes away smiling. On most trips, though, I can never get much beyond the prime rib, which is mouthwatering and tender beyond belief. Should your tastes run toward the lighter side, the Irma Philly Sandwich and London Broil Salad are worth checking out.

Awesome scenery
on the North Fork.

The Proud Cut Saloon (1227 Sheridan Ave., 307-527-6905) has "kick-ass" Western cuisine featuring buffalo burgers, choice steaks, and exotics such as Rocky Mountain oysters. It's both good and popular, so be sure to make reservations early. For a little New West ambiance and dinner, try Maxwell's (937 Sheridan Ave., 307-587-7749).

Good coffee joints are sprouting faster than noxious weeds these days, and every Wild West burg has at least one. The Cody Coffee Co. (1702 Sheridan Ave., 307-527-7879) brews great coffee and has a breakfast and lunch menu that ranks highly, as well.

Camping along the river is always our first choice, although high summer can get crowded in the several (there were 10 last time I counted) USFS campgrounds along US 14-16-20 between Cody and Yellowstone. Newton Creek is typical of the offerings: 37 miles up the road, with 31 units offering picnic tables, fire rings and grills, water and toilets for $9 per. There is also ample camping available in Buffalo Bill State Park on the shores of the reservoir.

There are many nice motels in Cody. We've enjoyed our stays at the Best Western Sunset Motor Inn (1601 8th St., 307-587-4265), and closer to the action the Yellowstone Valley Inn (3324 Yellowstone Park Hwy., 1-877-587-4656 or 307-587-3961) offers tent and RV sites, as well as cabins and motel rooms. They also have a full-service bar and a pretty good restaurant and coffee shop.

Nearby Fisheries

South Fork Shoshone River

While driving up the South Fork valley out of Cody and gawking at the pastoral hay meadows and well-kept private ranches, the idea that you're in bear country is a bit hard to swallow. It looks more like some sort of green fairy-tale kingdom than the picture most of us hold of the stronghold of the mighty grizzly. But that's just what the sign at the trailhead warns.

"You have the pepper spray?"

"Yep."

"There's just two of us. The sign says 'three or more.'"

"Maybe we'll luck out, and run into a grizz that can't count."

On the South Fork you don't have many choices: hassle the land barons downstream for access through private land or hike into the Washakie Wilderness upriver and take a chance getting "et" by a hungry grizzly. Do you want to catch a fat South Fork brown trout or don't you?

It would be nice if we could just jump in the water right at the trailhead and avoid traveling too far up the trail into bear territory, but the water immediately surrounding the gate is not the best. The closest serious trout water lies a few miles upriver in a narrow canyon.

"Nothing left, but to suck it up," I tease, silently crossing fingers and toes for both our sakes that we don't actually suffer a run-in.

Mostly in deference to Gale's bear phobia, we depart a bit later than usual, hike a bit faster than normal, talk a bit louder and longer, and quit a little earlier. We know full well that the best hatches often occur in the last light of evening, but hiking out anywhere near dark is "totally unacceptable," as my partner so bluntly puts it. The reward for all this work is the chance to hook a really big trout on a dry fly. Twenty inch browns and rainbows are not at all uncommon, and dry flies are often the ticket, although afternoons of high skies and bright sun sometimes do mandate making the switch to deep-drifted nymphs.

The South Fork in the canyon upstream of the trailhead really is serious bear country, but it's also a fine piece of trout water and shouldn't be passed up. Just take the proper precautions, as you owe it to yourself and the bear to avoid surprises. From what I've seen, bears don't want to meet you any more than you want to meet

Bighorn sheep are common on the rocky ridges above the river.

them. But some grizzlies, especially sows with cubs, don't react well to surprise encounters. So be especially alert and noisy when traveling through closed-in areas. And heed the advice of experts: invite a couple of friends, don't go alone.

You'll spend a whole lot more time catching trout than sighting bears, and actual encounters are probably less likely than getting struck by lightning.

Nearby Attractions and Activities

For the angler trying to get on the water, the town of Cody holds more than a few dangerous pitfalls. For example, stop at the Buffalo Bill Historical Center (720 Sheridan Ave., 307-587-4771) and before you know it a day's fishing is lost. Five museums make up the complex: the Buffalo Bill Museum (life and times of the scout, hunter, guide, and showman), the Whitney Gallery of Western Art (masterworks by the most famous painters and sculptors of the West, including Catlin, Bierstadt, Remington, Russell, Moran, Sharp, and others); Plains Indian Museum (Native American artifacts); Cody Firearms Museum (foremost collection of American firearms in the world); and the newest addition, the Draper Museum of Natural History.

Just down the street is the Foundation for North American Wild Sheep national headquarters (720 Allen Ave., 307-527-6261). If you're a wild sheep hunter you already know about this place, but for the rest of you wild sheep lovers out there, the mounted heads are awesome and there's a whole lot more to it than just a few trophies on a wall.

Author's Tip

Generally speaking, the river fishes best upstream from Wapiti Ranger Station to the headwaters above Pahaska Teepee. Find an empty pool or run and start with a large attractor dry, such as the Double Ugly Tickler. If you hit a good hatch, get the size and silhouette reasonably close and you should do okay.

Favorite Fly

Double Ugly Tickler

Hook	Mustad 94831 or Tiemco 5212 #6-16
Tail	Black, white, or yellow rubber or Sili Legs
Body	Peacock herl
Hackle	Rear, grizzly; middle, brown; front, grizzly

North Fork Special

Hook	Tiemco 2457 #10-16
Head	Silver, copper, or black bead (brass or tungsten)
Weight	0.015-0.020 lead wire (optional)
Tail	Natural goose biots
Rib	Fine gold, red, or copper wire
Body	Abdomen and thorax, fine black dubbing
Wing Pads	Three black goose biots (clipped and optional)
Legs	Natural goose biots

Fast Facts

North Fork Shoshone River

Location	Parallels US-14-16-20 between Cody, Wyoming, and Yellowstone National Park
Water Type	Typical mountain trout water from headwaters to Wapiti Ranger Station; rocky riffles and runs, deep green pools; lower river above Buffalo Bill Reservoir runs through wide sagebrush valley.
Primary Gamefish	Rainbow, Yellowstone cutthroat, occasional brown trout and mountain whitefish
Best Time	July and October, September will do in a pinch
Best Flies	Attractor patterns like Stimulator, Madam X, Humpy, Wulff, or a meaty nymph like a Girdle Bug, Bitch Creek, or Yuk Bug.
Equipment	9-foot, 5- or 6-weight, floating line, tapered leader, tippet to match the fly
Conditions	Spring runoff often begins in April and extends into July. The best fishing is mid- to late July through October.
Drive Time	From Casper: appx. 5 hours From Billings: 2.25 hours From Bozeman: 4 hours
Directions	From Casper, take US 20-26 west to Thermopolis, WY 120 west to Cody; from Billings, take I-90 east to Ranchester, WY, US 14 west to Greybull, US 14-16-20 west to Cody; from Bozeman, take I-90 east to Livingston, MT, US 89 south to Gardiner, MT, Mammoth Hot Springs-Cooke City road, US 212 east to WY 296 (Chief Joseph Hwy.) to WY 120 east to Cody.

Local Fly Shops

Yellowstone Troutfitters
239 Yellowstone Ave.
Cody, WY 82414
307-587-8240

North Fork Anglers
1438 Sheridan
Cody, WY 82414
307-527-7274

Aune's Absaroka Angler
754 Yellowstone Ave.
Cody, WY 82414
307-587-5105

Guides

Bill Cody Ranch
307-587-2097

Grub Steak Expeditions
1-800-527-6316, 307-527-6316

Crescent B Outfitting
307-587-6925

Dean Johnson Outfitting
1-800-843-7885, 307-587-4072

Contacts

Wapiti Ranger District
203A Yellowstone Highway
Cody, WY 82414
307-527-6921

Wyoming Game and Fish Dept.
Region 2 Fisheries Supervisor
2820 Hwy. 120
Cody, WY 82414
1-800-654-1178/307-527-7125

A North Fork rainbow in the net.

CHAPTER 19

THE RUBY RIVER
Forgotten Southwest Montana Gem

The summer our grandson Brian worked down in Wyoming, he would sometimes drive up to Dillon, Montana, on his days off. Naturally, we'd spend our time together fishing. One August morning we headed for Cliff and Wade Lakes. The fishing did not go well. A major wind literally and figuratively blew us off both lakes. Frustrated, we headed home early. As we crested the Ennis divide, he suggested we check out the Ruby River. Never one in need of much arm twisting when it comes to fishing the Ruby, I pointed the truck toward the Ruby Island Access just south of Alder and stopped on the bridge to check out the water.

"They're rising, Pap."

"Yep."

"Looks like a spinners. PMDs?"

"Yep."

Brian grabbed his rod, strung it up on the fly, and dove into the brush. He crept through the thick willows to an opening and zeroed in on a small pod rising eagerly along an undercut bank. Pitching a #16 yellow-bodied Adams Parachute, his first shot landed in an overhanging branch. When he yanked it free the branch broke and fell among the risers. Not the most auspicious start.

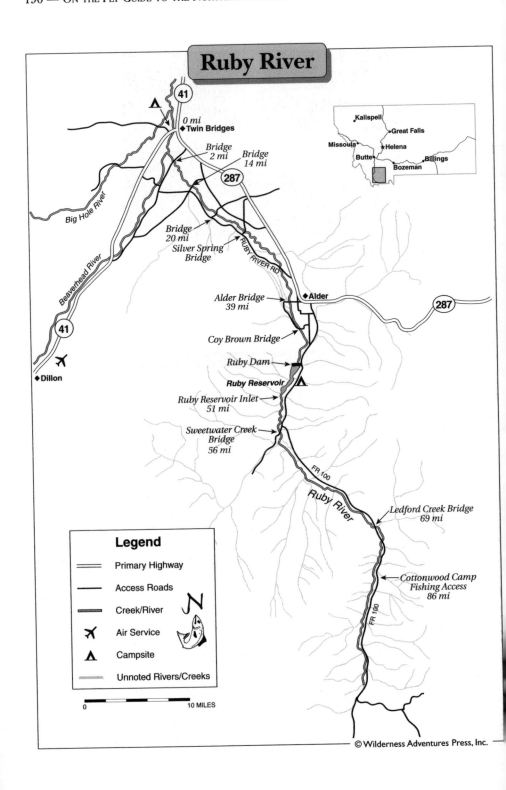

Ruby River

41

0 mi
◆ Twin Bridges

*Bridge
2 mi*   *Bridge
14 mi*

287

*Bridge
20 mi
Silver Spring
Bridge*

RUBY RIVER RD

*Alder Bridge
39 mi*   ◆ Alder

287

Coy Brown Bridge

Ruby Dam

Ruby Reservoir ⋀

*Ruby Reservoir Inlet
51 mi*

*Sweetwater Creek
Bridge
56 mi*

FR 100

Ruby River

*Ledford Creek Bridge
69 mi*

*Cottonwood Camp
Fishing Access
86 mi*

FR 100

Big Hole River

Beaverhead River

41

✈

◆ Dillon

Kalispell
Great Falls
Missoula   Helena
Butte
Bozeman   Billings

Legend

═══ Primary Highway

─── Access Roads

▬▬▬ Creek/River

✈ Air Service

⋀ Campsite

〰〰 Unnoted Rivers/Creeks

0   10 MILES

N

© Wilderness Adventures Press, Inc.

Onward and upward.

Just upstream the current split around a small rock, and a single trout was working the edge of the thin current seam between the rock and the bank. Taking careful aim this time, he directed the fly just inches above where the trout was swirling. It floated momentarily and then disappeared. When he raised the rod a lively brown came splashing across the surface. After a brief struggle he brought it to hand, posed the scrappy brown for the camera, then twisted the hook free.

Now it was my turn. Two casts a little farther up the same seam produced takes, but no hook-ups. When several more floats failed to spur any interest we moved on.

Where the current flattened out to form a narrow, elongated pool, several trout swirled—easy targets were it not for the bush jutting out from the bank halfway between. No problem. I'm more than good enough to curve the cast around the bush. I wound up and let fly.

Not even close. The fly centered the bush dead-on and hung there.

Not wanting to spook the pod, I left it hanging and beckoned for the kid to go for it.

He approached the obstacle as I should have, by slipping across the creek, and in short order hauled out a twin to his first catch. On the next cast he hooked and quickly lost what turned out to be the trout of the day. From my vantage point, still hanging on stupidly to the fly rod connected to the hung-up fly, the lost brown might have easily gone 18 inches or more.

But these things happen. Undaunted, Brian eventually ran the table, so to speak, catching or at least hooking just about every trout in the pod above the bush. Finally, after several casts went untouched, he allowed me to retrieve my fly and get back into the fray.

And so it went. Provided the caster of the moment managed to steer his flies clear of the bushes, one chunky brown after another gobbled them. When the spinner fall abated an hour or so later, the action slowed and we reeled up. A great ending to what had started out as a tough day on the water.

Fishing the Ruby River

The river begins deep within the Beaverhead-Deerlodge National Forest in the Snowcrest and Gravelly Ranges. A hundred river miles or so downstream it dumps into the Beaverhead River near Twin Bridges, which shortly thereafter meets up with the Big Hole to form the Jefferson. At about the halfway mark lies Ruby Reservoir, a good point of separation between the upper and lower river.

For 25 miles or so above the dam, private ranchlands (some of which are part of Ted Turner's sprawling Snowcrest Ranch) dominate, and access is fleeting to nonexistent. The upper river is really too small for easy floating, so it's wade fishing or forget it.

Above the ranches, however, the Beaverhead-Deerlodge National Forest provides anglers with unlimited access to modest numbers of rainbows, cuttbows, and recently reintroduced arctic grayling. It's not world class by any stretch, but we still find the upper Ruby pleasant and inviting, a place we fish often each summer.

On average, upper Ruby trout aren't big, probably less than 12 inches, although we've never actually measured one. While we've probably never landed a for-sure 20-incher, a couple have come danged close. Like the big rainbow that grabbed my dry fly while I gawked absentmindedly at the aerial acrobatics of a flight of bank swallows busily swooping in and out of a mud nest glued to a high, eroded bank. Somehow the trout managed to suck in the fly and hook itself, as I was clueless until I picked up the line for another cast.

Our upriver catch consists mostly of cuttbow hybrids, although every now and then when fishing way up we hook what looks to our amateur ichthyologist eyes to be a pure-strain cutthroat. But real scientists tell me you can't tell by just looking.

Below the reservoir, the river flows entirely through private land. Like the upper river, this lower section is not conducive to floating—too small, too many obstacles, etc. For the wade fisher there are just seven public access points to the lower 50

A beautiful view on
the upper Ruby.

miles. But seven are better than none, with plenty of opportunities for those willing to work at it.

The stretch from the dam down to Alder fishes well year-round. The dam releases a fairly constant flow, and the river produces frequent and prolific insect hatches. Armed with a Parachute Adams or Elk Hair Caddis coupled with a beadhead nymph, it's a rare day that we can't drum up some action. If the river is off color, or if fishing at dawn or dusk or during nasty weather, pitching #6-10 Buggers and Clousers often works like magic.

Hale and hearty brown trout dominate the lower river these days. Rainbows once shared equal billing, but whirling disease has since taken a toll. Redsides appear to be making pretty good comeback up near the dam, though. The lower Ruby trout run 12 to 14 inches, with an 18-incher in the mix every now and then. There are some surprisingly large fish residing in the deep bends of this small river, too.

Bottom line: While the Ruby may not quite measure up to the more famous big rivers in the area, it shouldn't be passed over, either. The lower river is open year-round, but the upper river's season runs from the third Saturday in May to November 30.

Restaurants and Accommodations

The Sheridan Bakery (201 S. Main St.) is a great breakfast stop. The food is good, the coffee hot, and the service fast and friendly. Before you head to the river be sure to stop at the Sunflower Deli (Main St., 406-842-5464). The sack lunches are made to order, and the local liquor store is well stocked.

The area's New West dinner spot is the Old Hotel in Twin Bridges (101 E. Fifth Ave., 406-684-5959). The homey atmosphere belies an experience that can only be labeled "serious fine dining." Choose from daily specials featuring fish, pork, beef, and poultry, as well as vegetarian delights. Our insider tip would be to try the Spinach Lasagna (Gale's favorite) or Rack of Lamb with Chipolte Sauce (mine). There is an extensive wine and beer list to match the menu.

If your tastes run a bit more toward Old West, try the primo steaks at the Alder Steakhouse (Alder, 406-842-5159). For something unique, head down the road to the Roadmaster Grille (Virginia City, 406-843-5234) where you can sit in genuine "car seat" booths centered around a genuine and beautifully 1950 Buick Roadmaster. And the food ain't bad, either.

The doors to the four private suites read "Sage, Remington, Powell, and Winchester," leaving little doubt who the Rod and Rifle Inn (301 Mill Street, Sheridan, 406-842-5960) caters to. It's quaint, clean, and reasonably priced, so why not? More traditional digs are found at the Moriah Motel (220 South Main, Sheridan, 406-842-5491) or Kings Motel (307 South Main, Twin Bridges, 1-800-222-5510 or 406-684-5639).

Healing Waters Lodge (270 Tuke Lane, Twin Bridges, 406-684-5960) is typical of the several area lodges that cater exclusively to the flyfishing crowd. Each guest room includes two queen beds (seven rooms total), fluffy down comforters and down pillows, private decks and patios, mountain views, and art and antiques that reflect the history of southwest Montana.

Five Rivers Lodge (13100 Hwy. 41 N, 406-683-5000), a large retreat just north of the town of Dillon, boasts outstanding service and wonderful cuisine. The lodge provides comfortably elegant accommodations, and the spacious living room with stone fireplace makes a great spot for cocktails or just mingling. There is a fly-tying area with a large, well-lit table and a library with hundreds of flyfishing books and videos. Outside, there's a large wraparound deck and Jacuzzi for relaxing and two spring-fed ponds for casting to huge trout.

The USFS Cottonwood Campground, 36 miles upriver from Alder, is a nice place to bivouac if you don't relish the idea of driving the long, dusty road to and from the upper river on same day. There are 10 individual sites with water and toilet facilities. The surrounding national forest also provides unlimited opportunities to find a campsite all to yourself.

Nearby Fisheries

The Ruby Reservoir fishes well, particularly at ice-out. I like to suspend sparsely feathered jigs (black) beneath a hot-pink bobber, but Gale calls this highly questionable flyfishing. If you agree with her, by all means, try midging or stripping nymphs and streamers.

After July, and until the fall freeze-up, several drive-in trout lakes high in the nearby Tobacco Root Mountains provide a nice diversion to the sweltering summer heat in the valley. The Branham Lakes above Sheridan (Mill Creek Road) hold surprising numbers of wildly colorful 10-inch brookies. Upper and lower Boulder Lakes (accessed via Bear Gulch Road in Twin Bridges) and Noble Lake (Wisconsin Creek Road between Sheridan and Twin Bridges, to Noble Fork turnoff) are more or less accessible by vehicle. The former can be reached in dry weather with any high-clearance vehicle, but reaching Noble is a little dicier. Cutthroat and brook trout are found in the Boulder Lakes, while Noble contains cutthroat. None of these are trophy lakes, but they are fun to fish, and Noble's resident mountain goats provide a little extra incentive.

Nearby Attractions and Activities

Virginia City, once the capital of Montana and now the state's best-preserved ghost town, affords a nice diversion to the angling. While in town be sure to arrange time for the Brewery Follies, which are presented nightly during the summer season. Be prepared to laugh until it hurts.

For serious rod builders, a stop at R. L. Winston Rod Co. (MT 287 south) on the outskirts of Twin Bridges is mandatory.

Author's Tip

The lower Ruby looks more like a meandering spring creek than a real river. Below the dam there are decent hatches throughout the year, including winter, when almost any sunny day produces a prolific midge hatch.

Favorite Fly

Parachute Adams (Russ Mowery style)

Hook	Tiemco 100 #14-22
Tail	Brown and grizzly fibers
Body	Fine gray dubbing
Hackle	Grizzly or brown or both
Post	White or dun poly yarn
Wing	Cut hen hackle tied spent

The famous fly-tier Al Troth of Dillon, Montana, has a unique and durable way of tying the Parachute Adams.

Cut a 3-inch piece of poly yarn and separate it into three strands. Lay the yarn (one strand) perpendicular to the hook spent-wing fashion. Bind it down with two or three wraps. Wrap one end of the poly around and under the hook to form a U-shape. Hold both ends of the poly up and take several turns with the thread in front of and behind it. Wrap the thread around its base to form a post.

Secure a hackle in front of the wing. Position the feather so that it is at a 90-degree angle from the hook.

Attach the tail material so that it butts up against the wing.

Dub the body and thorax area. Wrap the thread forward to the eye of the hook; apply dubbing and dub back to the wing. You have now created the head portion of the fly. Rotate the fly a quarter turn so the wing is sticking out to the side. Take several wraps of thread at the base of the wing. Point the eye of the hook toward yourself; the wing should be sticking out to the right with the thread hanging down at its base. Wrap the hackle so that each turn is below the thread.

Once you have completed hackling the fly, gently secure the hackle to the wing as you would to a hook. Trim the excess. Whip finish on the wing. Rotate the fly back to its original position. Pull the poly yarn apart gently so that it compacts the hackle at the base. Trim the poly to length.

Fast Facts

Ruby River

Location	Southwest Montana; access upper river by turning south on MT 357 off MT 287 at Alder; between Alder and Twin Bridges, MT 287 more or less parallels the river
Water Type	Upper river is typical mountain trout water, intimate pool-riffle configuration; lower river meanders like a snake through hay meadows, tends to shrink rapidly in summer
Primary Gamefish	Upper river, primarily cuttbows and rainbows, planted arctic grayling; lower river, predominantly brown trout, with a smattering of rainbows
Best Time	Upper river after June runoff; lower river fishes well year-round; my favorite is early spring from the dam to Alder
Best Flies	Generic dries, Sparkle Dun, Elk Hair Caddis, San Juan Worm, Beadhead PT, Zug Bug, Prince, and Copper John Nymphs, soft-hackle wets, Buggers, Zonkers, Clousers
Equipment	8½- to 9-foot, 1- to 5-weight, floating line, leaders to match the conditions and tippets to match air resistance on the fly
Conditions	Upper river seldom fishable until July, sudden summer storms can muddy it up when other streams in the area are running clear; lower river suffers from irrigation demands in dry summers.

Drive Time   From Bozeman: 2.25 hours
                        From Billings: 4 hours
                        From Salt Lake City: 6.75 hours
Directions   From Bozeman, I-90 west to Whitehall, MT 55/41 south to
                        Twin Bridges, US 287 south to Alder; from Billings, I-90
                        west to Exit 309, US 191 south to MT 84, west to US 287,
                        south to MT 287, north to Alder; from Salt Lake City, I-15
                        north to Dillon, MT 41 north to Twin Bridges, MT 287
                        south to Alder.

Local Fly Shops

Harman's Fly Shop   Hemingway's Lodging & Fly Shop
310 South Main Street   409 North Main Street
Sheridan, MT 59749   Twin Bridges, MT 59754
406-842-5868   1-888-434-5118/406-684-5648

Four Rivers Fishing Company
205 South Main Street
Twin Bridges, MT 59754
1-888-474-8377

Guides

King's Flat Line Outfitters   Ruby Springs Lodge
406-684-5639   1-800-278-7829/406-842-5250

Crane Meadow Lodge   Broken Arrow Lodge
406-684-5777   1-800-775-2928406842-5437

Healing Waters Lodge   Upper Canyon Outfitters
406-684-5960   1-800-735-3973/406-842-5884

Contacts

Beaverhead-Deerlodge National Forest   Montana Fish, Wildlife, and Parks
Dillon, MT 59725   Region 3
406-683-3913   1400 South 19th
                                            Bozeman, MT 59715
                                            406-994-4042

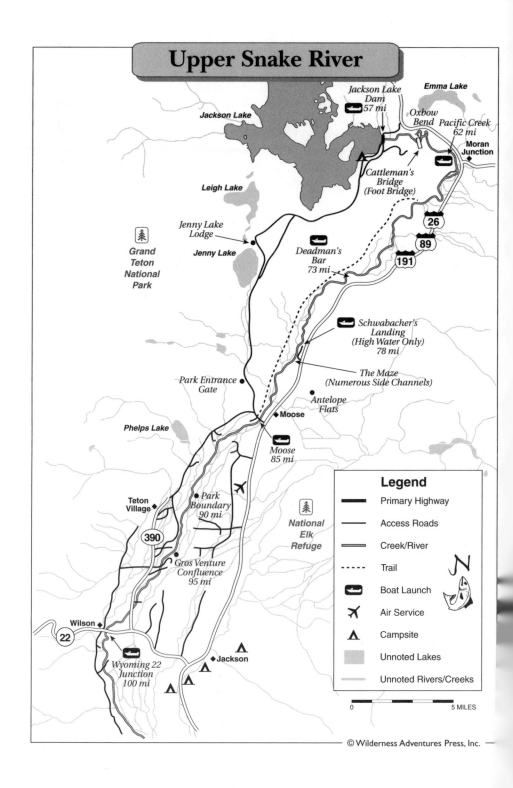

Upper Snake River

Emma Lake

Jackson Lake
Dam
57 mi

Oxbow
Bend

Pacific Creek
62 mi

Jackson Lake

Moran
Junction

Cattleman's
Bridge
(Foot Bridge)

Leigh Lake

26

89

191

Grand
Teton
National
Park

Jenny Lake
Lodge

Jenny Lake

Deadman's
Bar
73 mi

Schwabacher's
Landing
(High Water Only)
78 mi

The Maze
(Numerous Side Channels)

Park Entrance
Gate

Antelope
Flats

Phelps Lake

Moose

Moose
85 mi

National
Elk
Refuge

Teton
Village

Park
Boundary
90 mi

390

Gros Ventre
Confluence
95 mi

Legend

▬▬▬	Primary Highway
────	Access Roads
▬▬▬	Creek/River
------	Trail
🛥	Boat Launch
✈	Air Service
⚠	Campsite
	Unnoted Lakes
	Unnoted Rivers/Creeks

Wilson

22

Wyoming 22
Junction
100 mi

Jackson

0   5 MILES

© Wilderness Adventures Press, Inc.

CHAPTER 20

THE UPPER SNAKE RIVER
Teton Delight

The upper Snake River valley is a wonderful place in the last days of September, with the scent of fall in the air, the Tetons splashed by early snow, and the aspens and willows waving in the breeze like some giant yellow sea. It might sound maudlin, but I think it hits the mark. The crowds are gone, and the river's flow is nothing like it was just a couple of months earlier, when runoff raged well into midsummer.

In late September Schwabacher's Landing is no longer the place to launch or land your driftboat; you'd be hard pressed to float a toy boat here, let alone a real drift-fishing rig. With the gates at Jackson Lake shut down for the season, the river all but disappears in the channel that leads to this popular site. We're forced to march straight up the nearly dry riverbed until we come upon a magnificent pool. Grand Teton National Park forms a spectacular backdrop to the water, with the famous peaks looming behind the river and eagles and ospreys winging overhead. At any given moment an antelope, beaver, bison, deer, elk, moose, otter, or even the occasional bear might wander by.

The pool is perhaps a hundred yards long, and deep—one false step off the exposed gravel bar and you'd best know a swimming stroke or two. Gale rigs her favorite #14 Orange Stimulator, of course. But I've decided to go native today, opting for a #6 JJ Special, a local concoction invented by Jim Jones that was thrust upon me in a Jackson fly shop, with rave reviews I might add.

"Mister, don't be conned by the copycats showing up around town," warned the obviously devoted clerk, "the original's way better." Little did the innocent lad know that he'd already made the sale since rumors of the JJ's effectiveness were what drew us to the shop in the first place. But I let him finish the sale's pitch before plunking down $4.50 for a pair of flies. The Special is basically a grizzly-hackled brown-and-yellow Bugger with yellow rubber legs and a few strands of Krystal Flash for added pizzazz. Admittedly, it has a rather unique color pattern, and it's said to be most effective when jigged.

Back to my magnificent pool. Gale heads downstream, while I hike up to the head and arc a long cast to the edge of the fast water spilling in from the far side. The JJ lands with a rock-like *kerplunk*! The current immediately drowns it, pulling down a substantial length of floating line. I allow it to tumble and roll with the current for a few seconds before pumping (jigging) it back. On about the third pump a slight tap evokes an instinctive reaction on my part: line hand tightens, rod hand and arm shoot straight up. I can feel a heavy headshake being telegraphed up the line through the rod to my hand. Way to go JJ! One cast, one trout, can't beat it.

It would be difficult to find
a prettier place to fish.

But just when the first silvery flashes begin to confirm my early suspicions that this is indeed a serious Snake River cutthroat, the line goes slack. Worse, I discover that the trout has absconded with the JJ. A bad knot job strikes again. Well, at least this time I was smart enough to buy two...

Checking the knot more carefully this time, I send JJ number two tumbling down the same path as the first fly. Nothing. A couple dozen more drifts net similar results. By now I've fished my way well down the long pool and am seriously beginning to doubt the JJ's magic. Then, just as I start to pick up for yet another cast and retrieve, I feel a savage strike. I strike back hard and roll over what looks to be another hefty trout—roll over, but fail to hook, that is.

I make a quick pitch toward midstream and quickly bounce it back, once, twice, three times. *Bang!* Another hit, another miss. I toss the fly right back to the same spot and jig it my way a few times. *Bang!* Really wired for action now, I rip the line and raise the rod hard enough to cross any trout's eyes. Unfortunately, I find myself parted from my second, and last, JJ Special; the victim of a fly-eating sunken log.

I dig deep in my "uglies box" and come up with a well-chewed Yellow Yummy, which immediately takes a fat 15-inch cutthroat that I actually manage to land. A few casts later a foot-long cutt grabs and holds on. The next cast scores its twin. This is more like it. Following two quick misses, I'm latched fast to a feisty 14-incher. Thoroughly convinced the Yellow Yummy is today's real Snake River poison, I'm finally warmed up and ready to go just as the skies darken and a howling wind roars unchecked through the river valley. Hot damn fishing gone to hell in a hurricane—or something that feels very close.

Fighting to get my gear together for the mad dash to the truck, I glance downstream where Gale seems to be fighting a losing battle with a wind-stiffed line. Finally, she gives up, reeling the fly tight against the rod tip. With one hand clamping down her hat, she leans into the blow and makes her retreat.

Fickle fall weather in the northern Rockies, you gotta love it.

Fishing the Upper Snake River

Born in the backcountry of Yellowstone National Park, the Snake River gets its name from its curling nature and deep oxbow bends. Home to native Snake River fine-spotted cutthroat and introduced browns, it's a river famous for big fish that like to eat big flies—especially big dry flies.

From Jackson Lake Dam in Grand Teton National Park downstream, the upper Snake is really a floater's river, much of it suitable only for expert oarsmen. There are four floatable stretches within the Park, a delicious blend of braided channels, deep oxbows, long pools, shallow gravel bars, and steep dropoffs. Ten to 25 fish days are not uncommon, with most trout running 8 to 15 inches and one or two 16- to 20-inch fish showing up on most days. The biggest fish, some as large as 25 inches, usually fall to giant streamer patterns early and late in the season.

Due to its high-country origins, the Snake can be quite cold in early season, its trout reluctant to come to the surface. Popular early season patterns include Woolly Buggers, Clousers, Zonkers, local concoctions such as the Double Bunny and J. Special, and big ugly stonefly nymphs. "Anything with rubber legs," is something we consider sound advice.

But as runoff subsides, which can be as late as mid-July or mid-August, dry fly action begins to heat up, with Wulffs, Humpies, Stimulators, Trudes, Parachute Adams and Elk Hair Caddis all taking a fair share of fish. On sunny afternoons, especially in late August and early September, chucking big terrestrials (Parachute Hoppers are our favorite) and attractors can pay big dividends.

Fishing season on the Snake generally runs from April to the end of October with time off during peak runoff—unless, of course, you have a death wish that needs to be satisfied.

Restaurants and Accommodations

The Snake runs right through Jackson Hole, Wyoming, so there's plenty of services available for traveling anglers. For breakfast, head to Jedidiah's House of Sourdough (135 E. Broadway, 307-733-5671). The Early Riser Special includes two eggs, ham or bacon, home fries and all the sour jacks or biscuits and gravy you can stand. The Original Sour Jacks with blueberries gets this writer's highest praise.

Bubba's Bar-B-Q (515 W. Broadway, 307-733-2288) is a popular breakfast, lunch and dinner spot. For dinner, the Gun Barrel Steak & Game House (862 W. Broadway 307-733-3287) wins hands down. The locally owned and operated restaurant opened in 1993 in what used to be the Wyoming Wildlife Museum & Taxidermy. Named after the small, East Texas town of Gun Barrel City, the town's original 1950s hand-painted sign now hangs here, as do many of the original museum's big game trophies. In addition to the indigenous trophy mounts, there are numerous others from around the world, many of which were collected by the owners.

The bar is stocked with single-malt scotch and all the best bourbon and there are enough draft beer taps to make any connoisseur drool. The food is great and the taxidermy adorning the walls awesome. While choosing between Mesquite Steak and Velvet Elk Tenderloin Medallions with mushroom sauce, leeks, and sun-dried tomatoes puts me in the usual quandary, Gale keeps it simple by just ordering the Mixed Game Grill, a combo of elk, buffalo prime rib, and venison bratwurst.

There are literally dozens of other excellent eateries scattered around town, the only limit will be your expanding waistline and depleted wallet.

As to sleeping arrangements: Whatever your style, Jackson Hole has you covered. While there are several campgrounds in Grand Teton National Park, we like the
Gros Ventre Campground just beyond the border. It's right along the Gros Ventre River
(pronounced *gro-vaughn*), but best of all it comes complete with resident moose
and mule deer—always a plus. There are dozens of individual sites of every size and
description that can accommodate the largest RV and the smallest one-person bivy
sac. With community flush toilets and hot- and cold-running water, camping can't be
much cushier and still be camping.

If you're on your way to Yellowstone, stop in at Flagg Ranch Resort (south
entrance to Yellowstone, 307-543-2861) or Colter Bay Lodge, RV Park, and Tent Cabins
on Jackson Lake, 307-543-2811). Both are popular resorts that offer a wide range of
accommodations.

Elk feeding in the sage in Grand Teton National Park.

In the town of Jackson you'll find motels, hotels, and B&Bs galore, far too man
to list here. But for a good place to start try the Virginian Lodge (750 W. Broadwa
307-733-4063). It's friendly, clean, comfortable, and not too pricey, which can be a ser
ous concern in this high-priced resort town. Arriving between the summer and wir
ter tourist seasons will likely net you better rates.

Nearby Fisheries

Flat Creek in the National Elk Refuge just might be the best meadow trout stream i
the northern Rockies. Its flat water fishes more like a spring creek than, well, a sprin
creek. The trout are wise, spooky, and selective, so bring your A-game and be pr(
pared for some humbling days on the water. However, the rewards for skilled, patier
anglers are high. The cutts run 14 to 18 inches, and many surpass the two-foot marl
With the wispy leaders and smallish hook sizes required to fool these fish, landin(
them sometimes proves challenging. There are about 3 miles of open creek withi
the Refuge, and the season runs August 1 to the end October.

Nearby Attractions and Activities

With two national parks, a famous ski resort, and a bounty of lakes and rivers in th
surrounding national forests, Jackson Hole caters to just about every outdoor pursu
imaginable. If you want a break from the fishing, but don't want to leave the water, tr
the whitewater in the Snake River canyon. A host of outfitters offer daily trips dow
this wild stretch of water.

Located just outside of Jackson, the National Elk Refuge serves as winter rang
for a herd in excess of 7,500 head. Across the road, the National Museum of Wildlif
Art (307-733-5771) displays many works of the finest wildlife artists past and presen

Author's Tip

Mid-September to the end of October is a magical time on the upper Snake. Lo\
water, no crowds, and big trout on big flies make for a spectacular trip.

Favorite Fly

Parachute Hopper

Hook	TMC 5262 #6-12
Body	tan, brown, or yellow dubbing (Antron, rabbit, commercial mix)
Wing	Mallard duck quill coated with Flexament, folded over dubbed body
Post	White poly yarn
Hackle	Grizzly
Legs	Knotted pheasant tail or rubber strips or Sili Legs tied X-style

Fast Facts

Upper Snake River

Location	Grand Teton National Park, Wyoming
Water Type	Typical big, brawling Western river; extended runoff can last into August
Primary Gamefish	Snake River fine-spotted cutthroat and brown trout of good size
Best Time	Prior to runoff and August through October
Best Flies	Big attractor dry flies; meaty, rubber-legged nymphs; Buggers, Double Bunnies, JJ Specials; hoppers in season
Equipment	9-foot, 5- to 7-weight rod, floating and sink-tip lines
Conditions	Wading is difficult except during low flows. Float with caution, as swift currents, logjams, and sweepers pose problems for novice oarsmen. High country variable weather, expect chilly and wet anytime.

Drive Time	From Salt Lake City: 5.5 hours
	From Casper: 6.5 hours
	From Bozeman: 4 hours
Directions	From Salt Lake, I-15 north to Idaho Falls, US 26 east to ID 31 north to ID 33 south to WY 22 east to Jackson; from Casper, US 20/26 west to Jackson; from Bozeman, US 191 south to West Yellowstone, follow park roads to south entrance and then Grand Teton National Park to Jackson or bypass the parks to the southwest through Idaho.

Local Fly Shops

West Bank Anglers
3670 N. Moose-Wilson Road
P.O. Box 523
Teton Village, WY 83025-0523
307-733-6483

Orvis Jackson Hole
485 W. Broadway
Jackson, WY 83002-6029
307-733-5407

Jack Dennis Sports
50 E. Broadway
Jackson, WY 83001-3369
307-733-3270

High Country Flies
185 N. Center St.
Jackson, WY 83001
1-877-732-7210/307-733-7210

Guides

Reel Women Outfitters
208-787-2657

Camp Creek Inn and Outfitters
1-877-338-4868/307-733-3099

Upstream Anglers and Outdoor
Adventures
307-739-9443

Signal Mountain Fishing Guides
307-543-2831

John Henry Lee Outfitters, Inc.
307-733-9441

Grand Teton Lodge Company Fishing
Trips
307-733-3270

Flat Creek Ranch
1-866-522-3344/ 307-733-0603

Coy's Wilderness Fishing Trips
307-733-6726

Mangis Flyfishing Guide Service
1-800-850-1220/307-733-8553

Contacts

Grand Teton National Park
Moose, WY 83012-0170
307-739-3399

Jackson Hole Chamber of Commerce
Box E
Jackson, WY 83001
307-733-3316 or 5585

The upper Snake River in fall.

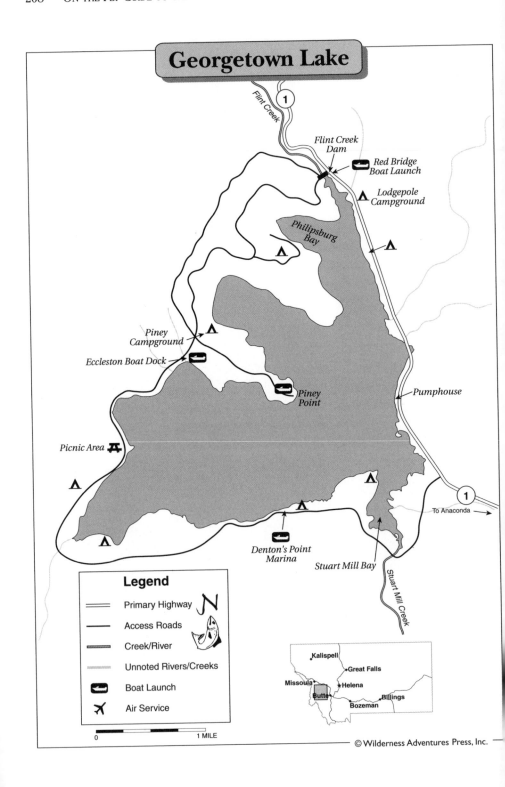

Georgetown Lake

Flint Creek

1

Flint Creek Dam

Red Bridge Boat Launch

Lodgepole Campground

Philipsburg Bay

Piney Campground

Eccleston Boat Dock

Piney Point

Pumphouse

Picnic Area

Denton's Point Marina

Stuart Mill Bay

Stuart Mill Creek

To Anaconda →

1

Legend

N

═══ Primary Highway

─── Access Roads

═══ Creek/River

─── Unnoted Rivers/Creeks

🛥 Boat Launch

✈ Air Service

Kalispell

Great Falls

Missoula

Helena

Butte

Billings

Bozeman

0   1 MILE

© Wilderness Adventures Press, Inc.

CHAPTER 21

GEORGETOWN LAKE
Big Trout, Classy Setting

Especially in spring, just after the ice recedes, Georgetown Lake in southwest Montana is one of those "Wow! What a spot to hook a trout" sort of places. And with all that beautiful water surrounded by black timber and the snow-splashed peaks of the Pintlar Range, it quickly becomes obvious that this isn't your normal run-of-the-mill Montana trout lake. But keep your eyes off the scenery because nothing—and I mean nothing—takes precedence over Georgetown Lake's trout.

To say that Georgetown has a widespread reputation for bigger-than-average trout is to understate the reality in a big way. Many of the rainbow and brook trout here are "pigs" in the most literal sense of flyfishing jargon.

In early June we we would like to pound the southeastern shoreline from the Pumphouse around to Denton's Point Marina, especially Stuart Mill Bay. But this part of the lake is under special regulations to protect spawning rainbows, and the shoreline and entire bay are closed to fishing from opening day (the third Saturday in May) through June 30. So today we launch our pontoon and tube elsewhere, across the lake in Rainbow Bay.

Gale mans the pontoon boat and, unusual for her, she drifts various beadhead nymphs beneath a big strike indicator, hoping to hook anything that comes along. I on the other hand, am on a mission. And a brookie measured in pounds, not inches is the only thing that will scratch my itch—no wimpy kokanees, no small brookies, no rainbows no matter how large. For me, it's big brook trout or nothing. I'm determined to land a truly big Georgetown Lake brook trout, just one, before I end up as fertilizer.

I kick the float tube into gear and alternate between trolling big home-brewed Clouser-style streamers and stripping magnum rubber-legged olive damsel creations. The former, I hope, imitates a red-sided shiner, which is a minnow said to be high on the favorite chow list of Georgetown brookies according to my insider source, a veteran FWP fisheries technician. The latter I know to be an ever-present food form, and one of those universal go-to patterns wherever trout swim in still water. I've tied these extra large in the hope that they will appeal to an extra large brookie.

In two hours—all the time we can spare today—the Clouser nabs two trout, both rainbows best measured in inches. The damsel nymph goes untouched. Based on my past quests to catch one of those elusive monster brookies, the results are not unexpected. Where Georgetown Lake and its famed fish are concerned, I am, as they say, snake bit. Maybe next time...

Next time turns out to be 7 a.m. on a mid-July morning. Apparently, even in the Pintlars summer has arrived, as the Butte-based weatherman promises "Georgetown's in for a real scorcher, mid-90s at least."

"Oh, how wonderful," says Gale, "the lake should just be brimming with jet skis and other noisome pests."

But at this early hour Georgetown is actually bathed in quiet. Not a ripple, not a wake, not a sound, except for the splashing, slashing sounds of surface feeding trout! With reckless abandon, the trout of Stuart Mill Bay seem bent on destroying the swarm of low-flying adult damselflies darting to and fro above the calm surface, clear wings glistening in the early morning sunshine.

Gale wonders aloud, "Where is everybody?"

But I'm already attached to a fish, and her question goes unanswered. It rips a semicircle around the float tube, bowing the rod double and bucking like a wild cayuse until suddenly the hook pulls free.

"What was it?"

"Damned if I know, never saw it. Didn't really fight like a rainbow, though." My mind wants to believe it was a huge brookie, even though I know Georgetown brookies aren't likely up on top gorging flying damsels in high summer. But a guy can dream, can't he?

Two casts later, a savage bucket-sized swirl engulfs the floating Deer Hair Damsel, swiping it from the surface. There's no doubt this time, as an instant later a arge rainbow leaps from the water like a tail-walking tarpon. Damn! Out comes the hook again.

"That looked like a nice rainbow. You better check your hook."

"No dice, the point is sharp, the hook is flawless."

I false cast a few times and drop the fly next to a real damsel that's sitting on a weed poking through the mirror-smooth surface. It no sooner lands than it too disappears in a savage swirl. This time a short, circular underwater battle ensues, as an unseen fish tears hell-bent in a semicircle around the tube. This time, however, I manage to haul it to the net—a fat 14- or 15-inch rainbow. Certainly no monster, but a fun trout on a dry fly, and there's no complaining about that.

Meanwhile, Gale has been hooking and landing or losing a mix of similar-sized rainbows and, somewhat surprisingly, even a couple of smaller kokanees.

All in all, the morning turns out better than expected considering the first onslaught of jet-ski noise and motorboat wakes doesn't reach us until nearly eleven. And by that time the hatch and the fishing are in the process of fizzling and the air is sizzling. No big brookies once again, not that we really expected any, but one can always hope.

Georgetown Lake with the snow-covered Anaconda-Pintlar Range in the background.

Fishing Georgetown Lake

Once the shoreline fishing restrictions are lifted July 1, our Georgetown game plans are largely confined to Stuart Mill, or sometimes Fin Bay. You can hardly go wrong in either spot by stripping damsels, nymphs, leeches, Buggers, or Clousers in and around the weed beds. When insects are actually hatching, we switch to the appropriate dries or emergers and usually trail a nymph behind. An especially effective rig when Callibaetis hatch (#12 early on, #14 midsummer, and #18 later on) is to rig a parachute-style dun trailed by a bubblehead emerger and a sinking nymph.

Damselflies begin hatching in earnest around the beginning of July. Damsel nymphs can be effective at any time, but are especially so just before and after the peak hatch period.

In August look for a big skimming caddis to appear. Assuming you possess a sound heart, hit the water just before dark, taper your leader to stout, and tie on a high-floating caddis like #6 or #8 Goddard Caddis, Stimulator, or heavily dressed Elk Hair Caddis. Make a long cast, tuck the rod in your armpit, and strip like hell with both hands—and good luck landing what hits.

Georgetown's big, colorful brook trout remain ghost fish so far as we're concerned, but my sources swear I should continue diligently stripping that old Redside

The Warm Springs Settling Ponds outside Anaconda produce large rainbow trout of a slightly different hue.

Clouser every chance I get, particularly during the late fall spawn. Assuming the big brookies really do exist and you happen to nail one, please protect and enhance this unique and fragile fishery by severely curtailing your casting to active spawners. And if you land a trophy, remember that good photos make for nice wall mounts and stuffed fish look best in museums.

Restaurants and Accommodations

The Haufbrau (111 Highway 1, Anaconda, 406-563-9982) is open for breakfast, lunch, and dinner, and specializes in friendly service, good food, and reasonable prices. Granny's Kitchen (1500 E. Commercial, 406-563-2349), among other sumptuous treats, serves delicious homemade soups and pies, and the Tortellini Chicken Salad is a particular favorite.

One of southwest Montana's best dinner spots is the Acoma Restaurant and Lounge in Butte (60 E. Broadway, 406-782-7001), which is built on a narrow site over a historic mine shaft in downtown Butte. Gale usually leans toward one of the veal dishes, particularly the Veal Acoma, sautéed with artichoke hearts and mushrooms and served in a white wine sauce, while I drool just thinking about the Halibut Imperial, a generous filet sautéed and topped with shrimp, crabmeat, and Hollandaise sauce. If you enjoy a before-dinner cocktail, hook a left inside the front door before heading upstairs to dine. The best bartender in all of Montana stands ready and waiting to mix your pleasure.

If you find yourself in Butte at lunchtime, the Acoma serves seven salads, a mean Top Sirloin Steak Sandwich, and meaty burgers; the Pasta of the Day is always a good bet.

One of the planet's more delightful dining experiences is found at the Pekin Noodle Parlor (117 S. Main St., 406-782-2217). Butte's oldest Chinese restaurant, it has been serving dishes like the delectable Pekin Extra Special in private, curtained, salmon-pink booths since 1916. The ambiance alone is worth the trip.

There are a whole host of good camping spots around the lake and in the nearby national forests. Piney and Rainbow Bay Campgrounds are right on the lake, while the North Fork Flint Creek Campground located on FR 65 requires a few miles of driving, although it's usually quieter. Same goes for the campground at nearby Echo Lake.

For those who enjoy outings in somewhat higher style, the Georgetown Lake Lodge and RV Park (Denton's Point Rd., 406-563-7020), offers clean, reasonable rooms and full hook-ups in the campground. A bit farther away, just outside Anaconda, is the ever-popular Fairmount Hot Springs Resort (1500 Fairmount Rd., 1-800-332-3272 or 406-797-3241). Following a hard day's fishing, you can relax in the hot springs then stay in one of the 152 rooms—high style and then some.

Anaconda, Montana

Anaconda is the town that Marcus Daly built. Butte had the ore, and Anaconda had the water necessary to refine it. (The town was originally named Copperopolis by its founder, but was renamed Anaconda when it was discovered that another Montana town already claimed the name.) The "Copper King" built the world's largest smelter the 585½-foot high, 86-foot wide Washoe stack, which still stands as a Montana icon (also a State Park/Interpretive Center, 406-563-2400). He also established the Butte, Anaconda, and Pacific Railroad specifically to transport the ore from his mines, and the town prospered.

In its heyday, Anaconda was one of Montana's most politically powerful cities, nearly hedging out Helena in the bid for the permanent state capital. The margin of victory was less than 2,000 votes.

When the Butte mines eventually faltered, the Anaconda Company closed the Washoe Smelter in 1983, and today the town struggles to survive. Despite its economic woes, Anaconda has managed to preserve its historic town center. City Hall and the Deer Lodge County Courthouse, with it fabulous rotunda, copper-clad cupola and curving staircases and ingenious dumbwaiter, are worth seeing, as is the Washoe Theater and the imposing Hearst Free Library, an 1898 gift from William Randolph Hearst's mother, Phoebe.

Nearby Fisheries

Anaconda's Copper King left behind a whole string of legacies, among them the nation's worst Superfund site. And while this isn't the place to describe the environmental trashing in detail, suffice it to say that Warm Springs Creek, the Washoe Smelter's primary source of water, did not fare well. By the time the mines and smelter closed their doors, the little creek (as well as much of the Clark Fork River it feeds into) was already DOA.

Then, for reasons well beyond my understanding of big oil business dealings, Arco bought Anaconda's remaining assets, and with them inherited a huge multi-million dollar cleanup. While the project is still ongoing, trout fishers have already cashed in. The famous Hog Hole and other ponds have proven to be real trophy-trout factories, home to brown trout as large as 14 pounds and equally outlandish rainbows in excess of 10 pounds.

But don't expect pushovers, as these trout can present some tedious fishing. Hogs aside, average trout in the ponds run 2 or 3 pounds, and somewhat less than that in the creek's moving water. Six to ten fish days are considered good, and based on personal experience, hooking up with a real pig once every six to ten outings is about average. Landing one, at least for me, is another story. For, you see, when it

:omes to actually landing really big trout anywhere on the planet, I am as "snake bit" is it gets.

Warm Springs' trout grow fat because, despite past atrocities, the waters are extremely fertile and produce prodigious amounts and varieties of foodstuffs, from)utsized leeches to diminutive aquatic insects. This means that any number of pat-erns and methods are apt to work at any given moment.

We've hooked trout on everything from tiny midges to huge snake-like stream-ers. And while we have hooked a few monsters, the biggest fish we've actually land-ed in the ponds has yet to break the 2-foot mark. My largest to date actually came rom the creek, an enormous rainbow that measured around 25 or 26 inches. Don't get me wrong; in my book any trout over 20 inches is special. But I understand only oo well that such a piddling specimen would be little more than a bothersome pest o a real Warm Springs hog hunter.

The Warm Springs Hog Ponds live by a complex set of regulations: All ponds and :anals are open August 15 through September 30, catch-and-release only; exceptions ire portions of the creek itself. The Kid's and Gravel Pit ponds are open year-round. 'ond 3 and the Hog Hole are open May 25 through September 30.

Nearby Attractions and Activities

t seems rather curious to me since I know nothing about golf, but Anaconda boasts)ne of the country's finest golf courses, the Old Works (406-653-5827). Designed by lack Nicklaus, it stands as a unique revival of a former Superfund site. Anyway, I sup-)ose it's as good a place as any to break out the clubs in between hatches.

Should you be into history, mining history in particular, the Anaconda/Butte area s perhaps ground zero. In addition to the Anaconda Stack, see the Copper Village Museum (406-563-2422), the Granite County Museum in Philipsburg (406-859-3020), ind the ghost town Southern Cross, east of Georgetown Lake on MT 1. In Butte, visit he World Museum of Mining (406-723-7211), the Anselmo Mine Yard and Granite Mountain Mine Memorial (1-800-735-6814 or 406-723-3177), and, of course, the notori-)us Berkley Pit, once the largest open-pit copper mine in the U.S. At 7,000 feet long, 5,600 feet wide, and 1,800 feet deep, it's quite a hole.

Author's Tip

From July through fall it's best to stick to weedy bays like Stuart Mill. The mud bot-om limits wade fishing, so tote along some sort of watercraft. We do nicely with a float tube and pontoon kick boat, but any sort of boat is better than none. A good actic during any hatch is to rig a long leader, 15 feet or more, pattern the rhythm of an individual surface feeder, and drop the fly in its path. During the damsel hatch,)oth dry flies and nymphs can be effective.

Favorite Fly

Damsel Nymph

Hook	1-2X long nymph hook #8-14
Bead	Copper, gold, or black; brass or glass
Tail	Light olive marabou/Krystal Flash
Body	Light olive marabou twisted and wrapped
Legs	Barred partridge
Collar	Olive marabou

Fast Facts

Georgetown Lake

Location	20 miles west of Anaconda, Montana, on MT 1, Anaconda Pintlar Scenic Byway
Water Type	Manmade reservoir at 6,000 feet elevation
Primary Gamefish	Brook and rainbow trout and kokanee salmon
Best Time	Opening day to late fall; July damselfly hatch, August skimming caddis, fall brook trout spawn
Best Flies	Midge, caddis, Sparkle Duns, damsels, mohair and bunny leech patterns, olive, brown, black Woolly Buggers, red-sided shiner imitations
Equipment	9-foot, 5- or 6-weight, floating, sink-tip, and full sink lines, leaders built stout enough to haul big fish out of weeds
Conditions	Expect the chilly weather in spring and fall; summer days are usually pleasant due to the high elevation. It can storm anytime, so be prepared. Wind is not a big factor most days.

Drive Time   From Missoula: 1.75 hours
                    From Bozeman: 2.5 hours
                    From Idaho Falls: appx. 4 hours
Directions   From Missoula, I-90 east to Drummond, MT 1 south to
                    lake; from Bozeman, I-90 west to MT 1 north to lake; from
                    Idaho Falls, I-15 north to I-90 west to MT 1 north to lake.

Local Fly Shops

Fish On Fly and Tackle   Kesel's Four Rivers
3346 Harrison Ave.   501 S. Higgens
Butte MT 59701   Missoula, MT 59801
406-494-4218   406-721-4796, 1-888-349-4796

Bugs and Bullets   Grizzly Hackle
Harrison Ave.   215 W. Front St.
Butte MT 59701   Missoula, MT 59801
406-782-6251   406-721-8996

Rock Creek Mercantile   Missoulian Angler
15995 Rock Creek Road   420 N. Higgens
Rock Creek, MT 59825   Missoula, MT 59801
406-825-6440   406-728-7766

Guides

Tom's Fishing and Bird Hunting Guide   Fran Johnson's
     Service   406-782-3322
406-723-4753

Contacts

Anaconda Chamber of Commerce   Butte Chamber of Commerce
306 E. Park Ave.   2950 Harrison Ave.
Anaconda MT 59711   Butte MT 59701
406-563-2400   1-800-735-6814, Ext. 10

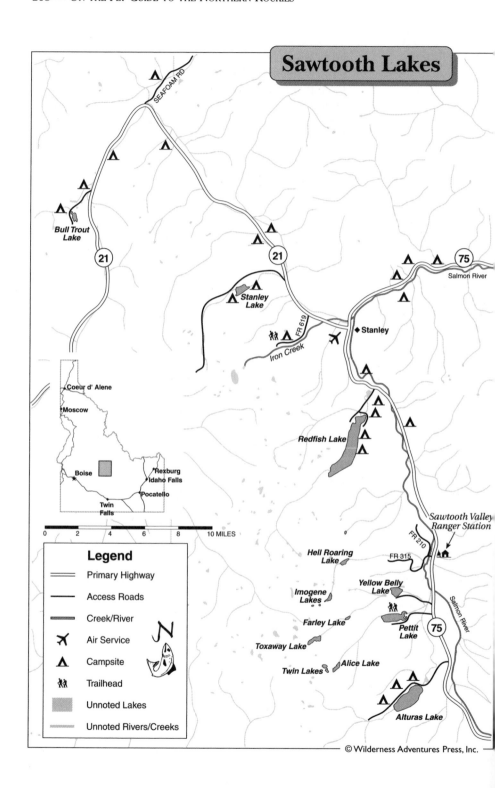

Sawtooth Lakes

SEAFOAM RD

Bull Trout Lake

21

21

75

Salmon River

Stanley Lake

FR 619

Stanley

Iron Creek

Coeur d' Alene

Moscow

Boise

Rexburg
Idaho Falls

Pocatello

Twin Falls

Redfish Lake

Sawtooth Valley Ranger Station

FR 210

FR 315

Hell Roaring Lake

Yellow Belly Lake

Imogene Lakes

Farley Lake

Pettit Lake

75

Salmon River

Toxaway Lake

Twin Lakes

Alice Lake

Alturas Lake

0   2   4   6   8   10 MILES

Legend

Primary Highway

Access Roads

Creek/River

✈ Air Service

Λ Campsite

🚶 Trailhead

Unnoted Lakes

Unnoted Rivers/Creeks

N

© Wilderness Adventures Press, Inc.

CHAPTER 22

THE SAWTOOTH LAKES

Idaho's Alpine Marvels

In the northern Rockies, opportunities to cast flies and catch a wild trout amid picturesque surroundings are as common as town rodeos, though very few top those
found among the craggy peaks of Idaho's Sawtooth Mountains. There are more than
a thousand pristine lakes in the area, and their icy waters eventually help build the
Salmon, Payette, and Boise Rivers. Within the boundaries of the Sawtooth Wilderness
alone, there are more than 150 lakes with bull, brook, lake, cutthroat, and rainbow
trout. While the trout rarely reach lunker size, they are as handsome as the scenery,
and bigger individuals are caught occasionally in some of the more remote, more
fertile lakes.

The drive-up lakes, like Bull Trout, Alturas, Petit, Redfish, and Stanley, host fishing
that can be so-so to good. For example, last fall we fished Bull Trout and caught 10- to
12-inch rainbows on dry and wet ant patterns until we tired of the game. While hunting for trout at Alturas Lake on the same trip, we instead found kokanee salmon on
the rise.

But even on their best days the drive-up lakes are just a warm-up for the fishing
that awaits up the trail. And no matter how good those days are, they lack the adven-

ture and solitude found in the backcountry. To really experience the Sawtooths one needs to strap on a pack and wear out a little shoe leather.

We usually do our damnedest to duck anything like crowds, so we try to time our visits for soon after Labor Day. The number of summer hikers dwindles somewhat, especially on weekdays, and many backcountry anglers are turning their attention toward hunting. While we don't always find empty trailheads, they're rarely anything like full.

Typically, we establish a base camp at one of the many USFS campgrounds within the Stanley Basin. Iron Creek on FR 619 is a favorite, but we also enjoy camping at Bull Trout Lake, and on the headwaters of the Middle Fork Salmon River on Beaver Creek.

From base camp we make daily forays to lakes within day-hike range; something on the order of 10 miles or so round trip works for us. And yes, we realize that at least half the fun is staying overnight, but at our age serious backpack excursions no longer hold the same appeal they did when we were 30 or 40.

In lake-filled country like the Sawtooths, a week of 10-mile day hikes still reveals a world of pretty fishing holes. Lakes like Hell Roaring (just 5 miles in) are full of feisty brook trout that are almost always willing to gobble a well-presented fly. To reach the trailhead follow FR 315 near the Sawtooth Ranger Station on ID 75 south of Stanley.

A little farther off the beaten path, the Imogene Lakes contain healthy populations of brook and rainbow trout. In the same general area, Decker Lake holds larger rainbows that are sometimes difficult to entice to the surface. The trailhead is reached off FR 210 north of the ranger station. Petitt Lake, south of Stanley off ID 75, is the jumping-off spot to Yellow Belly, Farley, Toxaway, Twin, and Alice Lakes. The sweeping vistas around Alice Lake, with its tiny forested islands and spectacular alpine backdrop, are almost enough to make you forget the cutthroats.

Our backcountry kit is a minimalist's dream. One pack contains the fishing gear, light pack rod, one reel/floating line, a spare spool containing sink-tip line, tippet in 3X to 5X, fly floatant, forceps, a film canister with a few split shot, one fly box with a spartan assortment of attractor dries, nymphs, and a few Buggers and Clousers. The same pack also carries the camera, spare camera lens, flash-unit, spare film, etc.

The second pack contains spare socks, sweaters, rain jackets (never go without, as high country storms are common, sudden, and often violent), gorp, energy bars, empty water-filter bottle, knife, matches, fire-starter paste, space blanket, GPS unit, compass, and map.

Admittedly, packing in a float tube, waders, two rods instead of one, and a larger fly assortment, to say nothing of extra personal gear, would without question increase both our range and our catch rate, but lugging that stuff around takes some of the fun out of the hike.

Bull Trout Lake.

Local outfitters offer all sorts of options if you'd prefer to explore beyond day-hike range without doing any heavy lifting: llama treks, horse-pack trips, trips where you hike while they pack the gear.

In mid-September one year we camped at Bull Trout Lake and spent the afternoon and evening trading off the pontoon boat and catching a passel of feisty rainbows. The next morning we drove up Beaver Creek (Seafoam Road) and hiked into a string of little lakes, none of which were named on our map. At the first, probably 3 miles in, we drew a blank, so we headed to the second, which lay a mile beyond. After hooking a pair of skinny 8- to 10-inch cutthroats, we placed it into the "not much" category and moved on. The third lake, just a quarter-mile uphill of the second, also produced meager results, and we started to think about cutting things short. But checking the map we saw that the fourth lake was only another mile or so farther on, so we figured on one last try.

The area around the outlet was uncharacteristically low and marshy (many Sawtooth Lakes are ringed by nothing but solid rock), but the upper end looked deep and inviting. We hiked up the mountainside, contoured across, and then dropped back down to the lake. Rising trout dimpled the ruffled surface and, judging the swirls, at least some were of decent size.

Using the shoreline boulders for a casting platform, Gale launched the first cast. The #10 Red-Ass Parachute Ant bobbed on the tiny waves for just a second or two before disappearing in a splashy rise. Soon she bent down and released a pretty, slightly snaky-looking cutthroat of about 12 or 13 inches. Taking the rod, it wasn't long before I too stooped low to release a twin of the first fish.

Taking turns and casting our way around the lake's upper end, we caught trout after trout, some fat, some not so fat, and all on the surface and on the ant. By late afternoon the ant was thoroughly chewed up, but still the rises and takes continued unabated. Our fish-catching urge satisfied for the day, we reeled in and headed back down the mountain.

Another fine day of exploring and fishing in some of the prettiest mountains in the West.

Happiness is an alpine lake and a good float tube.

Restaurants and Accommodations

In Stanley, Idaho, winter comes early and stays late. While frost is no stranger in any month of the year, after Labor Day you can always bet on frost, or even snow, in the high country. Many of Stanley's part-time residents flee for warm climes, but enough winter over to keep at least some of the town services running year-round. The Mountain Village Resort (208-774-3317)—lounge, restaurant, lodge, and mercantile—becomes sort of the village hub. They serve home-style breakfast, lunch, and dinner, and we've always found the staff friendly and fast and the food good.

In Lower Stanley, the recently opened Bridge Street Burger and Brew puts out a delicious sourdough pancake breakfast, and Papa Brunee's (208-774-2536) is the place to head for pizza, sandwiches, and a cold beer.

Population-wise Stanley ranks way down on Idaho's list, but don't let that statistic fool you into thinking it might be hard to find a place to stay. Within the Stanley Basin there exist, without doubt, far more rental rooms and cabins than permanent residents. In addition, there are dozens of USFS campgrounds and unimproved pull-outs within the surrounding national forests and other public lands, making for an almost limitless number of possibilities.

The Mountain Village Resort (1-800-543-5475) provides clean rooms at reasonable rates, especially after Labor Day. The Riverside Motel (1-800-284-3185 or 208-774-3409), with its modern log rooms with kitchenettes, is one of the newest additions to Stanley. The upside is that all rooms are non-smoking, the downside no pets allowed. Smiley Creek Lodge (208-774-3547) boasts "the longest view in the valley" and is widely known for rustic charm, burgers, rental cabins, and RV spots. The Triangle C Ranch (1-800-303-6258 or 208-774-2266) offers rentals, backcountry pack trips, and caters to flyfishers.

Stanley, Idaho

In 1873 Alvah Challis and Henry Sturkey found gold in Stanley Creek and set up a profitable hydraulic mining operation. Their operation, and others that soon followed, pillaged much of the nearby landscape until the vein petered out around 1920.

When the mines faltered, Stanleyites more or less turned their attentions toward tourism—hikers, hunters, anglers, river rats—cattle ranching, and logging, not necessarily in that order. Today the friendly little mountain village bustles year-round despite a winter population of just 70 hardy souls.

Nearby Fisheries

The mainstem Salmon River parallels Highway 75 for many miles down to the town of Salmon and beyond. Best known as a steelhead and salmon fishery, the upper reaches, particularly above East Fork, hold decent populations rainbows, cutthroat, and whitefish. Finding access is often as easy as simply pulling off the road, although there are a few private stretches.

The Middle Fork of the Salmon heads off US 21 south of Stanley and cuts a swath through the Frank Church-River of No Return Wilderness. Except for the very top end, access involves a long hike, horses, or a good raft and a better oarsman. This is one river where only expert rowers need apply. The trip downriver takes five to eight days and there are many Class IV and V rapids and falls to negotiate, making it no place for beginners. A permit is required to float, and these are doled out by lottery (Salmon-Challis National Forest, Middle Fork District Office, Challis, Idaho; 208-879-5204).

Fishing doesn't begin until after runoff peaks, in July most years. The rewards, however, can be high. Twenty-five to 50 fish days are not uncommon, and while most run 12 to 14 inches, some stretch the tape to 18 inches or more. Large steelhead and bull trout (all Idaho bull trout must be released immediately) are always a distinct possibility, as are chinook salmon and steelhead smolts.

The Yankee Fork (Salmon) between Stanley and Challis is another popular, albeit much smaller, option. It runs down a series of rocky canyons from one inviting riffle, run, and rock-lined pool to the next. The Payette and Boise Rivers get their start to the southwest, and they're a pair of mountain fisheries well worth exploring.

Author's Tip

Flyfishing here is not about big fish by any stretch of the imagination. Actually, the fishing often takes a back seat to the awesome vistas of the high country, the thrill of exploring new country and breathing clean air. Take the time to appreciate the clean, cold water and wild trout, and don't worry so much about nailing a 20-inch fish to brag about back at the lodge.

Favorite Fly

Red-Ass Parachute Ant

Hook	TMC 100 #12-20
Wing	White poly yarn tied as post
Abdomen	Red or rust dubbing
Thorax	Black dubbing
Hackle	Grizzly, parachute style

Fast Facts

Sawtooth Lakes

Location	Stanley, Idaho, midway between Ketchum and Challis
Water Type	High mountain lakes, with slower growth rates for trout
Primary Gamefish	Native cutthroat and bull trout, planted rainbow trout and grayling
Best Time	July to freeze-up; crowds dwindle after Labor Day
Best Flies	Basic attractor dries, terrestrials, nymphs, and streamers
Equipment	9-foot, 5- or 6-weight pack rod; floating, sink-tip, and full-sink lines, leader and tippet to suit fly pattern and method
Conditions	Expect it to be chilly; storms are frequent and often violent; summers can be buggy.
Drive Time	From Boise: 3 hours
	From Idaho Falls: 6 hours
	From Salt Lake City: 10 hours

Directions   From Boise, I-84 east to ID 21 north to Stanley; from Idaho Falls, US 20/26 west to Arco, US 93 north to Challis, ID 75 south to Stanley; from Salt Lake, I-15 north to I-84 west to Twin Falls, US 93 north to Shoshone, ID 75 north to Stanley.

Local Fly Shops

McCoy's Tackle Shop
P.O. Box 210
Stanley, ID 83278
208-774-3377

Mountain Village Mercantile
P.O. Box 150
Stanley, ID 83278
208-774-3661

The Bent Rod
Main St.
Challis, ID 83226
208-879-2500

Silver Creek Outfitters
Highway 75
Ketchum, ID 83340
208-726-5282

Lost River Outfitters
171 N. Main Street
Ketchum, ID 83340
208-726-1706

Guides

Middle Fork River Expeditions
1-800-801-5146

Sawtooth Adventure Co.
1-866-774-4644

Sawtooth Fishing Guides
208-774-2264

Silver Spur Sports
208-756-2833

Contacts

Sawtooth National Forest, Supervisor's
   Office
2647 Kimberley Rd. E.
Twin Falls, ID 83301

Sawtooth National Recreation Area
HC 64, Box 8291
Ketchum ID 83340
208-727-5000

SNRA Visitor Center
208-727-5013

Sawtooth National Forest
Stanley Work Center
HC 64, Box 9900
Stanley ID 83728
208-774-3000

CHAPTER 23

THE SOUTH FORK BOISE RIVER

Winter Games

Deep winter trout fishing is not everyone's bag, but winter happens to be our favorite time to fish those rivers that are, shall we say, a bit too crowded for comfort during the warm season. And if one of those rivers happens to be located where winter makes itself scarce on most days, so much the better. Southwest Idaho's South Fork Boise is such a river, although Old Man Winter does rear his nasty head on occasion.

The South Fork, at least the stretch we're most interested in, heads at Anderson Ranch Reservoir at the bottom of a deep and awesome canyon, accessible via a steep, winding gravel road. There are no guardrails (or even side berms) to ricochet off if you lose control on the snowy and/or icy road, so pay attention. Slip over the edge, and it's a long way down to level ground. However, the road is well maintained throughout the winter, and with a little careful planning you should be able to hit one of the nice January days for which the region is famous.

As with most winter trout fishing, the daily window of opportunity is short. And in this case, it's further shortened by the narrow canyon. Even when there's not a cloud in sight the low winter sun doesn't reach the river until near midday. And now, as I stand here at four in the afternoon, it's gone once again.

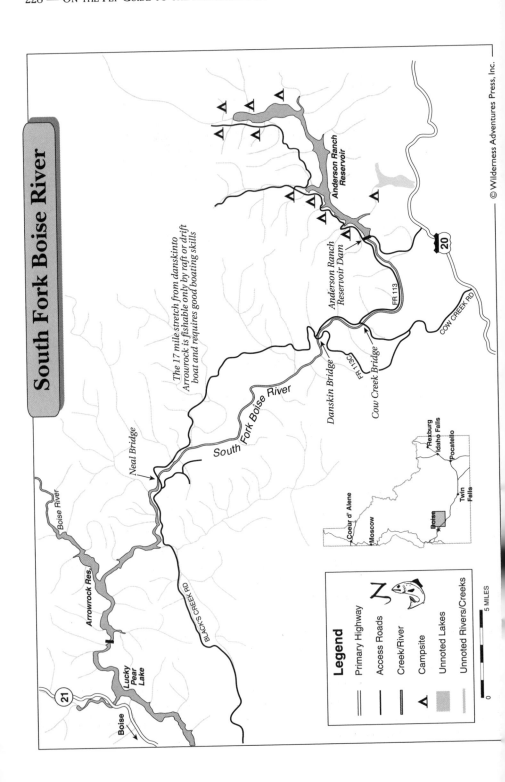

South Fork Boise River

The 17 mile stretch from danskinto Arrowrock is fishable only by raft or drift boat and requires good boating skills

Anderson Ranch Reservoir

Anderson Ranch Reservoir Dam

FR 113

Danskin Bridge

FR 113C

Cow Creek Bridge

COW CREEK RD

South Fork Boise River

Neal Bridge

Boise River

Arrowrock Res.

Lucky Pear Lake

BLACK'S CREEK RD

Boise

Coeur d' Alene

Moscow

Rexburg

Idaho Falls

Pocatello

Boise

Twin Falls

Legend

‖	Primary Highway
		Access Roads
		Creek/River
▲	Campsite
	Unnoted Lakes
	Unnoted Rivers/Creeks

0   5 MILES

© Wilderness Adventures Press, Inc.

For the past two hours I've been busily engaged with a pod of feeding rainbows that are gorging on a surprisingly heavy hatch of midges. I've been mesmerized by the constant dimpling and swirling trout, the towering rock walls, and the deep, inviting pool. Standing in icy water up to my waist and suddenly thrust into shadow, I've gone from slightly chilled to damn cold in a heartbeat. Oh well, great hatch, great rise, much fun—a fitting way to end a fabulous day on a fabulous river. (Any day of fishing we can steal from winter's clutches deserves a host of superlatives.)

When the rise began I switched from a #6 Bitch Creek and a #10 Brown Stone Nymph to a #20 Griffith's Gnat trailing a #20 Black Disco Midge. The pair of little flies proved deadly, and they were a lot more fun to fish with than the bottom dredgers. Whitefish, some approaching 20 inches, gobbled the stones pretty well, but except for one heavy 14-inch rainbow, they provided the sole source of early afternoon entertainment, unless you count the bald eagles and mule deer or the chukars and valley quail Katie spent the afternoon sniffing out. It wasn't until the midge hatch began that the rest of the rainbows came up to feed.

From a fishing standpoint, winter is a good time to fish the South Fork. Weekdays are virtually crowd-free, and the low flow makes for easy (relatively speaking) wading. For example, the above episode took place with the flow just above 300 cfs, a far cry from the 1,500 cfs typical in June.

Unfortunately, the best fishing doesn't usually occur on days with the most pleasant weather. Winter hatches are confined to midges and the ubiquitous Blue-Winged Olives. Midges tend to hatch on sunny days, but the trout don't always get after them with enthusiasm. When the BWOs come out to play, however, the trout are all over them. And we all know how that hatch favors nasty weather.

During non-hatch periods, drifting stonefly nymphs through deep holes and runs can provide fairly consistent underwater action, particularly if you don't mind catching the South Fork's big whiteys.

Fishing the South Fork Boise

With a blue-ribbon label and a national reputation, the South Fork Boise draws a lot of attention from anglers during the summer season. And because the river is just 60 miles from Boise, Idaho's capital and largest city, the crowds are particularly thick on weekends and holidays. Relatively easy access makes it even more appealing. Below the dam, a good gravel road parallels the river's Wild Trout Management stretch for 10 miles or so down to the Danskin Bridge Access. The remaining 17 miles are accessible only by floating.

Early spring hatches begin with Baetis and midge activity, followed by caddis and early stoneflies. The river's most consistent and long-lived hatch, the Pink Albert, a color variation of the Light Cahill, begins in July. Dry fly patterns should include

Sparkle Duns, Parachute Adams, Elk Hair Caddis, and stonefly patterns such as the Yellow Sally and Golden Stone in a variety of sizes and colors.

Popular nymphs include the Beadhead Pheasant Tail, Beadhead Prince, Copper John, Flashback, Brassy, Beadhead Hare's Ear, various caddis emergers, the Disco Midge, Bitch Creek, and George's Brown Stone. Streamers might include the brown and black Woolly Bugger, the ever-popular Egg-Sucking Leech and Clouser Minnow and various bunny strip patterns.

Rainbow trout and mountain whitefish, many of which run 15 to 18 inches, predominate, with enough in the 20-inch-plus class to make big fish fans salivate. There's also a small, remnant population of native bull trout.

Restaurants and Accommodations

For anglers who don't cotton to camping beside the river, Mountain Home makes a good base camp. Originally called Rattlesnake Station, the town was renamed when it was moved closer to the railroad tracks that opened up the area.

Today, the Rattlesnake Station Steakhouse (135 Bitterbrush, Old Hwy. 30 West 208-587-3691) is Mountain Home's unique fine-dining spot. Unique hardly does justice to the interior décor, which includes covered wagon booths, a mine shaft, and walls covered in art deco and customer autographs. And the food, drinks, and friendly service are unmatched. The Bergh family—matriarch Jan, patriarch Dave, concierge Salle, and maitre d' Benjamin—goes all out to make sure your dining experience is everything you hoped for and more. As you might expect, this is a seriously informal place; anything beyond jeans and sweaters would no doubt be considered overdressed.

More traditional dining can be found at AJ's Restaurant and Lounge (1130 Hwy. 20, 208-587-2264), which serves a great all-you-can-eat daily breakfast buffet. For lunch and dinner the salad bar is among the best in the area, and the steaks aren't too shabby, either.

If you're hankering for Italian food, check out the Smoky Mountain Pizza and Pasta (1465 American Legion Blvd., 208-587-2840). They have a great microbrew draft beer selection and wine list and delicious pizza, subs, and pasta in a snazzy, modern atmosphere. There is also a daily self-serve salad and pasta bar and lunch smorgasbord.

There are USFS campgrounds at the dam and beside the river. Our first choice is the one at parking area six. Other sites are available a half-mile below the dam and at the Village, Cow Creek, and Danskin Accesses. They provide a flat spot to set up camp and toilet facilities, but no water and anything like full hook-ups.

The Sleep Inn (1180 Hwy. 20, 1-800-627-5337) allows pets and is the town's newest motel. The Best Western Foothills Motor Inn (1090 Hwy. 20, 208-587-8477) is

*Sight-fishing during an
afternoon midge hatch.*

ist next door and allows pets. There is a busy truck stop across the street, however,
ɔ be sure to request rooms on the far side in the back unless, of course, all-night
ruck traffic doesn't bother you.

Nearby Fisheries

or purported desert country, there sure are a lot of fishing possibilities. The main
oise River, even in downtown Boise, is a decent rainbow fishery, and when supple-
iented each winter by steelhead releases it gets even better. Below town to its con-
uence with the Snake River savvy locals hunt for big browns and a burgeoning
opulation of feisty smallmouth bass.

There are also numerous ponds, lakes, and reservoirs within easy driving dis tance of Mountain Home and Boise; some hold trout, but many are home to warmwater species such as crappie and smallmouth and largemouth bass. Check out Anderson Ranch, Brownlee, Camas, C.J. Strike, Hell's Canyon, Lucky Peak, Lucky Strike, and Oxbow Reservoirs, Bruneau Dunes and the so-called Boise Urban Ponds and Lake Lowell, just to name a few. Stop in at the local fly shops or call Idaho Game and Fish to find out what's hot and what's not.

Nearby Attractions and Activities

The town of Mountain Home boasts one of the largest American Legion Posts around, and the town square comes complete with a mounted Delta-winged fighter jet in take-off mode. Neither of these facts should be too surprising once you learn that just 10 miles down the road is the Mountain Home Air Force base.

For natural wonders, visit the awesome Bruneau Sand Dunes (208-366-7919) and the Snake River Birds of Prey Area. A few miles east of town you'll find Glenn's Ferry the site of the most treacherous river crossing on the entire Oregon Trail, in the Three Island State Park (208-366-2394), which is one of the nicest and best maintained state parks anywhere. During the warm season you can even experience teepee living here.

If you're a wine connoisseur, I'm sure you are already well aware of southwest Idaho's wineries. A visit to one the many area vineyards makes for a nice side trip. We've visited Carmela Vineyards in Glenn's Ferry (795 W. Madison, 208-366-2313) Sawtooth Winery in Nampa (13750 Surrey Lane), which gets my distinguished vote for best bottle; Hells Canyon Winery in Caldwell (18835 Symms Road), which is open Saturday and Sunday noon to five or by appointment; and Ste. Chapelle Winery in Caldwell (19348 Lowell Road), a close tie for "Chuck's Best of Show Award." There are, of course, many more to options to explore, as well.

For bird hunters, southwest Idaho supports excellent chukar and valley quail populations, and much of the best hunting is on public land.

In Boise the M-K Nature Center (208-368-6060) is a must-stop for anglers. It's an indoor/outdoor facility that features the life of a mountain stream, both above sur face and below, as well as interpretive and interactive exhibits. The bird life and humongous rainbow trout make the stop worthwhile, but the whole place is pretty amazing as it's right in the midst of a major city.

The World Center for Birds of Prey (south of Boise, 208-362-8687) gives visitors a glimpse of how endangered species of hawks, falcons, eagles, and other birds of prey are saved. Several birds are on display year-round.

The Boise Greenbelt is a unique trail system that connects the city's parks. Better yet, more than 25 miles of trails provide walking access to the midtown section of

ιe Boise River. Watch your back cast here, though, as you may very well hook some
οor unsuspecting jogger or skateboarder.

Author's Tip

he South Fork fishes well year-round, but winter holds a special appeal. Low flows
ιake for easier wading, weekdays are virtually crowd-free, and profuse hatches of
ιiniscule flies often tempt sizeable trout to the surface. When there's no surface
ctivity, I tandem rig a #6 Bitch Creek with a cranefly larva pattern like the Walt's
γorm and go at them on the bottom.

Favorite Fly

Walt's Worm

Hook	Tiemco 5263 #8-14 weighted with 0.015-0.020 lead wire
Body	Heavily dubbed gray rabbit, cigar-shaped

Fast Facts

South Fork Boise River

Location	Off US 20 below Anderson Ranch Reservoir, 20 miles east of Mountain Home, Idaho
Water Type	Moderate-sized year-round tailwater, swift and rocky
Primary Gamefish	Rainbow and bull trout, mountain whitefish
Best Time	Late summer to spring runoff
Best Flies	Baetis, midge, and streamers in winter; Elk Hair Caddis early spring to June; Pink Alberts July to October; Bitch Creek, George's Brown Stone, cranefly larva all seasons

Equipment   9-foot, 4- to 6-weight with a floating line; chest waders
                   with felt soles and cleats and/or a suitable drift rig
Conditions   After spring runoff peaks, the flows generally
                   moderate to wade fishing levels by July. From the dam tc
                   Danskin Bridge river is mostly wader friendly; from
                   Danskin to Neal Bridge it's float fishing for experienced
                   rowers only.
Drive Time   From Boise: 1.5 hours
                   From Idaho Falls: appx. 5 hours
                   From Salt Lake City: appx. 5.5 to 6 hours
Directions   From Boise, I-84 east to Mountain Home, US 20 east to
                   the Anderson Ranch Reservoir turnoff, a good gravel
                   road parallels the river 10 miles to Danskin Bridge; from
                   Idaho Falls, I-15 south to I-86 west to I-84 west to
                   Mountain Home, then US 20 east to Anderson Ranch
                   Reservoir turnoff; from Salt Lake City, I-15 north to Ogden
                   I-84 west to Mountain Home, then US 20 east to Andersor
                   Ranch Reservoir turnoff.

Local Fly Shops

Idaho Angler
1682 S. Vista
Boise, ID 83705
1-800-787-9957, 208-389-9957

Bear Creek Fly Shop
5521 W State
Boise, ID 83703-3337
208-853-8704

Anglers (Orvis Dealer)
7097 Overland Rd.
Boise, ID 83709-1910
208-323-6768

South Fork Anglers
832 S Vista Ave.
Boise, ID 83705-2423
208-433-8844

Idaho Sporting Goods, Inc.
1001 W State
Boise, ID 83702-5443
208-344-8448

River Keeper Fly Shop
1224 Broadway Ave
Boise, ID 83705
208-344-3838

Stonefly Angler
625 S Vista Ave.
Boise, ID 83705-1759
208-338-1333

Guides

Idaho Outdoor Outfitters
208-467-5961

American West Sports
208-375-3376

Idaho River Sports
208-336-4844

Contacts

Boise National Forest
500 S. Walnut, P.O. Box 25
Boise, ID 83707
208-334-3700

Idaho Game and Fish
Southwest Region
3101 S. Powerline Rd.
Nampa, ID 83686
208-465-8465

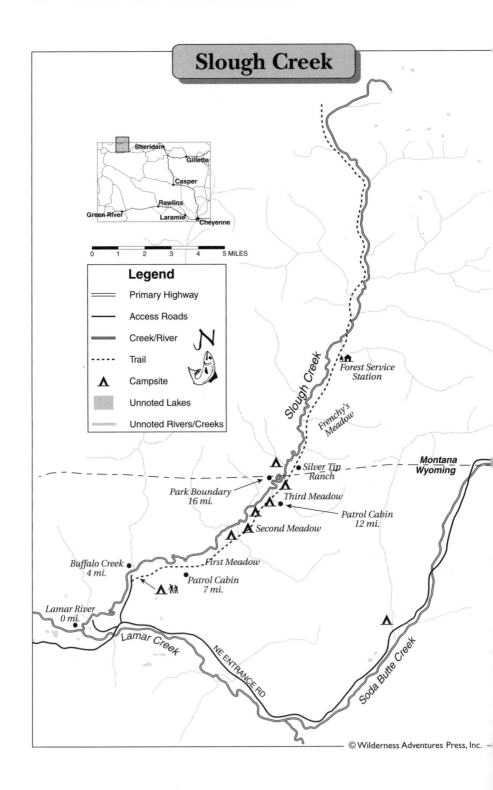

Slough Creek

Sheridan
Gillette
Casper
Rawlins
Green River
Laramie
Cheyenne

0   1   2   3   4   5 MILES

Legend

===== Primary Highway

—— Access Roads

===== Creek/River

----- Trail

Λ Campsite

Unnoted Lakes

Unnoted Rivers/Creeks

N

Slough Creek

Forest Service Station

Frenchy's Meadow

Silver Tip Ranch

Montana
Wyoming

Park Boundary 16 mi.

Third Meadow

Patrol Cabin 12 mi.

Second Meadow

Buffalo Creek 4 mi.

First Meadow

Patrol Cabin 7 mi.

Lamar River 0 mi.

Lamar Creek

NE ENTRANCE RD

Soda Butte Creek

© Wilderness Adventures Press, Inc.

CHAPTER 24

SLOUGH CREEK

Yellowstone National Park Gem

ach September we make a pilgrimage to fish northern Yellowstone National Park, specially Slough Creek. We usually make the hike to the famous first meadow, a relatively easy jaunt of just over 3 miles. The trek used to take us about an hour, although of late an hour and a half sometimes doesn't even cut it. And no, they haven't moved the meadow. I like to think it's because we take the time to search for wildlife and enjoy the scenery, but the reality is that things just take longer when the beard turns gray and the knees get a little rickety.

Since this is high country, it can turn winter-like in a hurry, even in September. Last year we timed our visit almost perfectly with the arrival of one of those cold snaps. The day started out cloudy, raw, and nasty and just got worse. By early afternoon it was feeling like late December. While we don't duck cold-weather fishing, there is a time and place for everything, and mid-September just didn't fit the bill.

Worse than the discomfort, though, was that the cold snap killed the hopper action and apparently put the trout in a funk, since even the small dark mayflies that hatched sporadically during mid-afternoon drifted down untouched.

Slough Creek's meadows can get crowded, but downstream of the trailhead there's a good chance to find a little solitude.

Thankfully, I read the handwriting on the wall from the get-go for once. I skipped the dry flies and started out stripping a #6 Conehead Black Woolly Bugger, stirring the interest of just enough cuts to make all the misery, while not quite worthwhile, at least tolerable. Probably no better than one in every 50 casts resulted in a hook-up or at least a rollover, and the number of fish actually brought to net was nothing to brag about.

Poor Gale stubbornly stuck to her guns, pitching just about every dry fly in both our boxes. She didn't tell me how many fish she raised, but I heard no squeals of glee from her direction all day.

In the end, we made what amounted to a mad dash down the mountain to get back to the truck before dark, as we'd seen a big grizzly bear earlier in the day digging up the hillside across the creek. A day like this wasn't worth chancing a bear encounter in the dark.

Still, if we had judged the results on parameters besides comfort and catch rates, the day would have ranked as one of the best. We competed for space with but one other angler, heard a bugling bull elk, spied a pair of coyotes and a grizzly bear, saw gray wolf tracks, and gazed upon one of the prettiest places in the Rockies. Even without the stellar fishing we were used to, I guess it could have been a whole lot worse.

Fishing Slough Creek

There aren't many small fish in Slough Creek, and few real monsters, but there are plenty of fat 14- to 18-inchers, all wild and colorful Yellowstone cutthroats. I've done no research to back it up, but Slough's cutts seem heavier on average than those found in other Park waters. Regardless, like cutts everywhere, these trout dine mostly at the surface, which, for us, provides the main attraction.

While all cutthroats can be pushovers at times, those in Slough Creek often break with tradition and become quite fussy. When they key on a single stage of a single hatch during periods of multiple, overlapping hatches the fishing can get a might tough. You might find #18 PMDs and #10 Gray Drakes, and #16 tan caddis coming off at the same time, and it's worth the time to do a bit of reconnaissance before jumping headlong into the fray.

When I run into multiple hatches I tend to assume the trout are eating one of the mayflies, usually the biggest I can see. Even though I know better than to assume anything, I usually waste precious time flailing the water with the wrong pattern before the light finally comes on and I take a closer look at the water. One trick that works at least some of the time on Slough is to forget what's hatching and go at them with terrestrials. The cutts here seem to have an affinity for ants, beetles, and hoppers.

Beyond the trailhead are three meadows. The first is about 3 miles up the trail, the second 5.5 miles, and the third a good 8 miles in. It should come as no surprise to learn that the first meadow gets the prize for heaviest angler use, and the fishing is generally considered easier the farther you're willing to walk.

If we arrive to find the trailhead parking lot a bit too full, or if we just don't feel quite up to the hike, we simply do an about-face and head downstream. The trout are just as big between the campground and the confluence with the Lamar River, although not quite as plentiful and maybe a little harder to catch. It's been our experience that we need to fish hard if we expect to do well in this stretch. As the years wear on, we find ourselves looking downriver more and more.

The day following the above episode turned out to be such a day. We arrive at the trailhead to find four vehicles already parked there, so we head downstream instead of hiking in to perhaps find the first meadow full of waving fly rods.

In a wide, clear pool Gale spots a big cutt circling an eddy; every so often it tips up to the surface to sip down a tidbit, then continues doing laps. For the next hour or so we take turns casting a variety of patterns in a variety sizes to this fish. Some are ignored completely, others seem to tempt it but are ultimately ignored. Egos deflated, we finally quit the stubborn trout and go hunting for a more willing adversary.

Presently, along the edge of another wide, shallow pool, we spy the telltale spreading concentric rings of a cautious riser. I creep into casting range and make my toss without much confidence, fully expecting a repeat of the rude treatment we've already endured. The fish rises and takes, which my sloppy concentration fails to detect quickly enough. It spits the fly out and disappears.

However, this trout is evidently not put off so easily. Its fright lasts but a few seconds and up it comes again. Gale is still snickering at my ineptitude as she lets fly a perfect pitch. Trout on! But her encounter lasts just seconds longer than mine, for just as the line comes tight it goes slack.

"Oh, too bad," I guffaw.

Shooting me a look that could kill, Gale reels in and starts up the bank, "Let's go see what's happening on Soda Butte."

As pointed out earlier, the cutts of Slough Creek aren't pushovers, and they certainly see their share of flies and fishermen.

Slough usually settles down after spring runoff a little faster than nearby Soda Butte Creek and the Lamar River, but it's still a rare year when the water is fishable before July. And in heavy snow years the Park's northern rivers have been known to remain blown out well into August.

Restaurants and Accommodations

Gardiner, Montana, with its 28 motels and B&Bs, 11 restaurants and bars, and 33 shops, is one of our favorite Montana towns. The Town Café (corner of Hwy. 89 and Park St.) serves a great breakfast, which often includes the local hot stove league's daily roundtable discussion of such varied topics as crooked local politicians, the feds' wolf management "boondoggle," sordid love affairs, and the outrageously low price of beef.

High Country Espresso, Books, and Gifts brews a great cup of coffee, and the pastries go down pretty easy, too. For lunch, the Two-Bit Saloon cooks up good homemade soup on a daily basis. Depending on our appetite we either head to Outlaws Pizza (Hwy. 89) for quality pizza and cold draft beer or the Yellowstone Mine Restaurant in the Best Western Motel (Hwy. 89, 406-848-7336) for good scampi and better steaks.

With so many lodging possibilities, I feel somewhat guilty recommending just three, but we've had such good service at all three that we haven't bothered to check out many others. And even then we find it difficult to choose a favorite. Chico Hot Springs, 30 miles north of the Park in Paradise Valley, ranks as our last choice, but only because it's farther from the action. The comfortable historic ambiance, gourmet dining, and unparalleled wine list, to say nothing of the chance to soak in the hot springs, make it tough to drive by on our way to the Park. And they welcome dogs, which makes Katie happy.

Still, we usually wind up staying at the Best Western in Gardiner (406-848-7311 or -800-828-9080) because it's a bit closer. Were it not for the "no pets allowed" sign in he lobby of the Yellowstone Village Inn (406-848-7417 or 1-800-228-8158) we'd proba-bly stay there more often. It's more reasonably priced than some motels in the area nd has actual drinking glasses in the rooms instead of those cheap plastic jobs.

We've had some unusual camping experiences outside the Park near Gardiner. 'or example, one night we hurried to set up camp before dark at a USFS camp-ground just outside town. We had just settled in when several trucks pulled up near-by. Soon the night air was filled with loud rap music as an all-night party kicked off.

Following a sleepless night, we moved camp farther up the road into the nation-al forest to an empty campsite above Jardine. After some strong coffee and a hearty breakfast, we headed off to the Park to fish. At dusk we returned to a campsite no onger empty. Our new neighbors had pitched what appeared to be a semi-perma-nent camp of cardboard, plywood, and plastic and were apparently well into the throes of some weird religious ceremony.

Fearing a repeat of the previous night's festivities, we decided to move again before the party really got cranking. This time we drove deep into the hills, pitching camp for the third time in two nights. We built a spirit-lifting campfire and had just begun cooking dinner when the music started.

Fishing Soda Butte Creek in late fall.

It was just a dull thump at first, but it gradually grew into an ear-shattering disco like blare. Pissed, I grabbed my pistol and charged into the blackness intent on stop ping the offenders from ruining another night's sleep. I quickly came to a bonfire that revealed a dozen or so young bikers encircled by Harleys and passing around a half-gallon jug of Jack Daniels and sharing a pipe full of something I didn't want to identify. Surprisingly, the apparent leader of the group did promise to "keep it down man," although I can't say he sounded very sincere.

Ever since that trip we've found it more to our liking to camp in the Park wher fishing the northern rivers; either Slough Creek Campground, 29 sites, picnic table fire ring, grill, toilet and water, no hook-ups, $10 per night, fills up early, or at Pebble Creek Campground, 32 sites, same amenities and price, and generally among the las campgrounds in the Park to fill up. If those two happen to be full we forgo conven ience and head on past Cooke City to our favorite, Fox Creek Campground.

Slough Creek, Soda Butte Creek and the Lamar River are the premier fisheries in northern Yellowstone Park.

Nearby Fisheries

Soda Butte Creek and the Lamar River

The Lamar River was running a milky gray due to runoff from a series of heavy thunderstorms that had swept through the high country the day before. And as we continued on past the mouth of Soda Butte Creek all the way upstream to Round Prairie and the confluence of Pebble Creek, we saw hordes of anglers. Deciding to pass on the well-known roadside fishery, we parked in a pullout above Pebble Creek Campground and hiked a quarter-mile or so to the creek, which was empty except for two giant old bull bison that lay chewing their cuds beside the water. Here Soda Butte, unlike the Lamar, ran low and clear, almost perfect for what we had in mind.

We rigged just one rod, Gale's 8-foot, 4-weight Loomis, and tied a #14 Parachute Adams to the end of a 12-foot leader tapered to 4X. As usual on smaller waters, we would trade off shooting casts and photos.

The first stretch began with a narrow run against the far grassy bank and ended in a deep green pool guarded by several bushes and a downed pine tree. Up first, I crept into casting position well below the pine, cast the fly, and watched expectantly for it to disappear. Didn't happen. Nor did the fly interest any takers on subsequent casts up through the pool and run and on to the next riffle. Odd, I though, since the place appeared to be as perfect a trout hangout as I had ever seen.

"Let's drop down a couple sizes. You give it a try," I suggested, tying on a #18 Parachute Adams and handing the rod over.

Gale got into position, practically standing in my original boot tracks, and made a cast to the fallen pine. Trout on! Next, I took the rod and made a cast several feet farther up, hooking another. And so it went. Apparently, the Soda Butte trout crowd preferred a #18 Parachute Adams to a #14, at least on this day. Proof positive came later upstream when we lost the #18 and tied on a #14 just for the hell of it. When it received the same rude treatment, we switched back to a #18 and immediately hooked a trout. Not yet fully convinced, we fiddled around with #12 and #14 caddis patterns to no avail, then switched to a #18 caddis and quickly took another fish.

Then the action really heated up. In one long pool Gale hooked eight or ten trout on as many casts. Still wishing to test the trout, I rigged a #18 Prince Nymph in tandem with the Adams and pitched it to almost the same spot where Gale had hooked the last trout. Almost before the nymph had time to settle below the surface, a fat 13-incher grabbed it. A second cast netted one only slightly smaller, and a third rolled one that I failed to hook.

Without picking up, I allowed the nymph to continue drifting and soon another trout (or the same one, who knows?) was on. The run continued, with trout after trout taking the nymph or the dry every couple casts. How high we might have run the count from just that one pool is anybody's guess. But eventually, enough was enough, and we reeled up and hiked back to the truck.

Soda Butte fishes well from Cooke City to the confluence with the Lamar River in Yellowstone Park, though by far the most popular stretch is immediately upstream of the confluence. This popularity is due to the fact that the cutthroats, often averaging as big as 18 inches, tend to stack up in the lower reaches, particularly when the Lamar is running high or off color. The fishing often requires nothing more sophisticated than stripping a black Woolly Bugger to catch all the hefty trout an angler can stand. The only downside is the crowds. But what's a little crowding when all those fat trout are just waiting to be hooked? We usually pass on the roadside circus, though, and opt for a quieter experience upstream.

A clear Lamar River often translates to hot-damn fishing action. On average, the cutthroat and rainbows we catch run around 12 inches here, but there are plenty of bigger specimens. As a bonus, you never know when a randy bull bison or a rogue grizzly or two might show up. Watching the parade of wild critters being chased by roadside tourists often provides more excitement than the fishing.

On one occasion, we watched in horror as a couple with a young child tried to pose the youngster on the back of a docile-looking cow bison. No kidding. Thank goodness the cow spooked just in the nick of time—and in the opposite direction—narrowly avoiding a for-sure tragedy. Abandoning my rod for a moment, I gave what I thought was an eloquent speech on the proper respect for wildlife and life and limb, but it didn't seem to go over too well. Oh, well, that's the way it goes when fishing near the road in Yellowstone.

Nearby Attractions and Activities

Yellowstone National Park is one humongous attraction and, much as I hate to admit it, activities other than fishing abound. One could, without doubt, spend a lifetime just gawking at the Park's thermal wonders, not to mention the endless array of trails open to hikers.

Since the reintroduction of gray wolves to the Park, a whole new sport (cult?) of wolf watching has sprung up. And photographers have long flocked here in all seasons hoping to capture on film the perfect wildlife shot, scenic shot, sunrise, sunset, etc.

Author's Tip

Don't even think of fishing Slough Creek, or the Lamar or Soda Butte, before July. And if you want to avoid the crowds and biting bugs, wait until mid- to late September. In late summer and early fall you can hardly go wrong fishing a favorite "hopper and dropper" tandem. Good fishing can be had below the trailhead, but don't expect it to be easy. Multiple hatches can make Slough Creek cutts fussy in the extreme. Observe first, cast second is a good rule to live by even up in the meadows.

Favorite Fly

Pheasant Rump Hopper

Hook	2X long dry fly (Dai-Riki 270) #12-16
Tail	Pheasant marabou
Rib	Ginger grizzly
Abdomen	Yellow floss
Thorax	Hot orange dubbing
Hackle	Grizzly
Wing	Pheasant rump/Krystal Flash
Head	Red thread

Fast Facts

Slough Creek

Location	Yellowstone National Park between Gardiner and Cooke City, Montana
Water Type	The three meadow sections upstream of the trailhead and the stretch below the campground offer nice riffles and pools.
Primary Gamefish	Yellowstone cutthroat trout, rainbow and cuttbow hybrids
Best Time	Mid- to late September; runoff can last well into August; seldom fishable before July

Best Flies	Dry flies to match the profuse and prolific hatches, hoppers, ants and beetles, and Buggers, leeches, and Clousers when nothing else works
Equipment	9-foot, 3- to 6-weight, floating lines, long tapered leaders (12 to 15 feet), tippet size to suit the fly
Conditions	High country variable; expect cool to cold anytime, only rarely unbearably hot; can and does rain, snow, sleet, hail, and blow without a moment's notice; prime grizzly territory
Drive Time	From Billings: 4.25 hours
	From Bozeman: appx. 3 hours
	From Salt Lake City: appx. 7 hours
Directions	From Billings, take I-90 west to Livingston, US 89 south to Gardiner, Park roads toward Cooke City; from Bozeman, take I-90 east to Livingston, US 89 south to Gardiner, Park roads toward Cooke City; from Salt Lake City, take I-15 north to Idaho Falls, US 20 north to West Yellowstone, Park roads to Tower and on toward Cooke City.

Local Fly Shops

Park's Fly Shop
Hwy. 89
Gardiner, MT 59030
406-848-7314

Hatch Finders Fly Shop
113 W. Park St.
Livingston, MT 59047
406-222-0989

George Anderson's Yellowstone Angler
Hwy. 89 S
Livingston, MT 59047
406-222-7130

Big Sky Flies and Guides
Hwy. 89
Emigrant, MT 59027
406-333-4401

Dan Bailey's Fly Shop
209 W. Park St.
Livingston, MT 59047
406-222-1673

Guides

Rendezvous Outfitters
406-848-7967

Blue Ribbon Flies
406-995-5000

Blue Ribbon Fishing Tours
406-222-7714

Contacts

Gardiner, Montana Chamber of
    Commerce
406-848-7971

Yellowstone National Park Visitor's
    Service
P.O. Box 168
YNP, WY 82190
307-344-7381, 307-344-2386

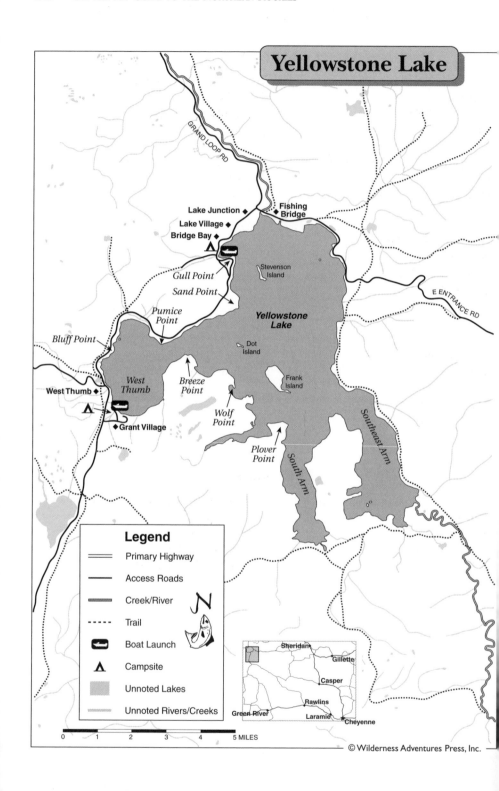

Yellowstone Lake

GRAND LOOP RD

Lake Junction ◆
Lake Village ◆
Bridge Bay ◆

♦ Fishing
Bridge

E ENTRANCE RD

Stevenson
Island

Gull Point
Sand Point

Pumice
Point

*Yellowstone
Lake*

Bluff Point

Dot
Island

West
Thumb
*West
Thumb*

Breeze
Point

Frank
Island

West Thumb ◆

Southeast Arm

△
🛥

Wolf
Point

◆ Grant Village

Plover
Point

South Arm

Legend

═══	Primary Highway
────	Access Roads
═══	Creek/River
- - - -	Trail
🛥	Boat Launch
△	Campsite
▨	Unnoted Lakes
▤	Unnoted Rivers/Creeks

N

Sheridan
Gillette
Casper
Rawlins
Green River
Laramie
Cheyenne

0   1   2   3   4   5 MILES

© Wilderness Adventures Press, Inc.

CHAPTER 25

YELLOWSTONE LAKE

Stillwater Champion

Early summer is far and away our favorite time to fish Yellowstone Lake. We like to be on the big lake right on the June 15 opener, or as soon after as our schedules will allow, because this is the best time to find cutts cruising the shallows like packs of hungry wolves.

We head for West Thumb's somewhat geothermally enhanced waters on the theory that warmer water equals more active trout, although I'd be lying if I said that warmer water didn't hold a similar appeal for us, too. "Springtime in the Rockies" is truly wonderful and all that, but it also can be damn chilly, especially when sitting partially submerged in 30-something-degree water.

Almost any point, sandbar, inlet, or shallow bay holds the potential for gangbuster action, but the hottest spots change from year to year. Our favorites are Pumice, Sand and Gull Points, and the shoreline immediately north of the West Thumb Geyser Basin. We usually launch the tube and pontoon, but in truth the roving trout could probably be caught just as well by wading right off the bank at this time of year.

Moose lend a unique flavor to the Yellowstone Lake flyfishing experience.

This year we made Yellowstone Lake the last stop on a whirlwind tour of south-west Montana and eastern Idaho fishing holes, hitting Cliff, Wade, Hebgen, and Henry's Lakes and the Madison (in and out of Yellowstone Park) and Firehole Rivers. We left camp (Lonesomehurst on Hebgen) before daylight on opening morning and drove to Pumice Point, stopping first at Grant Village for breakfast and to let a line of rumbling thunderstorms pass.

Gale fishes from her pontoon craft, seeking to tempt trout near the surface by pitching various topwater patterns on a floating line. I struggle into my float tube and go immediately to a full-sink line and a heavily weighted #6 Egg-Sucking Leech trailing a #12 red Chironomid, a rig that has worked here for me in the past. I remind myself that I'm out here more for the process than anything else, as the importance of racking up high numbers of fish has taken a back seat to just being outside finning around in one of the most beautiful spots on the planet.

But this time around so much B.S. is easy, since I make about two kicks and the same number of strips before I feel a heavy weight tugging on the other end of the line. In typical cutt fashion, the fish thrashes briefly then gives in and comes to net. Gale rows over, and we admire the crimson-splashed beauty before sending it on its way.

It's an auspicious start, and before long I've landed three cutts and made a couple of long-range releases. Not bad considering the lackadaisical mood I was in.

While we're not exactly knocking them dead, we are doing okay, and that's more than good enough. Actually, Gale is really doing better than okay, considering that she's been flinging a fly pattern that probably hasn't been seen on Yellowstone Lake since about 1968—a #10 Brown Hackle Peacock wet fly. Can you believe it? Nobody fishes Brown Hackle Peacock wets anymore, especially not in Yellowstone Lake on opening day.

I reel up, bobbing in the tube and silently cheering my partner on. She is by now really into fishing the different rig. Her method appears quite simple: cast out, raise the rod to about 45 degrees, skitter the fly just under and in the surface film with quick 6-inch strips. This creates a continuous wake that apparently drives some of the trout crazy, since about every tenth cast or so seems to bring an explosive strike. Not all result in solid hook-ups, but a wide grin passes her lips at each surface explosion.

Remarkably, we haven't seen a single trout break the surface except to attack her fly. The Brown Hackle Peacock used to be Gale's go-to fly before she discovered the Orange Stimulator, and it's nice to see that this classic pattern can still bring fish up when nothing else seems to be going on.

Fishing Yellowstone Lake

Yellowstone Lake is the largest freshwater lake above 7,000 feet in the U.S. It's an impressive 20 miles long and 14 wide, with a surface area of 196 square miles and an average depth of 140 feet.

Despite the amazing depth and breadth of fishing available in the Park, the big lake is by far the most popular angling destination. Fully a third of Park anglers fish the lake, most in search of the famous 14- to 18-inch Yellowstone cutthroats. To the chagrin of Park Service biologists, only a relative few target lake trout, an introduced species that threatens to wipe out the natives. The current regulations require anglers to kill all lake trout; no catch and release for those suckers.

Flyfishing the big lake is about as straightforward as it gets, although it might surprise you to learn that despite its large size many anglers fish from shore, wade, or use a float tube because the cutts tend to feed close to shore. And with the unpredictable wind that can kick up at a moment's notice, fishing close to shore is often a good idea. The June 15 opener finds the trout in pre-spawn mode, as both cutts and lakers are spring spawners. And this is the best time to catch both species on a fly rod; the annual fall shut down prior to freeze-up would rank a close second.

Admittedly, most days involve methods and flies other than skittering Brown Hackle Peacock wet flies, although I'm sure we could all profit by breaking them out once in a while. Most of my Yellowstone Lake hook-ups involve stripping smallish #6-10 leeches, Buggers, and Clousers. Black seems to be the best color, with brown or olive close behind, although sometimes blood red or even purple leeches can turn a dead morning into something tolerable.

Stripping weighted nymphs like chironomids, Princes, Pheasant Tails, Hare's Ears, scuds, etc. on a sink-tip or full-sink line is also effective. I often rig tandems of a Bugger and nymph, dry and nymph, caddisfly and ant, and so on. During a rise I like to pattern a line of swirls and then drop the fly where I next expect to see a rise form. A little twitch at just the right moment sometimes helps.

One little regulation you should know about is that all watercraft are required to have a Park permit (this applies to any body of water in the Park), and approved life vests are required for all boaters. The fees are reasonable: $20 annual, $10 weekly for motorized vessels; $10 annual, $5 weekly for non-motorized. You also need a Park fishing license, which costs $20 per season or $10 for 10 consecutive days, but you don't need a state license.

Restaurants and Accommodations

The food in the various Park restaurants is actually pretty good, although some of it can be pricey. On the plus side, the service is always friendly and there's almost always entertaining conversation.

Breakfast at the Grant Village Restaurant is always a treat—good omelets, fluffy pancakes, and a great breakfast buffet. For dinner, try the Huckleberry Chicken made with a "special in-house-made huckleberry sauce."

We like to hang out at the Lewis Lake Campground, so that would be our first choice when it comes to lodging, although it's not usually open by June 15. From time to time, we've stayed in various West Yellowstone motels such as the Gray Wolf Inn and Suites (250 S. Canyon, 406-646-0000) and the Kelly Inn (104 S. Canyon, 406-646-4544). Both are quite nice, but like Lonesomehurst on Hebgen, almost too far from the action to really suit our needs. Campgrounds within easier striking distance can be found at Bridge Bay, Grant Village, and Fishing Bridge, though all three tend to be busy and noisy.

Nearby Fisheries

Riddle Lake, south of Grant Village off the Loop Road, is an easy 2-mile-plus hike, and the cutthroats are of decent size, 12 to 13 inches on average. We've had some good sessions with surface feeders early morning and late evening, although we've stopped hiking in or out at these times ever since Gale noticed the ominous sign at the trailhead, "Warning—Grizzly Bears Frequent This Area."

The Yellowstone River and tributaries in the Park open July 15 to a large crowd. The big, naive cutthroats are in the river in various stages of spawning. In the first few days, you can often chuck whatever you want and still catch 15- to 18-inchers until your arm grows weary. But the bonanza is short-lived, and before you know it only the gifted few are hauling them in. Despite the increasing difficulty, it's easy to spot trout in the clear, smooth-surfaced pools like those around Buffalo Ford, and there's no end to the parade of hopeful anglers trying their damnedest. One ploy to beat the crowd is to park at Fishing Bridge and hike the trail down the other side of the river. (The first mile is closed to fishing.)

Nearby Attractions and Activities

Wildlife viewing and other Park attractions should more than adequately fill up any blank spots in the itinerary. If you get bored with Yellowstone's wonders, Grand Teton is just down the road to the south and the North Fork Shoshone River and Cody to the east.

Fishing Yellowstone Lake.

Author's Tip

Plan on fishing from dawn until the wind comes up, generally sometime around noon. If no fish are rising, start off stripping smaller streamers, wets, or nymphs. When a hatch does start, try to match the natural's silhouette and relative size, pattern a line of swirls, and then cast to intercept. And remember the old bird-hunting adage: Flock shooting rarely puts birds on the table.

Favorite Fly

Brown Hackle Peacock Wet Fly

Hook	Mustad 3906B
Thread	Red 6/0
Tail	Brown hackle fibers
Rib	Fine gold wire
Body	Peacock herl, tied to form a tapered body
Hackle	Brown hen hackle wrapped soft-hackle style

Fast Facts

Yellowstone Lake

Location	Yellowstone National Park, near the east entrance
Water Type	Large, deep, and windy lake at over 7,000 feet
Primary Gamefish	Native Yellowstone cutthroat and illegally planted lake trout; cutts average 14 to 18 inches
Best Time	June 15 through July; late September to November
Best Flies	Leeches, Buggers, Clousers #6-10; Beadhead Prince and Hare's Ear, damsel nymphs, scuds; Elk Hair Caddis, Stimulator, Humpy, Wulffs, Adams, and Callibaetis dries
Equipment	9-foot, 5- or 6-weight, floating, sink-tip and full-sink lines;

	leader and tippet to suit method
Conditions	Big lake, wind often restricts fishing to morning and evening hours. Can turn chilly even at high noon in high summer. Storms are sudden, frequent, and often violent. If you don't like crowds avoid peak summer season. Even though the lake is big enough to get away from the worst of it, the road to and from is usually hell to drive at best.
Drive Time	From Bozeman: 3 hours
	From Billings: 4 hours
	From Salt Lake City: 7 hours
Directions	From Bozeman, US 191 south to West Yellowstone, follow Park roads to lake; from Salt Lake City, I-15 north to Idaho Falls, US 20 west to West Yellowstone, follow park roads to lake; from Billings, I-90 east to Livingston, US 89 south to Gardiner, follow Park roads to lake.

Local Fly Shops

Arrick's Fly Shop
37 N. Canyon
West Yellowstone, MT 59758
406-646-7290

Madison River Outfitters
117 Canyon
West Yellowstone, MT 59758
406-646-9644

Blue Ribbon Flies
315 N. Canyon
West Yellowstone, MT 59758
406-646-7642

North Fork Angler
1107 Sheridan Ave.
Cody, WY 82414
307-527-7274

Bud Lilly's Trout Shop
39 Madison
West Yellowstone, MT 59758
406-646-7801

Yellowstone Troutfitters
239 Yellowstone Ave.
Cody, WY 82414
307-587-8240

Jacklin's Fly Shop
105 Yellowstone
West Yellowstone, MT 59758
406-646-7336

Aune's Absaroka Angler
754 Yellowstone Ave.
Cody, WY 82414
307-587-5105

Contacts

Yellowstone National Park Information
307-344-7381

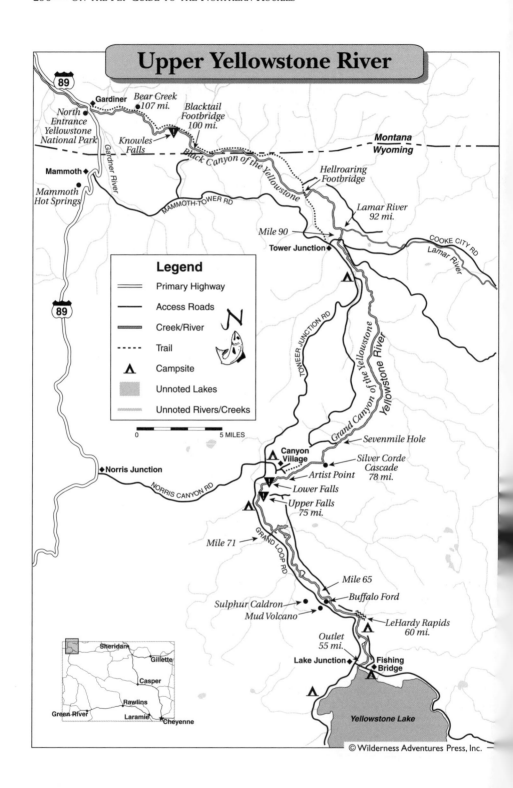

Upper Yellowstone River

Gardiner
Bear Creek
107 mi.
Blacktail
Footbridge
100 mi.

North
Entrance
Yellowstone
National Park

Knowles
Falls

Black Canyon of the Yellowstone

Montana
Wyoming

Mammoth ◆

Mammoth
Hot Springs

MAMMOTH-TOWER RD

Hellroaring
Footbridge

Lamar River
92 mi.

Mile 90

COOKE CITY RD

Lamar River

Tower Junction ◆

Legend

	Primary Highway
	Access Roads
	Creek/River
- - -	Trail
⋀	Campsite
	Unnoted Lakes
	Unnoted Rivers/Creeks

N

0   5 MILES

TOWER JUNCTION RD

Grand Canyon of the Yellowstone

Yellowstone River

Sevenmile Hole

Canyon
Village

Silver Corde
Cascade
78 mi.

◆ Norris Junction

NORRIS CANYON RD

Artist Point

Lower Falls

Upper Falls
75 mi.

Mile 71

GRAND LOOP RD

Mile 65

Buffalo Ford

Sulphur Caldron
Mud Volcano

LeHardy Rapids
60 mi.

Outlet
55 mi.

Lake Junction ◆

Fishing
Bridge

Sheridan

Gillette

Casper

Rawlins

Green River

Laramie

Cheyenne

Yellowstone Lake

© Wilderness Adventures Press, Inc.

CHAPTER 26

THE UPPER YELLOWSTONE RIVER
Yellowstone Park's Centerpiece Fishery

While I'm not exactly what you'd call religious, each time I wade the cold, clear, insect-laden waters of the upper Yellowstone I can't shake the feeling that He must be watching how we treat what had to be one of his pet projects. Just the idea of again wetting a line in this hallowed Western water brings a grin to my face. And should I manage to hook one of the magnificent, fat, and colorful cutthroats that swims here, I treat it with respect bordering on reverence.

Grandson Brian and I hit the river shortly before noon midweek following the July 15 opener. We found it clear, not especially high, and amazingly, all but deserted around Buffalo Ford—one truck in the pullout, one angler in the water. A round of vicious thunderstorms with a devilish brew of high winds, sleet, hail, and rain had apparently chased everyone else away, leaving just three deranged souls to feed our madness.

Despite the lack of competition and the iffy weather, we decided to stick to our original game plan of starting at Fishing Bridge. We rigged up between downpours and then hiked the trail downriver on the opposite bank from the popular Loop Road access points. As alluded to earlier, this is a good strategy for avoiding the usual highway mob scene because the river's deceptively strong current keeps all but the most adventurous from wading across.

In the slow water we could see trout occasionally dimple the surface or flash beneath it, evidently picking off straggler Flavs (*Drunella flavilinea*, one of several important species of Blue-Winged Olive) and tan caddis emergers. I went with a #14 Orange Stimulator and dropped a #12 North Fork Special off the bend; Brian tied on a #12 tan Elk Hair Caddis and a Beadhead Prince Nymph.

Two casts and I was fast to a fat 17-incher, but even before I could land it the wind kicked into high gear and angry black clouds once again dumped on us. The savage wind hurled buckets of rain that quickly changed to pea-sized hail. While attempting to horse the fish in quickly to avoid any more abuse than necessary, I put too much pressure on the leader and the fish and I parted ways.

But before I could join Brian up in the trees the hail squall suddenly stopped and the sun came out. I scurried back into the river and got in only a few more casts before the skies opened up with rain and a mix of snowflakes and thumbnail-sized hail. We did our best to stick it out, diving for cover during the worst of it and toughing it out the rest of the time, but we eventually gave up in late afternoon, soaked and chilled to the bone.

Eye-popping scenery is just another reason to flyfish the Yellowstone River in the Park.

Truth be told, it really wasn't all that bad, at least not as I reflect on it from the comfort of home as I write this. After all, we did manage to hook a few, land a few, and lose a few, and we shared a few laughs while huddled under the trees.

Fishing the Upper Yellowstone River

South of sprawling Yellowstone Lake, the Yellowstone River's headwaters rise in the Thorofare region—perhaps the wildest place left in the Lower 48. Access, whether by long walk, horseback, or boat, requires a commitment of several days. Compared with the casual fishing experience found at, say, Buffalo Ford below the big lake, where finding an empty spot to park your vehicle along the tourist-infested Loop Road is often the hardest part, the two experiences are like night and day.

The Loop Road parallels the river from Fishing Bridge to the Grand Canyon of the Yellowstone, where access is easy to moderate. Below the falls, however, is another story. Excursions into Grand and Black Canyons involve steep descents on rugged, switchback trails that aren't for the faint of heart. Wading in the heavy current of the canyons is never a good idea. Leave the waders in the truck, wear hiking boots, and plan on fishing from the bank. And remember to take lots of water and limit the fly-fishing gear to the bare essentials. (A backcountry permit is required for overnight stays.)

The Yellowstone's cutthroat trout are wild, not particularly fussy about what they eat, and always of good size since smaller cutts migrate early to the lake and stay there until of spawning size and age. You just don't catch many trout less than 14 inches or greater than 18 inches, but of course you'll never hear us bitching when our catch averages 15 or 16 inches.

Cutthroats are the most gullible of all trout, extremely vulnerable to being caught, and except for those hanging out in the vicinity of Buffalo Ford, they can be downright foolish at times. Studies showed that individual fish were caught so many times in the heavily fished waters that catch-and-release regulations were implementation in 1973. Fishing Bridge and the first mile downriver were closed to all angling, and the season was pushed back to July 15 to protect spawning cutts. The results are evident in the wonderful fishery that exists today.

Throughout the season a variety of hatches, often overlapping, provide anglers plenty of chances at rising trout. Caddis, mayfly, and stonefly hatches range in size from the huge Salmonfly, often imitated on #4 and #6 hooks, to the diminutive Pale Morning Duns, Blue-Winged Olives, and Tricos best imitated by #16-22 offerings. Blizzard hatches sometimes cause Yellowstone River cutts to feed selectively, but even then a decent imitation will take fish.

While closely matching the hatch is one way to go, it's often a better idea to toss them a curve. For example, a large caddis pattern during a Trico spinner fall or an ant when the flock is obviously eating Green Drakes. Mayfly spinner falls on August evenings can rival those found on any fertile tailwater.

In September and October the still waters of Buffalo Ford crawl with Micro Caddis and Baetis. To play the hatch-matching game when these diminutive insects are on the water requires tiny hooks and long, thin leaders and tippets. Add in the fact that the once foolish trout of spring have become educated, and fishing these late hatches can be quite challenging.

After getting in our early season licks around Buffalo Ford, we usually confine most of our later trips to the canyons or hike as far from the road as possible. Combined with fishing early and late in the day, this greatly reduces the crowd hassle.

The Park enforces its own set of fishing rules, and one rule that is strictly enforced is the mandatory use of nontoxic weight—no lead. Pick up the current regulations when you stop to purchase a fishing license.

Restaurants and Accommodations

An upscale dining experience can be had at the Lake Yellowstone Hotel (307-242-3899), which serves breakfast, lunch, and dinner, although evening meals are often the biggest treat. The nightly specials include wild game dishes such as Pan-Seared Elk and Red Deer Medallions and Breast of Duck, while seafood lovers can check out the Pan-Seared Salmon or Fettuccine with Scallops and Shiitake Mushrooms. High on our list is the Pork Scaloppini served with a wonderful mustard sauce and baked polenta, but if you really want to get the juices rolling try the Angus Sirloin with Bourbon Sauce Glaze. And be sure to make your reservations early during the summer, for the Lake Yellowstone Hotel is a popular eatery.

Besides the famed Irma Hotel in Cody, Buffalo Bill built several lodges, summer hotels, and fall hunting lodges in the Yellowstone area. Pahaska Teepee Resort (183 Yellowstone Highway, 1-800-628-7791) just outside the Park's east gate is the best known, still going strong after nearly a century in operation. With a lounge, restaurant, gift shop, gas station, and cabins, the resort sees a lot of traffic.

For campers who don't want to stay inside the Park, there are three USFS campgrounds just outside the east entrance: Sleeping Giant, Pahaska, and Deer Creek. All provide dozens of individual campsites, picnic tables, fire rings with grills, water, and toilets. As you might expect, these fill up early during the summer season.

Bison cross the Yellowstone River at Buffalo Ford.

Nearby Fisheries

Lewis-Shoshone Lake Channel

he kid in the West Yellowstone fly shop said, "Yep, the browns are already in the hannel. You guys should have fun." The next morning, as we anxiously prepared our acks for the hike in, a Park Ranger stopped by to visit.

"How's the fishin' in the channel?" I asked.

"I hear the browns are still in the outlet bay in Shoshone Lake, and the host own at the Lewis Lake Campground tells me they're staging in the Lewis outlet bay o, but far as I know haven't showed up in the channel or the river yet. I figure the ın should start in about a week. Well, you two have a nice day. Keep an eye peeled or bears."

Now what?

Well, we hiked the 3 miles and change to the channel anyway and stripped uggers and leeches and tried various meaty-looking attractor dries and nymphs for veral hours. We managed to turn one big brown, but saw no other trout, so we iked back out, drove to the campground, hiked the mile or so into the Lewis Lake utlet, flailed the Lewis River to a froth downstream for several hundred yards, ooked nothing, and saw nothing. There was nothing left to do, so we hiked back to ıe campground, built a drink, lamented our bad timing, and shrugged it off as just nother one of those things.

If your mid-fall timing is better than ours was you can expect some of the best fishing of your life on streamers and big uglies. Don't except to be fishing alone though, as the cat has been out of the bag on this fishing event for years now.

Author's Tip

Fishing the canyons of the upper Yellowstone requires an effort, but it's a great way to escape the crowds of anglers unwilling to walk when they can access the river right on the roadway. We rig big, high-floating attractor dry flies and drop a medium to large nymph off the hook bend and cast the rig to the deeper pools and runs. The Yellowstone is deceptively powerful and thus dangerous to wade. Keep an eye out for all types of wildlife, but particularly grizzly bears, which are plentiful in this area.

Favorite Fly

Egg-Sucking Leech

Hook	Mustad 36890 SF, #2-8
Tail	Black marabou/Krystal Flash
Rib	Fine copper wire
Body	Black chenille
Hackle	Palmered black saddle
Head	Pink, orange, chartreuse, or peach Glo-Bug Yarn wrapped around a tungsten barbell; similar colored coneheads are a good alternative

Fast Facts

Upper Yellowstone River

Location	Born in remote wilderness south of Yellowstone Lake; exits lake at Fishing Bridge in YNP, flows generally north through the park
Water Type	Broad, heavy current, wild river; especially dangerous to wade in some sections
Primary Gamefish	Yellowstone cutthroat trout of good size, average 14 to 18 inches; scattered rainbow and brown trout lower down and mountain whitefish
Best Time	July 15 opener to close of Park's fishing season in early November; in the hardest fished sections expect more difficult fishing as the season progresses
Best Flies	Attractor dries, except during hatches, when a relatively close match works best; medium to large nymphs and streamers
Equipment	9-foot, 5- or 6-weight, floating and sink-tip lines, long leaders help in bigger pools, but trout generally aren't leader shy; tippets of 3X or 4X usually work
Conditions	High country, so expect chilly and wet any day; storms are often sudden and violent; wind can play havoc with casting in the canyons
Drive Time	From Bozeman: appx. 2.5 hours From Billings: appx. 4 or 5 hours From Salt Lake City: appx. 5 or 6 hours
Directions	From Bozeman, US 191 south to West Yellowstone, follow Park roads to lake; from Salt Lake City, I-15 north to Idaho Falls, US 20 west to West Yellowstone, follow Park roads to lake; from Billings, I-90 east to Livingston, US 89 south to Gardiner, follow Park roads to lake.

Local Fly Shops

Arrick's Fly Shop
37 N. Canyon
West Yellowstone, MT 59758
406-646-7290

Blue Ribbon Flies
315 N. Canyon
West Yellowstone, MT 59758
406-646-7642

Bud Lilly's Trout Shop
39 Madison
West Yellowstone, MT 59758
406-646-7801

Jacklin's Fly Shop
105 Yellowstone
West Yellowstone, MT 59758
406-646-7336

Madison River Outfitters
117 Canyon
West Yellowstone, MT 59758
406-646-9644

Park's Fly Shop
Hwy. 89
Gardiner, MT 59030
406-848-7314

George Anderson's Yellowstone Angler
Hwy. 89 S
Livingston, MT 59047
406-222-7130

Dan Bailey's Fly Shop
209 W. Park St.
Livingston, MT 59047
406-222-1673

Hatch Finders Fly Shop
113 W. Park St.
Livingston, MT 59047
406-222-0989

Big Sky Flies and Guides
Hwy. 89
Emigrant, MT 59027
406-333-4401

Guides

Madison River Outfitters
406-646-9644

Bear Trap Outfitters
406-646-9642

Rendezvous Outfitters
406-848-7967

Blue Ribbon Fishing Tours
406-222-7714

Contacts

West Yellowstone Chamber of
    Commerce
30 Yellowstone
West Yellowstone, MT 59758
406-646-7701

Yellowstone National Park Information
307-344-7381

Gardiner Chamber of Commerce
406-848-7971

Lamar Underwood ponders a fly selection at Buffalo Ford.

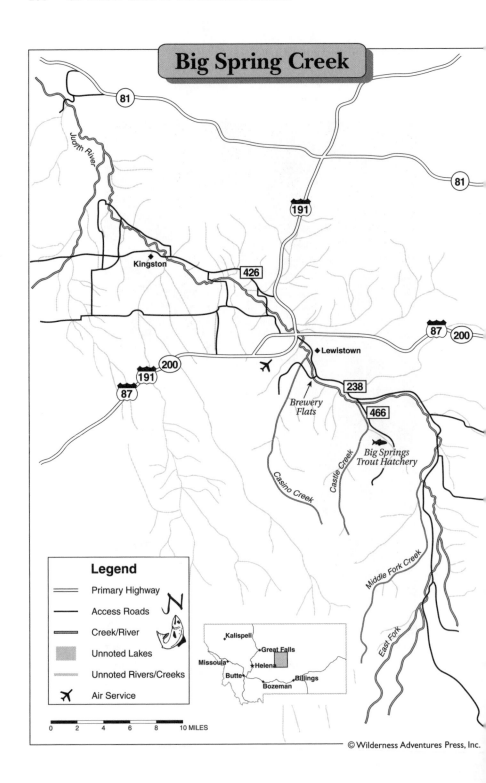

CHAPTER 27

Big Spring Creek

81

Judith River

81

191

Kingston

426

87 200

Lewistown

200
191
87

238

466

Brewery
Flats

Casino Creek

Castle Creek

Big Springs
Trout Hatchery

Middle Fork Creek

East Fork

Legend

═══	Primary Highway
───	Access Roads
───	Creek/River
▨	Unnoted Lakes
┈┈┈	Unnoted Rivers/Creeks
✈	Air Service

N

Kalispell
Great Falls
Missoula
Helena
Butte
Billings
Bozeman

0   2   4   6   8   10 MILES

© Wilderness Adventures Press, Inc.

BIG SPRING CREEK

An Oasis in Dry Country

We "discovered" Big Spring Creek quite by accident many years ago. With a two-week whirlwind tour of famous Big Sky trout spots fast winding down, we found ourselves on the Yellowstone River near Big Timber, Montana. The only problem was that our plane home was due to depart Great Falls early the next day. Since we'd never been up that way we decided to take the scenic route—Harlowton up toward Lewistown then on to Great Falls. To make a long story short, we stopped for gas and lunch at Eddies Corner, where the guy on the next stool asked what we were doing on our visit. We said fishing, to which he replied, "You best try Big Spring Creek."

We drove into town, got directions to the creek, and stopped at the first access we came to. I tied on a pair of smallish nymphs and sent the rig swimming down the first juicy-looking run off the parking lot. I immediately caught a fat 14-inch rainbow, then another, and another. We've been catching Big Spring Creek trout off and on ever since.

Just yesterday, yet again on my way to somewhere else, I stopped off at the newly renovated Brewery Flats Access just east of town. I fished several bends and hooked and released several rainbows and a couple of whities.

Brewery Flats was once the channelized poor sister of an otherwise nearly perfect trout stream. No more. Now, perhaps excepting the Big Spring itself, the Flats have been transformed into the creek's showplace. The once straight-as-an-arrow, largely unproductive channel beside the road has been turned into a meandering model of what a real spring creek is supposed to look like. And judging from my early prospecting the trout are loving the new digs too.

Fishing Big Spring Creek

Big Spring Creek differs a bit from a true spring creek in that it feeds off several tributaries—Castle, East Fork, and Casino Creeks—so it does get muddy from spring snowmelt and hard rains. Nonetheless, it derives much of its flow from Big Spring, which delivers 64,000 gallons of cold fertile water per minute.

Thirty miles or so downstream it merges with the Judith River. In that relatively short run can be found some of Montana's best trout fishing, and some of the toughest if you're not paying close attention.

There aren't a lot of hatches to contend with here. In fact, day in and day out, it's the nymph specialist who tends to catch the most trout. But take a page from the spring creek specialist's notebook and stock your vest with the precise patterns known to work their magic. Caddis are major player here so be sure to bring a wide variety of patterns and styles—think small in spring, larger in summer, and small again in fall. Peacock bodies are almost always a good choice. Tie on an Elk Hair dry and put an Antron pupa or soft hackle on the dropper, weighted for non-hatch or pre-hatch times and unweighted during a hatch. The most important aspect of fishing any flies is to achieve a natural drift that doesn't tip off the trout.

Big Spring Creek supports a huge wild trout population, with as many fish per mile as the Missouri River below Holter Dam, although not as large. And despite the fact that it gets channeled right through the town of Lewistown, it's a beautiful little stream with loads of wildlife. Chokecherries grow as thick as a hedge along its lush banks—Lewistown isn't known as the "Chokecherry Capital of Montana" for nothing

We like Big Spring Creek so much that we always make a least one pilgrimage each year. Our visits have run the gamut from early spring through late fall, and no one time have we come away feeling anything like cheated. In early spring we've hit Baetis hatches that rival those found anywhere. Some days the trout gobbled our #18 Comparaduns and Sparkle Duns like candy, and some days only #18 and 20 Pheasant Tail Nymphs would interest the trout. When the Baetis weren't out, the trout seemed to prefer nothing more exotic than the good old spring creek stand-by, a red (or brown) San Juan Worm.

In midsummer we've found trout apparently on a strict diet of Sparkle Pupa and beadhead caddis larva imitations. When we've hit town in July the various PMD atterns—soft hackles, emergers, and duns—have often done the trick. I have to dmit, though, that I probably stick with a well-drifted ant 90 percent of the time, per- aps trailed by a tiny Pheasant Tail. We've had summer and early fall afternoons vhen Big Spring trout jumped all over our terrestrials. We had to remind ourselves iat, yes, this really is a spring creek, and yes, the trout really are tough most of the me.

For about two hours on one late August dawn, the trout absolutely went bonkers ɔr a deep drifted #18 Red-Ass Black Ant. And when that action finally slowed, there eemed to be a trout under every bush waiting to gobble a well-pitched #14 Red and •lack Parachute Ant (dry). Of course, that was highlight film stuff, and we've had lenty of days when even "tough" wasn't a strong enough description.

Big Spring Creek browns and rainbows aren't known for being hefty; the large iajority we catch run less than 14 inches. On occasion, however, we get lucky and ɔol one in the 16- to 18-inch range. Bigger fish are in there, but we haven't seen iem—yet.

Dave Stover of Lewistown releases a fat brook trout taken on a damsel nymph at the Trophy Trout Springs Ranch near Hobson, Montana.

Restaurants and Accommodations

Following a cold, snowy early April bout of feeding various Baetis patterns to Big Spring Creek trout on the newly renovated Brewery Flats section we stopped at the Hackamore Supper Club, 2 miles west Lewistown on Hwy. 87 (406-538-5685), and were treated to a couple of the best steaks we'd ever had.

Actually, when it comes to dining out in Lewistown variety is not big on our agenda. In fact, it's nonexistent. For breakfast, it's oatmeal at the Empire Café (21 Main St., 406-538-9912); for lunch, something from the Whole Famdamily Restaurant (206 W. Main St., 406-538-5161). The Cobb Salad and Turkey Gobbler deli sandwich are particularly good, as are any of the soups and the chili.

We usually camp out toward Hobson (Hwy. 87 west of Lewistown) at Achley Lake State Park. It's free and usually quiet, often all but deserted. The downside is the 25-mile drive back and forth to the creek, but we find that the lake's rainbow trout and kokanee salmon and the drive through pretty country filled with ring-necked pheasants more than offset the added time in the truck.

Big Spring Creek in Lewistown, Montana, is an inviting and productive trout fishery.

If you want to be closer to the action we can recommend the famous Yogo Inn (211 E. Main, 406-538-8721) or the not so famous yet equally comfortable and friendly Super 8 (102 Wendell Ave., 406-538-2581). If you opt for the latter late in the season, be aware that getting a room might be difficult with all the bird hunters and dogs that descend on the town.

Lewistown, Montana

Lewistown is the geographical center of Montana. Surrounded as it is by four mountain ranges—the Judiths, Moccasins, and Big and Little Snowies—it's sort of a last refuge for tree lovers before the largely treeless expanse of east-central Montana, otherwise known as the "Big Empty."

Many out-of-staters envision it as just another slowly dying railroad and cattle town, but they would be wrong in this case. Besides its spectacular scenery, Lewistown has a thriving and historical downtown business district and a surrounding valley that's dotted with prosperous looking farms and ranches. This is also the major jump-off point to the remote and wild Missouri Breaks and the C. M. Russell National Wildlife Refuge.

Nearby Fisheries

Brown trout fishing on the Judith River was once a jealously guarded local secret, but the recent drought, increased irrigation demands, and the continuing proliferation of locked gates in the region have all but killed off the once fine fishery. One way to access a portion of what's left is to arrange a stay in one of the comfortable log cabins on the Leininger Ranch (406-538-5797).

Upstream in the Lewis and Clark National Forest, the Middle and Lost Forks provide anglers limited opportunities to catch smallish wild trout, but even the forks are beset with problems. In summer both are diminished to slight trickles by the ongoing drought, and the upper Middle Fork suffers from too many ATVs following its course.

Warm Spring Creek is a decent rainbow trout and smallmouth bass fishery. The fish aren't large, but they are fair in number. One thing this little gem has plenty of, though, is fanged serpents.

Nearby Attractions and Activities

The Charlie Russell Chew-Choo (406-538-8721, ext. 312 or 1-800-860-9646) is without doubt a unique dining experience. Saturdays from June through September you can ride the rails from Kingston Junction, 10 miles northwest of Lewistown, to Denton

(28 miles). The train crosses three wood trestles and passes through a tunnel while you enjoy a prime-rib dinner catered by the Yogo Inn of Lewistown. There is also entertainment on board, as well as several historic towns to view and "watchable wildlife" throughout.

You can also visit the Big Spring itself, which locals say is flat out "the prettiest spot on the planet." While you're there stop by the hatchery, one of the West's largest facilities, where 3 million trout are added annually along with kokanee salmon.

Author's Tip

If nothing is hatching, begin the hunt with a pair of smallish nymphs, such as a #16-18 Pheasant Tail, Copper John, or Flashback, or rig a dry with a nymph trailer. Both weighted and dry ants are a good choice from early summer through fall—all black, all red, and black and red have worked well for me in the past. Caddis are an almost daily event spring through fall, so be ready with a variety of imitations.

Favorite Fly

Beadhead Black-Ass Red Ant

Hook	Standard wet fly #12-18
Front Abdomen	Copper bead
Rear Abdomen	Dubbed black Antron
Hackle	Dark brown (sparse)
Wing	None

Fast Facts

Big Spring Creek

Location	Lewistown in central Montana
Water Type	Spring creek with freestone characteristics
Primary Gamefish	Brown and rainbow trout; average size 12 to 14 inches
Best Time	March through October; also fishes well in winter, but pick your days carefully
Best Flies	Midge, Baetis, PMD, and caddis patterns, never leave home without a good assortment in smallish sizes; the Pheasant Tail, Copper John, and Prince Nymph, caddis emergers and pupa, terrestrials both wet and dry the San Juan Worm in red or tan. Dry flies will take fish, but nymphs and other wet stuff work better; especially noticeable during non-hatch periods.
Equipment	8- to 9-foot, 3- to 5-weight rods, floating line, tapered leaders; be prepared to fish long, fine tippets
Conditions	Except during brief runoff in early spring and after hard rain showers the creek generally runs clear, cold, and constant
Drive Time	From Billings: 3.5 hours
	From Bozeman: 3 hours
	From Great Falls: 2.5 hours
Directions	From Billings US 87 north to Grass Range, Hwy. 200 west to Lewistown; from Bozeman I-90 east to Big Timber, US 191 north to Lewistown; from Great Falls US 87/Hwy. 200 west to Lewistown.

Local Fly Shops

Don's
P.O. Box 780
Lewistown, MT 59457
406-538-9408

The Bait Shop
638 NE Main
Lewistown, MT 59457
406-538-6085

Sport Center
320 W. Main
Lewistown, MT 59457
406-538-9308

Guides

Linehan Outfitting Co.
406-295-4872

Contacts

Montana FWP Field Office
Airport Rd.
Lewistown, MT 59457
406-538-4658

Lewistown Chamber of Commerce
408 NE Main St., P.O. Box 818
Lewistown, MT 59457
406-538-5436

CHAPTER 28

THE BIGHORN RIVER
Montana's Fantastic Fishery

Reborn at the base of Yellowtail Dam 42 miles south of Hardin at Fort Smith, Montana's Bighorn River—at least the first 13 miles—is without question among the best and most fertile trout fisheries anywhere. The river's legendary fly hatches occur nearly nonstop year-round.

The 3-mile run from the Afterbay dam (actually the start of the tailwater fishery) to Lind Access (locally known as "Three-Mile") boasts some 6,000 catchable trout per mile. The average runs somewhere around 15 or 16 inches, with 20-plus-inchers far from uncommon. The 10-mile float from Three-Mile down to Bighorn Access is much the same, just longer. It's all as blue ribbon as blue ribbon gets, but the trade-off is the incredible crowds of anglers that flock here. On an almost daily basis through-out the year a floating armada of anglers plies the river, making it a frontrunner for the title "Most Overrun Trout River" right alongside such luminaries as New Mexico's infamous San Juan and Utah's Green to name just two.

It's gotten so bad that we don't even float the Bighorn any more, at least not very often. Rather than vie for position with other floaters, we hike in above Three-Mile early in the morning. We usually find plenty of elbowroom until the first floaters

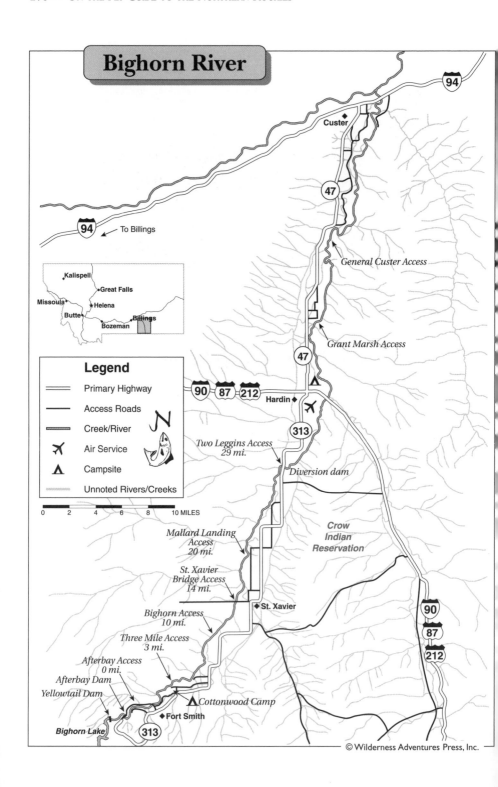

Bighorn River

94

Custer

47

94 ← To Billings

General Custer Access

Kalispell
• Great Falls
Missoula •
Butte • • Helena
Bozeman • Billings

Grant Marsh Access

47

Legend

═══	Primary Highway
────	Access Roads
══	Creek/River
✈	Air Service
▲	Campsite
~~	Unnoted Rivers/Creeks

90 87 212
Hardin ◆ ▲

313

Two Leggins Access
29 mi.

Diversion dam

0 2 4 6 8 10 MILES

Mallard Landing
Access
20 mi.

Crow
Indian
Reservation

St. Xavier
Bridge Access
14 mi.

◆ St. Xavier

Bighorn Access
10 mi.

90

Three Mile Access
3 mi.

87

Afterbay Access
0 mi.

212

Afterbay Dam
Yellowtail Dam

▲ Cottonwood Camp

◆ Fort Smith

Bighorn Lake 313

© Wilderness Adventures Press, Inc.

arrive. Another crowd-beating ploy is to wade fish the far side of the river just below the cable, immediately across from the boat launch. The floaters tend to launch and then dig like hell to get away from the busy parking lot, and we're left to a piece of water with more than enough trout and few anglers. You can also try fishing above the cable (no boating or wading allowed), although it's a popular spot among the bait and hardware slingers.

The shelving riffle in midriver just below the cable is a small honey hole that houses a large number of hungry trout, but getting to it at anything beyond minimum flows requires some sort of watercraft. We often take turns with our pontoon boat, rowing out, anchoring just off the main flow, and having at it. The rules are simple: catch or hook a trout then row back to the landing and turn over the oars.

As this treasure trove never seems to run out of willing trout, there is really no reason to float on down among the crowds. No shuttle hassle, either, although in today's inflated times Fort Smith shuttle rates really aren't all that bad. By the way, the local fly shops, the Dam Restaurant, and Cottonwood Campground all provide shuttle services.

Fishing the Bighorn River

The Bighorn fishes like a typical Western tailwater. In winter and early spring, fly patterns such as the Ray Charles (pink scud), Skinny Nelson, Disco Midge, Palomino Midge, Orange Scud, San Juan Worm, egg patterns, and bigger stuff like Bighorn Buggers, Blood Leeches, and Clousers all work at various times.

Baetis appear in April and there follows a progression of popular and productive hatches through the summer: Little Yellow Stoneflies, Pale Morning Duns, Tricos, caddis, fall Baetis, with midges, scuds, sow bugs, and San Juan Worms producing throughout. Finding out what's hot at the moment is as easy as reading the "board" at any of the local fly shops.

Frankly, the biggest problem for floating anglers is usually finding a run at which to stop and fish, as boats and anglers seem to swarm over the water like a hatch of insects.

Restaurants and Accommodations

Almost as good as the fishing was dining at Polly's, but when she died in 2001 the restaurant closed, leaving only the Dam Restaurant (in Fort Smith) and Carol's Café (13 miles up the road toward Hardin) available for walk-in dining.

In season, Ok-A-Beh Marina (406-666-2349) serves pretty good steaks, burgers, and sandwiches. Forrester's Big Horn Resort (406-666-2502) accepts reservations for a nicer dining experience.

The Bighorn Reservoir is a great fishery in its own right.

If you decide to go it alone, be sure to pack along your groceries, as there are none to be had in Fort Smith. Only the basics are sold at the marina, and beer, wine, and liquor are scarce.

Cottonwood Campground (406-666-2391), located at the turnoff to the Three-Mile access, offers 20 campsites and 15 full RV hook-up sites, a fly shop, public showers, and cozy cabins with kitchens and baths. There are two public campgrounds where camping is free, but there is a $5 entrance fee to the national recreation area, which is covered by a National Parks or Golden Eagle Pass. They are located on each side of Afterbay, with 12 sites on the near side and 28 on the far side.

Nearby Fisheries

The Bighorn Reservoir once provided a great mixed-bag fishery, but the recent drought has left most launch sites high and dry. There's now a hell of a long hike down to water in most areas.

But, of course, it's hard to leave a river like the Bighorn to fish anywhere else anyway.

Nearby Attractions and Activities

The Little Bighorn Battlefield National Monument (I-90 and Hwy. 212, Exit 510, 406-638-2621) is where General George Custer and the Seventh Cavalry met their maker at the hands of a swarm of angry Sioux and Cheyenne warriors.

The Bighorn Canyon above Yellowtail Dam is awesome, stunning, and very photogenic. And the nearby Pryor Mountains are home to a thriving herd of wild horses.

Author's Tip

Early spring, late fall, and winter are the best times to avoid the rush, although it's always tough. Rig a Ray Charles and a Skinny Nelson or Disco Midge beneath a strike indicator and drift through anything that even looks fishy, as trout lurk just about everywhere. The more water you cover, the more likely you are to find pods of rising trout.

Favorite Fly

Pink Scud

Hook	Mustad 9527(or equivalent)
Body	Dubbed pink dyed rabbit, picked out for legs
Rib	Fine gold wire
Shellback	Several strands Krystal Flash

Fast Facts

Bighorn River

Location	Fort Smith, Montana, 42 miles south of Hardin on MT 313
Water Type	Fertile and famous tailwater fishery
Primary Gamefish	Rainbow and brown trout of better than average size
Best Time	Anytime; least crowded is late fall, winter, and spring; worst crowds from July to September
Best Flies	Midge patterns, Griffith's Gnat #18-20, Palomino Midge #16-20, Brassie #16-20, Disco Midge #16-20; PMD Sparkle Dun #16-18, CDC Emerger #16-18, Pheasant Tail Nymph #16-20, Black Caddis Pupa and X-Caddis #16-18, Spent-Wing Trico #18-22, Stimulator and Elk Hair Caddis #16-18, Parachute Adams #16-22, Olive CDC Emerger #16-22, San Juan Worm #6-10, scuds, sow bugs #14-20, soft hackles #16-20, Woolly Buggers, Clousers #2-10
Equipment	9-foot, 5- or 6-weight rod, floating line, long tapered leaders, tippet to suit method and fly
Conditions	Extreme weather; winter can be 50 degrees above zero to 50 below; wind can blow hard anytime; summer can be pleasant to brutal, with sudden and violent storms. The river itself is a model of consistency, but dam releases do alter the flows from low in winter to high in summer. There are no dangerous rapids.
Drive Time	From Billings: 2.5 hours From Bozeman: 5 hours From Casper: 5 hours
Directions	From Billings, I-90 east to Hardin, south to Fort Smith on MT 313; from Bozeman, I-90 east to Hardin, south to Fort Smith on MT 313; from Casper, north I-25 to Buffalo, west I-90 to Hardin, MT, south MT 313 to Fort Smith.

Local Fly Shops

Fort Smith Fly Shop and Cabins
P.O. Box 7872
Fort Smith, MT 59035
406-666-2550

Big Horn Angler
P.O. Box 577
Fort Smith, MT 59035
406-666-2375

Big Horn Trout Shop
P.O. Box 7477
Fort Smith, MT 59035
406-666-2375

Big Horn Fly Shop
1426 N. Crawford Ave
Hardin, MT 59034
406-665-1321

Big Horn Fly Shop
P.O. Box 7597
Fort Smith, MT 59035
406-666-2253

Big Horn Fly Shop
485 S. 24th Street W
Billings, MT 59102
406-656-8257

Rainbow Run Fly Shop
2244 Grand Ave.
Billings, MT 59102-2619
406-656-3455

Quill Gordon Flyfisher's
Fort Smith, MT 59035
406-666-2375

Guides

Forrester's Big Horn River Resort
1-800-665-3799

Big Horn River Lodge
1-800-235-5450

Big Horn River Country Lodge
406-666-2331

East Slope Outfitters and Guest House
406-670-8998

Rimrock Outfitters
406-248-4861, 1-800-655-5715

Bighorn Yellowstone Outfitter
406-252-5859

Two Leggins Outfitters
406-665-2825

Eagle Nest Lodge
406-665-3711

Royal Bighorn Lodge
406-665-1321

Tight Lines Lodge
406-666-2240

Contacts

Yellowtail Dam Visitor's Center
406-666-3218

In August, the daily armada of driftboats on Montana's Bighorn River nearly overwhelms the landscape.

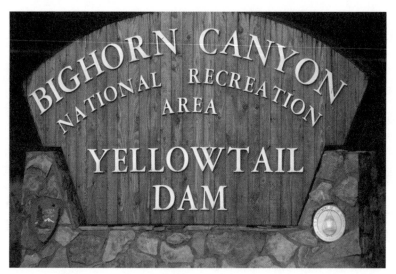

Yellowtail Dam created this fine tailwater trout factory.

CHAPTER 29

THE BITTERROOT RIVER

Western Montana's Embattled Jewel

The fishing on western Montana's Bitterroot River remains top shelf, despite the rampant development that threatens to destroy one of the prettiest spots around. Like so many popular places in the West, it's literally being loved to death as more and more people move into the area.

The West Fork Bitterroot, born high in the Bitterroot Mountains hard by the Idaho-Montana border, boils and seethes downslope until eventually slowed by Painted Rocks Reservoir. Throughout its run, above and below the reservoir, to just below Connor, the West Fork's waters teem with westslope cutthroat trout. Above the reservoir the trout are typical mountain-bred wild trout, colorful though not all that big. But below the reservoir these wild fish are bigger-than-average small-stream cutts.

The river below the dam is clear, though bank-full with icy snowmelt when I arrive. Gingerly wading as close as I dare to the near edge of a roaring current tongue, I pitch a pair of heavily weighted stonefly nymphs (a Bitch Creek and Rubber-Legged Black Stone) to a wide seam on the far edge of the torrent. Like a pair of anvils tossed in a quiet slough, the pair splash water then sink to the bottom.

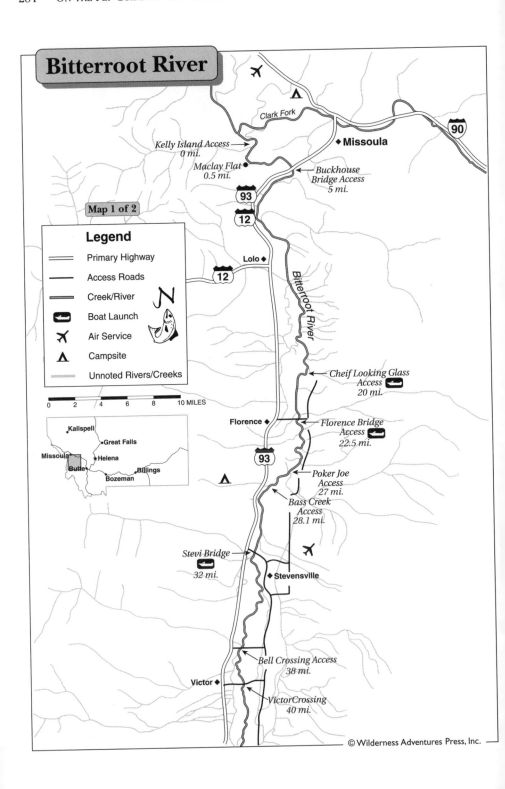

Bitterroot River

Clark Fork

♦ **Missoula**

Kelly Island Access
0 mi.

Maclay Flat
0.5 mi.

Buckhouse
Bridge Access
5 mi.

90

93

12

Map 1 of 2

Legend

═══ Primary Highway

─── Access Roads

─── Creek/River

▱ Boat Launch

✈ Air Service

▲ Campsite

▭▭ Unnoted Rivers/Creeks

Lolo ♦

12

Bitterroot River

Cheif Looking Glass
Access
20 mi.

Florence ♦

Florence Bridge
Access
22.5 mi.

93

Poker Joe
Access
27 mi.

Bass Creek
Access
28.1 mi.

0   2   4   6   8   10 MILES

Kalispell
★Great Falls
Missoula ★Helena
Butte
Bozeman Billings

▲

Stevi Bridge
32 mi.

♦ Stevensville

Bell Crossing Access
38 mi.

Victor ♦

VictorCrossing
40 mi.

© Wilderness Adventures Press, Inc.

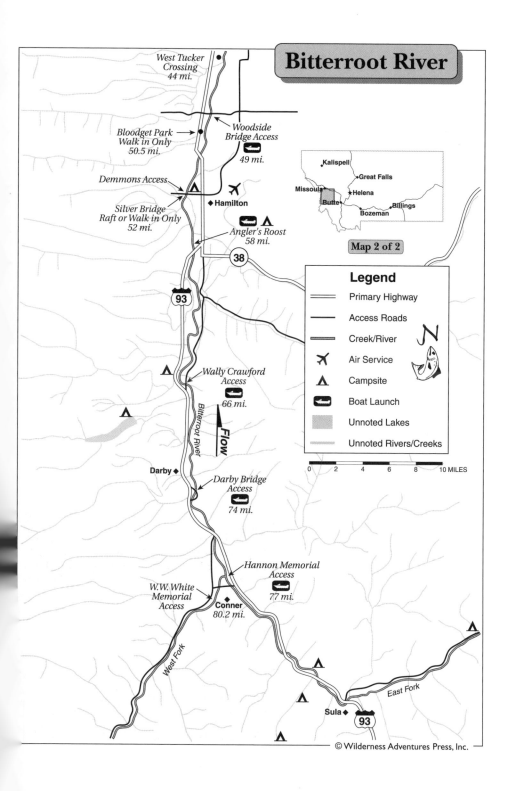

Bitterroot River

Map 2 of 2

West Tucker
Crossing
44 mi.

Woodside
Bridge Access
49 mi.

Bloodget Park
Walk in Only
50.5 mi.

Demmons Access

Silver Bridge
Raft or Walk in Only
52 mi.

♦ Hamilton

Angler's Roost
58 mi.

38

93

Kalispell
Great Falls
Missoula
Helena
Butte
Billings
Bozeman

Legend

═══	Primary Highway
───	Access Roads
───	Creek/River
✈	Air Service
▲	Campsite
🚤	Boat Launch
▨	Unnoted Lakes
∿	Unnoted Rivers/Creeks

N

Wally Crawford
Access
66 mi.

Bitterroot River

Flow

Darby ♦

Darby Bridge
Access
74 mi.

0 2 4 6 8 10 MILES

Hannon Memorial
Access
77 mi.

W.W. White
Memorial
Access

Conner
80.2 mi.

West Fork

East Fork

Sula ♦

93

© Wilderness Adventures Press, Inc.

Tic, tic, tic, tic, they bounce along until suddenly the big hot-pink bobber shoots upstream. I lift the rod and give the line a hard jerk, and immediately feel a heavy throbbing.

Moments later Katie the wirehair is giving the fat 16-inch cutthroat the once over, while I proudly pose for the camera. Pretty day, pretty river, fat wild trout, no competition, no million dollar palaces or Hummers in sight—hell, this is as good as it gets, at least to my way of thinking.

Fishing the Bitterroot

Heavy mountain snowpack in western Montana means major runoff can go on for some time. Typically, mid-May to mid-June is something of a bust no matter how deep the snow, but severe winters can put the river off into early July. Wading the Bitterroot is tough during high flows, and float fishing obviously maximizes the number of opportunities you have—and all but eliminates potential run-ins with irate landowners.

The closer you get to Missoula, the harder it is to find public land, but thanks to Montana's stream access law wade fishing is limited only by how far you can hike as long as you stay below the high-water mark. Numerous public fishing accesses make a variety of long or short floats possible. For example, the float from Connor to

Painted Rocks Reservoir separates the upper and lower West Fork Bitterroot.

lannon Memorial is a quickie, while doing Woodside Bridge to Bell Crossing is a marathon at anything less than maximum flows.

Pre-runoff is our favorite time to fish the Bitterroot. Starting in March we hunt for trout and the mysterious and flightless Skwala stonefly. While decent fishing can be had without hitting the hatch, we're always a little disappointed when the big flies fail to show, which is all too common where we're concerned. Our luck at pinning down the Skwala runs about on par with pinning down its Salmonfly cousin. But each spring we give it our best shot. And while we seldom stumble upon many trout actually eating Skwala dries, we do at least find some willing to eat the nymph.

We find it much easier to get the timing right on the Bitterroot's other hatches: Baetis, PMDs, Green Drakes, and the variety of lesser stoneflies and caddisflies. Spring through fall the nearly constant parade of hatches keep Bitterroot trout looking up, creating the perfect opportunity to cast our dry flies to rising trout. Skwala, Trico, whatever—we'll take that any day.

From mid-July into fall we often begin our Bitterroot adventures with a Parachute Hopper, ant pattern, Stimulator, or Madam X, to which I almost always add a dropper nymph.

Restaurants and Accommodations

top in at Dotson's Saloon and Fat Mac's Pizzeria in Darby (114 Main St., 406-821-024). Over the past 80 years or so the Dotson has grown to become something of a Bitterroot icon, and Fat Mac's, with its rustic log cabin atmosphere, isn't too shabby as a pizza place, either. Another Bitterroot mainstay is the "Knob" (6065 US 93 S, Connor, 406-821-3520), where delectable menu items like the Hickory Smoked Ribs are off-the-charts good.

Perhaps the pinnacle in fine dining can be found "amongst the pines" at the Triple Creek Restaurant in Darby (5551 West Fork Rt., 406-821-4408). The elegant, glass-encased dining room and the cozy upstairs lounge provide spectacular views of the Bitterroot Mountains—the perfect backdrop for one of the West's best dining experiences. With a menu dotted with such exotic entrees as Phyllo- and Spinach-Wrapped Beef Tenderloin or Wild Mushroom Stuffed Free Range Chicken Breast antt, you're in for quite a treat.

On to lodging. But before I climb back down to my lower level of angling on the road, I should probably mention the Triple Creek's Ultimate Montana Angler experience; a four-night stay in a luxury cabin, complete with fireplace, living room, and bedroom, fully-stocked bar, satellite TV, VCR/DVD, steam shower, and private hot tub on your own outside deck. The flyfishing includes casting instruction, guided wade fishing on the West Fork, and a guided float trip on the mainstem Bitterroot for rainbow, cutthroat, and brown trout. Each guest receives a custom Triple Creek flyfishing vest, and, of course, someone else does the cooking and dishwashing chores. I makes for an amazing vacation.

After all that, it's probably something of a letdown to hear that, as usual, we drag along the tent-trailer and camp. We like the USFS Rombo Campground 4 miles south of Darby on US 93, 18 miles southwest on Hwy. 473 (16 sites, water, vault toilets, picnic table, and fire ring) or the East Fork at Jennings Campground, 1 mile west of Sula on US 93, 10 miles northeast on Hwy. 472.

Ross's Hole, Montana

This beautiful valley is named for Alexander Ross of the Hudson Bay Company who with 55 Indian and white trappers, 89 women and children, and 392 horses, camped here in March 1824 en route from Spokane House to the Snake River country. It took nearly a month of backbreaking labor for the party to eventually make it across the pass to the Big Hole valley, prompting Ross to call the basin, "Valley of Troubles."

Earlier, in 1805, the valley hosted another desperate crew. The Corps of Discovery frantically searching for a passable route through the mountains to the Pacific, struggled to the top of the Salmon-Bitterroot Divide and staggered down the north side to the valley. Here they met up with a band of Salish Indians. Clark wrote, "Those people recved us friendly, threw white robes over our shoulders & smoked in the pipes of peace, we encamped with them and found them friendly." Badly in need of rest, they stayed here for two days, visiting with and taking notes on the Salish (Lewis and Clark mistakenly called them "Flatheads") vocabulary and trading for and purchasing much needed horses to continue the journey.

Nearby Fisheries

Numerous small tributaries spill down the flanks of the Bitterroots to the west and the Sapphires to the east. Nearly all can provide anglers willing to hike a bit with a pleasant small-stream flyfishing experience. And some hold bigger trout than one might expect at first glance.

The little creeks aren't technical fisheries. They're just fun places to enjoy a little solitude, cast a fly, and perhaps catch a wild trout or two. If you're willing to explore a little, you may just find a special little fishery that you'll never read about in a national sporting magazine.

Nearby Attractions and Activities

On August 9, 1877, the Big Hole National Battlefield (406-689-3155), just across the pass, was the site of a ferocious and bloody fight between Chief Joseph's beleaguered band of Nez Perce and the Seventh Infantry. An extensive network of trails links the various sites on the battlefield, and the Nee-Me-Poo Trail, a 1,500-mile hiking and backpacking trail, passes through as it traces the Nez Perce flight from Oregon to the Bears Paw Mountains in north-central Montana. Be sure to pack along your fly rod because the North Fork Big Hole also passes through.

The Lee Metcalf National Wildlife Refuge, just south of Stevensville, is a haven for waterfowl, raptors, songbirds, and whitetail deer. And down near Missoula you'll find another famous stop on the Lewis and Clark trail, Traveler's Rest.

The Bitterroot Lily is Montana's state flower, and what better place to look for its pale pink blooms than in its namesake valley. Indians relished the roots, and legend has it that the plant sprang from the tears of a Flathead matron whose family was starving. Hearing her sobs, the sun sent a messenger bird to turn the tears into a nutritious, though bitter, root whose beautiful flowers reflected the mother's piety.

Author's Tip

Wade fishing upstream of a public fishing access in the morning and downstream later on is a good strategy to stay ahead of the float-fishing crowd. Bitterroot trout seem to prefer feeding on the surface (at least we like to think so). On most days we start with a dry fly and a dropper nymph, and only dredge the bottom when the trout leave us no choice.

Below the Painted Rocks, westslope cutts like this one are not uncommon.

Favorite Fly

Skewala Stone

Hook	Mustad 94831 (or equivalent)
Body	Orange foam, wrapped with tying thread to form segmented
Under wing	White Z-lon
Overwing	Deer or elk body hair and Krystal flash mixed wrapped back to form a bullet head
Legs/Feelers	Brown rubber or Sili-legs tied in at sides

Fast Facts

Bitterroot River

Location	Western Montana, south of Missoula
Water Type	Freestone mountain river; rowdy and rocky up high, more placid lower down
Primary Gamefish	Westslope cutthroat, rainbow, and brown trout and mountain whitefish
Best Time	Pre-runoff in March and April and September to November
Best Flies	Stonefly patterns in early spring; large attractors and species-specific patterns to mimic excellent PMD, Green and Brown Drake, and various caddis hatches
Equipment	9-foot, 4- to 6-weight rods, floating lines, and tapered leaders and tippets to suit. Excellent float and/or wade fishing exists from the forks to the mouth, except during peak runoff when the fishing is perhaps best left to ospreys, eagles, kingfishers and otters.

Conditions	Major spring runoff, usually mid-May into June; otherwise typical variable Montana weather. Water temps can become marginal on lower river during hot summers.
Drive Time	From Bozeman: 4 hours
	From Spokane: 4 hours
	From Idaho Falls: 6 hours
Directions	From Bozeman, I-90 west to Missoula, US 93 south; from Spokane, I-90 east to Missoula, US 93 south; from Idaho Falls, I-15 north to Sage Junction, Hwy. 33 southto Mud Lake, Hwy. 28 north to Salmon, Hwy. 93 north to Hamilton.

Local Fly Shops

Riverbend Flyfishing
P.O. Box 594
Hamilton, MT 59840
406-363-4197

Kesel's Four Rivers
501 S. Higgens
Missoula, MT 59801
406-721-4796, 1-888-349-4796

Grizzly Hackle
215 W. Front St.
Missoula, MT 59801
406-721-8996

Missoulian Angler
420 N. Higgens
Missoula, MT 59801
406-728-7766

The Kingfisher
926 E. Broadway
Missoula, MT 59801
1-888-542-4911

Angler's Roost
815 Hwy. 93 S
Hamilton, MT 59840
406-363-1268

Bitterroot Anglers Fly Shop
4039 US 93 N, Ste. B
Stevensville, MT 59870
406-777-5667

Anglers Afloat
2742 Alpenglow Rd.
Stevensville, MT 59870
406-777-3421

Guides

Flyfishing Always
406-363-0943

Foust's Flyfishing
406-363-0936

Joe Biner's Rainbow Guide Service
406-821-4643

Rocking W Outfitters
406-821-3007

Thunder Bow Outfitters
406-754-2406

Backdoor Outfitters
1-888-330-3861

Five Valley Flyfishing
406-728-9434

Lewis and Clark Trail Adventures
406-728-7609, 1-800-366-6246

Montana Flyfishing Co.
406-549-4822

River Resource Outfitters
406-543-3358

Trouthawk Outfitters
406-721-6121

Western Water and Woods
406-251-5212

Contacts

Bitterroot National Forest
Hamilton, MT 59840
406-363-3131

Lee Metcalf NWR
Stevensville, MT 59870
406-777-5552

Montana FWP
Region 2
Missoula, MT 59801
406-542-5500

Sula State Forest
Hamilton, MT 59840
406-363-1585

Painted Rocks State Park
406-542-5500

The upper East Fork Bitterroot.

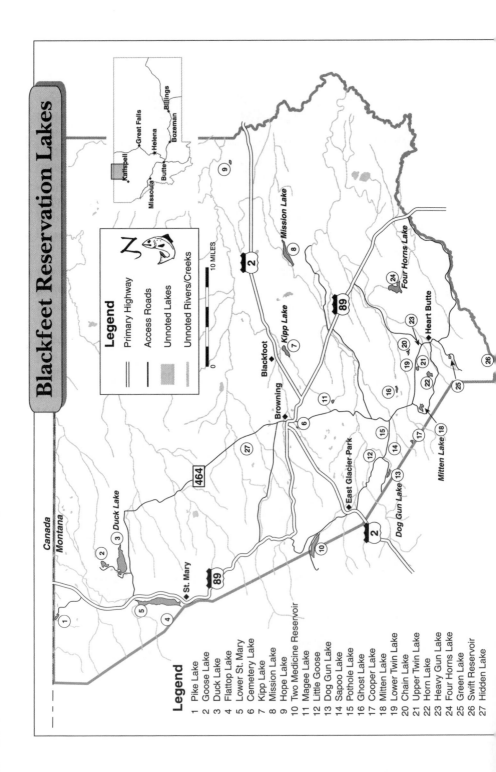

Blackfeet Reservation Lakes

Legend

Primary Highway
Access Roads
Unnoted Lakes
Unnoted Rivers/Creeks

10 MILES

0

Legend

1 Pike Lake
2 Goose Lake
3 Duck Lake
4 Flattop Lake
5 Lower St. Mary
6 Cemetery Lake
7 Kipp Lake
8 Mission Lake
9 Hope Lake
10 Two Medicine Reservoir
11 Magee Lake
12 Little Goose
13 Dog Gun Lake
14 Sapoo Lake
15 Pothole Lake
16 Ghost Lake
17 Cooper Lake
18 Mitten Lake
19 Lower Twin Lake
20 Chain Lake
21 Upper Twin Lake
22 Horn Lake
23 Heavy Gun Lake
24 Four Horns Lake
25 Green Lake
26 Swift Reservoir
27 Hidden Lake

Canada
Montana

Duck Lake

St. Mary

East Glacier Park

Browning

Blackfoot

Kipp Lake

Mission Lake

Four Horns Lake

Heart Butte

Dog Gun Lake

Mitten Lake

Kalispell
Great Falls
Helena
Billings
Bozeman
Missoula
Butte

CHAPTER 30

BLACKFEET LAKES
Where Huge Really Isn't a Superlative

Let's begin with a little quiz: What two nations border the north and east boundaries of Glacier National Park? And no fair looking at a map.

Hopefully, all of you named our northern neighbor, Canada. But unless you've been there, I'll bet you missed the Blackfeet Nation to the east. On the other hand, if you're a flyfisher who focuses on trophy trout, you're probably well aware that Montana's Fish, Wildlife, & Parks Department manages the fisheries at Kipp, Mission, Mitten, Dog Gun, and Four Horns Lakes on the Reservation. And that Duck Lake hosts some of the biggest rainbows you'll find anywhere.

Over the years big rainbow trout and Duck Lake have become almost synonymous. And considering the countless articles and videos that have touted Duck Lake as one of the state's primo big-trout spots, it's no wonder. Duck is also probably the most consistent of the Blackfeet Lakes, as other lakes sometimes turn on and off quickly.

Mission Lake, normally a hotspot, suffers from some sort of salinity problem that occasionally causes the fishing to sour. Mitten Lake's trophy fishery suffers at times due to the stocking of too many trout. It's often difficult to drag anything by the 12-

inchers that swarm in front of the bigger boys and girls. Kipp is usually off in the early season, but later turns on to produce good catches of large fish. Meanwhile, Duck Lake gets all the ink and most of the crowds because day in, day out the fishing stays the same—pretty darn good.

Wind is always a big player on these lakes. On our trip last April, the wind didn't stop blowing for three days and nights, and the fishing (at least my fishing) sucked. Four Horns, Mitten, Mission, and Kipp Lakes—it didn't matter where, the action was slow to nonexistent. Even the pack of hungry 12-inchers at Mitten shut down.

I ran into a friend of a friend who happened to be there at the same time, and he didn't hesitate to erase any doubt I might have had that I was just hitting the wrong lakes at the wrong times: "Duck flat out sucked!" I guess it should have been some small consolation that everyone else was experiencing the same miserable fishing we were, but we'd rather have been sharing a few stories of all the big ones we landed.

I did learn a new (to me) technique for tubing in hurricane-like wind. Hunt up a shoreline where the whitecaps are running more or less parallel to shore, strap on the flippers, and launch the tube. Fish as best you can while allowing the wind-blown surf to hurl you along until the truck is about to disappear from view. Then reel in, land the tube, tie the tube and gear fast to the nearest sagebrush or anything

Blackfeet Nation: a land of many lakes.

that won't blow away, and hike to the truck. Bring the truck to the gear and repeat the entire operation.

The technique, revealed to me at Mission Lake by a young guy from Cut Bank, worked flawlessly, although neither of us managed to land a single trout. The few we hooked got off, and I couldn't help thinking that maybe we weren't the only ones blown off by the wind.

Later that afternoon, after windsurfing Four Horn's 3-foot waves for several hundred yards and three moves of the truck, I was suddenly startled by a hard jolt. Rearing back, I felt a heavy throbbing on the line. "Got one!" I hissed to no one in particular, since I was the only fool still out there, "And it's a goddamn dandy." I gritted my teeth, settling in for the great battle that was sure to unfold. Then the trout splashed to the surface and in no time I leaned over to twist the hook free on the 10-inch "goddamn dandy." It just might have been the smallest trout ever taken from the Blackfeet Lakes.

After dragging the #10 Green Damsel and a #16 Orange Scud under the surface of the raging waves all day while sleep deprived from the screaming wind the previous night, I'd had enough. It was a fitting end to a tough trip, but that's the way it goes sometimes.

Fishing the Blackfeet Lakes

The official Non-Member Sportsman Regulations you get when buying the requisite Reservation fishing permit include a map showing the location of 27 fishing lakes. Rainbow trout are the main attraction, but the lakes also harbor brown, brook, lake, and bull trout, and even a few warmwater species like bass, walleye, and northern pike.

While you can usually just follow the crowds to Duck Lake, finding some of the others can be challenging. Of course, it goes without saying that the best way to find your way around the sprawling Reservation is to start out with a guide. (See the end of this chapter for a list of Blackfeet Tribal Licensed Outfitters.) Otherwise, expect to lose a little fishing time while hunting the various lakes. Only a very few highway turnoffs sport signs for the lakes, and the Reservation is vast and largely unpopulated.

Once you find the lakes, the fishing is straightforward and pretty good, at least it is when the wind abates, although just like fishing anywhere it can be awful, great, or just about anything in between on any given day. The surest time for hot action is early spring right after the ice goes off, usually around the beginning of April. Rainbows migrate shoreward, and for a month or so you don't even need a float tube; just wade in and do your thing.

Following the annual spring fling, the trout tend to hang out in deeper water, and you'll need a boat or float tube to reach the hottest action. On windy days, which is almost every day in Blackfeet country, you can often still find action on the windward side of the lakes, right at the transition line between muddy and clear water.

Damsel nymphs are good almost anytime, but in June the trout start looking up for the adults. Rumors fly around of catching 50 trout or more a day that run 15 to 20 inches. And even if such tales are exaggerated by half, that's still a better day than most flyfishers expect anywhere.

In September and October, after the heat and crowds of summer start to wane, the fishing picks up again. Hoppers can bring 5- to 10-pound fish to the surface. As the water cools later in fall, the lakes offer up some of the best fishing of the year when browns begin staging for the annual spawn and all trout go on a pre-winter feeding spree. By the way, for the upland bird and waterfowl hunter, the Reservation is a great place to set up a cast-and-blast operation.

Fly patterns run the gamut from the Adams, Elk Hair Caddis, Renegade, and other attractor dries to #2-6 leeches and Buggers in black, brown, chartreuse, olive, and orange. Olive, orange, or yellow #14-16 scuds; various egg patterns; #8-12 damsel nymphs; #14-16 Callibaetis nymphs, emergers, duns, and spinners; #12-20 midges; #6-10 Skating Caddis; and assorted nymphs, hoppers, ants, and sculpins should cover whatever hatches, swims, or crawls in the lakes.

The constant wind and heavy trout make wimpy 1- to 4-weight rods a poor choice. I like a long 6-weight rod with plenty of backbone, and I often rotate between floating, sink-tip, and full-sink lines in a single day's fishing. Leaders sometimes need to be as long as 15 to 20 feet, but tippets should remain on the stout side. Seldom do we go less than 3X.

You don't need a Montana fishing license to fish the Reservation, but you do need a Blackfeet permit: $20 daily, $30 for three days, or $65 for the season. As of this writing you don't need a float-tube permit, but you do need one for all watercraft propelled by oar, motor, or wind. Among other places, permits are available in Browning at the Fish and Game Department Headquarters, in Dupuyer at the North Trail Trading Post (Hwy. 89, 406-472-3336), where you can also find friendly conversation and current info on the Reservation lakes, and at Scheel's All Sports in Great Falls (Holiday Village Shopping Ctr., 406-453-7666).

Restaurants and Accommodations

The Restaurant Thimbleberry in East Glacier (Hwy. 49, 406-226-5523) serves breakfast, lunch, and dinner; all good fare to be sure, but the breakfasts are particularly appealing. The Whistle Stop (Hwy. 49, 406-226-9292) serves great barbeque chicken and a whole passel of mouthwatering homemade desserts.

For Mexican food, Serrano's (406-226-9392) ranks right up there with any we've found. The area's fine-dining honors go to the Two Sisters Café (4 miles north of St. Mary, 406-732-5535). And yes, there really are two sisters, Beth and Susan Higgins, the former trained as a chef in New Orleans, the latter in San Francisco. In addition to a unique décor and menu, the margaritas are said to be spellbinding. Not especially fond of being spellbound, Gale and I usually opt for something less exotic, like a double Tanqueray Gin on the rocks with a twist of lime.

The Mountain Pine Motel (Hwy. 49 N., 406-226-4403) and Jacobsen's Cottages (1204 Hwy. 49 N., 406-226-4422 or 1-888-226-4422) are friendly, clean, and reasonable. As B&Bs go, the Bison Creek Ranch (20722 US 2 W., 406-226-4482 or 1-888-226-4482) is about as nice as it gets.

Camping is allowed at any of the Blackfeet Lakes, although you might not want to drag your 40-foot trailer down some of the roads. None allow open fires, and don't expect amenities of any sort. Organized camping can be found on US 2 between Browning and Cutbank at the Meriwether Meadows Campground and RV Park (Camp Disappointment) and at the Sears Motel and Campground (1023 Hwy. 49, 406-226-4432).

Nearby Fisheries

In addition to its famous lakes, the Reservation boasts something like 1,500 miles of streams that are open to nontribal members from June 1 through September 15. And there is some decent backcountry fishing amid the awesome surroundings of neighboring Glacier National Park.

Nearby Attractions and Activities

Glacier National Park would always be a must-stop for us, except that we usually fish the Blackfeet Lakes in early spring before the Going-to-the-Sun Highway opens. Snow blocks this main road through the Park until early summer.

Anytime we're near Freezeout Lake (US 89 north, between Fairfield and Choteau) in early spring we make the detour to check out the waterfowl and shorebird migration. Thousands of birds representing many species stop off there, which creates quite a spectacle. For birders, it's a good chance for photographs and a way to pad the life list.

If you haven't yet seen the new Lewis and Clark Interpretive Center in Great Falls (406-727-8733) be sure to check it out on your way through town.

Author's Tip

If it's your first time at the Blackfeet Lakes, by all means head for Duck Lake. It's easy to find and is usually the most consistent. Inquire at one of the area fly shops to find out what patterns and methods are currently hot. Floating, sink-tip, and full-sink lines should always be in your gear, and don't forget your float tube or boat, even if everyone you talk to says, "Don't bother, you can catch 'em right from shore." I would much rather have an unused float tube in the truck than one that's still hanging in the garage when I need it. And be prepared mentally to deal with wind, lots and lots of wind.

Favorite Fly

Orange Scud

Hook	#12-18 Mustad 9527 (or equivalent) weighted with 0.015 lead wire
Body	Dubbed orange rabbit, picked out for legs
Shellback	Several strands of Krystal Flash

Fast Facts

Blackfeet Lakes

Location	Blackfeet Indian Reservation east of Glacier National Park
Water Type	Fertile prairie pothole lakes
Primary Gamefish	Rainbow, brown, brook, and bull trout
Best Time	April and May and again September to November

Best Flies	Brown, black, olive Buggers and leeches; orange, yellow, olive scuds; damsel nymphs; and egg and midge patterns; hoppers later on
Equipment	9- to 10-foot rods, 5- to 7-weight floating, sink-tip, and full-sink lines, leaders to suit the situation, seldom necessary to go less than 3X
Conditions	Wind is a constant companion. Early spring weather can be brutal, with extremes from 80 above to well below zero; spring blizzards are common; summers usually include blistering hot, sunny days. Whenever it rains or snows, gumbo-laden roads can make access difficult.
Drive Time	From Billings: 8 hours
	From Bozeman: 6.5 hours
	From Great Falls: 3 hours
Directions	From Billings, I-90 west to US 287 north to Helena, I-15 north to Shelby, US 2 east to Reservation, follow Reservation roads to various lakes; from Bozeman, I-90 west to US 287 north to Helena, I-15 north to Shelby, US 2 east to Reservation; from Great Falls, I-15 north to Shelby, US 2 east to Reservation.

Local Fly Shops

Montana River Outfitters
1401 5th Ave.
Great Falls, MT 59403
401-761-1677

Shannon's Fur, Feather, & Fly
2514 2nd Ave. S
Great Falls, MT 59405
406-452-7727

Wolverton's Fly Shop
210 5th St.
Great Falls, MT 59405
401-454-0254

Guides

Morning Star
406-338-2785

Milk River Outfitters
406-336-2721

Cutbank Creek
406-338-5567

Glacier Gateway
406-338-7767

Montana Ranch Adventures
406-336-3810

Old West Outfitters
406-336-7767

Rising Wolf Adventures
406-863-9430

Contacts

Blackfeet Fish and Game Department
P.O. Box 850
Browning, MT 59417
406-338-7207

Mission Lake at dawn.

CHAPTER 31

THE BLACKFOOT RIVER

Forever Changed by "The Movie"

Prior to the blockbuster 1992 film, *A River Runs Through It*, the Blackfoot was just another Montana trout river. Because it hadn't yet fully recovered from a long history of logging and mining abuse and was off the beaten path to more famous rivers, it was still a relatively unknown flyfishing commodity. But the movie forever changed all of that, and these days it's pretty hard to find a flyfisher who has visited Montana without fishing the Blackfoot at least once.

At about the same time the movie hit the streets, the Blackfoot received another jolt of publicity due to a proposal for a cyanide-heap-leach gold mine near the river. In the past few years the river has really come on as a top-notch fishery and to again subject it to potential peril just to line the pockets of few would be a sorry act, but for the time being voters have put on hold all new cyanide-related mining operations. Even with the comeback and enormous publicity, the Blackfoot is a second-tier fishery compared to the state's most popular trouting destinations.

We didn't come to the Blackfoot because of the movie or the publicity. We were just following another squiggly blue line on the Montana map during our early explorations of the state. While the fishing that day turned out to be nothing to write

Blackfoot River

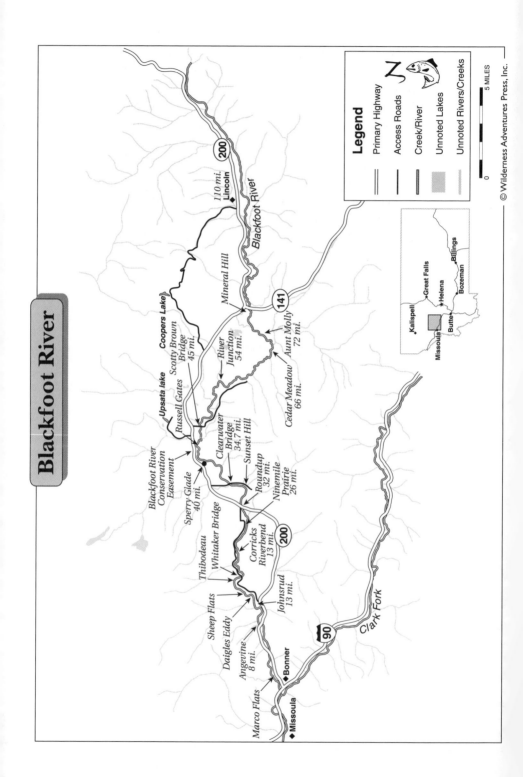

Legend

Primary Highway
Access Roads
Creek/River
Unnoted Lakes
Unnoted Rivers/Creeks

5 MILES
0

© Wilderness Adventures Press, Inc.

200
110 mi.
Lincoln
Blackfoot River
Mineral Hill
141
Aunt Molly 72 mi.
Cedar Meadow 66 mi.
River Junction 54 mi.
Coopers Lake
Scotty Broun Bridge 45 mi.
Upsata lake
Russell Gates
Blackfoot River Conservation Easement
Sperry Glade 40 mi.
Clearwater Bridge 34.7 mi.
Sunset Hill
Roundup 32 mi.
Ninemile Prairie 26 mi.
Thibodeau
Whitaker Bridge
Corricks Riverbend 13 mi.
200
Sheep Flats
Daigles Eddy
Johnsrud 13 mi.
Angevine 8 mi.
Bonner
90
Clark Fork
Marco Flats
Missoula

Great Falls
Helena
Billings
Bozeman
Kalispell
Missoula
Butte

ome about, the drive up from Helena via Stemple Pass produced a memorable experience. Just outside Lincoln we passed a strange-looking fellow, dressed in agged Army fatigues and riding a beat-up bicycle. Watching him coast out of sight in he rearview mirror, I made the comment to Gale: "Now there's an old boy that's een in the woods a bit too long." Little did we know that a couple of years later the whole country would learn about this man whose name turned out to be Ted Kaczynski (a.k.a. the Unibomber).

Below Lincoln we found a spot to park beside MT 200, which was all but desert-ed. (Don't expect it to still be deserted these days, though. We've run into a bunch of raffic every time we've been up there lately.) We strung up rods and hiked through he timber to the river. I don't recall all the details, but at some point I quit trying to ound up trout on dry flies and switched to pounding 'em up with streamers, as that tretch of river had numerous bends, undercuts, brushy banks, and logjams. A few undred probing casts resulted in about six or eight decent trout and few more links.

The next time we fished the river was in early September, the first cool days fol-owing a long, hot, dry, and dusty Montana summer. On our way from the Missouri to he Bitterroot we stopped at Sunset Hill FAS and fished upstream toward Clearwater Bridge. My fishing journal reveals that we started midmorning using hoppers and ended in late afternoon still fishing the same flies: "Both mine and G's are so chewed hey look like toys the pup's been playing with rather than actual fly patterns—sorry ooking, but the trout don't seem to care." The notes make no mention of numbers or izes, but obviously that was one day neither of us got skunked.

Fast forward to last spring, in the period between the low snow runoff of April and the major runoff of late May and early June. I fished the lower river in several dif-erent locations, but generally Johnsrud Park up toward Corrick's. Here the Blackfoot s characterized by minor rapids, heavy riffles, and numerous fast-water runs inter-upted by deep pools. The river is a veritable rock garden in this area and a bitch to wade.

I rigged a dark body #12 Elk Hair Caddis dry that trailed a #14 beadhead caddis upa imitation and proceeded to slap the pair into all the trouty-looking spots I ould reach without drowning or twisting a knee among the rocks and current. There was no apparent hatch, but the trout were on the hunt for caddis since about one out of every three casts elicited some sort of response, and every now and then an actual hook-up. The final tally showed several small to middling fish, a couple medium-sized, and a brown I might stretch a little to call big. There were a few browns, more rainbows, and just a couple of cutts—not a bad outing.

Fishing the Blackfoot

Floating is the best way to avoid the roar of traffic and the unsightly development along the highway. But boaters beware: The Blackfoot is a big, powerful, high-gradient river and no place for newbie oarsmen, especially in high water. Wade fishing during runoff borders on suicidal, and even at lower flows it's often difficult to remain upright among the many slippery boulder fields—a wading staff is not a bad idea.

Despite the lack of many trophy-caliber fish, the Blackfoot is a fun river to fish, full of non-picky trout that like to look up for a meal. July through fall can be a dry fly angler's dream. The Salmonfly hatch kicks off the festivities, though it usually hits just when the annual June runoff is peaking. But if you can get on the water during this time and consistently bang the banks with bushy dries or heavily weighted nymphs or streamers you just might find yourself fast to a brown trout over 20 inches, which aren't that uncommon at this time of year.

Once the water drops to normal levels, usually by July, the river hosts a parade of stonefly and caddis hatches and enough mayflies to keep things interesting. While the hatches certainly energize the trout, matching the hatch is often simply a matter of slapping something of reasonable size and color in as many juicy-looking spots as possible. Blackfoot trout live in an environment where everything is moving at a rapid pace; they either pounce on food quickly or go hungry.

From late summer into early fall you can often tie on a hopper and dropper and leave it rigged until lost or mauled beyond further use. The exceptions would be during local explosions of the spruce moth (doesn't happen every year or even everywhere on the river) or when the large orange-body October Caddis is in town.

While Blackfoot trout aren't fussy, don't misconstrue that to mean uneducated or foolish. Drag-free floats are still mandatory, and any fly box should contain a variety of patterns and sizes, from attractor dries and nymphs to big uglies.

Restaurants and Accommodations

The historic Hotel Lincoln (north at the blinking light off Hwy. 200, 1-888-362-4396) has replaced the famous 7-Up Ranch Supper Club, which burned down, as Lincoln's fine-dining spot. Custom-cut steaks, seafood, and chicken entrees round out the menu.

Farther downriver in Ovando lies another Montana landmark, Trixis (Hwy. 200, 406-793-9611). This is one of those real Montana bars, where the sign on the door warns, "leave the guns outside." But don't let a little thing like that keep you from trying the delicious food served inside: Mexican every Wednesday night, prime rib Friday and Sunday, and barbeque ribs on Saturday. And if you are a big eater you can opt for the 18-, 25-, or, believe it or not, 32-ounce steak. There is live music and dancing in the saloon most weekends.

On the lodging side, the Hotel Lincoln has recently undergone a complete facelift and now includes 11 rooms and 3 suites, all with private bath and log furnishings. Camping is available at the Johnsrud Park, Thibodeau, Corrick's Riverbend, Russell Gates Memorial, and River Junction fishing accesses. All have toilets and individual sites, but require a fee, and there's a 7-day stay limit. You will generally find weekdays much quieter than weekends, and the fishing is better then anyway.

Nearby Fisheries

A turn north on Highway 83 at Clearwater Junction takes you through the Seeley-Swan Valley where you'll find just about every sort of fishing Montana has to offer. Brown's Lake, east of Ovando off Highway 200, is a popular spot to tube for rainbow

The author releases a heavy Blackfoot rainbow.

and cutthroat trout; north of the highway, Cooper's Lake offers excellent fishing for average-sized cutthroats; and Upsata Lake, east and north of Ovando off Hwy. 200, provides the tubing flyfisher a chance at both rainbow and largemouth bass. Milltown Dam, which might be history any day now, offers flyfishers one of the best shots around at pike of decent size.

Author's Tip

In recent years, the Blackfoot has become a real summer hangout for floaters and tubers who come not to fish, but rather just to play. If you like a little quiet with your flyfishing, then skip all weekends between Memorial Day and Labor Day. And be sure to bring along a box of big dry flies, as chances are good that the trout will be slurping goodies from the surface. A guide friend told me, "It's a rare day on the Blackfoot from summer through fall that we don't tie on a Chernobyl Ant or one of the other popular, high-floating foam jobs."

Favorite Fly

Elk Hair Caddis

Hook	#12-18 Mustad 94840 (or equivalent)
Body	Dubbed, color to match naturals
Hackle	Palmered, color to match the naturals
Wing	Elk hair, tied spent

Fast Facts

Blackfoot River

Location	Flows generally southwest between Lincoln and Bonner, Montana; prime fishing in the 60 or so river miles below the confluence of the North Fork
Water Type	Typical freestone river; gentle in some spots, brawling in others; can be dangerous at peak runoff, mostly a pleasant experience later on
Primary Gamefish	Browns and rainbows, with cutthroats on top
Best Time	Fishes well early spring prior to runoff and again in summer through fall, except in the driest, hottest summers
Best Flies	Great dry fly stream in summer, #12-16 Parachute Adams, Royal and Gray Wulff, Stimulators, #6-10 Chernobyl Ant, Hoppers, #4-8 Salmonfly, #10-16 Beadhead Hare's Ear, Prince, and Pheasant Tail Nymphs
Equipment	8- or 9-foot, 4- to 6-weight floating lines, tapered leaders and tippets to suit the situation
Conditions	Major runoff can kill fishing for several weeks during the period of mid-April to June. After that, barring severe drought, the river fishes well through fall. Fickle Montana mountain weather.
Drive Time	From Bozeman: appx. 2.5 to 3.5 hours
	From Spokane: appx. 3.5 hours
	From Missoula: 15 minutes (to lower river)
Directions	From Bozeman, I-90 west to Bonner exit, Hwy. 200 upriver; from Spokane, I-90 east to Bonner exit; from Missoula, I-90 east to Bonner exit.

Local Fly Shops

Riverbend Flyfishing
P.O. Box 594
Hamilton, MT, 59840
406-363-4197

The Kingfisher
926 E. Broadway
Missoula, MT 59801
1-888-542-4911

Kesel's Four Rivers
501 S. Higgens
Missoula, MT 59801
406-721-4796, 1-888-349-4796

Angler's Roost
815 Hwy. 93 S
Hamilton, MT 59840
406-363-1268

Grizzly Hackle
215 W. Front St.
Missoula, MT 59801
406-721-8996

Bitterroot Anglers Fly Shop
4039 US 93 N, Ste. B
Stevensville, MT 59870
406-777-5667

Missoulian Angler
420 N. Higgens
Missoula, MT 59801
406-728-7766

Guides

Blackfoot River Outfitters
406-542-7411

Anglers Afloat
406-777-3421

Flyfishing
406-363-0943

God's Country Outfitters
406-362-3070

Foust's Flyfishing
406-363-0936

Five Valley Flyfishing
406-728-9434

Joe Biner's Rainbow Guide Service
406-821-4643

Lewis and Clark Trail Adventures
406-728-7609, 1-800-366-6246

Rocking W Outfitters
406-821-3007

Montana Flyfishing Co.
406-549-4822

Thunder Bow Outfitters
406-754-2406

River Resource Outfitters
406-543-3358

Backdoor Outfitters
1-888-330-3861

Trouthawk Outfitters
406-721-6121

Contacts

Montana FWP
Helena Office
406-444-4720

Helena National Forest
406-449-5201

Montana DNRC
Lincoln Field Office
406-362-4999

Montana FWP
Region 2
Missoula, MT 59801
406-542-5500

Lolo National Forest
Missoula, MT 59801
406-329-3750

Clearwater State Forest
406-244-5857

Author casts to a trouty-looking piece of the Blackfoot River.

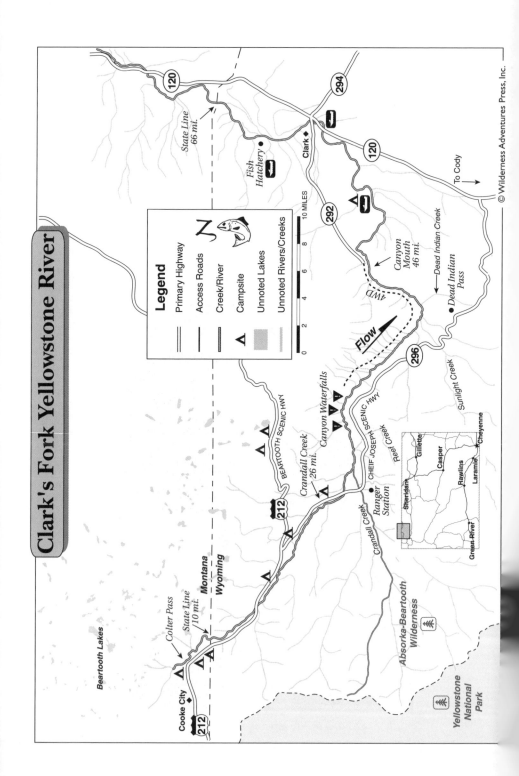

Clark's Fork Yellowstone River

Legend

- Primary Highway
- Access Roads
- Creek/River
- Campsite
- Unnoted Lakes
- Unnoted Rivers/Creeks

0 2 4 6 8 10 MILES

© Wilderness Adventures Press, Inc.

State Line 66 mi.

Fish Hatchery

Clark

To Cody

Canyon Mouth 46 mi.

Dead Indian Creek

Dead Indian Pass

4WD

Flow

Sunlight Creek

Canyon Waterfalls

Crandall Creek 26 mi.

BEARTOOTH SCENIC HWY

CHEIF JOSEPH SCENIC HWY

Reef Creek

Ranger Station

Crandall Creek

Absorka-Beartooth Wilderness

Montana
Wyoming

Colter Pass

State Line 10 mi.

Beartooth Lakes

Cooke City

Yellowstone National Park

Sheridan
Gillette
Casper
Rawlins
Laramie
Cheyenne
Green River

CHAPTER 32

THE CLARK'S FORK OF THE YELLOWSTONE RIVER

Wyoming's Wild and Scenic River

The upper canyons of the Clark's Fork, north and east of US 212 between Cooke City and the Beartooth Pass, are among the most picturesque trout waters anywhere, although many anglers don't even think they're the prettiest places on the river itself, preferring instead the awesome gorge partway down the mountain beside the Chief Joseph Highway.

Standing on the brink of one of those minor canyons not far from the Montana-Wyoming line, it seemed imperative that Gale or I climb down to cast across the plunge pool beneath the roaring waterfall to check out the fishing and procure a "socko photo," as one of my editors puts it. We do, after all, write and photograph for a living, and such photos help put bread on the table. Eyeballing the steep drop, I suggested a friendly coin toss—loser gets to climb down and do the fishing, winner gets to crawl to the precipice and take the photo.

Gale won. Pity me.

But she doesn't like heights even a little bit, so she wasn't exactly jumping for joy: "Seems to me nothing but lose, lose—die falling with camera in hand or die falling with a fishing pole in your mitt."

Obviously, we both survived, but I must admit that my short end of the stick turned out to be a lot of fun. On 25 or 30 casts in the canyon, I probably hooked 24 or more trout. Maybe I got a little carried away, but in a long career of wielding a fly rod to harass wild brook trout in a wide variety of places, the experience ranked right up there. The colorful and no doubt slightly starved brookies in the plunge pool barely let the #14 Royal Wulff touch down before one rocketed up from the dark green depths and blasted it. No missing the subtle sip, these were serious slam-bam takes.

How far I might have run up the score is anybody's guess. All I know is that on the last cast a brookie came to the fly just as quickly and enthusiastically as the first. Although by then I'd already moved into the realm of hoggishness. An idea brought home by the look on the camera operator's face as she clung precariously to her narrow perch on the rock cliff above.

Pilot Peak acts as a beacon to anglers.

Fishing the Clark's Fork

The Clark's Fork of the Yellowstone is Wyoming's only Wild and Scenic river. It begins in Montana, north of Cooke City, in a rugged landscape known as the Absaroka-Beartooth Wilderness, which is among the most remote and scenic areas in the Lower 48. The river fits right in, tumbling and roaring down rugged rocky canyons and spilling over cliffs in frothing waterfalls beneath dagger-like, 11,000-foot-plus Pilot Peak.

The uppermost reaches contain primarily brook trout, while rainbows and a remnant population of cutthroats hold sway through the midsection. Some anglers claim grayling are present too, but we've never caught them. Waterfalls within the canyon confine browns to the lower end of the river.

The most adventuresome, and arguably the best, fishing lies within the rugged canyon, 1,200 feet deep and with several high impassable waterfalls. It continues for 20 miles below the confluence of Crandall Creek. This is no place for anyone with weak knees or a weak heart. Tim Wade's (North Fork Anglers, Cody, WY) guides actually "reserve the right to decide whether or not you are fit enough." And floating the canyon is not an option. So access is by foot only, and much if it is straight down to fish and straight up to get back to the truck. But for those willing and able, the rewards are true wilderness fishing just a hop, skip, and long jump from the highway.

A 12-inch brook trout in the upper river is a big one, but like wild brook trout anywhere, what they lack in size is more than made up for in beauty and feistiness. Lower down, you'll find rainbows and some cutts that average 12 to 14 inches, with an occasional 16- to 18-incher showing up.

While all the canyon sections seem like prime habitat for big trout, so far we've not hooked any. Those in the lower canyon do seem to run a bit larger, but that may be just wishful thinking resulting from the extra effort required to get there. Below the canyons, where the river spreads out and flows through high desert sagebrush and ranchlands, browns show up and your chances of hooking a trophy increase.

With wild and colorful trout throughout, remarkable fly hatches, solitude, and stunning scenery just off the highway it's hard to fault this river for a lack of monstrous fish.

As you no doubt already suspect, trout here are seldom selective. When a hatch of something like big, gray mayflies shows up, we tie on something close and go fishing. When no insects show themselves, we toss whatever looks good to us at the time—Stimulator, Turck's Tarantula, Humpy, Madam X, ant, hopper, etc. As long as the flies are presented in a reasonably competent manner, the trout don't seem to care too much about the rest.

For those rare occasions when we can't pound 'em up top fast enough, we add a dropper nymph such as a Beadhead Prince, Hare's Ear, Bitch Creek, Girdle or Yuk Bug, or strip ugly black, olive, or brown leeches or Woolly Buggers or small Clousers.

Restaurants and Accommodations

Any fishing expedition to this part of the country should include a stop for breakfast, lunch, or dinner at the Beartooth Café in Cooke City (US 212, 406-838-2475). Check out the breakfast omelets or the chili for lunch; the steaks rank among the best we've had. The café also boasts over a hundred brands of beer.

Right across the street, the Prospector Restaurant (209 US 212, 1-800-527-6462) runs a close second on our list of favorite Cooke City eateries. They have good sandwiches and soup for lunch, great steaks for dinner, and a bartender who doesn't skimp on the hard stuff.

We have a friend who's been staying at the Soda Butte Lodge in Cooke City (209 US 212, 1-800-527-6462) each September for so long we half expect the owners to change the name in his honor. It hasn't happened so far, but since we trust his judgment implicitly we have to believe the place has a lot going for it, even though we've never stayed there.

We usually choose to camp outside Cooke City at Fox Creek, right off US 212 and conveniently located right beside the upper Clark Fork. By the time you read this the Soda Butte Campground (USFS, off US 212 just outside Cooke City) renovations should be completed, which might give us a new favorite camping spot in the area.

Cooke City, Montana

Each time we visit Cooke, I can't help but wonder whose idea it was to make this a Montana community. Why not Cooke City, Wyoming? It would seem to make more sense, since all the roads that lead here are Wyoming highways, and the only other direct connection to civilized Montana traverses miles and miles of rugged wilderness. Actually, I think most of the 90 or so permanent residents rather like not having a direct umbilical to the mother-state anyway.

No doubt it's largely because of this separation that Cooke comes off as an independent place with a big reputation for societal misfits. We have, however, always found it a delightful place to visit. The natives seem especially friendly and good-humored folks, although some do get a might testy during the height of the summer and winter tourist seasons. But who can blame them.

While there's not much fishing up here in January, it's worth a visit just to see the immense amount of snow. By New Year's, the snow is literally piled up to the eaves of single-story structures. But with the snow comes a huge armada of snarling snow machines.

In summer most of the Cooke City's tourists seem to have their sights set on hiking and biking the nearby Beartooth Plateau and Yellowstone National Park. But the sly fly angler can still ferret a ton of insider info from savvy locals. In other words,

A picturesque stretch of water.

tone down the arrogant outsider attitude and strike up a little friendly conversation down at the pub or general store. By the way, you can buy your Wyoming fishing license here.

Nearby Fisheries

The Absaroka-Beartooth Wilderness

The pursuit of wild trout has a lot going for it, not the least of which is the chance to hang out in some of the wildest, prettiest places around—the Absaroka-Beartooth Wilderness, for example. Named for the encompassing Absaroka and Beartooth Mountains, the vast wilderness straddles the Montana-Wyoming line. Montanans call it "the roof of Montana," while down Wyoming way they know it as "the top of the world." Here, we'll concentrate on the Wyoming version, though there's little difference from one side of the boundary to the other.

Three blacktop roads access the Wyoming side. You can drive up Sunlight Basin out of Cody via the Chief Joseph Scenic Highway or come down from Red Lodge, Montana on the winding Beartooth Highway or take the less spectacular, though far from ho-hum, route through northern Yellowstone Park. For scenic splendor, we give all three rave reviews.

The trout in the area's waters, though wild and colorful, aren't known for their huge size. This is high country, with most of the terrain at or above 10,000 feet. Hence, there's a short growing season. Snow and ice often linger well into July, and the first fall snow is likely to fall before Labor Day. And the heavily glaciated, granite-lined lakes make for less than ideal food factories, further limiting trout growth. Bottom line, with very few exceptions, flyfishing the Beartooth Lakes is not about catching big trout.

But picture this: a mirror-smooth high mountain lake, the surface ruffled only by the spreading concentric rings of dozens of rise forms made by trout dimpling and swirling, frantically trying to take full advantage of a sparse hatch of dark mayflies. Then frame the scene in every direction with 12,000-foot peaks and a pale blue sky.

Within the Absaroka-Beartooth there are about 450 alpine lakes that hold fish, and the only real question is how far to hike. And since most of the lakes lie inside the wilderness boundary, where motorized vehicles are prohibited, you will indeed be hiking unless you bring a horse. There are a few vehicle-accessible lakes near the highway, though, and these can be fun fishing when you want to stretch your legs after a long drive.

Also, many of the more popular trailheads are found at the drive-in lakes. Several other lakes scattered just outside the wilderness boundary can be accessed by 4-wheel-drive vehicles with high clearance.

The area receives more than passing interest from backpackers and the horsy set. Some fish, but many just go to experience the wilderness. In an ideal world, fly-fishers who want a lake all to themselves would need only hike a little farther, but in the real world we all know the ideal is rarely the reality. Put bluntly, if you want to be alone forget the July Fourth and Labor Day weekends, and just hope for the best on the days in between.

The lakes contain a surprising variety of trout: brook, cutthroat, golden, lake, rainbow, and splake, as well as arctic grayling. Most are 4 to 12 inches on average, but the occasional lunker does show up. A few of the more fertile lakes produce larger trout, but nothing to rival the monsters more typical of lowland lakes.

The best flyfishing occurs during a hatch or when the wind drops land-born insects like ants and beetles all around your float tube—a phenomenal occurrence known as a vortex. It's impossible to predict where or when such events might occur, so you just get lucky or you don't.

A prime example occurred one August afternoon last summer as I sat in my float tube on a little lake partway up the trail from the Beartooth Lake Campground. All morning and half the afternoon I'd been trying just about every trick in the book, with nothing to show for the effort. Just as I was about to give up, suddenly the lake came alive. Trout swirled and slashed the surface around my tube. When a big black carpenter ant bounced off the tube and lit struggling on the surface, I had all the clues I needed. I fumbled around my fly boxes for a #10 Deer Hair Ant and for the next hour or so enjoyed some fast fishing. No monsters, but the 8- to 12-inch rainbows provided nearly nonstop action, and their appearance turned a sure bust into a wonderful day.

During an aquatic insect hatch, high mountain trout can on rare occasions become a bit finicky. But the trout are usually so thrilled to find an easy meal for a change that they'll gobble just about anything that lands in the cruising lane.

On our last trip to the lakes, we hit a series of major thunderstorms that sent us packing for the highway. Of course, the sun came out as soon as we reached the trailhead, so we drove to Beartooth Lake right beside the road, ate lunch on the tailgate, and watched the lake fill with the concentric rings of rising trout. We launched the float tube, made a few casts, and caught a couple of brookies and a 14-inch cutthroat before the day's worst lightning, wind, rain, and hail again forced a retreat to the truck. Soon the sun came back out and the dimples reappeared. Once again we launched the tube, and, of course, this time they quit rising almost before we could manage a cast.

Meanwhile, a truck bearing Wisconsin plates parked next to ours, and a guy got out, pulled on waders, strung a fly rod, waded in, and began stripping what looked like a black Woolly Bugger. He started catching trout right away. Impressed (or impressionable), we immediately switched to a black Woolly and were tight to fish.

Finally, another thundercloud with all the fixings rolled by, and we dashed to the truck for the last time. Just another day of fishing in the high country.

Nearby Attractions and Activities

The triangle formed by Red Lodge, Montana; Cody, Wyoming; and Yellowstone National Park is an outdoor lover's paradise. If you like it natural and wild there's no better place to be in the northern Rockies.

The Chief Joseph Highway may not be "the most scenic drive in America," but it's damn close.

Author's Tip

If you really want an awesome flyfishing experience, venture down into the gorge below Crandall Creek. Get in shape and pare down the outfit: rod, reel, small box of high-floating attractor flies, spare tippet (3X is usually fine), forceps, and a stiff hiking staff. No waders are necessary, as they just get in the way. Early fall is by far the best time.

Favorite Fly

Orange Stimulator

Hook	#6-16 Mustad 94841 (or equivalent)
Tail	Dark elk or deer hair
Abdomen	Orange dubbing
Thorax	Hot-orange Antron
Hackle	Palmered grizzly rear (sized short), palmered grizzly front
Wing	Dark elk or deer hair

Fast Facts

Clark's Fork of the Yellowstone River

Location	Access off US 212 and the Chief Joseph Scenic Highway between Cooke City, Montana, and Cody, Wyoming
Water Type	Wyoming's only Wild and Scenic river, fast flowing, rugged canyons, mountain river
Primary Gamefish	Brook trout in upper reaches, rainbows and a smattering of cutthroats in midsections, brown trout lower down, and a few grayling

Best Time	Anytime after runoff in the canyons and lower section; usually fishable by July; upper sections best in fall
Best Flies	Incredible fly hatches throughout; but trout aren't fussy. Carry a good selection of basic dries, nymphs, and streamers, and you should have it covered.
Equipment	9-foot, 4- to 6-weight rod, floating line, leaders tapered to suit the fly and method; trout aren't leader shy
Conditions	Wade fishing in the upper reaches, but not recommended in the canyons; extremely difficult getting around in lower canyon, bouldering skills help; floating is not an option; lower river is floatable but some take-outs require advance planning; check locally prior to launch.
Drive Time	From Cody to the upper river: appx. 2 hours From Bozeman to midsection: appx. 3.5 hours From Billings to the upper river: appx. 2 hours
Directions	From Cody, take WY 120 north to WY 296 (Chief Joseph Highway) to US 212, access from highway; from Bozeman, take I-90 west to Livingston, MT 89 south to Gardiner and Yellowstone NP north entrance, follow park roads to the northeast entrance, US 212 and WY 296 to access river; from Billings, take I-90 east to Laurel, MT, US 212 to Red Lodge, the Beartooth Highway to WY 296 to access river.

Local Fly Shops

Yellowstone Troutfitters
239 Yellowstone Ave.
Cody, WY 82414
307-587-8240

Aune's Absaroka Angler
754 Yellowstone Ave.
Cody, WY 82414
307-587-5105

North Fork Anglers
1438 Sheridan
Cody, WY 82414
307-527-7274

Outdoor Sports Center
1131 12th St.
Cody, WY 82414
307-587-9526

Park's Fly Shop
P.O. Box 196
Gardiner, MT 59030
406-848-7314

Guides

Bill Cody Ranch
307-587-2097

Grub Steak Expeditions
1-800-527-6316/307-527-6316

Crescent B Outfitting
307-587-6925

Dean Johnson Outfitting
1-800-843-7885/307-587-4072

Contacts

Wyoming Game and Fish Department
Region 2 Fisheries Supervisor
2820 Hwy. 120
Cody, WY 82414
1-800-654-1178/307-527-7125

Almost every plunge pool holds hungry trout.

CHAPTER 33

Coeur d'Alene Lakes
Variety in Small Packages

For variety, the Coeur d'Alene Chain Lakes—Anderson, Black, Blue, Bull Run, Cave, Killarney, Medicine, Rose, Swan, and Thompson—in northern Idaho's panhandle are hard to beat. On any given cast you may hook up with a bass, bluegill, crappie, northern pike, or perch. There are rumors of cutthroat and rainbow trout too, though we've never caught any.

In late May last year we found the lakes suffering from a serious lack of water due to an abnormally low snowpack in the surrounding mountains. Many normal hotspots were high and dry, and we spent a large portion of four days searching out new places with enough water to make casting our flies worthwhile. But when we did find enough water the fish were willing.

One cloudy, breezy afternoon on Thompson Lake was typical of the fishing we experienced. After a frustrating morning of fish hunting, around lunchtime I suddenly got into the crappies. For the next two hours one after another grabbed my #10 olive and yellow Woolly Bugger.

Meanwhile, Gale had rowed around the corner into a small bay full of weeds and lily pads, and just as suddenly she found a whole swarm of hungry bass willing

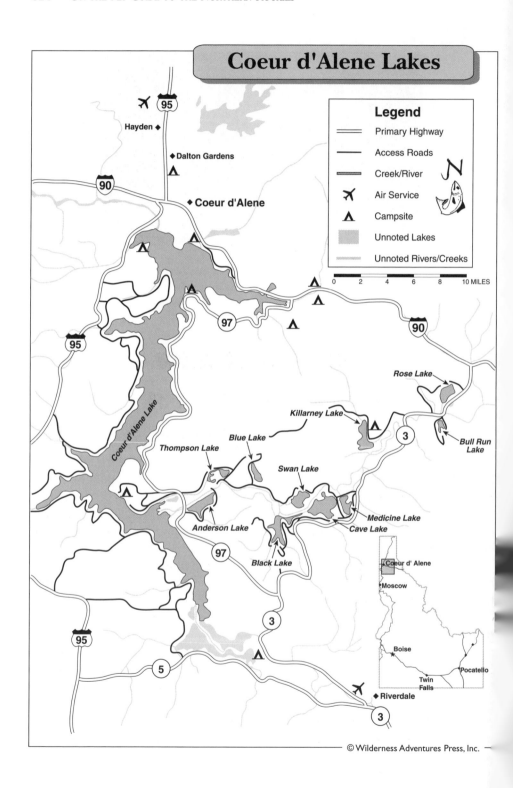

Coeur d'Alene Lakes

Legend

Primary Highway	
Access Roads	
Creek/River	
Air Service	
Campsite	
Unnoted Lakes	
Unnoted Rivers/Creeks	

N

0   2   4   6   8   10 MILES

Hayden

Dalton Gardens

Coeur d'Alene

Coeur d'Alene Lake

Rose Lake

Killarney Lake

Blue Lake

Thompson Lake

Bull Run Lake

Swan Lake

Medicine Lake

Anderson Lake

Cave Lake

Black Lake

Coeur d'Alene

Moscow

Boise

Pocatello

Twin Falls

Riverdale

© Wilderness Adventures Press, Inc.

to gobble her Chartreuse Slider. When the bass action slowed, she tied on a small Prince Nymph trailer and topped off the action with a bunch of hand-sized bluegills and a few fat perch.

Fishing the Coeur d'Alene Lakes

As lakes go, with the exception of Coeur d'Alene Lake itself, these are on the small side and can easily be fished from a float tube or kick boat, but electric- or gasoline-powered boats, skiffs, or canoes provide more mobility and easier access. You can put your boat in via the river and simply motor between the lakes.

Public access to individual lakes varies. For instance, about the only way to access Swan Lake is from the river by boat, while Killarney Lake offers a public boat ramp and campground right off the road. Of course, for tubers and kick-boaters public access does not necessarily jive with the best fishing spots—probably the best argument for bringing a motor.

Fly patterns for the lakes depend a lot on what species you're after. Pike like big flies that create a big fuss in the water, 6-inch Double Bunnies, leeches, and magnum Clousers and Dahlberg Divers. Chartreuse and white, yellow and white, and red and white are good color combinations for exciting the toothsome predators.

Bass can often be teased into blasting surface flies. Try a deer hair or cork popper, slider, or Dahlberg Diver in #1/0 to #6. On other days it pays to go subsurface with leeches, Buggers, Clousers, and the like. Bluegills and crappie fall for smaller versions of the above patterns, as well as small feathered jigs and weighted nymphs suspended under a strike indicator. Bluegill are usually much more willing than crappie to feed on the surface.

Restaurants and Accommodations

The Coeur d'Alene area is so blessed with good eateries that naming just a couple isn't really fair, but here are a few favorites. For lunch, check out Blondee's Deli-Café (1527 Northwest Boulevard, 208-667-9998). They serve great sandwiches, huge and delicious fresh salads, and two homemade soups of the day, as well as daily and weekly specials.

For dinner, try the broiled halibut or top sirloin steak at Crickets Steakhouse and Oyster Bar (424 Sherman Ave., 208-765-1990), or if you like a little jazz and blues with your dinner try the Wine Cellar (313 Sherman Ave., 208-664-9463).

Capone's Sports Pub and Grill (751 North 4th) boasts 41 taps, a more than ample variety of suds to slake any thirst. The hotspot for serious after-dark partying is the Iron Horse (664 Sherman Ave., 208-667-7314).

The USFS campground at Bell Bay (Coeur d'Alene Lake) ranks high on our list of favorites sleeping spots. It also gets high marks for its central location to the Chain Lakes; however, there is no launch ramp to the big lake.

Hidden Creek Ranch (7600 E. Blue Lake Rd., 1-800-446-3833) not only sits in one of the prettiest little valleys imaginable, it's also close to the main action. As is the Osprey Inn Bed and Breakfast (208-689-9502), which overlooks Coeur d'Alene Lake and is close to Thompson and Anderson Lakes.

Coeur d'Alene, Idaho

Known in some circles as the "Playground of the Pacific Northwest," Coeur d'Alene sprang to life in 1847 with the building of the Mission of the Sacred Heart just up the road at Cataldo. Held together by wooden pegs, straw, and river mud it is Idaho's oldest standing building.

Casting the evening rise.

The famous (or infamous from an environmental standpoint) and historic Silver Valley, lying just to the east of Cataldo, was once home to the richest lead and silver mines in the country. Silverwood, just north of town, is said to be the world's largest theme park.

One local bragged, "Once you've seen Coeur d'Alene it may be hard to leave." And many writers have labeled the town and surroundings among the nation's most spectacular. While I doubt they were speaking of flyfishing, they actually hit the nail pretty well on the head.

Nearby Fisheries

The myriad smaller bays of sprawling Coeur d'Alene Lake provide even kick-boaters and tubers with an endless variety of flyfishing opportunities, although adding motor power obviously provides a lot more. The big lake contains cold and warmwater fishes, from cutthroat trout and chinook salmon to outsized northern pike.

Rocky points, steep banks, and dropoffs are good places to start looking for trout and salmon, while warmwater species tend to hang out in the back bays near weeds, lily pads, and other structure.

Rising trout can often be found in the bays, especially early morning and late evening. For example, on our late May trip we spied rising trout from our campsite overlooking Bell Bay almost every morning and evening. All I had to do was launch a float tube to get in on the action.

March Browns were the attraction, and during May and early June they're one of the lake's best hatches. A good strategy is to mimic the swimming action of the nymphs. We rig a sink-tip line, or sometimes a full-sink, tie on a pair of suggestive, buggy-looking nymphs, and slowly strip the line as we kick along, concentrating on steep banks, rip-rap, or other trouty-looking spots.

Two other events flyfishers plying the big lake should note are the annual carpenter ant dispersion flights of early summer and the wind-borne stink bug beetles, or "leptos" as the locals call them, in October.

Nearby Attractions and Activities

While I'm no bike enthusiast, if I were I'd have a new address pronto. The 72-mile-long Trail of the Coeur d'Alene bicycle trail has to be one of the best cycling facilities around. Built at a cost of around $30 million with funds supplied by the Union Pacific Railroad, it was part of an environmental cleanup agreement.

The paved trail follows the old railroad bed between Mullan and Plummer, mostly right beside the Coeur d'Alene River. There are numerous access points with fancy steel benches and clean and sparkling restrooms, so you can bite off just about whatever chunk of trail suits you. Actually, the whole deal so impressed me the first time I saw it that I came very close to switching avocations. Well, not really, but it *is* a wonderful trail.

An interesting way to kill an hour or so in downtown Coeur d'Alene is to take a stroll on the "World's Longest Floating Boardwalk," which is a 3,300-foot chance to gawk at the fancy architecture and luxurious boats (many of which seem more appropriate for the open ocean than a large inland lake).

Flyfishers who also golf will no doubt want to play the nearby Coeur d'Alene Resort Golf Course. It's the one with the floating green—of course.

Author's Tip

Access to the Chain Lakes begins via two terribly narrow and crooked roads, Highways 3 and 97. The former is crooked, narrow, and too damn busy (truck traffic galore), while the latter is merely crooked and narrow. So, with safety and sanity in mind, it pays to base your operation as near the action as possible. Harrison or one of the nearby campgrounds or the many fishing accesses that also allow camping are all good choices. While staying in Coeur d'Alene sounds cushy, it would be a nightmare drive to and from the lakes each morning and evening.

Favorite Fly

Dahlberg Diver

Hook	#1/0 to #6 3X-long streamer hook
Tail	Bunny strip
Head	Spun and clipped deer hair with a distinct collar makes the fly dive when stripped

Fast Facts

Coeur d'Alene Lakes

Location	Series of lakes on the Coeur d'Alene River generally south and east of the city of Coeur d'Alene, Idaho
Water Type	Warmwater lakes varying in size from huge Coeur d'Alene Lake to 1,720-acre Cave Lake to 100-acre Bull Run Lake
Primary Gamefish	Pike, largemouth bass, crappie, and bluegill; some of the bigger lakes have cutthroat trout
Best Time	While bait and hardware fishing heats up as early as February or March, the best time to flyfish is May through November
Best Flies	Clousers, Dahlberg Divers, sliders, poppers, leeches, Woolly Buggers. March Brown and carpenter ant "hatches" of May and June and "leptos" beetles of October can provide top-notch cutthroat action, especially in the smaller bays of Coeur d'Alene Lake.
Equipment	Some sort of boat is almost mandatory; motorboats can access nearly all the lakes from a single put-in on the Coeur d'Alene River; even electric motors allow anglers to cover a lot of water.
Conditions	Expect warm to cool weather, but come prepared for hot to cold; not particularly windy, but it can still be rough for tubers.
Drive Time	From Spokane: 45 minutes From Missoula: 2.75 hours From Idaho Falls: 7.5 hours

Local Fly Shops

Northwest Outfitters/Orvis
402 Canfield & Hwy. 95
Coeur d'Alene, ID 83815
208-772-1497

Black Sheep Sporting Goods and Toys
308 W Seale Ave.
Coeur d'Alene, ID 83815
208-667-7831

Castaway Flyfishing Shop
350 Bosanko
Coeur d'Alene, ID 83815
208-765-3133

Pine Street Pawn and Flyfishing Shop
525 Pine
Sandpoint, ID 83864
208-263-6022

Dig-In Outfitters
2425 N. Government Way
Coeur d'Alene, ID 83815
208-664-7922

St. Joe Sport Shop
402 College Ave.
St. Maries, ID 83861
208-245-4417

Fins and Feathers Tackle Shop and
    Guide Service
1816 Sherman Ave.
Coeur d'Alene, ID 83815
208-667-9304

Blue Goose Sport Shop
621 Main St.
St. Maries, ID 83861
208-245-4015

Guides

Panhandle Outfitters, Inc & Orvis
    Endorsed Flyfishing
1-888-300-4868

St. Joe Outfitters and Guides
208-245-4002

Priest River Guide Service
208-661-1146

Contacts

IDFG
Panhandle Region
2750 Kathleen Ave.
Coeur d'Alene, ID 83814
208-769-1414

CHAPTER 34

HAYDEN LAKE
Not Wilderness, But Still Good Fishing

Hayden Lake is one of the best warmwater flyfishing lakes around, with 16-inch-plus largemouth and smallmouth bass, lunker pike, and crappie as big as they get in the northern Rockies. The bad news is that public shore access sucks. Combine this with the region's heavy highway traffic and what might just be the world's most crooked road, and you have to really love to fish to enjoy your visit here. But, of course, you *do* love to fish or you wouldn't be reading this book.

Hayden is not the biggest lake in Idaho, but it's no small puddle—4,000 acres and 40 miles of shoreline. For flyfishers without a motorboat, the access issue is major since there are just two official public accesses to the entire lake, one at the south end, the other in downtown Hayden. Both require a hell of a long kick to the better flyfishing spots at the north end of the lake.

An alternative, also far south of what we consider the best fishing area, is a private marina that extracts a fee to launch. So, that leaves Sportsman's Park or jumping in at one of the rare spots where the road touches the lake but isn't posted or lined with houses. Of course, you could also search for a soft touch who will allow you to

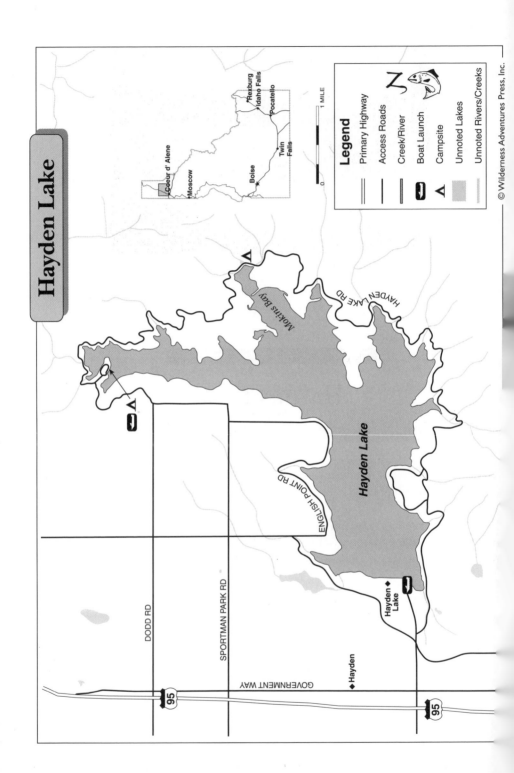

Hayden Lake

launch at a private dock. At first glance, the latter idea doesn't sound too appealing, but as a Hayden Lake regular told Gale, "There are 359 docks, you know!"

How the two got around to discussing that little bit of trivia was never made entirely clear to me, but such a number also means a host of potential casting targets, since just about anyone who fishes Hayden on a regular basis will tell you that everything that swims eventually ends up under or around one of those docks.

Our normal procedure here involves pitching camp at the USFS campground at Mokins Bay, lugging the tube and pontoon down the road to the water, and launching while no one is looking. I can't really say whether or not this is legal, but no one has ever told us it isn't.

Anyway, casting poppers, sliders, and deer hair bugs, or a #8 Shenk's White Streamer in around the lily pads usually provides hours of entertainment and a mixed bag of largemouth bass, crappie, the occasional pike, and even a perch or two. Just outside the lily pads can be a hotspot for crappie, but catching a bunch often requires a change in tactics from topwater patterns to dangling something tempting underneath a bobber. The above-mentioned Shenk's White or perhaps a #10 olive and yellow Conehead Woolly Bugger works well, particularly if you give the fly a gentle twitch every now and then.

The lake is relatively skinny up there, so with little or no wind even I can kick around a bunch of docks in a day. A more mobile flyfisher would without doubt run out of daylight long before running out of targets.

Restaurants and Accommodations

There isn't all that much right in Hayden itself, but in Coeur d'Alene, just 5 miles down the road, there are enough eateries to keep you from going hungry. For starters, check out GW Hunters Steak and Pub (2108 N. Fourth St., 208-765-9388), which has a unique and varied menu, microbrews, and a nifty hunting lodge atmosphere. If you develop a craving for a little junk food, or just a snack, head for I.C. Sweets (602 E. Sherman Ave., 208-664-1549) and pig out on frozen custard ice cream made in house daily. Or try a Chicago-style hotdog, homemade pretzel, or a bunch of other decadent diet busters.

The USFS campground at Mokins Bay is nestled in the trees on the north end of the lake, and as pointed out above, it's just a relatively short hop to the water. In spring and fall, the campground is usually uncrowded. On weekends, of course, all bets are off. Sportsman's Park, a few miles closer to Hayden, gets more traffic, but stick to weekdays both early and late in the season and the ruckus shouldn't be too bad.

Author's Tip

Get a motorboat and cruise out to one of the smaller bays to pound the boundless private docks. Bring a fly box full of hair bugs, poppers, and sliders in chartreuse, black, white, and yellow; brown and black leeches and Woolly Buggers, also olive and yellow Woolly Buggers; chartreuse and white, red and white, and yellow and white Clousers; and Shenk's White Minnows. Once the summer rush starts, the best fishing—often the only fishing—is early and late in the day before the boat traffic gears up.

Favorite Fly

Shenk's White Minnow

Hook	#1/0 to 6 Mustad 9672 (or equivalent), weighted with lead wire
Tail	White marabou/Krystal Flash
Body	Clipped white rabbit

Fast Facts

Hayden Lake

Location	5 miles north of Coeur d'Alene, Idaho via Hwy. 95
Water Type	Warmwater lake, 4,000 acres with 40 miles of shoreline, highly developed with difficult shore access
Primary Gamefish	Large- and smallmouth bass, crappie, pike
Best Time	April through June and again in September and October
Best Flies	Poppers and sliders, leeches, Buggers, and Clousers

Equipment	9- to 10-foot rods, 6- to 9-weight floating, sink-tip and full-sink lines with tapered leaders to suit the fly and species; wire or heavy shock tippet for pike
Conditions	Biggest drawback is the lack of shoreline access; motorized boats make for less hassle and obviously allow anglers to cover far more water.
Drive Time	From Spokane: 45 minutes From Missoula: 2.75 hours From Idaho Falls: over 7 hours
Directions	From Spokane, I-90 east to Coeur d'Alene, north on Hwy. 95 to Sportsman's Park Road; from Missoula, I-90 west to Coeur d'Alene, north on Hwy. 95 to Sportsman's Park Road; from Idaho Falls, north on I-15 to I-90 west to Coeur d'Alene, north on Hwy. 95 to Sportsman's Park Road.

Local Fly Shops

Northwest Outfitters/Orvis
402 Canfield & Hwy. 95
Coeur d'Alene, ID 83815
208-772-1497

Castaway Flyfishing Shop
350 Bosanko
Coeur d'Alene, ID 83815
208-765-3133

Dig-In Outfitters
2425 N. Government Way
Coeur d'Alene, ID 83815
208-664-7922

Fins and Feathers Tackle Shop and
    Guide Service
1816 Sherman Ave.
Coeur d'Alene, ID 83815
208-667-9304

Black Sheep Sporting Goods and Toys
308 W Seale Ave.
Coeur d'Alene, ID 83815
208-667-7831

Pine Street Pawn and Flyfishing Shop
525 Pine
Sandpoint, ID 83864
208-263-6022

St. Joe Sport Shop
402 College Ave.
St. Maries, ID 83861
208-245-4417

Blue Goose Sport Shop
621 Main St.
St. Maries, ID 83861
208-245-4015

Contacts

IDFG
Panhandle Region
2750 Kathleen Ave.
Coeur d'Alene, ID 83814
208-769-1414

Idaho Travel Dept.
700 W. State St., 2nd Floor
Boise, ID 83720
1-800-VISIT ID, 208-334-2470

Supervisor
Idaho Panhandle National Forest
1201 Ironwood Dr.
Coeur d'Alene, ID 83814
208-765-7223

*Moxins Bay on northern Idaho's Hayden Lake; a good spot
to hunt bass, crappie, and pike.*

CHAPTER 35

MONSTER LAKE

Serious Trout, for a Few Dollars More

I no longer engage in arguments about whether it's more fun to catch one 10-pound trout or 10 one-pounders because there is no resolution. To each his own. But having said that, and after giving the matter serious thought, I've concluded that we all deserve at least one truly big trout—a trout so big that nobody even thinks to ask it's length, just "How the hell much does that sucker weigh?"

The northern Rockies has more than its fair share of big trout spots: Clark Canyon Reservoir, Warm Springs Settling Ponds, Henry's Lake, the Beaverhead and Bighorn Rivers, to say nothing of numerous private ponds and spring creeks. However, few measure up to Hugh and Melissa Fraser's Monster Lake (8 miles south of Cody on Hwy. 120, 1-800-840-5137). When you consider that Monster's rainbows and browns run 18 to 28 inches, with some over 10 pounds, and that the brookies run 15 to 22 inches, with some to 5½ pounds, it becomes obvious that these are serious trout by any angling standard.

Steve Bassett, lake manager and chief guide, generously agreed to pose a few of his pet rainbows for our benefit. So cameras locked and loaded, we spent a beautiful April morning stalking him as he cast over the mirror-smooth surface of the lake.

Monster Lake near Cody, Wyoming, is home to big trout.

Despite the pretty day, however, some of the trout apparently had other agendas. In particular, the male rainbows had territorial grievances on their minds and weren't the least bit interested in his offerings. Brown and brook trout too, regardless of gender, were conspicuous in their absence. As for the buck rainbows, time after time he laid down what looked to us like perfect casts only to have the fish scoot off in hot pursuit of interlopers.

But the hen rainbows were another matter. Evidently not quite ready to spawn, the girls were far more cooperative. One of every dozen or so casts resulted in a take. While fishing, Steve maintained a nearly nonstop banter concerning Monster's history, which began nine years ago when the trout averaged a whopping 8 pounds. He described the array of hatches from damsel, Callibaetis, midge, and caddis to a mysterious tiny mayfly and the great hopper fishing, and told anecdotes like the one about the celebrity bass angler who insisted on "lipping" countless big trout until both thumbs were mangled and bleeding profusely or the guide who was bitten by a rattler while catching hoppers to chum trout for the delight of a visiting cameraman.

Meanwhile, in a far corner of the 180-acre lake, three clients were knocking 'em dead, having caught well over 50 fish between them by midmorning. When you consider that nearly every 'bow caught measures between 18 and 21 inches, that is a mindboggling fishing record.

Fishing Monster Lake

Throughout the fishing season, the weather can be hot, arctic, or anything in between—sometimes all in the same day.

Mid-March means ice-out, chironomids, egg patterns, ravenous trout, and often iced-up rod guides. Anglers typically rack up some of the biggest numbers of the year at this time. May brings the first Callibaetis hatch and signals the start of the long dry fly season, which more or less lasts until freeze-up kills off the last hoppers. June is damsel time, and big fish cruise the shallows looking to ambush the lively nymphs. July through October is hopper time, and some of the most exciting hopper fishing occurs after dark.

Imagine the lake, glass smooth and cloaked in inky darkness, the only sounds the dip of oars and the far off yodeling of a coyote family. Suddenly you hear *kersploosh!* and find yourself hanging on for dear life as a double-digit brown trout runs off with your hopper, putting a serious hurt on your reel's drag system, to say nothing about the strain on your pounding heart.

There's a hefty rod fee to fish on this private lake, but it certainly offers one of the best chances to land that fish of a lifetime in the northern Rockies.

Restaurants and Accommodations

Nearby Cody has enough variety to satisfy even the most eclectic tastes, but three eateries rate high on our list. The Proud Cut Saloon (1220 Sheridan Ave., 307-527-6905) is a great dinner spot. Cassie's Supper Club (214 Yellowstone Ave., 307-527-5500) is a popular restaurant and for good reason: great seafood and even better steaks, with live music and dancing on the weekends. And Zapata's Mexican Restaurant (1362 Sheridan Ave., 307-527-7181) serves tasty salsa, tamales, and enchiladas, and the fried ice-cream dessert is beyond description.

Monster Lake (29 Nielson Rd., 1-800-840-5137) can accommodate up to 14 guests in comfortable, quiet, well-appointed rooms with kitchen facilities. Three-bed units run $80 per night; four-bed units $100 per night. Washer and dryer facilities are available, as well.

If you opt to stay in nearby Cody, the Sunset Best Western (1601 8th St., 307-587-4265) and the Rainbow Park (1136 17th St., 1-800-710-6930) are just two of many great places to stay.

Nearby Fisheries

The Shoshone River from the Buffalo Bill Reservoir down through the town of Cody holds some very good trout and fishes particularly well in late winter and early spring. But once irrigation starts, you can forget it, since dam releases are too erratic for good fishing. Browns to 25 inches and good numbers of 10- to 16-inch cutts and rainbows are the attraction when river flows are stable. The river all the way down to Powell is a popular winter fishery.

Author's Tip

It's worth hiring a guide for at least the first day of your first visit to Monster Lake. Even if you're a veteran fly angler, you'll learn a lot from Steve Bassett and his crew about the nuances of Monster and about stillwater flyfishing in general.

Favorite Fly

Clouser Minnow

Hook	#2-6 streamer hook with lead eyes
Wing	Dark bucktail on the back; Krystal Flash in the center; white bucktail on the bottom. (Remember that this fly rides hook-point up, so build the wing accordingly— sparse works best.)

Fast Facts

Monster Lake

Location	10 miles south of Cody, Wyoming, on Hwy. 120
Water Type	Fertile, 180-acre private lake (fee access)
Primary Gamefish	Primarily rainbows, with brown and brook trout
Best Time	Ice-out to freeze-up, generally April to November, reservations required
Best Flies	Steve Bassett will advise upon reservation
Equipment	Rods must be 5-weight or heavier, floating and sink-tip lines depending on conditions. Tippets on the heavy side are recommended.
Conditions	Typical high-desert weather; wind is common, and sudden changes should be expected. Fishing is from shore, float tubes, pontoon craft, and small skiffs with electric motors only.
Drive Time	From Casper: appx. 5 hours
	From Billings: 2.25 hours
	From Bozeman: 4 hours
Directions	From Casper, take US 20-26 west to Thermopolis, 120 west to Cody; from Billings, take I-90 east to Ranchester, US 14 west to Greybull, US 14-16-20 west to Cody; from Bozeman, take I-90 east to Livingston, US 89 south to Gardiner, take Mammoth Hot Springs-Cooke City road, US 212 east to WY 296 (Chief Joseph Hwy.) to WY 120 east to Cody.

Local Fly Shops

Yellowstone Troutfitters
239 Yellowstone Ave.
Cody, WY 82414
307-587-8240

Aune's Absaroka Angler
754 Yellowstone Ave.
Cody, WY 82414
307-587-5105

North Fork Anglers
1438 Sheridan
Cody, WY 82414
307-527-7274

Outdoor Sports Center
1131 12th St.
Cody, WY 82414
307-587-9526

Guides

Fishing is by reservation only, guide can be arranged through the Monster Lake staff:

Monster Lake
29 Nielson Rd.
Cody, WY 82414
1-800-840-5137

Steve Bassett, manager and head guide, hooks into a typically fat rainbow.

CHAPTER 36

THE NORTHWEST LAKES
Enough Variety to Last a Lifetime

Pull out your trusty copy of the *Montana Atlas and Gazetteer* and refer to pages 54, 65, 66, 67, 82, and 83; notice all the lakes. There's enough variety in both water and species to keep even the most devout fly caster going for several lifetimes. For example, consider the Thompson Chain Lakes off US 2 west of Kalispell: Banana, Bootjack, Crystal, Horseshoe, Loon, McGregor (Big and Little), and Upper, Middle, and Lower Thompson. The lakes all contain bass and rainbow and/or cutthroat trout, but Middle Thompson also holds brown trout and northern pike, while McGregor is home to some giant lake trout. The lakes vary widely in size, but all can be fished readily with nothing more exotic than a float tube.

The confluence of the Blackfoot and Clearwater Rivers, where Highways 83 and 200 converge, marks the lower end of the Seeley-Swan Valley. Here you'll find a whole string of lake-fishing possibilities, beginning with Harper's Lake and ending with Swan Lake just south of Bigfork, Montana. In between, strung out like pearls on a necklace, are Salmon, Placid, Seeley, Inez, Alva, Rainy, and Clearwater Lakes.

Whenever we find ourselves on Highway 83 we make it a point to sample one or more of these gems. So far, we've caught rainbow and cutthroat trout and north-

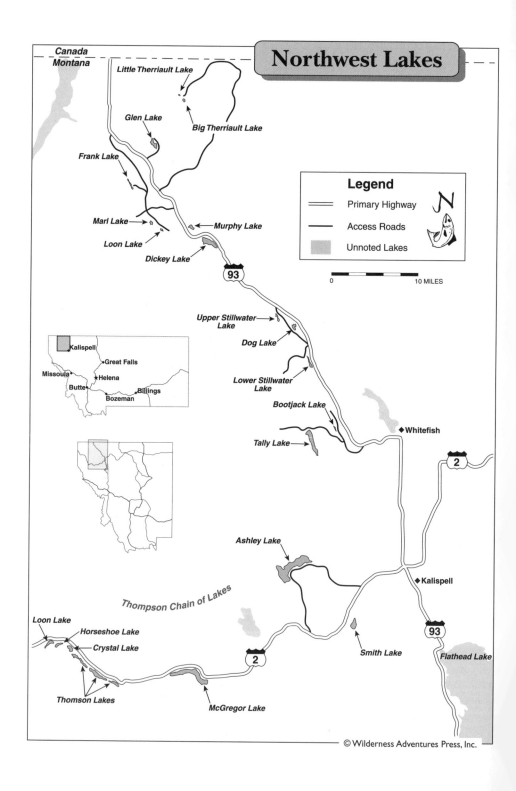

Northwest Lakes

Canada
Montana

Little Therriault Lake

Glen Lake

Big Therriault Lake

Frank Lake

Marl Lake

Murphy Lake

Loon Lake

Dickey Lake

93

Legend

Primary Highway

Access Roads

Unnoted Lakes

0   10 MILES

Upper Stillwater Lake

Dog Lake

Lower Stillwater Lake

Kalispell

Great Falls

Missoula

Helena

Butte

Billings

Bozeman

Bootjack Lake

Whitefish

Tally Lake

2

Ashley Lake

Kalispell

Thompson Chain of Lakes

Loon Lake

Horseshoe Lake

Crystal Lake

2

93

Smith Lake

Flathead Lake

Thomson Lakes

McGregor Lake

© Wilderness Adventures Press, Inc.

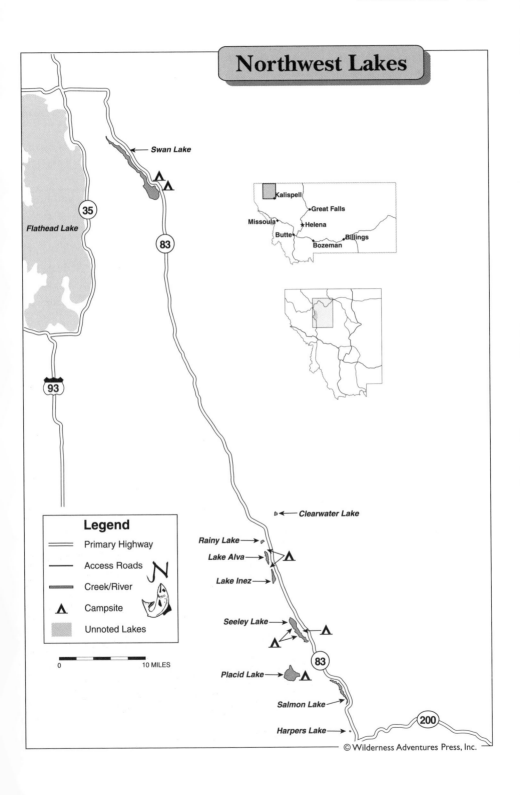

Northwest Lakes

Swan Lake

35

Flathead Lake

83

93

Kalispell

Great Falls

Missoula

Helena

Butte

Billings

Bozeman

Clearwater Lake

Legend

Rainy Lake

Lake Alva

━━━ Primary Highway

━━ Access Roads

━━ Creek/River

Lake Inez

Λ Campsite

Unnoted Lakes

Seeley Lake

0   10 MILES

Placid Lake

83

Salmon Lake

Harpers Lake

200

© Wilderness Adventures Press, Inc.

ern pike from several lakes, had a fun fall afternoon catching modest-sized kokanee salmon on dry flies and nymphs in Placid Lake, and drooled over the giant rainbows plainly visible in the clear water of Harper's Lake. Other lakes within the chain hold many of the above species plus largemouth bass, whitefish, bull trout, and sunfish and perch.

Smith Lake, on US 2 just west of Kalispell, is a fun place to catch ferocious northern pike as well as planted rainbows. And a little farther out of town Ashley Lake is a hotspot for 3- to 5-pound rainbows, with occasional specimens pulling the scales down to double digits. This is a large lake, but not a particularly windy one, although it's also quite the summer playground for water skiers, jet-skiers, and the like. We avoid it completely on weekends from Memorial Day to Labor Day.

It fishes best early in the spring and later in fall. As with most lakes, the best strategy is to fish the shoreline dropoffs by stripping and/or trolling nymphs, Buggers, and leeches. If you do go during the summer, stick to dawn and dusk or cloudy, rainy, windy days. Any insect event here usually brings a rise from the resident cutthroats and rainbows.

Clearwater Lake in the Seeley-Swan Valley with the Bob Marshall Wilderness as backdrop.

US 93 north of Whitefish opens up a whole new world of lake fishing at Upper and Lower Stillwater, Big and Little Therriault, Dog, Murphy, Dickey, Marl, Eureka, Loon, Frank, and Glen Lakes, and a little map study will reveal a host of others. While there isn't room here to cover all the fishing found even in this partial list of waters, I can testify that Dickie, Frank, and Murphy Lakes are fertile and churn out fat rainbows in the 2-pound-plus category with pleasing regularity.

Troll and strip olive or orange scuds or perhaps a nymph, midge, or streamer pattern during non-hatch periods. If you hit a rise, switch to a suitable dry fly trailing a nymph, and match both closely to the naturals. We've had fun days chucking hair bugs and poppers to Dickey Lake largemouth bass, and Dickey also fishes well for fat perch.

Nearby Sophie holds northern pike and sunfish. On summer mornings and evenings strip 6-inch chartreuse and white Double Bunnies to catch the pike. The sunfish are suckers for Rubber-Leg Foam Spiders allowed to sink slowly on a sink-tip line. Tally Lake, by the way, is Montana's deepest natural lake at 492 feet, and it's a pretty place to launch a tube in search of cutthroat, brook, and rainbow trout of average size, along with lake whitefish. However, this is another lake with a lot of curb appeal, so it attracts a large summer horde.

Restaurants and Accommodations

An out-and-out smorgasbord of good eateries abound throughout this region of northwest Montana. Some are pricey, some reasonable. In Seeley Lake, we've enjoyed dining at the Chicken Coop and Lounge (Seeley Lake, 406-677-2980) and Lindy's Prime Steak House (Seeley Lake, 406-677-9229). In Bigfork, the Bigfork Inn (604 Electric Ave., 406-837-6680) is our pick for fine dining. The Top Sirloin does it for me, while Gale is usually torn between the Cajun Shrimp Pasta and Cashew Chicken. After dinner, you can dance to the Big Band sounds of yesteryear and have fun, but that's usually my cue to exit.

At the Painted Horse Grill in Kalispell (110 Main St., 406-257-7035), be sure to try the excellent seafood and game dishes. For a great breakfast, check out the 1950s-style Bojangles Diner (1319 Highway 2 West, 406-755-3222). The diner also serves up pretty tasty salads, chicken, and seafood dishes for lunch and dinner, but the homemade pies and hot fudge sundaes put it off the charts.

Some of the best pizza in the region is concocted in the brick ovens at Truby's Wood Fired Pizza in Whitefish (115 Central Ave., 406-862-4979). This is also the spot to slake your thirst with something from the extensive microbrew and wine list.

For accommodations, the Seeley-Swan Wilderness Gateway Inn (406-677-2095 or 1-800-355-5588) is high on our list of favorites, and the Laughing Horse Lodge in Swan Lake (406-886-2080) comes highly recommended by trusted friends. There are also a host of other motel options in towns like Whitefish, Kalispell, and Bigfork.

If you're into campgrounds, there is a whole bevy of good choices, like Lake Alva (8 miles north of Seeley Lake off Hwy. 83), which has 43 campsites, toilets, and a boat launch. (Call the Seeley Lake Ranger District, 406-677-2233, for reservations.) There is also public camping at many of the other two-dozen or so sizeable lakes within the Seeley-Swan corridor. Farther north, McGregor Lake Campground (32 miles west of Kalispell on Hwy. 2) boasts 22 campsites, water and toilets, but don't bring trailers longer than 32 feet. And up toward Eureka, off US 93, North Dickey Lake Campground provides 25 individual sites, water, and toilets.

Nearby Attractions and Activities

Glacier National Park is just up the road from Kalispell, offering unsurpassed hiking, fishing, whitewater rafting, and wildlife viewing. To the south lies the Seeley-Swan Valley, which borders the rugged Bob Marshall Wilderness and the equally rugged, though smaller, Mission Mountains Wilderness. Hiking and camping opportunities are nearly boundless, and the hunting for ruffed grouse and whitetail deer is among the best Montana has to offer.

Flathead Lake is itself an attraction. At 28 miles long and 7 or 8 wide, it's the largest natural freshwater lake west of the Mississippi. Wild Horse Island is worth a look, as it's home to wild horses, bighorn sheep, and a plethora of birds.

A float tube isn't the most mobile form of transportation, but it sure is handy.

Author's Tip

Toss in the camping gear, fly rod, and a float tube and head up Seeley-Swan or take US 93 north or US 2 west from Kalispell. Stop off at the first lake you come to and give it a go. If things are slow, just move on down the road—it won't be far to the next lake. Camp where and when your casting arm wears out. Watch it, though, as you may never want to go home.

Favorite Fly

Lead-Eye, Rubber-Leg Krystal Bugger

Hook	#1/0-10 streamer hook with lead eyes
Tail	Marabou with Krystal Flash
Body	Chenille, Ice-chenille, Esatz, etc.
Hackle	Palmered over body, collar-style front
Legs	Sili Legs

Fast Facts

The Northwest Lakes

Location	Generally northwest of Clearwater Junction, over to Eureka and west of Kalispell, Montana
Water Type	Mostly natural lakes, varying in size from huge to tiny
Primary Gamefish	Brook, bull, rainbow, and cutthroat trout, largemouth bass, northern pike, kokanee salmon, sunfish, and lake whitefish
Best Time	May and June and again September and October. The bigger lakes, especially on weekends, host a mob of boaters and other non-fishing recreationists in July and August.

Best Flies	Depends on species, and to some extent time of year. Patterns that work for trout and bass in other places work here.
Equipment	9- to 10-foot, 6- to 8-weight rod; full array of floating, sink-tip, and full-sink lines; tapered leaders and tippets to suit the situation. Some sort of watercraft is highly recommended, and motor power helps on bigger lakes.
Conditions	Bigger lakes can be windy and dangerous to small craft and tubes, while smaller lakes are usually safer. Fickle mountain weather can run the gamut daily from cold to hot; storms can be sudden and frequent.
Drive Time to Kalispell	From Bozeman: 6 hours From Missoula: 3 hours From Spokane: appx. 5 hours
Directions to Kalispell	From Bozeman, I-90 west to Missoula, US 93 north to Kalispell; heading to Seeley-Swan, I-90 west to Bonner, Hwy. 200 east to Clearwater Junction, Hwy. 83 north toward Kalispell; from Missoula, US 93 north to Kalispell; heading to the Seeley-Swan, I-90 east to Hwy. 200 east to Hwy. 83 north toward Kalispell; from Spokane, I-90 east to Coeur d'Alene, US 95 north to Bonners Ferry, US 2 east to Kalispell.

Local Fly Shops

Lakestream Fly Shop
15 Central Ave.
Whitefish, MT 59937
406-892-4641

Kootenai Angler
13546 Hwy. 37
Libby, MT 59923
406-293-7578

Glacier Country
945 4th Ave.
Kalispell, MT 59901
406-756-7128

Libby Sports Center
116 E. 9th
Libby, MT 59923
406-293-4641

Open Season
119 E. Idaho
Kalispell, MT 59901
406-755-1298

Green Mountain Sports Center
800 US 93 N
Eureka, MT 59917
406-296-2566

Contacts

Kalispell Chamber of Commerce
15 Detroit Loop
Kalispell, MT 59901
406-752-6166

Kootenai National Forest
Libby, MT 59923
406-293-6211

Lolo National Forest
Missoula, MT 59801
406-329-3750

Eureka Ranger Station
406-296-2536

Clearwater State Forest
406-244-5857

Murphy Lake Ranger Station
406-882-4451

Flathead National Forest
Kalispell, MT 59901
406-758-5204

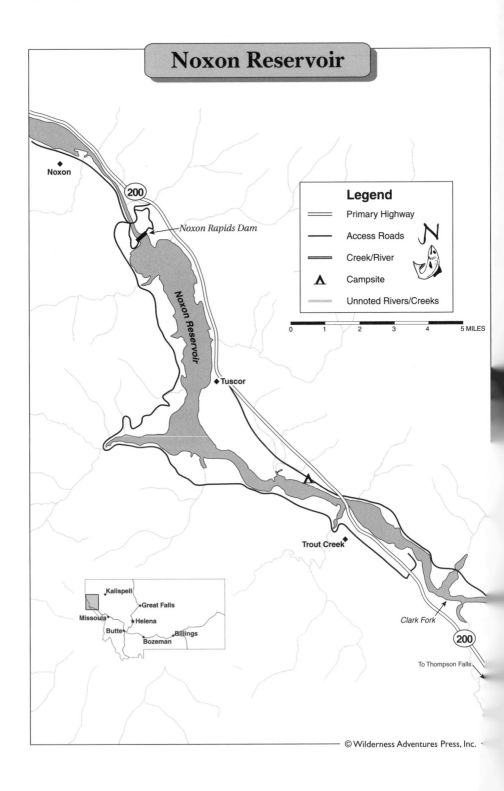

Noxon Reservoir

Noxon

200

Noxon Rapids Dam

Noxon Reservoir

Tuscor

Legend

Primary Highway

Access Roads

Creek/River

▲ Campsite

Unnoted Rivers/Creeks

N

0   1   2   3   4   5 MILES

Trout Creek

Kalispell

Great Falls

Missoula   Helena

Butte   Billings

Bozeman

Clark Fork

200

To Thompson Falls

© Wilderness Adventures Press, Inc.

CHAPTER 37

NOXON RESERVOIR
Northwest Montana Hotspot

Noxon Reservoir, at 30 miles long and nearly 2 miles wide, is a pretty big chunk of bass water for the average small boater to cover. Lacking motorized transport, we usually concentrate our efforts close to the docks, in bays, and in and around the mouths of various tributaries.

Last year, we headed to the reservoir the first week in June, using Highway 472 north of Thompson Falls State Park and the Forest Road between Trout Creek and Noxon to access the lake's smaller nooks and crannies. We found the smallmouth bass in feeding mode, no doubt fattening up for the upcoming spawn. Using sink-tip and full-sink lines, we trolled, stripped, and twitched streamers off the banks and around the smaller flats, finding enough action to make the long drive up from Dillon more than worthwhile.

On another trip we stopped to set up camp at North Shore late one afternoon in September, midway through a week-long cast-and-blast expedition across northwest Montana. We decided there wasn't enough daylight left to launch much of an attack on the local grouse population, so we chose to hunt up a little bass action instead. As the float tube and fly gear are always handy in the truck, we were on the water in no time.

Kicking up toward the railroad bridge, I bombarded the near shoreline with surface and subsurface offerings until a smallie finally smacked a yellow-and-white Clouser. The fish instantly performed two aerial summersaults, then took the fight deep before I was able to wrestle it close enough to hold its lower jaw and twist the hook free. Several casts later I caught one slightly smaller. Then in quick succession I caught a largemouth and a smallmouth, each around a foot long.

I still hadn't quite kicked to the halfway point between the bridge and camp when the sun dropped behind the mountains, bathing the lake in deep shadow. Switching to a Chartreuse Slider, I retraced my path, and before darkness ended the affair I landed three more fat smallies and one similarly robust largemouth.

It was a beautiful evening, and seeing the fish assuaged my guilt for leaving the dog in camp. Best of all, there wasn't another flyfisher in sight.

The author about to release a nice bass.

Restaurants and Accommodations

In nearby Thompson Falls, try Granny's Homecooking (915 W. Main St.) or the Rimrock Lodge (1 mile west on Hwy. 200, 406-827-3356). Granny's gets the nod for breakfast and lunch, while Rimrock is a great spot for dinner.

We've enjoyed stays at the Trout Creek Motel and RV in Trout Creek (406-827-3268) and at the aforementioned Rimrock Lodge. They're nothing fancy, but clean, friendly, and reasonable.

For campers, Marten Creek, located on the lake 7 miles from Trout Creek (FR 2229) in the Kootenai National Forest, is a nifty little campground with just four sites. North Shore, a couple of miles northwest of Trout Creek on Highway 200, is a little bigger (13 sites) and closer to the action. Six miles north of Noxon on Highway 200 you'll find Bull River campground, with 26 sites.

Nearby Fisheries

The Thompson River, just outside of Thompson Falls, is not on many lists of destination hotspots for fly anglers, and probably rightly so. Compared to Montana's many blue-ribbon trout fisheries, the Thompson pales both in numbers of trout and average size. However, what it lacks in those departments, it makes up for in scenic splendor. The Thompson is a pretty little trout stream by almost any standard.

The river supports brook, rainbow, brown, and cutthroat trout, as well as mountain whitefish and protected bull trout. It's fun water to fish as well, with meadows, forested canyons, deep pools and runs, shallow riffles, and boulder-strewn pocket water. Many of the normal Western hatches show up, including mayflies from big Gray Drakes to diminutive Tricos, caddis of every size and description, and stoneflies, including the elusive Salmonfly.

Most trout run 12 inches or less, but bigger fish occasionally enter the river from the Clark Fork and stay a while. The river is too small to float, so come prepared to walk and wade. It should go without saying, but we've had the most fun in the places where the river and the road part company.

Author's Tip

Noxon is a quality bass fishing lake that gets lost in the shuffle as anglers hop from one famous trout river to the next. It's big water to be sure, but there are plenty of intimate little spots just made for float tubes and small boats. Once the water warms up, it pays to get out early and stay late. Cast to the dropoffs and to any structure near the banks—rocks, overhanging limbs, brush, boat docks, and bridge pilings.

Favorite Fly

Clipped Deer Hair Bug

Hook	#1/0-6 Sproat style
Tail	Marabou or deer-hair mixed
Body	Spun and clipped deer body hair
Legs	Sili Legs or rubber band (optional)

Fast Facts

Noxon Reservoir

Location	Noxon Rapids Dam, just east of Noxon, Montana, on Hwy. 200, heads the 30-mile-long impoundment on the north-flowing Clark Fork River
Water Type	Manmade reservoir
Primary Gamefish	Warmwater species include largemouth and smallmouth bass and northern pike; coldwater species include rainbow, brown, cutthroat, and bull trout and mountain whitefish
Best Time	Early spring and late fall are best for pike; May and June and again in September and October are the best bass fishing months. Trout fishing peaks in spring and fall.
Best Flies	Dahlberg Divers, sliders, poppers, deer hair bugs, Buggers, leeches, and Clousers, and crayfish imitations
Equipment	9- to 10-foot, 6- to 8-weight rods, with full array of floating and sinking lines; weight-forward, bug-taper lines facilitate casting heavy wind-resistant patterns

Conditions	Montana's version of the Banana Belt, though weather is still fickle. For example, in June one year we saw it snow 7 inches one day and rise to 70 degrees the next.
Drive Time	From Missoula: 3.75 hours From Bozeman: 7 hours From Spokane: appx. 3.5 hours
Directions	From Missoula, I-90 west to St. Regis, Hwy. 135 north to Hwy. 200 west to Noxon; from Bozeman, I-90 west to St. Regis, Hwy. 135 north to Hwy. 200 west to Noxon; from Spokane, I-90 east to Coeur d'Alene, US 95 north to Sandpoint, Hwy. 200 east to Noxon.

Local Fly Shops

Krazy Ernie's
602 Main St.
Thompson Falls, MT 59873
406-827-4898

Contacts

Kootenai National Forest
2693 Hwy. 200
Trout Creek, MT 59874
406-827-3533

Thompson Falls Chamber of
Commerce
P.O. Box 493
Thompson Falls, MT 59873
406-827-4930

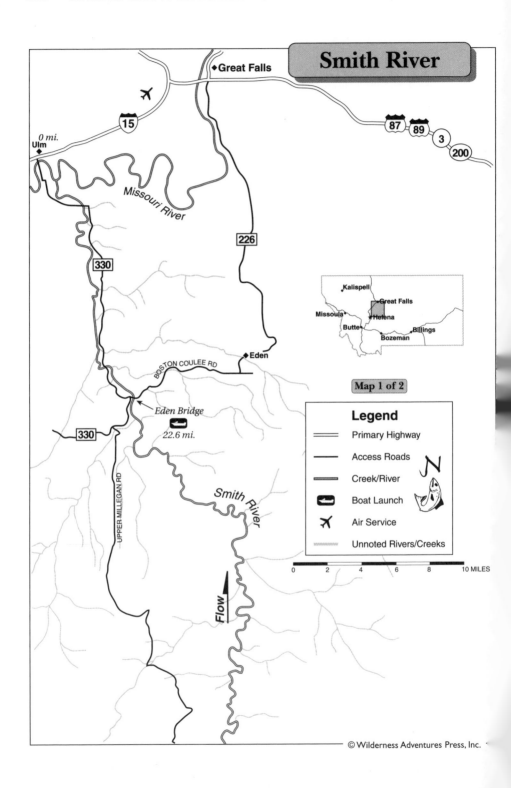

Smith River

Great Falls

15

87 89 3 200

0 mi.
Ulm

Missouri River

226

330

Kalispell
Great Falls
Missoula Helena
Butte Billings
Bozeman

Eden

BOSTON COULEE RD

Map 1 of 2

Eden Bridge
22.6 mi.

UPPER MILLEGAN RD

Smith River

Flow

Legend

═══	Primary Highway
───	Access Roads
───	Creek/River
⬛	Boat Launch
✈	Air Service
∿∿∿	Unnoted Rivers/Creeks

N

0   2   4   6   8   10 MILES

© Wilderness Adventures Press, Inc.

CHAPTER 38

THE SMITH RIVER

Wilderness Gem in Central Montana

To float fish Montana's Smith River in the roadless 60 miles or so between Camp Baker and Eden Bridge is a highlight of the northern Rockies trouting experience. But it takes a lot of work to plan the multi-day float and set up the incredibly long shuttle. And as the much-sought-after permits are distributed via lottery, a little luck doesn't hurt, either. If you get shot down in the permit draw, you can still hire an outfitter with an open launch date or hang out at Camp Baker waiting to see if a party doesn't show up on their scheduled launch date, which does happen. Of course, hiring the services of an outfitter will set you back somewhere between $2,700 and $3000—no small sum.

If you are able to get on the water, though, you're in for a unique wilderness experience and great fishing without a lot of other anglers around. (Only nine launches are allowed per day.) However, should the weather turn foul, or the fishing sour, there's no turning back, no getting out partway down and hitchhiking back to the truck. Once committed, you are in for the long haul. And as you don't always get to pick the floating dates you are assigned, you might be on the river in an April snowstorm or after summer irrigation drawdowns drastically reduce the flow.

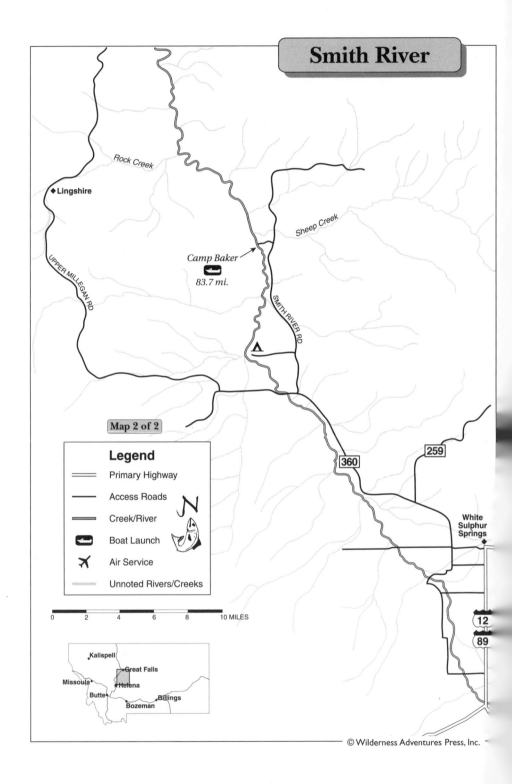

Smith River

Rock Creek

◆Lingshire

UPPER MILLEGAN RD

Sheep Creek

Camp Baker
83.7 mi.

SMITH RIVER RD

Map 2 of 2

259

360

White
Sulphur
Springs

Legend

Primary Highway	
Access Roads	
Creek/River	
Boat Launch	
Air Service	
Unnoted Rivers/Creeks	

N

0   2   4   6   8   10 MILES

12

89

Kalispell
Great Falls
Missoula
Helena
Butte
Billings
Bozeman

If, for whatever reason, you can't swing the float but would still like to fish the Smith I have good news. There is another way.

In mid-April I packed up the tent-trailer and left Dillon a couple days earlier than necessary to keep an appointment in Lewistown. Taking the scenic route from Townsend up Deep Creek and over to White Sulphur Springs, I hooked a left in town on Highway 360N and drove 15 miles to the Camp Baker turnoff. At the big wood sign that reads "Smith River Wildlife Management Area," I hooked another left, switched the truck into 4-wheel high, and careened across the muddy two-track hoping momentum and a silent prayer would get the trailer and me safely to the river.

Not only did the rig make it to the river with relative ease—only two really bad spots brought the lump up in my throat and turned my knuckles white—the campground was deserted and the river, though slightly off color, looked great.

The window of opportunity for early spring trouting is often as short as 11 a.m. to 3 p.m., and it was already 1:30 when I arrived, so I left pitching camp for later. Struggling into waders and stringing my rod on the fly, so to speak, I was on the water in no time. I rigged a San Juan Worm and a pink-and-yellow Glo-Bug (hey, when you only have a short time on a river far from home, I say aesthetics be damned) 5 feet below a big hot-pink strike indicator and crimped on a couple of split shot with my teeth. I then pitched the whole mess into the juicy-looking run beneath a low cliff.

The first drift turned up nothing, and it seemed like the flies might not be running deep enough. So I stripped in, bit on another split shot, and tried again. Tic, tic, tic…hung up. Too much lead. So I stripped in again, removed one split shot, switched the unweighted Glo-Bug for one with a gold beadhead, and cast a third time.

I guess the third time really is a charm because when the bobber wiggled I raised the rod and felt a heavy head shaking. Following a brief struggle, I pulled a slightly skinny 14-inch brown in close and twisted the hook from the corner of its upper jaw. For the next couple of hours the Smith River browns seemed almost as delighted as I was with my pedestrian fly choices.

But around 4 o'clock the action suddenly stopped. I cycled through several patterns and tried different drifts, all to no avail. Finally, I switched to a Black Woolly trailing a bright, flashy Prince Nymph and banged the banks back to my starting point below the rig. I rolled another six trout or so, but landed just one. Oh well, it was good while it lasted, and it's not often that a flyfisher can hit the water these days without seeing another angler.

Fishing the Smith River

As I alluded to earlier, a float from Camp Baker to Eden Bridge is a unique and wonderful experience, and if you enjoy a little solitude and wilderness with your flyfishing it's well worth the effort. The river routinely serves up 25 or so brown and rainbow trout in the 12- to 16-inch range during a good day. The actual float is relatively painless, with no serious whitewater to worry about. In fact, the most difficult floating conditions arrive with low summer flows instead of high spring flows. Good campsites are easy to find, and there's more than enough wildlife and scenery to watch when the fishing slows down.

Step one for the do-it-yourselfer is to apply for and draw a launch permit. The drawing is held in February. For the latest information, contact the Fish, Wildlife & Parks (FWP) office in Great Falls (406-454-5840). Unused launches are issued on a first-come, first-served basis.

Step two is to plan your float—camping and fishing gear, meals, campsites, etc. One of the most difficult logistic problems is making the required number of river miles each day in order to complete the float within the allotted timeframe. Covering 60 river miles in four days means fishing and floating 15 miles a day, which isn't easy to do even at normal flows, much less at low flows. If you're new to the river you might want to get in touch with FWP officials or a Smith River veteran for advice.

My friend Shawn Jones has floated parties down the Smith for many years, and every time the subject comes up he speaks to that very issue, "You know that if you don't make your 10 miles or whatever today, you've got to make up the extra tomor-

Floating is the only way to experience the wilderness flavor of the Smith River.

row. And if you don't make it up tomorrow, well, pretty soon you're screwed and end up rowing instead of fishing."

The float season generally runs April through June, usually ending in early July. The hatches start in mid-April with the mysterious and elusive Skwala Stones. Early spring, before and after the midday hatch, is prime time for big uglies like Yuk Bugs, Woolly Buggers, and Clousers. The river also gets a good early Baetis hatch that anglers often don't get to fish due to the timing.

The Salmonflies hatch in mid-May, followed by Golden Stones (#10 or #12 Yellow Stimulators are the hot fly), and Brown Drakes (#10 Parachute Adams or extended-body patterns such as the Paradrake work on top). Fall is hopper time, and Baetis will show up again on nasty days. If there is enough water in the river, late September into October can be a really hot time, as pre-spawn browns are stacked up around the mouths of tributaries. It's also an easier time to find an open launch date.

One final word on the Smith: All is not well with this fishery. A new proposal being considered would allow for an incredible 2,500 new irrigation permits. Added to the 36,000 irrigated acres already draining the Smith to near dry at Eden Bridge by late summer, it would seem that such an outrageous increase could very well kill the fishery altogether. Cross your fingers—or better yet, raise holy hell with the powers that be.

Restaurants and Accommodations

Obviously there aren't any services on the river. But upriver in White Sulphur Springs, you'll find Dori's Café and the Truck Stop Café on the town's main drag. While neither counts as fine dining, they do put out good down-home meals at reasonable prices.

When you reach the take-out at Eden Bridge, you better have packed enough groceries for one last meal or you'll go hungry on the long drive back to civilization.

Almost everyone I know camps out the night before their launch at Camp Baker (Sheep Creek Fishing Access) or upriver at the Smith River Fishing Access. However, if you don't want to spend the extra night camping, nearby White Sulphur Springs is the place to go. The Spa Hot Springs Motel (202 W. Main, 406-547-3366) features two natural hot springs and clean rooms at reasonable rates, and the Sky Lodge B&B (4260 Hwy. 12 E., 406-547-3999 or 1-800-965-4305) offers visiting anglers an even cozier overnight option. The Super 8 (808 3rd Ave. SW, 406-547-8888) is the town's newest motel.

Author's Tip

Floating is the only way to experience the Smith River's fine wilderness fishery. Permits are, however, getting more and more difficult to acquire, especially during the popular May-June period. One strategy is to apply for early spring or later in the fall after irrigation demands end; another is to hang out at Camp Baker hoping for a no-show.

Favorite Fly

Trude

Hook	Mustad 94831 or equivalent
Tail	Golden pheasant tippets
Body	Peacock herl (fore and aft); crimson floss (center)
Wing	White Z-lon or calf-tail tied down-wing style
Hackle	Brown, tied heavy

Fast Facts

Smith River

Location	River flows north from White Sulphur Springs to Missouri River at Ulm
Water Type	Wilderness float is characterized as low gradient with a few minor Class I or II rapids
Primary Gamefish	Brown and rainbow trout, mountain whitefish
Best Time	April and September provide prime fishing with less

hassle drawing launch permit, but fickle spring weather can ruin a float trip.

Best Flies
: Usually requires little hatch matching; attractor dries and normal array of nymphs and streamers should suffice.

Equipment
: 8- to 9-foot rods, 3- to 5-weight floating lines, tapered leader and tippet to suit the fly; fine tippets aren't usually necessary

Conditions
: Expect high water in May and June; river muddies up easily. In low water years the fishing is dead (or even closed) in July and August; mid-September to freeze-up usually sees a rebound in river flow once irrigation ceases. Spring can turn wintry, summers are generally hot and dry, and fall can be ideal, with warm days and cool, bug-free nights.

Drive Time
: From Helena: 2.5 hours
From Billings: 3.5 to 4 hours
From Bozeman: 2.5 hours

Directions
: From Helena, I-15 north to Cascade, Hwy. 330 west to Hwy. 360 east to Smith River Rd. to Camp Baker; from Billings, US 87 north to Roundup, US 12 west to White Sulphur Springs, Hwy. 360 west to Smith River Rd. to Camp Baker; from Bozeman, I-90 east to US 89 north to White Sulphur Springs, Hwy. 360 west to Smith River Rd. to Camp Baker.

Local Fly Shops

Montana River Outfitters
1401 5th Ave.
Great Falls, MT 59401
401-761-1677

Wolverton's Fly Shop
210 5th St.
Great Falls, MT 59401
401-454-0254

Montana Fly Goods
2125 Euclid Ave.
Helena, MT 59601
406-442-2630

Flyfisher's Inn
2629 Old US Hwy. 91
Cascade, MT 59421
406-468-2529

Missouri River Expeditions
114 Forest Park Dr.
Clancy, MT 59634
406-933-5987

Guides

Big Sky Expeditions
1-800-466-9589

Osprey Expeditions
1-800-315-8502

Lewis and Clark Expeditions
406-449-4632

Camp Baker Outfitters
406-547-2173

Castle Mountain Flyfishers
406-547-3918

Big Hole/Beaverhead Outfitters
406-683-5426

Crow Creek Outfitters
406-266-3742

Birch Creek Outfitters
406-547-2107

Headwaters Angling
1-800-246-3759

Contacts

Great Falls Fish, Wildlife & Parks
4600 Giant Springs Rd.
Great Falls, MT 59405
406-454-5840

Lewis and Clark National Forest
4234 US Highway 89N
Niehart, MT 59465
406-236-5511

Turn at this sign on the way to Camp Baker and you'll find a public access to the Smith River where wade fishing is possible.

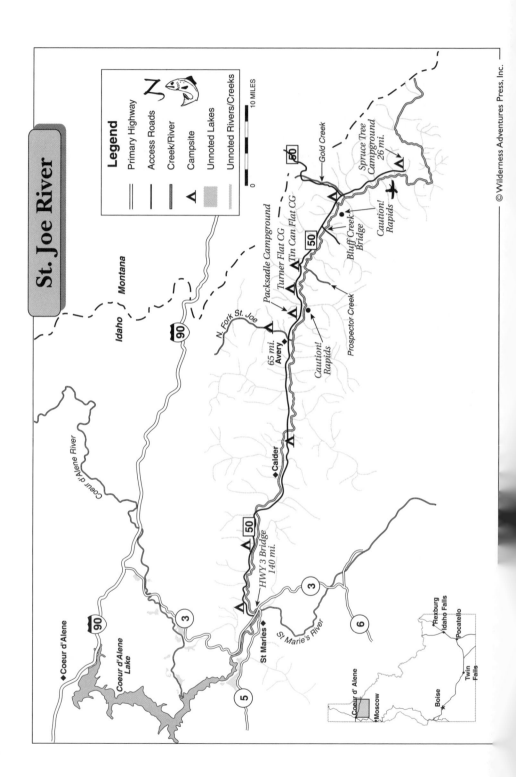

St. Joe River

Legend

≡	Primary Highway
—	Access Roads
—	Creek/River
▲	Campsite
	Unnoted Lakes
	Unnoted Rivers/Creeks

N

0   10 MILES

Idaho

Montana

Coeur d'Alene River

Coeur d'Alene

Coeur d'Alene Lake

St. Maries

St. Marie's River

HWY 3 Bridge 140 mi.

Calder

N. Fork St. Joe

65 mi. Avery

Caution! Rapids

Packsadle Campground

Turner Flat CG

Tin Can Flat CG

Prospector Creek

Gold Creek

Bluff Creek Bridge

Caution! Rapids

Spruce Tree Campground 26 mi.

Coeur d' Alene

Moscow

Rexburg

Idaho Falls

Pocatello

Boise

Twin Falls

© Wilderness Adventures Press, Inc.

CHAPTER 39

THE ST. JOE RIVER
Cutthroat Revival in Northern Idaho

Born high in the Bitterroot Range on the Montana border, the St. Joe River cuts a swath through the rugged forested mountains of northern Idaho's panhandle before eventually dumping into sprawling Coeur d'Alene Lake some 150 river miles to the northwest near the logging town of St. Maries. You'll still see legions of log trucks on area roads and tugboats still tie up to the dock after booming logs downriver to the big Potlatch Lumber Mill. Love it or hate it, the town's apparently still thriving logging industry is an increasingly rare sight these days throughout the northern Rockies.

Logging aside, St. Joe's cutthroat fishery is alive and well. After barely surviving a near knockout punch in the middle of the 20th century, the river has regained the star status it once claimed. This is somewhat surprising in light of the easy and plentiful public access along most of its length. In the catch-and-release water above Avery cutts average 12 inches or so, and we usually catch as many fish under 10 inches as we do over 14 inches.

This might disappoint hog hunters, but if you are in this for fun, the St. Joe is tough to beat. Thanks to enlightened catch-and-release management, the 50 miles from Prospector Creek upstream has grown into a primo fishery. And whether you choose to float or wade you'll find plenty of opportunities.

Our usual strategy here couldn't be much simpler. Leaving Packsaddle Campground, we drive upriver (the road closely parallels much of the river) to the confluence at Gold Creek, which is generally empty. We park the truck, rig up with the first dry fly in the box that catches our fancy, and have at 'em. Nine times out of ten, that's all it takes. Once you get above Avery, one spot is often as good as another, although we avoid the nasty whitewater sections until the flow drops.

In fact, I wasn't sure until I asked whether Gale had ever fished anything here but her go-to favorite, the Orange Stimulator. She replied, "Hardly ever, although sometimes I vary the size from the usual #14 to a larger one, say a #8, and sometimes smaller, like a #16. And every once in a blue moon I do shift from the orange to a yellow or red one, but lately I've been leaning toward this greenie." (Gale claims the "greenie" somewhat mimics a local pattern some guy showed her in a gas station in St. Maries.)

I, on the other hand, become very involved when it comes to choosing fly patterns. Take the thinking that goes into today's St. Joe start. I might first consider what Gale just told me. Maybe I should go with a "greenie," too. But since everyone knows that St. Joe cutts prefer big attractor dry flies, rummaging through my collection produces a host of possible choices. Or maybe I should try a Chernobyl Ant or one of the other foam and rubber-band concoctions I seem to rely on more and more for cutthroat fishing.

And I almost always go with two flies, so what to use as the dropper leads me on a whole new search. Finally, it occurs to me how much precious fishing time I'm wasting. Without further ado, I tie on a #12 Chernobyl and trail a #10 Prince Nymph 2 feet or so behind it and wade in.

Today turns out to be one of our better days. Leapfrogging up and down the river, we fish only the honey holes at the confluence and at various tributaries. Since the river's still running pretty high (mid-July) we fish only the near side. Later, when the flow drops, we'll cover both sides thoroughly.

But this morning it doesn't matter that we're only fishing half a river. The St. Joe cutts seem to be on a minor feeding binge, and more than once we both have trout on at the same time. After an hour or so we put one rod away and just take turns.

Fishing the easy way.

Restaurants and Accommodations

St. Maries has the usual small-town cafés, pizza places, and fast-food joints, but fine-dining options are few and far between in this part of Idaho. We usually treat an expedition to the St. Joe as just another good excuse to hone our camp-cooking

The area around the St. Joe sports one of the West's largest elk herds.

skills. The key is to plan your menu before leaving home so that you can be sure to bring the right groceries, which may be difficult to acquire on the road.

Whether to camp or not is also sort of a no-brainer here since there are almost no motels. But upstream of Avery there are a whole bevy of USFS campgrounds. Tin Can Flat, Conrad Crossing, and Spruce Tree are three that come to mind, all good places to headquarter for an assault on the river's cutthroats.

If you don't like camping but still want to stay upriver, head to the St. Joe Lodge (208-245-4002) up beyond where the road ends. It's a rustic, Orvis-endorsed operation that includes an older log cabin and bunkhouse, other cabins, and a wall tent to house the overflow.

St. Maries, Idaho

St. Maries, located at the confluence of the St. Maries and St. Joe Rivers, was once an important steamboat stop and major distribution center for raw logs. Today it's somewhat more diversified, taking advantage of the region's natural beauty and outdoor sporting opportunities to help fill the economic gap forced upon it by a dwindling logging industry, although logging is still somewhat of a thriving industry here.

In spring the town fills up with whitewater enthusiasts coming from or going to the challenging rapids upriver. Summer brings legions of campers and anglers, and in autumn hunters arrive to sample what may be the best elk hunting anywhere, to say nothing of the deer, bear, moose, mountain goat, turkey, pheasant, and waterfowl that also abound.

Nearby Fisheries

North Fork Coeur d'Alene River

Think of all the ways you might kill a river: pillage the surrounding timber, then allow the resulting slash to burn, leaving bare, steep slopes to slide into the river and fill its gravels with life-choking sediment; straighten its natural meandering course to facilitate poorly built roads; allow boomed logs to strip it clean during spring runoff; placer and dredge mine its gravels and alter its natural progression of riffles and pools; and then screw up taking care of what little is left. These, in a nutshell, are the abuses suffered by the once magnificent Coeur d'Alene River system, including the North Fork.

But killing off a river isn't easy, and despite years of abuse, neglect, and mismanagement the North Fork is still very much alive and kicking. Concentrate your efforts in the upper river above the confluence with Yellow Dog Creek, and you'll soon see what I mean. But remember that this is another westslope cutthroat fishery where the game is all about catching pretty, wild, native trout rather than extracting hogs from a fish factory. On average, the fish run 10 to 12 inches, but with plenty of slightly larger specimens to sweeten the pot.

A bunch of tributaries feed the upper river, and nearly all are trout water. Like wild cutts everywhere, they aren't too selective. So bring some attractor dries and hit the trail to explore some beautiful country.

Author's Tip

Fishing the upper St. Joe in September, especially in years when the spruce moths show up, can result in sensory overload. The cutts really turn on to the moths, and any fly pattern even remotely close to the naturals usually works—a White Wulff, for example. As with most insect events, timing is everything, so be sure to check in first with Blue Goose Sport Shop (208-245-4015) or the St. Joe Lodge (208-245-4002) for the latest river reports. Regardless of when you go, pattern choice isn't nearly as important as presenting the fly in the right places; for cutts, that generally means pounding the deep pools and runs, logjams, etc.

Favorite Fly

Renegade

Hook	TMC 100 or equivalent
Tag	Gold Mylar tinsel
Rib	Fine gold wire
Rear Hackle	Brown
Body	Peacock herl
Front Hackle	White

Fast Facts

St. Joe River

Location	Idaho panhandle, generally south of Coeur d'Alene Lake
Water Type	From the upper end to Avery, characterized by rapids, falls and deep pools; bottom half is flat and increasingly a warmwater fishery
Primary Gamefish	Westslope cutthroat and rainbow trout; also brook and bull trout (must be immediately released)
Best Time	July, August, and September
Best Flies	Attractor dry flies such as the hair-wing Wulff series, Stimulator, foam-body ties, and local ties such as the St. Joe Favorite and Special; Beadhead Hare's Ear, Prince, Copper John, Flashback, stonefly nymphs
Equipment	9-foot rod for 4- to 6-weight floating lines, tapered leaders and tippet to suit situation
Conditions	Typical mountain weather, but expect hot days and cool nights; mosquitoes and blackflies can be thick

Drive Time   From Spokane: 2 hours
                    From Missoula: 3.75 hours
                    From Idaho Falls: 8 hours
Directions   From Spokane, I-90 east to Hwy. 3 (White Pine Scenic
                    Byway) south to St. Maries, FH 50 (St. Joe River Rd.) to
                    upper river; from Missoula, I-90 west to Hwy. 3 (White
                    Pine Scenic Byway) south to St. Maries, FH 50 (St. Joe
                    River Rd.) to upper river; from Idaho Falls, I-15 north to
                    I-90 west to Hwy. 3 (White Pine Scenic Byway) south to
                    St. Maries, FH 50 (St. Joe River Rd.) to upper river.

Local Fly Shops

Northwest Outfitters/Orvis
402 Canfield & Hwy. 95
Coeur d'Alene, ID 83815
208-772-1497

Castaway Flyfishing Shop
350 Bosanko
Coeur d'Alene, ID 83815
208-765-3133

Dig-In Outfitters
2425 N. Government Way
Coeur d'Alene, ID 83815
208-664-7922

Fins and Feathers Tackle Shop and
    Guide Service
1816 Sherman Ave.
Coeur d'Alene, ID 83815
208-667-9304

Black Sheep Sporting Goods and Toys
308 W Seale Ave.
Coeur d'Alene, ID 83815
208-667-7831

St. Joe Sport Shop
402 College Ave.
St. Maries, ID 83861
208-245-4417

Blue Goose Sport Shop
621 Main St.
St. Maries, ID 83861
208-245-4015

Guides

Panhandle Outfitters, Inc & Orvis
Endorsed Flyfishing
1-888-300-4868

St. Joe Outfitters and Guides
(St. Joe Lodge)
208-245-4002

Priest River Guide Service
208-661-1146

Contacts

St. Maries Ranger District
P.O. Box 407
St. Maries, ID 83861
208-245-2531

The first of several nice USFS campgrounds you'll pass as you head upriver from St. Maries.

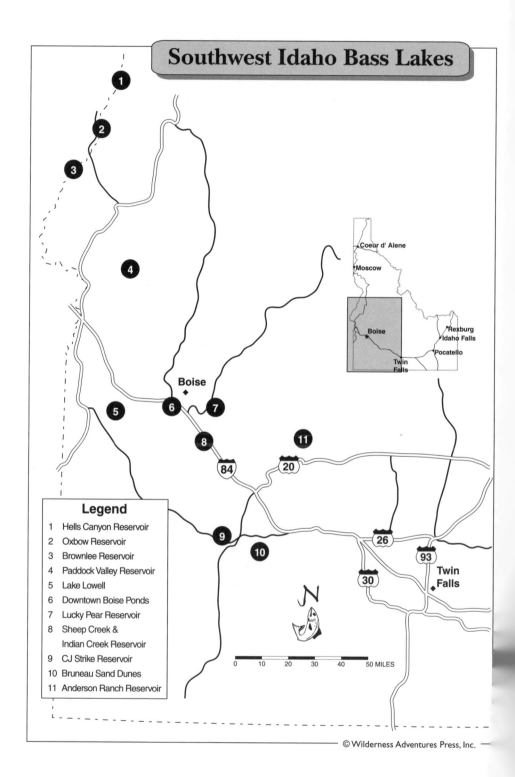

CHAPTER 40

Southwest Idaho Bass Lakes

Legend

1. Hells Canyon Reservoir
2. Oxbow Reservoir
3. Brownlee Reservoir
4. Paddock Valley Reservoir
5. Lake Lowell
6. Downtown Boise Ponds
7. Lucky Pear Reservoir
8. Sheep Creek &
   Indian Creek Reservoir
9. CJ Strike Reservoir
10. Bruneau Sand Dunes
11. Anderson Ranch Reservoir

Coeur d' Alene
Moscow
Boise
Rexburg
Idaho Falls
Pocatello
Twin Falls

Boise

84
20
26
93
30
Twin Falls

0   10   20   30   40   50 MILES

C H A P T E R   4 0

SOUTHWEST IDAHO BASS LAKES

Almost More Water Than Sand

Imagine yourself adrift in a float tube in the middle of C.J. Strike Reservoir's Cove Arm, when suddenly one air chamber goes flat. Nothing to panic about yet because you are sitting in a state-of-the-art tube with multiple air chambers and built-in floatation in the seat. Though knowing the episode isn't life threatening is small consolation since the shoreline is several hundred yards distant. It's going to be a serious kick across a pretty wide lake while listing hard to one side...

The afternoon I found myself in just such a predicament, Lady Luck, in the form of Gale and her pontoon boat, came to my rescue. She towed me to safety, although two adults aboard one small pontoon boat does not make for swift travel. Still, it would have run rings around my half-deflated tube.

Cove Arm is just one of many southwest Idaho fly rod bassin' hotspots. The list includes the Snake River impounds Brownlee, Oxbow, and Hell's Canyon, and Anderson Ranch, C.J. Strike, Indian Creek, Paddock Valley, and Lucky Pear Reservoirs, Crane Falls, Bruneau Sand Dunes, and Lowell Lakes, Hagerman Wildlife Management area ponds, and the downtown Boise ponds.

Bluegills are great fun on a fly rod.

At the risk of being labeled a pathetic whiner, it seems that whenever I send my flies in search of bass at Crane Falls I all too often come up with fat rainbows—what a pity, huh? Especially in early May, when the warmwater-loving bass motors are just starting to rev, the 'bows are already running full throttle, and unless you toss really big uglies pesky rainbows are just something you have to learn to live with. Or, of course, you could simply go someplace where there are no pesky rainbows, such as Bruneau Sand Dunes Lake.

Bruneau Dunes is managed as a trophy largemouth bass lake with a daily creel limit of two bass over 20 inches. If your luck runs like ours usually does, you can expect to catch bass ranging in size from 19 inches on down while sitting in your float tube waiting for that elusive 20-incher. At a size little bigger than a large farm pond, this is one bass lake tailor-made for float tubes, although you can use any watercraft without a gasoline motor.

Dunes Lake, situated in Bruneau Dunes State Park, is actually two lakes separated by a narrow channel. The smaller of the two, accessed at the Observatory, contains more and fatter bluegills but fewer and smaller bass. The bigger lake, accessed at the lower picnic and day-use area, holds fewer 'gills but more and bigger bass. It's a pleasant flyfishing destination that fishes surprisingly well, and sitting at the base of all that sand, it's certainly one of the most unique.

The drill is to pound the reedy shoreline with various topwater flies, deer hair bugs, cork poppers, or sliders early and late in the day, and then idle away the midday hours pounding the reedy shoreline by stripping underwater stuff like Clousers, leeches, and Buggers.

Fishing the Southwest Idaho Bass Lakes

No matter which lake(s) you choose to fish, some sort of watercraft will help you reach many more fishable areas. And wading shorelines is often difficult, as the majority of the lakes border on a landscape that can only be described as harsh— rocks, brush, steep slopes, to say nothing of the thriving snake population. But the best reason for bringing a boat or float tube is that the added mobility translates into more fish in the net.

Flyfishing for bass in still water requires a good selection of floating and sinking fly patterns, the usual array of full-sink, sink-tip, and floating lines, and long, powerful rods to help sling the bulky patterns. Reels with a good disc drag and adequate backing are nice, too, since even a mediocre smallmouth will put a big, fat trout to shame when it comes to fighting.

As bass fishing with a fly rod might be a new adventure for all the northern Rockies trout bums out there, I'd like to toss out a little fly rod bassin' theory that's proven effective for me.

Bass are not generally regarded as cerebral, certainly not in the sense that we revere fussy trout. Generally speaking, bass aren't leader shy. Short, stout leaders win out over the long, wispy variety if for no other reason than that short and stout handles big air resistant and heavy bass flies better. But once the bass water turns crystalline, it's a theory that often needs a little tinkering.

Bass lakes tend to vary in clarity from crystal-clear to downright murky, and some individual waters vary widely from season to season. C.J. Strike Reservoir is a prime example. Often C.J. is on the murky side, conditions made to order for stiff leaders, but last spring we found it just the opposite—so clear you could easily see bottom almost everywhere.

Obviously, the gin-clear water called for a change in leader and tippet strategy. We went with leaders as long as we could while still managing to turn over our flies. We stuck with 2X terminal tippet, but it worked much better when backed up by at least 10 feet of tapered leader with a heavy butt measuring 0.025 inch or so.

Restaurants and Accommodations

The town of Mountain Home gives visiting anglers a lot of choices, but it may be quite a drive depending on just where you happen to be fishing. Closer to the action is Tom and Donya Crenshaw's Bruneau One Stop, café and motel (Hwy. 51 and Hot Springs Rd.). The Crenshaws serve a mean breakfast, with the omelets and pancakes getting particularly high marks.

One of the nicest campgrounds around (with trees in the desert, no less) is located at Bruneau Dunes State Park (208-366-7919). The downside is that on weekends it fills up early, so reservations are a good idea.

Camping, both organized and primitive, is also available at several access sites on C.J. Strike Reservoir and at Crane Falls Lake. The newly renovated Cove Access would be at the top end, Cottonwood in the middle, and Jacks Creek more primitive. Most campsites are limited to around 10 consecutive days of camping. Call the BLM Bruneau Resource Area at 208-384-3300 for more information.

Nearby Fisheries

Catching bass, bluegill, and crappie on flies is not the only flyfishing game here in the desert, not by a long shot. Believe it or not, there are also many trout lakes and streams in the area. The Bruneau River in Bruneau-Jarbridge Canyon (follow the signs 18 miles south of Bruneau) holds redband trout and smallmouth bass, and the 1,200-foot hike down and back up tends to keep the crowds at bay.

The Duck Valley Indian Reservation's Sheep Creek and Mountain View Reservoirs and Lake Billy Shaw provide pay-to-play rainbow trout fishing. The latter costs $50 per day, while the other pair is a bargain at just $8 per day. Contact the Shoshone-Paiute Tribes Wildlife and Parks Department (P.O. Box 219, Owyhee, NV 89832; 1-800-761-9133) for more information. Or check in with one of the fly shops listed below.

Nearby Attractions and Activities

Kids just love Bruneau Sand Dunes State Park; after all, where else can one go tobogganing nearly year-round? On spring and fall weekends, the dunes come alive with youngsters toting all kinds of plastic contrivances, the sort usually reserved for snow sledding. Grownups can explore the unique flora and fauna around the continent's tallest sand dune, which soars some 470 feet above the surrounding desert floor, or simply sit and watch the horseplay.

The rugged Owyhee (a corruption of the word "Hawaii") Canyon is just a few miles down the road. It has a diverse bird and wildlife population, including desert bighorn sheep, sage grouse, and redband trout. The canyon is also a popular rafting spot.

Author's Tip

Spring and fall are the ideal times to fish Idaho's desert lakes. Summer days can be brutally hot, which usually kills the fishing. From July well into September the fishing is best in early morning, late evening, and after dark. While long leaders are not usually the norm when chasing warmwater species with a fly rod, before the weeds really get going these lakes can be gin-clear, so gear up accordingly.

Favorite Fly

Red/Chartreuse Deer Hair Bug

Hook	Mustad 9672 or equivalent, #1/0 to 2
Tail	Wood duck flank
Body	Spun and clipped deer hair; chartreuse rear two-thirds, red front third

Fast Facts

C.J. Strike Reservoir (with many other lakes in the area)

Location	South of Mountain Home, Idaho, on Hwy. 51 toward Bruneau
Water Type	Large, stable pool reservoir
Primary Gamefish	Largemouth and smallmouth bass, rainbow trout, panfish, catfish
Best Time	April to June and September to November
Best Flies	Clousers, leeches, Buggers, poppers, deer hair bugs

Equipment	9- to 10-foot rod, 6- to 8-weight, bug tapers, floating, full-sink, and sink-tip lines, tapered leaders to suit situation; float tube or other watercraft helps; only electric motors on Bruneau Dunes Lake
Conditions	Mild winters to scorching hot, triple-digit summers; most comfortable early spring and late fall; desert surroundings often windy and can be buggy
Drive Time	From Boise: 1.5 hours
	From Salt Lake City: 5 hours
	From Idaho Falls: 4 hours
Directions	From Boise, I-84 east to Mountain Home, Hwy. 51 south to reservoir; from Salt Lake City, I-15 north to I-84 west to Hammer, Hwy. 78 west to reservoir; from Idaho Falls, I-15 south to I-86 west to I-84 to Hammer, Hwy. 78 west to reservoir.

Local Fly Shops

The Fishin' Hole
Hwy. 51
Bruneau, ID 83604
208-845-2001

Idaho Angler
1692 Vista
Boise, ID 83701
1-800-787-9957, 208-389-9957

Angler's (Orvis)
7097 Overland Rd.
Boise, ID 83709
208-323-6768

Bear Creek Fly Shop
5521 W. State
Boise, ID 83703
208-853-8704

South Fork Anglers
832 S. Vista Ave.
Boise, ID 83705
208-433-8844

Stonefly Angler
625 S. Vista Ave.
Boise, ID 83705
208-338-1333

Riverkeeper
1224 Broadway Ave.
Boise, ID 83703
208-344-3838

Guides

MacKenzie Outfitters
208-433-8844

Mountain Sports
208-587-8858

Contacts

Idaho Game and Fish
Southwest Region
3101 S. Powerline Rd.
Nampa, ID 83686
208-465-8465

Largemouth bass.

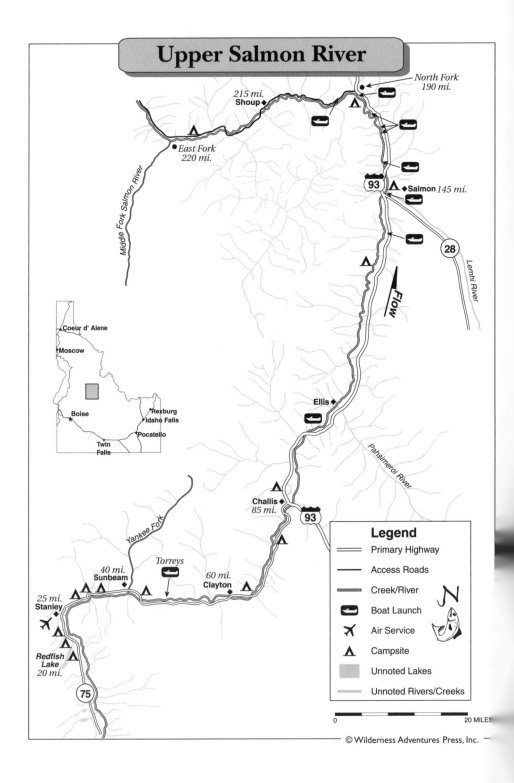

Upper Salmon River

North Fork
190 mi.

215 mi.
Shoup ◆

East Fork
220 mi.

93

Salmon 145 mi.

28

Middle Fork Salmon River

Lemhi River

Flow

Coeur d' Alene

Moscow

Boise

Rexburg
Idaho Falls

Pocatello

Twin
Falls

Ellis ◆

Pahsimeroi River

Challis ◆
85 mi.

93

Yankee Fork

Torreys

40 mi.
Sunbeam

60 mi.
Clayton

25 mi.
Stanley

Redfish
Lake
20 mi.

75

Legend

Primary Highway

Access Roads

Creek/River

Boat Launch

Air Service

Campsite

Unnoted Lakes

Unnoted Rivers/Creeks

N

0   20 MILES

CHAPTER 41

THE UPPER SALMON RIVER

Steelhead on the River of No Return

The steelhead swimming in the upper Salmon River near Stanley, Idaho, each spring are the survivors of a 980-mile odyssey from the Pacific. It's an amazing journey, made even more so by having to negotiate many dams (and avoid many anglers) on the Columbia and Snake Rivers. So when one grabbed my Egg-Sucking Leech the other morning and raced hell-bent downstream, I wasn't all that sad to see it get off.

Had one pulled the same stunt three days later, however, I'd probably still be cussing a blue streak. That hook-up was the only one I'd have on the entire trip, as far as steelhead go, anyway. But I know only too well that steelhead on the fly can be a bitch, so the result of my efforts came as no great surprise. At least the trout fishing was pretty good.

Indians called the Salmon the "River of No Return." It's an ominous nickname that Lewis and Clark found little reason to argue with after a quick peek at the raging rapids roaring through the unbelievably deep gorge below what is now Corn Creek. Daring, though hardly fools, the pair wasted little time in ordering the expedition to turn back to seek safer passage.

Modern fly anglers, goaded on by visions of somersaulting steelhead and legions of cutthroat and rainbow trout, are not so easily dissuaded. Fall through spring, the river hosts what amounts to a steelhead fishing army, although most aren't flyfishers. No matter what the weapon of choice, the Steelhead Army is apparently oblivious to the waterway's perils or the discomforts of nasty spring weather. But on weekends with nice weather the Army obviously grows exponentially. Don't expect to find yourself alone anywhere on the upper Salmon when the steelhead are running.

Let's divide the Salmon into two rivers. The lower river from the mouth of the Middle Fork Salmon downstream to the confluence of the Snake is largely inaccessible to anglers (except, of course, in the relatively short run beside the highway near Riggins). It provides great fishing, but is tough to get to without a jet boat. In contrast, access could hardly be better on the upper river from the Middle Fork upstream to Stanley. This stretch is paralleled by roads for the entire length and surrounded by public land. So let's focus on this 200-mile run.

Mid-March weather in the northern Rockies can be maddening, and its unpredictable nature makes for an iffy steelhead hunt. To understand why is to understand steelhead and steelhead fishing—sort of, anyway.

This steelhead was hooked on the upper Salmon, roughly 950 miles upriver from the Pacific Ocean.

Some steelhead enter the lower Salmon in fall, and depending on the circumstances, November and December can be hot times for casting flies. Temperature and water level dictate just how far upstream the run surges until winter shuts it down. Some years there are fresh-run steelhead in the Salmon above the Middle Fork, and some years there aren't. When they are there, sight fishing with a fly rod can be excellent during cold spells, as fish tend to stack up in eddies and behind boulders.

The ice breaks up and water temperatures start to rise in February or March, causing over-wintering steelhead to begin moving upriver once again. Once the water temperature reaches 40 degrees, the run picks up speed as the urge to procreate drives the steelhead racing toward natal spawning waters. The low snow begins to melt too, causing a mini-runoff period. But the faster it melts, the swifter and more discolored the river becomes—and the harder it is to catch fish on a fly.

In muddy water, steelhead tend to streak upstream, making flyfishing difficult at best. All you can do is cover a lot of water, as the fish don't stay put in traditional holding water.

Conventional fly rods are not the best instruments for covering a lot of water on a fast, high, discolored river. The best, and often the only, chance for fly-rod action is the narrow window on either side of dawn and after sunset, when steelhead are most likely to be resting in predictable lies between surges upriver. During the day, expect to do a lot of blind casting, or just switch to trout fishing until you see the bait and hardware guys hooking up.

Back on that three-day spring trip I alluded to earlier, the spring mini-spate started the very day my friend Shawn and I decided to drive over from Dillon. Across the mountains in Montana it was still winter, while in the Lemhi Valley spring had sprung. We arrived to find the Lemhi River running chocolate, spewing its off-color brew into the Salmon and rendering the main river virtually unfishable from the town of Salmon downstream.

Three steelhead-less days followed. And were it not for the pretty, wild rainbow trout willing to take up the slack, we might have pouted all the way home.

Fishing the Upper Salmon River

April fishing usually entails casting to actively spawning fish on redds. Some would say this is a no-no, and normally I would wholeheartedly agree, but in this case the spawners are merely play-acting. Despite the numerous redds, few actually produce smolts. It's sad but true that as we head into the 21st century the overwhelming majority of steelhead are spawned in hatcheries and released into the river as smolts. Only a small percentage of fish make their way downriver to the sea and return a year later as semi-wild adults.

In Idaho these days a truly wild steelhead is an increasingly rare (and precious) thing; thus the standing rule that all steelhead sporting an un-clipped adipose fin must be immediately released unharmed. The adipose fins of all hatchery fish are clipped prior to release, and these stockers make up nearly all of the catch.

Wild or otherwise, so-called "one-ocean," or "A-run," steelhead are those that return to their natal river after just one year at sea. "Two-ocean," or "B-run," steelhead return after two years at sea. A-run fish average 4 to 8 pounds and comprise most of the upper Salmon River steelhead run. B-run fish average 12 to 16 pounds, although some exceed 20 pounds.

B-run fish are far more common in the Clearwater River system and Middle Fork Salmon, but some still make their way to the upper Salmon. As proof, I offer the 35-incher a fellow Dillonite caught and released just last spring and the 42-inch, 25-pound-plus monster recently hauled from the Lemhi Hole just outside the town of Salmon.

Whether you're fishing in fall, winter, or spring, the key is to get the fly down to the steelhead. While I suppose it is possible to catch a Salmon River steelhead on a dry fly, far more are hooked on flies bounced on the bottom or swinging very close to the bottom. Unlike trout actively feeding a hatch of insects on or near the surface, steelhead only occasionally come up through the water column to attack a fly.

Except in the lowest flows and shallowest runs, getting to the bottom requires full- sink or sink-tip lines and heavily weighted flies (sparsely dressed jigs might be even better) suspended under a suitably-sized bobber. Granted, none of the above is pretty or classic in the traditional flyfishing sense, but if you want to catch steelhead with a fly rod in your hand, it's the best way to do it. If you really despise the idea of bobber-and-jig fishing, stick with the traditional down-and-across wet fly method, which works about as well as anything else on most days.

The upper Salmon River steelhead season closes on April 30, and after mid-April flyfishers should plan on fishing the river above Challis.

When steelhead clamp their mouths shut it's time to switch over to trout fishing. I replace the standard steelhead purples, blacks, and pinks with a lead-eyed orange black, and yellow concoction named the Salmon River Special. To trout on the upper Salmon River in early spring, the Special is nothing short of poison—especially gullible are the resident rainbows.

As trout fisheries go, the upper river is just okay. Even on the best days, it falls somewhat short of blue-ribbon status. Trout, primarily rainbow and cutthroats, are found in good numbers throughout the river, but they don't add up to what you'll find on more famous Idaho trout waters like the South Fork Boise or Kelly Creek. And while rumors of big trout persist, I must confess we've never found them. Still we usually find enough fish of descent size that we seldom bypass a chance to fish the river.

The run near the confluence of Yankee Fork is a particular favorite. In early fall, we've enjoyed days when trout after trout nabbed our flies—mostly modest-sized rainbows that are buckets of fun. In late winter and early spring, the trout fishing above and below the town of Salmon has saved more than one tough steelhead outing.

When the steelhead are in, almost no one fishes for trout. In high summer, with steelhead mania in recession, you can often find whole stretches of river void of human competition, which is all too rare these days anywhere in the northern Rockies.

Restaurants and Accommodations

In Salmon, when the lunch board on the sidewalk in front of Bertram's Brewery and Restaurant (corner of Main and Andrews, 208-756-3391) reads "Prime Rib Sandwich" steelheading takes a back seat. For that matter, any time we're near Salmon at mealtime we head for BB&R. The extensive wine list would be worth a look were it not for the fact that the brewery has eight delicious labels to choose from. I recommend the Mt. Borah Brown or the Lost Trail Amber Ale; they'll make even the worst steelheading day a whole lot better in a hurry.

Camping spots are available all along the river. The plushest is Cottonwood Campground, not far above Ellis and the confluence of the Pahsimeroi River. If there is a drawback to the many campsites along the river, it's the proximity to the highway

Shawn Jones wades the Upper Salmon.

and traffic noise, which seems to go on all night. In mid-March we camped at Shoup Bridge, and every time I was about to nod off along came another vehicle.

For more camping information, contact the Salmon Chamber of Commerce (one of most helpful Chambers around) at 1-800-727-2540; the Salmon/Challis National Forest (50 Hwy. 93) at 208-756-5100; Salmon Meadows Campground (400 North St. Charles) at 208-756-2640; or BLM (Idaho) at www.publiclands.org.

Motels can be found in North Fork, Salmon, Challis, and Stanley, and prices range from moderate to high, although most give you a break in the off season. The Challis Motor Lodge (Hwy. 93 and Main, Challis, 208-879-2251) and the Stage Coach Inn (201 Hwy. 93 N, Salmon, 208-756-2919) are two moderately priced motels that offer clean rooms and friendly service. There are a number of nifty lodges and bed and breakfasts in the area, such as the Broken Arrow in Gibbonsville (208-865-2241) and the Greyhouse Inn in Salmon (1-800-348-8097).

Nearby Attractions and Activities

As this region played a big role in the Lewis and Clark saga, there are a number of sites worth visiting. Lemhi Pass is just up the road from Salmon and, as mentioned above, the canyon below North Fork proved a pivotal turning point for the expedition. Just outside Salmon (Hwy. 28 E), the Sacajawea Interpretive Center is currently under construction. Among other things, the center will provide visitors with a look at Shoshone Indian fish traps and weirs (Lemhi River), traditional teepee construction, and various historical artifacts.

Author's Tip

Time your steelhead trip to coincide with good sight-fishing conditions—typically late fall/early winter and again in late winter/early spring before the low snow melts. Early April, after the low snow melts but before the major snowmelt runoff from the high country begins, is often a good time, too. But rain and constant snowmelt from early spring snowstorms can muddy the waters and kill the sight fishing, so be sure to call ahead to check current conditions. Carla Young at the Bent Rod in Challis (1 866-880-0451) is a good source of information, as are the folks at Silver Spur Sports in Salmon (208-756-2833). These shops can also arrange a guided trip, which isn't a bad idea if you are new to the steelhead game.

Favorite Fly

Purple Peril (Steelhead)

Hook	#2-6 Mustad 7999
Tail	Purple hackle fibers
Body	Purple yarn
Rib	Silver tinsel
Hackle	Purple
Wing	Fox squirrel tail

Salmon River Special (Trout)

Hook	#6-10 Mustad 7999/lead eyes
Tail	Black marabou
Body	Black chenille rear two-thirds; orange front third
Hackle	Grizzly palmered
Legs	Sili Legs

Fast Facts

Upper Salmon River

Location	Upstream of the Middle Fork Salmon confluence to Stanley, Idaho
Water Type	Moderate-sized, classic pool/riffle configuration with an increasing number of whitewater rapids lower down
Primary Gamefish	Steelhead, with good trout fishing for rainbow and cutthroat trout
Best Time	Steelhead: November, December, and April. Trout: pre-spring runoff and again late summer through fall
Best Flies	Steelhead: #2-6 black, purple, and pink (alone or in combination) wets, such as Boss, Green-Butt Skunk, Egg-Sucking Leech, Purple Peril, Popsicle, Double Sperm, egg patterns, etc.
Equipment	Steelhead: 9- to 14-foot rods, full-sink, sink-tip, and floating lines; multi-tip lines are ideal; 6-weight minimum; reels should have a reliable disc drag and hold lots of backing; leaders built to suit the situation. Trout: 9-foot, 4- to 6-weight rods, standard reels, tapered leaders to suit.
Conditions	Typical mountain weather: warm one minute, brutal the next. River levels vary with season, normally low and clear in late fall, mini-runoff sometime in late February or early March, low and clear through April until the major runoff begins in May or June.
Drive Time	From Boise: appx. 6 hours
	From Idaho Falls: 3.75 hours
	From Bozeman: 5.5 hours
Directions	From Boise, I-84 east to Hwy. 21 north to Stanley, Hwy. 75 south to Challis, Hwy. 93 south to Salmon; from Idaho Falls, I-15 north to Sage Junction, Hwy. 33 south to Mud Lake, Hwy. 28 west to Salmon; from Bozeman, I-90 east to Whitehall, Hwy. 55 and 41 south to Dillon, I-15 south to Clark Canyon Reservoir, Hwy. 324 west to Leadore, Hwy. 28 south to Salmon.

Local Fly Shops

Silver Spur Sports
403 Main St.
Salmon, ID 83467
208-756-2833

The Bent Rod
Main St.
Challis, ID 83226
208-879-2500

Contacts

Salmon Chamber of Commerce
200 Main St.
Salmon, ID 83467
1-800-727-2540

Salmon/Challis National Forest
50 Hwy. 93
Salmon, ID 83467
208-756-5100

Idaho Fish and Game
Salmon Region
1214 Hwy. 93 N. P.O. Box 1336
Salmon, ID 83467
208-756-6274

Eastern Idaho Visitor Information
Center
505 Lindsey Blvd.
Idaho Falls, ID 83401
1-800-634-3246, 208-523-1010

A-run steelhead are fish that have returned to their natal river after spending one year in the Pacific Ocean.

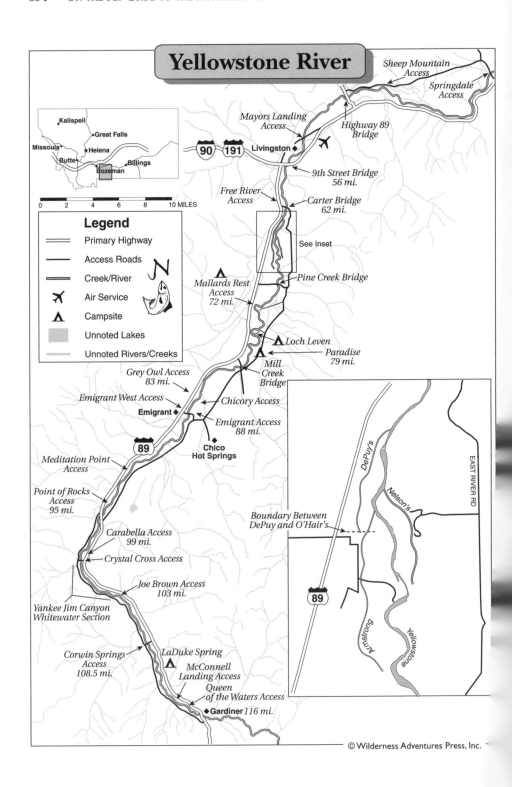

Yellowstone River

Legend

Primary Highway
Access Roads
Creek/River
Air Service
Campsite
Unnoted Lakes
Unnoted Rivers/Creeks

Sheep Mountain Access
Springdale Access
Mayors Landing Access
Highway 89 Bridge
Livingston
9th Street Bridge 56 mi.
Free River Access
Carter Bridge 62 mi.
See Inset
Pine Creek Bridge
Mallards Rest Access 72 mi.
Loch Leven
Paradise 79 mi.
Mill Creek Bridge
Grey Owl Access 83 mi.
Emigrant West Access
Chicory Access
Emigrant
Emigrant Access 88 mi.
Chico Hot Springs
Meditation Point Access
Point of Rocks Access 95 mi.
Carabella Access 99 mi.
Crystal Cross Access
Joe Brown Access 103 mi.
Yankee Jim Canyon Whitewater Section
Corwin Springs Access 108.5 mi.
LaDuke Spring
McConnell Landing Access
Queen of the Waters Access
Gardiner 116 mi.

Kalispell
Great Falls
Missoula
Helena
Butte
Bozeman
Billings

0 2 4 6 8 10 MILES

Boundary Between DePuy and O'Hair's
DePuy's
Nelson's
EAST RIVER RD
Armstrong
Yellowstone

© Wilderness Adventures Press, Inc.

CHAPTER 42

THE YELLOWSTONE RIVER

The Quintessential Northern Rockies Trout River

French explorers called it *Roches Jaunes* (Yellow Rocks) and the Minnetaree Sioux knew it as the *Mi tsi a-da-zi*, but a Canadian explorer, perhaps one whose French was a bit rusty, labeled it simply Yellow Stone, although over time the two words became one through common use. The namesake rocks are probably the yellow sandstone bluffs near Billings, Montana, once a favorite hangout for Minnetaree hunting parties in pursuit of bison.

Remote Yount's Peak, 20 miles south of Yellowstone National Park in the Teton Wilderness, overlooks the headwaters of the Lower 48's longest free-flowing river; 671 miles downstream it merges with the Missouri River at Williston, North Dakota. What a fishing jaunt it would be to float the portion of river that flows through Montana. It's an idea that has haunted my dreams ever since I first met old Yellow Rocks, though I'll admit it seems less likely with each gray hair that shows up in my beard. But I do keep carving away at it, if only in little pieces.

The first time I fished the Yellowstone was in late March as near as I can recollect. It was a cold day, way back when only a hardy few anglers were into winter fly-fishing. We were well into a helter-skelter road trip to wherever Montana trout might possibly be on the bite when a ferocious wind threatened to send us airborne off the interstate. How impressive that blow was to the average wind-beaten Livingston resident, I'll never know. But I can tell you the gale sure impressed us. It's the wind to which we compare all others to this day. Anyway, looking for respite in Livingston, we ducked into Dan Bailey's Fly Shop.

To my query about what was happening on the river, the kid behind the counter reached into one of the zillion fly bins, pulled out a woven-body stonefly pattern, and said, "Head upriver to Carter's Bridge, find a tailing riffle or a good shelf, drift this right on the bottom. Mister, it's the best game in town, but you best wait until the wind settles a little, it'd be tougher than shit out there right now."

The wind never did settle that day, but overnight it mellowed enough for casting. Unfortunately, it also turned cold; something like six above not counting wind chill. That's a little cold for me, even though I like winter fishing, but while stalling over breakfast it occurred to me that this was the Yellowstone and we were here to fish. It would be a shame to pass up the chance to take a few fish here, however slight. Against my better judgment, and because there wasn't anywhere else to go in the area that would be warmer, we headed up to Carter's Bridge.

Gale took one look at the thick hoarfrost on the bankside bushes, turned the car's heater to full blast, and buried her nose in a magazine. I bundled up and hit the river, for once following directions from a fly shop exactly. It turned out that the kid behind the counter had the Yellowstone's trout pretty well pegged. In short order I managed to bean several fat rainbows, a couple of snaky browns, and a bevy of plump and feisty whitefish. It was a good thing too, because a long fishing session was out the question.

After two hours or so, I reeled up, and shivered and shuttered my way to the car, where Gale inquired skeptically, "Well, how was it?"

"Damn fine," I replied without a hint of sarcasm.

The old *Roches Jaunes* might be a little more crowded these days, even in winter, but by God it still has pretty damn fine fishing.

Fishing the Yellowstone River

Paradise Valley in late September is among the prettiest spots on the planet, and I'd hate to miss a fall of fishing there. But if I were forced to choose just one time and place to fish the river it would be in April down around Big Timber. And I'd pray hard that my visit coincide with the annual spring caddis blizzard.

Last spring, we headed east from Livingston, confident the hatch would indeed be blizzard-like and the trout would be going bonkers. Didn't happen. We found beautiful river, but caddis not a one.

Yellowstone River above Big Timber.

Mornings, we dredged the bottom with the usual assortment of Buggers, Clousers, Yuk Bugs, flash-wrapped nymphs, San Juan Worms, and egg patterns and hauled out a few winter-thin browns and a couple of feisty rainbows. In the afternoons, we wiled away the time by luring modest-sized rainbows to the surface with small dry flies. All in all, not a bad way to spend a couple of early spring days on a great river, but not at all like fishing the same great river during the mother of all caddis hatches, either.

Restaurants and Accommodations

Anglers who rate fishing holes by the number of good eating and drinking establishments nearby will love Livingston. We give Martin's Café (406-222-2110) high marks for breakfast vittles. For lunch, check out the historic Murray Hotel (201 West Park St., 406-222-8336). The fine-dining spot is Russell Chatham's Livingston Bar and Grill (130 N. Main St., 406-222-7909). If you just want a good dinner without the bells and whistles, try the Buffalo Jump Steakhouse and Saloon (5237 Hwy. 89 South, 406-222-2987).

The Yellowstone is blessed with numerous public fishing accesses and associated campgrounds. There's not a whole lot of difference between them, so we usually just choose the closest one to where we want to fish. Down around Big Timber it might be the Gray Bear Access, although this is one spot where trains have not yet gone the way of dinosaurs, so be sure to pack along a set of good earplugs. South of

Livingston we've camped at the Mallards Rest, Paradise, Emigrant, and Joe Brown (Yankee Jim) accesses, as well as at the Forest Service campground up Pine Creek.

There are so many B&Bs, lodges, and resorts that cater to flyfishers in and around Paradise Valley that trying to mention them all would be problematic. With that in mind, I'll limit my comments to the few I know something about. Chico Hot Springs Lodge in Pray (#1 Chico Road, 406-333-4933) is probably the best known of these lodges, and surprisingly, it's also one of the most reasonable. The food is great, and the rooms are clean and comfortable—soaking in the hot springs is just an added bonus. While we've never been, close friends rave about the Blue Winged Olive, An Angler's Bed and Breakfast just south of Livingston (5157 Hwy. 89, 406-222-1141).

If you just want a clean, quiet, comfortable motel room, check out the Econo Lodge (111 Rogers Lane, 406-222-0555). They welcome dogs, too.

Livingston, Montana

The Union Pacific railroad arrived in 1882, and the branch line south to Yellowstone National Park carried countless tourists to Gardiner where they boarded a stagecoach. Farming and mining were the economic mainstays in the early days. Today's industries include tourism, flyfishing, lumber manufacturing, and locomotive repair.

The river is home to some sizeable brown trout.

The dominating theme of downtown is still railroading. The historic Northern Pacific depot has been restored to its original grandeur to accommodate art and history exhibitions. The imposing brick structure resembles an Italian villa, with its curved colonnade and rich terra cotta ornament along the track side. The original interior was lavishly decorated with mosaic trim, terrazzo floor, and wrought-iron ticket windows. The Livingston Chamber of Commerce is located in the depot complex.

The Firehouse 5 Playhouse provides visitors the chance to enjoy live theater year-round. The summer schedule includes classic modern-day vaudeville in a cabaret-style setting, while the winter lineup includes major musicals, concerts, and comedy acts. The theater itself is decorated with fire memorabilia and is complete with movie-style concessions.

There are also museums and art galleries to see and a whole flock of restaurants and bars, all set amid the pristine beauty of five surrounding mountain ranges. It's truly a vacationer's paradise, albeit an often windy one.

Nearby Fisheries

Paradise Valley Spring Creeks

Some of the best and most challenging fishing in Paradise Valley is not on the big river itself, but rather at the famous trio of spring creeks: Armstrong, Depuy's, and Nelson's.

Armstrong Spring Creek (O'Hair Ranch, 406-222-2979) averages about 80 feet wide and 3 feet deep over its mile-long run. A true spring creek, it flows clear and cold (46 to 55 degrees) and constant over the entire year. Its fertile waters provide ideal insect and trout habitat, producing a massive amount of trout food in the form of caddis, mayflies, midges, scuds, sow bugs, and other important macroinvertebrates. The Blue-Winged Olives and Pale Morning Duns often hatch in true blizzard fashion.

Trout numbers range from excellent to extraordinary—heavy wild rainbows, browns, and native cutthroats ranging from 14 to 20 inches, and with excellent staying power. While the clarity of the water and healthy trout population make spotting fish easy, catching them can be tough. It's the ultimate dry fly fishing experience, but it doesn't treat amateurs well.

The creek is on a private ranch owned by the O'Hair family and is open all year. Twelve rods are allowed daily, and fees run $75 (April 15-June 1), $100 (June 15-Sept. 14), $75 (Sept. 15-Oct. 14), and $40 (Oct. 15-April 14).

Depuy's Spring Creek (406-222-0221) consists of 3 miles of private spring creek ranging from riffles and runs to classic smooth flats. Like Armstrong, it is a true spring creek. Unaffected by runoff and rich in nutrients, it produces a host of insects: mayflies, midges, scuds, snails, and aquatic worms supplemented by a healthy supply of ants, beetles, and hoppers in warmer months.

Depuy's wild rainbows, browns, and native cutthroats are prolific and healthy, averaging around 12 to 17 inches, with larger fish a possibility. The creek is open year-round and allows 16 rods per day. Rod fees are $75 (April 15-June 14), $100 (June 15-Sept. 14), $75 (Sept. 15-Oct. 14), and $35 (Oct. 15-April 14).

If there is a more picture-perfect spring creek than Nelson's Spring Creek (406-222-6560) I can't wait to see it. Until then, when I dream of spring creeks, the vision will be of Nelson's gin-clear, long, smooth, and relatively shallow runs, dimpled by sipping 15- to 18-inch wild rainbows, browns, and cutthroats.

Like its two sisters, hatches are outstanding, and the amount of natural food available to foraging trout borders on awesome. Nelson's carries with it a reputation for being the toughest of the three Paradise Valley spring creeks. But almost every spring creek is tough. They all offer the ultimate test of flyfishing skills and knowledge, which is why we're willing to pay so much for the pleasure of fishing them.

All three are usually booked months in advance for June, July, and August, so be sure to make reservations early.

If you don't like to pay for your fishing, the mountains surrounding Paradise Valley abound with small tributaries and high mountain lakes. The fishing is far easier and there is plenty of solitude to be found. The local fly shops can also put you on a number of excellent private ranch lakes.

Nearby Attractions and Activities

The International Flyfishing Museum (corner of B and Lewis, 406-222-9369) is a museum and education center run by the Federation of Flyfishers. If you're interested in the history of flyfishing, this is the place to start.

Author's Tip

For the mid-April caddis blitz, be sure to pack along patterns for each stage of the emergence: larva, pupa, and adult. The Beadhead Peacock Caddis works for the larva; for the pupa it's difficult to top the LaFontaine Sparkle Emergent Pupa. Adult feeders can usually be fooled with either a dark-bodied X-Caddis or the good old Elk Hair Caddis.

Favorite Fly

Black Stonefly Nymph

Hook	#2-6 5263, weighted with wraps of lead wire
Antennae and Tail	Black goose biots
Abdomen, Thorax, and Head	Black Haretron dubbed
Rib	Black Schwannundaze
Wing Cases	Turkey quill sections coated with Flexament
Legs	Black round rubber

Fast Facts

Yellowstone River (Montana)

Location	Gardiner, Montana, to past Big Timber is a blue-ribbon coldwater fishery; below there to the North Dakota line is a diverse, but rarely flyfished, warmwater fishery.
Water Type	Freestone river with a broad and heavy current. The river may be blown out from mid-May through June and sometimes even well into July; despite its size and heavy current, it's relatively easy to float. The worst rapids occur in Yankee Jim Canyon downstream of Gardiner.
Primary Gamefish	Wild brown, rainbow, and native Yellowstone cutthroat trout, mountain whitefish
Best Time	Pre-runoff in March, April and early May; September through November

Best Flies	Best hatches are March Browns in late April and early May; Mother's Day caddis hatch during the same period; a variety of stonefly hatches, including a strong Salmonfly hatch in May and June (river is often blown out during peak hatch times); PMDs, caddis, Green Drakes, and Little Yellow Stoneflies hatch in late July through August, but in normal years hoppers rule from August into fall; late fall is giant streamer time.
Equipment	9-foot, 5- or 6-weight rods, floating lines, long tapered leaders, tippets to match the situation.
Conditions	Windy. You might have a better chance of spying a white buffalo than experiencing anything close to a calm day on the Yellowstone. Other than wind, expect typical Montana weather.
Drive Time	From Bozeman: 30 minutes From Billings: 1.5 hours From Idaho Falls: 4.5 hours
Directions	From Bozeman, I-90 east, for the upper river turn south at Livingston on Rt. 89; from Billings, I-90 east, for upper river turn south at Livingston on Rt. 89; from Idaho Falls, Hwy. 20 north to Hwy. 191 at West Yellowstone, I-90 east to Livingston, turn south to reach upper river.

Local Fly Shops

Dan Bailey's Fly Shop
209 West Park Street
Livingston, MT 59047
406-222-1673, 1-800-356-4052

George Anderson's Yellowstone Angler
Rt. 89 South, P.O. Box 660
Livingston, MT 59047
406-222-7130

Hatch Finders Fly Shop
113 West Park St.
Livingston, MT 59047
406-222-0989

Park's Fly Shop
P.O. Box 196
Gardiner, MT 59030
406-848-7314

Big Sky Flies and Guides
Rt. 89
Emigrant, MT 59027
406-333-4401

Montana Troutfitters
1716 W. Main
Bozeman, MT 59715
406-587-4707

River's Edge
2012 N. 7th
Bozeman, MT 59715
406-586-5373

Fins & Feathers
1500 N 19th Ave # B
Bozeman, MT 59715
406-586-2188

Bozeman Angler
23 E. Main
Bozeman, MT 59715
406-587-9111

Greater Yellowstone Flyfishers
31 Spanish Peak Dr
Bozeman, MT 59715
406-585-5321

Guides

Wilderness Outfitters
406-222-6933

Old West Outfitters and Supply
406-322-5472/4910

Cudney Guide Service
406- 333-4057

Long Outfitting
406-222-6775

Lone Willow Creek Guide Service
406-222-7584

Bear Paw Outfitters
406-222-6642

Curt Hall
406-333-4061

Bears Den Outfitters
406-222-0746

Tom Jenni's Reel Montana
406-539-6610, 1-866-885-6065

Eagle Vista Ranch
406-222-7952, 614-891-0489

Hubbard's Yellowstone Lodge
406-848-7755

Al Gadoury's 6X Outfitters
406-586-3806

Contacts

Livingston Chamber of Commerce
406-222-0850

Montana FWP
Region 3
1400 S. 19th
Bozeman, MT 59715
406-994-4042

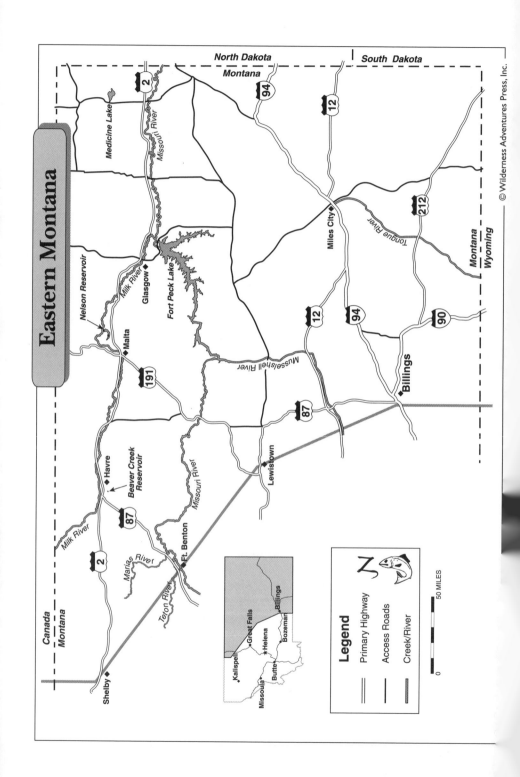

CHAPTER 43

EASTERN MONTANA
Untapped Flyfishing Smorgasbord

Few fly anglers know much about the flyfishing possibilities east of Billings or north of Lewistown. Even before the present drought, I doubt many flyfishers traveled to the Big Empty. And the run of dry years has really put a hurt on a large number of once-fine fisheries—by midsummer the Musselshell River is dry as a bone in places; the Tongue River is all but sucked dry; prairie potholes, once home to rainbow trout literally as long as your leg, are now lifeless or near death. Hopefully, the drought is starting to lose its grip, which should allow the fisheries to recover. But I'd recommend calling the nearest Fish, Wildlife & Parks office for an update before heading out.

Tongue River Country

One of our most memorable northern Rockies flyfishing experiences occurred a couple springs back on the Tongue River in southeastern Montana. We got into a pack of giant, though hard to catch, rainbows, and while trying to solve that puzzle a big storm hit, which not only canceled the fishing, it nearly canceled us as well.

We found the big rainbows rolling up for bugs swept into the river by a strong wind. Before the storm hit, we tied into a couple of real pigs. Both ripped a #8 Madam X from the surface and took off upstream toward the dam, leaving beaver-sized wakes and a sheared tippet behind them. I was on the way to winning a battle with the next fish when the ferocious storm struck, and I really did bust that one off on purpose.

The storm's highlights involved hurricane-strength wind bearing a deluge of sleet, marble-sized hail, pouring rain, and finally blinding snow, which was piled up some 3 feet deep outside the tent-trailer by the next morning. The odyssey continued when I foolishly tried to drive out later that morning and got bogged down in deep drifts a hundred yards short of the pass. We were lucky enough to be towed over the top by a good Samaritan who had kept his tire chains handy.

The afternoon before the storm we had launched the float tube in a bay beside the marina on Tongue River Reservoir and had great fun catching crappie and the occasional smallmouth bass by slowly stripping small Buggers. We also had good fishing with flies suspended beneath a floating strike indicator. There was a slight chop on the lake, and I guess the bobbing motion it imparted to the suspended flies proved too much temptation for the crappies because every few minutes down would go the bobber and up would come another scrappy crappie.

As an added bonus, we had coaxed a tom turkey off his roost tree just that morning.

Bird hunters flock "out east" as we say; more flyfishers might want to consider it.

Flyfishing Along the Hi-Line

In the fall we do a lot of upland bird hunting north and south of the Hi-Line (US 2) from Shelby east to the North Dakota border. I've no idea how many times we've hunted around Havre, but I must admit that until two falls ago I'd never even heard of 10,000-acre Beaver Creek County Park (10 miles south of Havre, Hwy. 234).

We were scoping out the bird-hunting possibilities at the Havre FWP office and overheard a fisheries biologist say, "Beaver Creek up in the Bears Paw Mountains has brook trout, and in Bear Paw Lake there are cutthroat and rainbow trout and smallmouth bass, and in Beaver Creek Reservoir you'll find walleye, pike, rainbow trout, smallmouth bass, and perch." The next time we're up this way, you can bet we'll pack a fly rod or two.

Farther east, walleye might still be king at Fort Peck Reservoir, but smallmouth bass seems to be closing fast. And while the big reservoir's vast windswept expanses are no place to carelessly float a tube, plenty of good flyrodding spots can be found right off shore. The breakwaters, docks, and the dam face should keep even a cautious flyfisher grinning for quite some time.

If you opt to bring a seaworthy boat, by all means point it toward the Big Dry Arm or between Rock and McGuire Creeks or around the rocky points between Hell and Devils Creek or along the dam itself. Fly patterns that work elsewhere for smallies work well here too, but minnow imitations like the Dahlberg Diver, Clouser Minnow, and various leech patterns are probably a good place to start. A word of caution: Fort Peck is more like an inland sea than a lake, turning from tranquil to white-capped fury in a heartbeat.

Fly anglers wanting to pad their life list of fish species might want to consider Nelson Reservoir just off US 2 east of Malta. You might catch a bigmouth buffalo, or even a smallmouth buffalo. Or perhaps you'd rather cast for carp, goldeye, or even sucker. And if such exotics aren't your bag Nelson is widely known for pike and walleye. (If you actually catch a bigmouth buffalo on a fly, you might want to quit fishing immediately and go play the lottery since bigmouth bufflers are pelagic feeders. They swim along with an open mouth, straining zooplankton through their gills, which makes flies a tough sell.)

It's about as far from our home in Dillon to Medicine Lake on the eastern end of the Hi-Line as you can get while remaining in Montana. The last time I checked the odometer read 621 miles, and the trip took over 11 hours. Not exactly the sort of place one picks for a casual afternoon of fishing, but despite the long drive we find ourselves out there at least once each fall. The real lure, of course, is feathered game, but there are pike available in good numbers. However, they are of modest size since a big fish kill in the mid-nineties decimated the population, which is just now rebounding.

The Lower Missouri River

The Missouri River at Loma, where the Teton and Marias Rivers add their flows, is another hotspot for the fly angler wishing to pad the life list. Says local FWP fisheries biologist Bill Gardner, "We've documented 47 species in the area, which is about as rich an aquatic environment as Montana has to offer." Of course, he wasn't inferring that all 47 can be induced to eat flies, but certainly some can. According to Gardner, "Goldeye, smallmouth bass, northern pike, channel cat, brown and rainbow trout, and carp are among the more common."

If for some reason you find yourself in the Glasgow area in late spring or early summer, the Milk River's confluence with the Missouri is another good spot for a variety of warmwater species. The Milk is among the lower Missouri's most important spawning tributaries, so just about everything that swims in the big river eventually heads up the Milk to spawn—channel catfish, walleye, sauger, northern pike, and a whole host of non-game species.

While most of these species would be pretty weird stuff for the typical fly angler, they are a wonderful change of pace. And if you're tired of fighting the crowds just to put your boat in the water on rivers like the Bighorn, head east and you'll have all the water to yourself.

Restaurants and Accommodations

Just about every little burg in the eastern half of the state has at least one decent eatery. Sam's Supper Club in Glasgow (307 Klein Ave., 406-228-4614) specializes in Montana char-broiled steaks. The menu also includes walleye, of course, and the bar serves single-malt scotch, too. Malta's version of fine dining is the Stockman Bar and Steakhouse (406-654-1919).

Like good eateries, just about every eastern Montana town has at least one cozy motel. In Malta, it's the Riverside (406-654-2310), which is reasonable and clean and allows dogs. In Havre, it's the Duck Inn (406-265-9615), which is a little fancier and includes a great supper club. In Glasgow, try the Cottonwood Inn (406-228-8213).

Most fishing access sites allow camping, and almost every town has a park that allows camping.

Nearby Attractions and Activities

I realize that in this case "nearby" doesn't really apply, but there are still a multitude of attractions. A few of the most interesting are Pompey's Pillar on I-94 between Billings and Forsyth as you explore the lower Yellowstone River; Makoshika State

Park near Glendive; the Charles M. Russell National Wildlife Refuge at the upper end of sprawling Fort Peck Reservoir; the Little Big Horn Battlefield on I-90 east of Billings at Hardin; and the Chalk Cliff, Medicine Rocks, Capital Reef complex down in the Powder River country east of Broadus.

Author's Tip

Eastern Montana flyfishing, like everything else "out east," is a far flung and eclectic affair. Unless you know specifically what you might catch on any given cast, my best advice is to tie on a #6 black or olive Woolly Bugger or Clouser and go for it. Of course, it doesn't hurt to check with the local FWP office, tackle and bait shops, or hardware and sporting goods stores for local updates.

Favorite Fly

Black Woolly Bugger

Hook	#2-10 Mustad 36890 SF
Tail	Black marabou
Body	Black chenille
Hackle	Black, palmered with a heavy collar

Fast Facts

Eastern Montana

Location	Roughly east of Shelby, Lewistown, and Billings
Water Types	Creeks, rivers, reservoirs, and potholes
Primary Gamefish	A variety of warm and coldwater gamefish
Best Time	Spring to early summer and again in fall, assuming, of course, there is still water
Best Flies	Buggers, leeches, Clousers, Bunnies, poppers, deer hair bugs, attractor dries and various meaty-looking nymphs
Equipment	9-foot, 4- to 6-weight rod, floating, sink-tip and full-sink lines, tapered leaders to suit, wire or heavy shock tippets for pike, some sort of watercraft
Conditions	Lots of wind. Spring and fall weather is typically unstable, and summers can be brutally hot and dry.
Drive Time	A long way from anywhere, but then that's part of the appeal.
Directions	From south to north, the main arteries are I-94, Hwy. 200, and US 2.

Local Fishing Shops

Don's
P.O. Box 780
Lewistown, MT 59457
406-538-9408

Sport Center
320 W. Main
Lewistown, MT 59457
406-538-9308

The Bait Shop
638 NE Main
Lewistown, MT 59457
406-538-6085

Big Horn Fly Shop
1426 N. Crawford Ave
Hardin, MT 59034
406-665-1321

Big Horn Fly Shop
485 S. 24th Street W
Billings, MT 59102
406-656-8257

Rainbow Run Fly Shop
2244 Grand Ave.
Billings, MT 59102-2619
406-656-3455

Scheel's All Sports
Rimrock Mall
Billings, MT 59102
406-656-9220

Sunshine Sports
304 Moore Ln
Billings, MT 59102
1-800-773-3723

Montana River Outfitters
1401 5th Ave.
Great Falls, MT 59403
401-761-1677

Missouri Breaks River Company
2409 4th Ave.
Great Falls, MT 59401
406-453-3035

Wolverton's Fly Shop
210 5th St.
Great Falls, MT 59405
401-454-0254

Falls Outfitters
1704 6th Ave.
Great Falls, MT 59401
406-727-2087

Many Rivers Outfitting
815 Grizzly Dr.
Great Falls, MT 59401
406-736-5556

Scheel's All Sports
Holiday Village Shopping Ctr.
Great Falls, MT 59405
406-453-7666

Contacts

Montana FWP
Region 4
4600 Giant Springs Rd.
Great Falls, MT 59406
406-454-3441

Montana FWP
Region 6
Rt. 1-4210
Glasgow, MT 59230
406-228-9347

Montana FWP
Region 5
2300 Lake Elmo Dr.
Billings, MT 59105
406-252-4654

Montana FWP
Region 7
P.O. Box 1630-1
Miles City, MT 59301
406-232-4365

Fly Shops, Sporting Good Stores, Lodges, Outfitters And Guides

Idaho

Name	Address	Phone
Fall River Fly & Tackle	PO Box 692, Ashton, ID 83420	208-652-7646
Three Rivers Ranch	PO Box 593, Ashton, ID 83420-0593	208-652-3750
B&B Tackle	211 S. Stout, Blackfoot, ID 83221-2924	208-785-3322
H. Koppel Co.	PO Box 198, Boise, ID 83701-0198	208-344-3539
Bear Creek Fly Shop	5521 W. State St., Boise, ID 83703	208-853-8704
Sunset Sports Center	5804 Fairview Ave., Boise, ID 83704	208-376-1100
Benchmark/Stone FlyAngler	625 Vista Ave., Boise, ID 83705	208-338-1333
Idaho Angler	1682 Vista Ave., Boise, ID 83705	208-389-9957
Intermountain Arms/Tackle	900 Vista Ave, Boise, ID 83705	208-345-3474
Anglers	7097 Overland Rd., Boise, ID 83709	208-323-6768
The Angling Craftsman	3355 N. Five Mile Rd., #300, Boise, ID 83713	208-375-4766
River 1	651 7th St., Challis, ID 83226	208-879-2589
Cast Away Fly Shop	3620 N. Fruitland Lane, Coeur D'Alene, ID	208-765-3133
Fin & Feathers	1816-½ Sherman Ave, Coeur D'Alene, ID 83814	208-667-9304
Black Sheep	308 W. Seale Ave., Coeur D'Alene, ID 83815	208-667-7831
Northwest Outfitters	402 W. Canfield, Coeur D'Alene, ID 83815	888-347-4223
Yostmark Mountain Equipment	12 E. Little Ave., Driggs, ID 83422	208-354-2828
Teton Valley Lodge	379 Adams Rd., Driggs, ID 83422-5356	208-354-2386
Angler's Catalog Company, LLC	PO Box 993, Eagle, ID 83616	800-657-8040
Fly Fishing Inc.	1403 Mace Rd., Eagle, ID 83616	208-939-9810
MacKenzie Outfitters	3210 E. Chinden Blvd. Ste. 128, Eagle, ID 83616	208-433-8844
Rae Brothers Sporting Goods	247 E. Main St., Grangeville, ID 83530	208-983-2877
Cast and Blast	PO Box 509, Hayden, ID 83835	208-772-3748
Trout Bum International	6724 N. Orlinda Lane, Idaho Falls, ID 83401	208-524-4890
XAT	366 N. Holmes Ave., Idaho Falls, ID 83401	208-528-9554
Hyde Outfitters Fly Shop	1520 Pancheri, Idaho Falls, ID 83402	800-444-4933
Jimmys All Seasons Angler	275 'A' Street, Idaho Falls, ID 83402	208-524-7160
Island Park Outfitters & Last	HC66, Box 483, Island Park, ID 83429	208-558-7068
Trouthunter	HC 66, Box 477, Island Park, ID 83429	208-558-9900
Henry's Fork Anglers, LLC	HC 65, Box 491, Island Park, ID 83429-9701	208-558-7525
Ram Sport Center	124 E. Main St., Jerome, ID 83338	208-324-3722
The Hatch	46 S. Overman Dr., Jerome, ID 83338	208-733-9111

Flying B Ranch	Rt. 2, Box 12C, Kamiah, ID 83536	208-935-0755
Lost River Outfitters	PO Box 3445, Ketchum, ID 83340	208-726-1706
Sturtevants of Hailey	PO Box 830, Ketchum, ID 83340	208-788-7847
Scott's Fly Shop	PO Box 3218, Ketchum, ID 83340-3218	208-788-4561
Silver Creek Outfitters	500 N. Main St., Ketchum, ID 83340	208-726-9056
The Traditional Sportsman	814 Main St., Lewiston, ID 83501	208-746-6688
Twin River Anglers	534 Thain Rd., Lewiston, ID 83501	208-746-8946
Lolo Sporting Goods	1026 Main St., Lewiston, ID 83501-1842	206-743-1031
Gart Sports	625 21st St., #A, Lewiston, ID 83501-3285	208-746-8040
The Bent Rod	PO Box 358, Mackay, ID 83251	888-Bent-Rod
www.reelflies.com	456 N. 400 W., Malad, ID 83252	208-766-4017
Outdoor Solutions	PO Box 735, McCall, ID 83638	208-634-5340
Intermountain Sports	1375 Fairview Ave., Meridian, ID 83642	208-888-4911
Malone Outfitters	149 . Adkins Way, Meridian, ID 83642	208-888-3240
Sportsman's Warehouse	3797 E. Fairview Ave., Meridian, ID 83642	208-884-3000
Husky Sport Shop	1006 Pullman Rd., Moscow, ID 83843	208-822-0205
Northwestern Mountain Sports	PO Box 9467, Moscow, ID 83843	208-882-0133
Gart Brothers Sporting Goods	121 E. 5th St., Moscow, ID 83843-2909	208-882-9547
Howard's Tackle Shoppe	1707 Garrity Blvd., Nampa, ID 83687	208-465-0946
Riverside Sport Shop	PO Box 2547, Orofino, ID 83544	208-476-5418
All Season's Angler	509 E. Oak St., Pocatello, ID 83201	208-232-3042
Lee Aikens Sport Shop	245 N. Main St., Pocatello, ID 83204-3196	208-233-3837
All Seasons Sports	160 W. Main St., Rexburg, ID 83440	208-356-9245
Rocky Mountain Flies & Supplie	1572 W. 930 St., Rexburg, ID 83440	208-356-0514
Fur-Feather & Fly	2955 W. 5200 S., Rexburg, ID 83440-4305	208-356-9522
Silver Spur Sports	403 Main St., Salmon, ID 83467-4218	208-756-2833
Outdoor Experience	314 N. 1st Ave, Sandpoint, ID 83864	208-263-6028
Pine Street Pawn & Fly Fishing	525 Pine St., Sandpoint, ID 83864	208-263-6022
House of Harrop Flies	Box 491, St Anthony, ID 83445	208-624-3537
Blue Goose Sport Shop	621 Main St., St. Maries, ID 83861	208-245-4015
McCoy's Tackle Shop	PO Box 210, Stanley, ID 83278	208-774-3377
Bill Mason Snug Outfitters	PO Box 127, Sun Valley, ID 83353	208-622-9305
Sun Valley Outfitters	PO Box 3400, Sun Valley, ID 83353	208-622-3400
Sun Valley Rivers Co.	PO Box 1776, Sun Valley, ID 83353-1776	208-726-7404
Drifters of the South Fork	Box 148, Swan Valley, ID 83449	208-483-2722
Sandy Mite Fly Shop & Cafe	HC 34, Box 10, Swan Valley, ID 83449	208-483-2609
South Fork Lodge	PO Box 22, Swan Valley, ID 83449	877-347-4735
Rainbow Fly Fishing Shop	1862 Addison Ave. E., Twin Falls, ID 83301	208-733-9632
Blue Lakes Sporting Goods	1236 Blue Lakes Blvd., ND, Twin Falls, ID 83301	208-733-6446

Snake River Outfitters	232 2nd St., E., Twin Falls, ID 83301-6245	208-735-1289
Stayner's Sporting Goods	PO Box 2367, Twin Falls, ID 83303-2367	208-733-8453
Simerly's Grocery, Pawn, Tackl	PO Box 207, Wendell, ID 83355	208-536-6651

Montana

East Slope Anglers	PO Box 160249, Big Sky, MT 59716	406-995-4369
Gallatin River Guides	PO Box 160212, Big Sky, MT 59716	406-995-2290
Lone Mountain Ranch	Lone Mountain Access Rd., Big Sky, MT 59716	800-514-4644
Two River Gear	PO Box 591, Bigfork, MT 59911	406-837-3474
Bighorn Fly & Tackle Shop	485 S. 24th St., W., Billings, MT 59102	406-656-8257
Gart Sports	100 24th St., W., Billings, MT 59102	406-656-3888
Gibson's	1313 Broadwater, Billings, MT 59102	406-252-8436
Rainbow Run Fly Shop	2244 Grand Ave., Billings, MT 59102	406-656-3455
Rimrock Scheels	300 S. 24th St. W, Billings, MT 59102-5650	406-656-9220
Big Bear Sports Center	2618 King Ave., W., Billings, MT 59102-6428	406-652-5999
Bob's Custom Rods & Flies	3803 Ben Hogan Lane, Billings, MT 59106-1032	406-652-6605
Fred's Fly Fishing Guide Serv	504 Henderson St., Bozeman, MT 59715	406-585-9235
Hawkridge Outfitters & Rodbuil	8000 Trail Creek Rd., Bozeman, MT 59715	406-585-9608
Montana Troutfitters	1716 West Main St., #4, Bozeman, MT 59715	406-587-4707
Powder Horn Sportsman	35 East Main St., Bozeman, MT 59715	406-587-7373
The Bozeman Angler	23 E. Main St., Bozeman, MT 59715	800-886-9111
The Rivers Edge	2012 N. 7th Ave., Bozeman, MT 59715	406-586-5373
Bob Ward & Sons	2320 W. Main St., Bozeman, MT 59718	406-586-4381
Fins & Feathers of Bozeman	1500 N. 19th, Bozeman, MT 59718	406-586-2188
Greater Yellowstone Flyfishers	31 Spanish Peak Dr., Bozeman, MT 59718	406-585-5321
Northern High Plains Out	Box 152, Browning, MT 59417	406-338-7413
Trail and Creek Outfitters	Hwy. 88, Browning, MT 59417	406-732-4431
Bob Ward & Sons	1925 Dewey Blvd., Butte, MT 59701	406-494-4452
Fish-On Fly and Tackle	3346 Harrison Ave, Butte, MT 59701	406-494-4218
Fran Johnson's Sport Shop	1957 Harrison Ave, Butte, MT 59701	406-782-3322
Great Waters Fly Inn	7 S. Excelsior, Butte, MT 59701	406-832-2180
Southwest Montana Flies	1814 Thornton Ave., Butte, MT 59701	406-832-3368
Beartooth Flyfishing	2975 Hwy 287 N., Cameron, MT 59720	406-682-7525
Wade Lake Resort	P.O. Box 107, Cameron, MT 59720	406-682-7560
Madison River Cabins	1403 US Hwy. 287 N., Cameron, MT 59720	406-682-4890
Fly Fisher's Inn	2629 Old US Hwy. 91, Cascade, MT 59421	406-468-2529
Missouri Riverside Outfitters	3103 Old US Hwy. 91, Cascade, MT 59421	406-468-9385
Coyote's Den Sports Shop	PO Box 239, Chester, MT 59522-0239	406-759-5305

Rock Creek Fisherman's Mercant	73 Rock Creek Road, Clinton, MT 59825	406-825-6440
Flathead River Outfitters	7343 Hwy 2E, Columbia Falls, MT 59912	406-892-2033
Montana Fly Co.	PO Box 2853, Columbia Falls, MT 59912	406-892-9112
Northern Rockies Outfitters	PO Box 2443, Columbia Falls, MT 59912	406-892-1188
Arends Tackle	514 Kokanee Cir., Columbia Falls, MT 59912	406-892-4923
Outdoor Supply	PO Box 1262, Columbus, MT 59019	406-322-4910
Riverside Fly Shoppe	Box 1035, Columbus, MT 59019	406-322-5472
Beartooth Plateau Outfitters	302 Main St. POB 1127, Cooke City, MT 59020	800-253-8545
Big Bear Lodge	PO Box 1029, Cooke City, MT 59020	406-838-2267
Missouri River Trout Shop	110 Bridge St., Craig, MT 59648-8715	800-337-8528
Bitterroot Fly Company	305 N. Main St., Darby, MT 59829	800-363-2408
Triple Creek Ranch	5551 W. Fork Stage Route, Darby, MT 59829	406-821-4600
Five Rivers Lodge	13100 Hwy. 41 North, Dillon, MT 59725	800-378-5006
Frontier Anglers	680 N. Montana St., Dillon, MT 59725	800-228-5263
The Watershed	11 Pierce Dr., Dillon, MT 59725	800-753-6660
Tom Smith's Backcountry Angler	426 S. Atlantic St., Dillon, MT 59725	406-683-3462
Uncle Bob's Fishing Supplies	PO Box 262, Dillon, MT 59725	800-708-5565
Watershed Adventures	600 N. Montana St., Dillon, MT 59725	406-683-4352
Great Divide Outfitters & Fly	Rt. 43, Divide, MT 59727	406-267-3346
Big Sky Flies & Guides	PO Box 4, Emigrant, MT 59027	406-333-4401
Hubbard's Yellowstone Lodge	Miner Basin, Emigrant, MT 59027	406-848-7755
Gary Evans Madison River Guide	PO Box 1456, Ennis, MT 59729	406-682-4802
Madison River Fishing Company	109 Main St., Ennis, MT 59729	800-227-7127
The Tackle Shop	PO Box 625, Ennis, MT 59729	800-808-2832
Bamboo Flyrod and Gun	PO Box 391, Ennis, MT 59729-0391	406-682-4176
Big Horn River Outfitters	Box 7483, Ft. Smith, MT 59035	406-666-9199
Bighorn Angler	Box 577, Ft. Smith, MT 59035	406-666-2233
Bighorn Fly & Tackle Shop	One Main St., Ft. Smith, MT 59035	406-666-2253
Bighorn River Lodge	PO Box 7756, Ft. Smith, MT 59035	406-666-2368
Bighorn Trout Shop	PO Box 7477, Ft. Smith, MT 59035	406-666-2375
East Slope Outfitters	Box 855, Ft. Smith, MT 59035	406-356-7799
Fort Smith Fly Shop	PO Box 7872, Ft. Smith, MT 59035	406-666-2550
George Kelly's Bighorn Country	PO Box 524, Ft. Smith, MT 59035	406-666-2326
Parks Fly Shop	PO Box 196, Gardiner, MT 59030	406-848-7314
Montana River Outfitters	923 10th Ave. N, Great Falls, MT 59401-1160	406-761-1677
Big Bear Sport Centers	121 NW Bypass, Great Falls, MT 59404	406-761-6300
Holiday Village Scheels	3 Holiday Village Mall, Great Falls, MT 59405	406-453-7666
Shadow Cast Outfitters	205 9th Ave., S., Great Falls, MT 59405	406-727-2119

Shannon's Fur, Feather, & Fly	2514 2nd Ave. S, Great Falls, MT 59405	406-452-7727
Wolverton's Fly Shop	210 5th Street South, Great Falls, MT 59405	406-454-0245
Scheels Sports - Great Falls	1200 10th Ave., S. #3, Great Falls, MT 59405	406-454-6775
Bob Ward & Sons	1120 North 1st, Hamilton, MT 59840	406-363-6204
Fishaus Fly Fishing	702 N. First St., Hamilton, MT 59840	406-363-6158
Kent Custom Rods	102 Vantage Lane, Hamilton, MT 59840	406-363-4356
River Bend Fly Fishing	PO Box 594, Hamilton, MT 59840	406-363-4197
Anglers Roost	815 US Hwy. 93 S., Hamilton, MT 59840	406-363-1268
Bighorn Fly & Tackle Shop	1426 N. Crawford Ave., Hardin, MT 59034	406-665-1321
Bing & Bob's Sport Shop	PO Box 1568, Havre, MT 59501	406-265-6124
Bob Ward & Sons	3323 Dredge, Helena, MT 59601	406-443-2138
Capital Sports & Western	1092 Helena Ave., Helena, MT 59601	406-443-2978
Cross Currents	326 N. Jackson, Helena, MT 59601	406-449-2292
Montana Fly Goods	2125 Euclid Ave., Helena, MT 59601	406-442-2630
Wolf Creek Guide Service	420 Broadway, Helena, MT 59601	406-442-5148
Trophy Trout Springs Ranch	PO Box 167, Hobson, MT 59452	406-423-5542
Snappy Sport Senter	1400 Hwy. 2 E., Kalispell, MT 59901	406-257-7525
Sportsman FF & Ski Haus	40 E. Idaho St., Kalispell, MT 59901	406-755-6484
Fish Montana Fly Shop	PO Box 455, Kalispell, MT 59903	406-752-7842
Sports Incorporated	333 2nd Ave. N., Lewistown, MT 59457	406-538-8261
The Sports Center	320 West Main, Lewistown, MT 59457	406-538-9408
Don's Inc.	120 2nd Ave. S., Lewistown, MT 59601	406-538-9408
Dave Blackburn's Kootenai Angl	115 W. 2nd St., Libby, MT 59923	406-293-7578
Yellowstone Angler	PO Box 629, Livingston, MT 59047	406-222-7130
Trailhead Sporting Goods	1014 W. Park St., #4, Livingston, MT 59047	406-222-7977
Yellowstone Gateway Sports	1106 W. Park St., Livingston, MT 59047-2955	406-222-5414
Groveland Hunts	PO Box 6, Martinsdale, MT 59053	406-572-3342
Sunrise Fly Shop	PO Box 85, Melrose, MT 59743	406-835-3474
Montana Fly Co.	PO Box 29, Melrose, MT 59912	406-835-2621
Brady's Sportsman Surplus, Inc	Tremper Shopping Center, Missoula, MT 58901	406-646-7801
Bob Ward & Sons	3015 Paxson St., Missoula, MT 59801	406-728-3220
Kesel's Four Rivers Fly Shop	501 S. Higgins Ave., Missoula, MT 59801	406-721-4796
Missoulian Angler	401 S. Orange St., Missoula, MT 59801	406-728-7766
Sportsman's Surplus	2301 Brooks St., Missoula, MT 59801	406-721-5500
Outdoor Adventures	153 Pattee Creek Dr., Missoula, MT 59801-8736	406-542-1230
Grizzly Hackle	215 W. Front St., Missoula, MT 59802	406-721-8996
The Kingfisher	926 E. Broadway, Missoula, MT 59802	406-721-6141
GE Russell Fly Fish	187 Fairway Dr., Missoula, MT 59803	406-721-5673

Blackfoot Angler & Supplies	PO Box 84, Ovando, MT 59854	406-793-3474
Philipsburg Hardware Co.	Box 39, Philipsburg, MT 59858	406-859-3561
Troutski Productions	306 2nd Ave. E., Polson, MT 59860	406-883-1481
High Country Outfitters Fly Fi	158 Bridger Hollow Rd., Pray, MT 59065	406-333-4763
Knoll's Yellowstone Hackle	104 Chicory Rd., Pray, MT 59065	406-333-4848
Headwaters & High Country Outf	13 N. Broadway, Red Lodge, MT 59068	406-446-1027
Sir Michaels Sport Shoppe	21 N. Broadway, Red Lodge, MT 59068	406-446-1613
Yellowstone Troutfitters	10 S. Broadway, Red Lodge, MT 59068	406-446-3819
Ronan Sports	PO Box 8, Ronan, MT 59864	406-676-3701
Harman Fly Shop	PO Box 668, Sheridan, MT 59749	406-842-5868
Brock's Fly Shop	116092 Buxton Rd., Silver Bow, MT 59750	406-446-3268
Anglers Passport	PO Box 712, Silver Star, MT 59751	800-440-2699
Clark Fork Trout & Tackle	103 Mullan Gulch Rd., St. Regis, MT 59866	406-649-2538
Royal Bighorn Lodge	PO Box 183, St. Xavier, MT 59075	406-666-2340
Sporting Adventures/Tightlines	County Rd #145, St. Xavier, MT 59075	406-666-2240
Bitterroot Anglers	4039 Hwy 93 N, Stevensville, MT 59870	406-777-5667
Tamarack Lodge	32855 S. Fork Rd., Troy, MT 59935	406-295-4880
Four Rivers Fishing Co.	205 S. Main St., Twin Bridges, MT 59754	800-276-8768
Hemmingway's Fly Shop	PO Box 428, Twin Bridges, MT 59754	406-684-5649
Twin Bridges Trout Shop	Box 303, Twin Bridges, MT 59754	406-684-5773
Trout Futures	PO Box 485, Twin Bridges, MT 59754-0485	406-684-5512
Blackbird's Fly Shop & Lodge	PO Box 998, Victor, MT 59875	800-210-8648
Glacier Anglers	PO Box 210, W. Glacier, MT 59936	406-888-5454
Glacier Wilderness Guides	PO Box 535, W. Glacier, MT 59936	406-387-5555
rrick's Fly Shop	PO Box 1290, W. Yellowstone, MT 59758	406-646-7290
lue Ribbon Flies	Box 1037, W. Yellowstone, MT 59758	406-646-7642
ud Lilly's Trout Shop	39 Madison Ave, W. Yellowstone, MT 59758	406-646-7801
agle's Tackle Shop	PO Box 280, W. Yellowstone, MT 59758	406-646-7521
acklin's Fly Shop	PO Box 310, W. Yellowstone, MT 59758	406-646-7336
adison River Outfitters	PO Box 398, W. Yellowstone, MT 59758	406-646-9644
J. Cain	30 Madison Ave., W. Yellowstone, MT 59758	800-358-7688
rehole Ranch	PO Box 686, W. Yellowstone, MT 59758-0686	406-646-7294
astle Mt. Fly Fisher	PO Box H, White Sulphur Springs, MT 596	406-547-2330
own Enterprises	6457 Hwy. 93 S., Whitefish, MT 59937	406-862-3111
kestream Fly Fishing Shop	15 Central Ave., Whitefish, MT 59937	406-862-1298
umptown Anglers	222 Central Ave., Whitefish, MT 59937	877-906-9949
llow Creek Fly Fishing Cente	101 Main St., Willow Creek, MT 59760	406-285-3885
g Hole River Outfitters	PO Box 156, Wise River, MT 59762	406-832-3252

Complete Fly Fishers	PO Box 127, Wise River, MT 59762	406-832-3175
Troutfitters	62311 Mt. Hwy. 43, Wise River, MT 59762-9709	406-832-3212
Montana River Outfitters	PO Box 101, Wolf Creek, MT 59648	800-800-8218
Bighorn Country Outfitters	Box 7524, Yellowtail, MT 59035	406-666-2326

Wyoming

Just Gone Fishing	PO Box 655, Buffalo, WY 82834	307-684-2755
Sports Lure	66 S. Main, Buffalo, WY 82834	307-684-7682
Ugly Bug Fly Shop	316 W. Midwest, Casper, WY 82601	307-234-6905
Dean's Sporting Goods	260 S. Center St., Casper, WY 82601-2524	307-234-2788
Fantasy Fly Co.	1321 N. Buck Creek Rd., Casper, WY 82604	307-265-5601
Platte River Fly Shop	7400 Hwy. 220, Casper, WY 82604-9229	307-237-5997
Sportsmen's Outlet	2115 E. Lincolnway, Cheyenne, WY 82001-5130	307-632-4868
Southside Tackle	605 S. Greely Hwy., Cheyenne, WY 82007	307-635-4348
Aune's Absaroka Angler	754 Yellowstone Ave., #A, Cody, WY 82414	307-587-5105
North Fork Anglers	1107 Sheridan Ave., Cody, WY 82414	307-527-7274
Whiskey Mountain Tackle	102 W.Ramshorn St., Dubois, WY 82513	307-455-2587
IGA Sports World	524 Front St., Evanston, WY 82930	307-789-6788
Spoke & Edge Sports	201 S. Gillette Ave., Gillette, WY 82716	307-682-9343
Green River Bait	2120 Grant Circle, Green River, WY 82935	307-875-5989
Highland Desert Flies	1700 Wilson St., # 39, Green River, WY 82935	307-875-2358
Outfitters of Green River	100 E. 2nd South, Green River, WY 82935	307-875-8700
Wind River Sporting Goods	420 Uinta Dr., Green River, WY 82935	307-875-4075
Wyoming Custom Tackle, Inc.	134 Hwy. 20 South, Greybull, WY 82426	307-765-4662
White Water Snake River Park	9705 S. Hwy. 89, Jackson Hole, WY 83001	307-733-1573
Orvis Jackson Hole	PO Box 9029, Jackson Hole, WY 83002	307-733-5407
High Country Flies	PO Box 3432, Jackson, WY 83001	307-733-7210
Jack Dennis Fly Fishing	PO Box 3369, Jackson, WY 83001	307-733-3270
Unique Outdoor Enterprises, In	155 W. Main St., Lander, WY 82520	307-332-3158
Sweetwater Fishing Expeditions	PO Box 524, Lander, WY 82520-0524	307-332-3986
Four Seasons Anglers	334 Fillmore St., Laramie, WY 82070	307-721-4047
Jim's Custom Rods	1932 Sheridan, Laramie, WY 82070	307-754-3789
West Laramie Fly Store	1657 Snowy Range Road, Laramie, WY 82070	307-745-5425
Snake River Angler	10 Moose St., Moose, WY 83012	307-733-3699
Grande Teton Lodge	PO Box 250, Moran, WY 83013-0250	866-646-0388
Ft. William Guest Ranch Lodge	PO Box 1588, Pinedale, WY 82941	307-367-4670
Great Outdoor Shop	332 West Pine St.POB 787, Pinedale, WY 82941	307-367-2440
Two Rivers Emporium, LLC	PO Box 1218, Pinedale, WY 82941	800-329-4353

Rocky Mountain Discount Sports	709 N. Federal Blvd., Riverton, WY 82501	307-856-7687
Gart Brothers Sporting Goods	1371 Dewar Drive, Rock Springs, WY 82901	307-362-4208
Walker's Wholesale	315 Gale St., Rock Springs, WY 82901-6426	307-382-2580
Rock Creek Anglers	HF Bar Ranch, Saddlestring, WY 82840	307-684-7304
Great Rocky Mountain Outfitter	PO Box 1677, Saratoga, WY 82331	307-326-8750
Hack's Tackle & Outfitters	Box 1225, Saratoga, WY 82331	307-326-9823
Old Baldy Club Fly Shop	PO Box 707, Saratoga, WY 82331	307-326-5222
Platte Valley Outfitters	PO Box 900, Saratoga, WY 82331	307-326-5750
Big Horn Mountain Sports	334 N. Main St., Sheridan, WY 82801	307-672-6866
Fly Shop of the Big Horns	227 N. Main, Sheridan, WY 82801	307-672-5866
Dave's Custom Shop	308 E. 2nd St., Sheridan, WY 82801-3715	307-674-4070
Westbank Anglers	PO Box 523, Teton Village, WY 83025	800-922-3474
Hitching Rail	300 Main St., Thayne, WY 83127	307-883-2302
Teton Troutfitters	Hwy 89 Hoback Jct., Wilson, WY 83014	307-733-5362
Crescent H Ranch	PO Box 347, Wilson, WY 83014-0347	307-733-3674
Bressler Outfitters	PO Box 766, Wilson, WY 83014-0766	307-733-4812
The Bearlodge Angler	612 Grace Ave., Worland, WY 82401	888-226-9258
The Outdoorsman	632 Big Horn Ave, Worland, WY 82401	307-347-2891

Sources of Information

Idaho

Idaho Fish and Game Offices
Headquarters
600 S. Walnut
P.O. Box 25
Boise, ID 83707
208-334-3700

Panhandle Region
2750 Kathleen Avenue
Coeur d'Alene, ID 83815
208-769-1414

Clearwater Region
1540 Warner Avenue
Lewiston, ID 83501
208-799-5010

Southwest Region
3101 S. Powerline Road
Nampa, ID 83686
208-465-8465

McCall
555 Deinhard Lane
McCall, ID 83638
208-634-8137

Southeast Region
1345 Barton Road
Pocatello, ID 83204
208-232-4703

Upper Snake Region
1515 Lincoln Road
Idaho Falls, ID 83401
208-525-7290

Salmon Region
99 Highway 93 North
P.O. Box 1336
Salmon, ID 83467
208-756-2271

Idaho hunting/fishing info, regulations
and nonresident applications
1-800-635-7820

License and tag sales -
Visa, MasterCard, American Express,
Discover
1-800-554-8685

Idaho Fish & Wildlife Foundation
http://www.ifwf.org

Citizens Against Poaching
http://www2.state.id.us/fishgame/Us/
Enforcement/cap.htm

Report a Poacher (Idaho)
1-800-632-5999

Ask Fish (Fishing reports)
1-800-ASK-FISH

Public Lands Information Center
(USFS / BLM maps)
www.publiclands.org/mapcenter

Idaho River Flow Information
(Mar. - Oct.)
1-208-327-7865

U.S. Bureau of Reclamation Reservoir
and Stream Conditions
1-208-334-9134

USGS Stream Flows Information
wwwidaho.wr.usgs.gov/
rt-cgi/gen_tbl_pg

Idaho Road Conditions
www2.state.id.us/itd/
ida-road/index.html

National Interagency Fire Center
www.nifc.gov/information.html

BLM Field Offices
 Coeur d'Alene
 1808 N. Third Street
 Coeur d'Alene, ID 83814
 208-769-5030

 Cottonwood
 House 1, Butte Drive
 Route 3, Box 181,
 Cottonwood, ID 83522
 208-962-3245

 Challis
 801 Blue Mountain Road
 Challis, ID 83226
 208-879-6200

Salmon
50 Highway 93 South
Salmon, ID 83467
208-756-5400

Idaho Falls
1405 Hollipark Dr.
Idaho Falls, ID 83401
208-524-7500

Burley
15 East 200 South
Burley, ID 83318
208-677-6641

Shoshone
400 West F Street
P.O. Box 2-B
Shoshone, ID 83352
208-732-7200

Pocatello
1111 N. 8th Avenue
Pocatello, ID83201
208-478-6340

Malad
138 S. Main
Malad City, ID 83252
208-766-4766

Four Rivers/Owyhee
3948 Development Ave.
Boise, ID 83705
208-384-3300

Jarbidge
2620 Kimberly Road
Twin Falls, ID83301
208-736-2350

National Forests

Idaho Panhandle
1201 Ironwood Dr.
Coeur d'Alene, ID 83544
208-765-7223

Clearwater National Forest
12730 Hwy. 12
Orofino, ID 83544
208-476-4541

Nez Perce National Forest
E. US 13, Rt. 2
P.O. Box 475
Grangeville, ID 83530
208-983-1950

Payette National Forest
106 W. Park St.
P.O. Box 1026
McCall, ID 83638
208-634-8151

Boise National Forest
1750 Front St.
Boise, ID 83702
208-364-4100

Sawtooth National Forest
2647 Kimberly Rd.
Twin Falls, ID 83301
208-737-3200

Challis National Forest
US 93 North
H/C 63 Box 1671
Challis, ID 83226
208-879-2285

Salmon National Forest
US 93 North
P.O. Box 729
Salmon, ID 83467
208-756-2215

Targhee National Forest
420 N. Bridge St.
P.O. Box 208
St. Anthony, ID 83445
208-624-3151

Caribou National Forest
Federal Building, Suite 294
250 South Fourth Ave.
Pocatello, ID 83201
208-236-7500

Sawtooth National Recreation Area
Star Route
Ketchum, ID 83340
208-726-7672

Indian Reservations

Fort Hall Reservation
Fort Hall Hunting and Fishing Dept.
208-238-3808

Duck Valley Reservation
Tribal Fish and Game Office
702-757-2921

Nez Perce Reservation
Nez Perce Tribe
208-843-2383

State and Federal Agencies
State Fish and Game Agencies
www.state.id.us/fishgame/
agencies.htm

Idaho Outfitters and Guides
www.state.id.us/oglb/oglbhome.htm

Idaho Dept. Parks and Recreation
www.IDOC.state.id.us/StateParks/
spdir.html

Sportsman Organizations
Idaho Fish and Wildlife Foundation
www.idfishhunt.com/~IFWF

Idaho Wildlife Federation
www.idahowildlife.org

Trout Unlimited (Idaho Council)
www.idfishnhunt.com/tutedt.htm

Idaho Bass Anglers Sportsman
 Society
www.idfishnhunt.com/idahobass.
html

Idaho Steelhead and Salmon United
www.idfishnhunt.com/issu.html

Idaho Rivers United
www.desktop.org/iru

Montana

Montana Fish, Wildlife and Parks
Headquarters
Montana Fish, Wildlife & Parks
1420 East Sixth Avenue
P.O. Box 200701
Helena, MT 59620-0701
406-444-2535

Region 1
490 North Meridian Road
Kalispell, MT 59901
406-752-5501

Region 2
3201 Spurgin Road
Missoula, MT 59804
406-542-5500

Region 3
1400 South 19th
Bozeman, MT 59718
406-994-4042

Region 4
4600 Giant Springs Road
Great Falls, MT 59405
406-454-5840

Region 5
2300 Lake Elmo Drive
Billings, MT 59105
406-247-2940

Region 6
Route 1-4210
Glasgow, MT 59230
406-228-3700

Region 7
P.O. Box 1630
Miles City, MT 59301
406-232-0900

BLM Offices
Montana/Dakotas
5001 Southgate Drive
P.O. Box 36800
Billings, MT 59107
406-896-5000

Butte
106 N. Parkmont
P.O. Box 3388
Butte, MT 59702
406 533-7629

Dillon
1005 Selway Dr.
Dillon, MT 59725-9431
406 683-8023

Glasgow
RR 1-4775
Glasgow, MT 59230-9796
406 228-3757

Great Falls
RR 1-4775
Glasgow, MT 59230-9796
406 228-3757

Havre
W. 1704 Highway 2
Drawer 911 Havre, MT 59501-0911
406 262-5891

Lewistown
Airport Road
P.O. Box 1160
Lewistown, MT 59457-1160
406-538-1945

Malta
501 S. 2nd Street E.
HC 65 Box 5000
Malta, MT 59538-0047
406-654-5113

Miles City
111 Garryowen Road
Miles City MT 59301-0940
406-233-2827

Missoula
3255 F. Missoula Road
Missoula, MT 59804-7293
406-329-3717

National Forests
Northern Region Headquarters
3255 F. Missoula Road
Missoula, MT 59804-7293
406-329-3717

Beaverhead-Deerlodge
National Forest
420 Barrett St.
Dillon, MT 59725-3572
406-683-3900

Bitterroot National Forest
1801 N. First
Hamilton, MT 59840-3114
406-363-7100

Custer National Forest
1310 Main Street
Billings, MT 59105
406-657-6200

Flathead National Forest
1935 3rd Ave. E.
Kalispell, MT 59901
406-758-5200

Gallatin National Forest
P.O. Box 130
Bozeman, MT 59771
406-587-6701

Helena National Forest
2880 Skyway Dr.
Helena, MT 59601
406-449-5201

Kootenai National Forest
1101 Highway 2 West
Libby, MT 59923
406-293-6211

Lewis and Clark National Forest
1101 15th St. N.
Great Falls, MT 59401
406-791-7700

Lolo National Forest
Fort Missoula Bldg. 24
Missoula, MT 59804
406-329-3750

National Parks
Glacier National Park
P.O. Box 128
West Glacier, MT 59936-0128
406-888-7800

Yellowstone National Park
P.O. Box 168
Mammoth, WY 82190-0168
307-344-7381

River Flow Data
www.waterdata.usgs.gov/mt.

Montana Road Information
www.mdt.state.mt.us/travinfo

Travel Montana
www.visitmt.gov

Poacher Hotline
1-800-TIP-MONT

Outfitters and Guides Associations
Fishing Outfitters Association of
Montana (FOAM)
Box 67
Gallatin Gateway, MT 59730
406-763-5436

Montana Outfitters and Guides
Association (MOGA)
P.O. Box 1248
Helena, MT 59624
406-449-3578

Indian Reservations
Blackfeet Nation
P.O. Box 850
Browning, MT 59417
406-338-7276

Flathead Reservation
Confederated Salish &
Kootenai Tribes
P.O. Box 278
Pablo, MT 59885
406-675-2700

Crow Reservation
Crow Agency, MT 59022
406-638-2601

Fort Belknap Tourism Office
R.R. 1, Box 66
Fort Belknap Agency
Harlem, MT 59526
406-353-2205

Fort Peck
Assiniboine and Sioux Tribes
P.O. Box 1027
Poplar, MT 59255
406-768-5155

Northern Cheyenne Chamber of
Commerce
P.O. Box 328
Lame Deer, MT 59043
406-477-6253

Rocky Boy
Chippewa-Cree Business Committee
Box 544, Rocky Boy Route
Box Elder, MT 59521
406-395-4282

Sportsman and Conservation Organizations
American Fisheries Society-MT
Chapter
www.fisheries.org/AFSmontana

Montana Trout Unlimited
www.montanatu.org

Federation Flyfishers
www.fedflyfishers.org

Missouri River Flyfishers
www.mrffish.net

Wyoming

Wyoming Game and Fish Department
Headquarters
5400 Bishop Blvd
Cheyenne, WY 82006
307-777-7014

Region 1
360 N. Cache
Jackson, WY 83001
307-733-2321

Pinedale
117 S. Sublette Ave.
Pinedale, WY 82941
307-367-4353

Region 2
2820 Hwy. 120
Cody, WY 82414
307-527-7125

Region 3
700 Valley View Dr.
Sheridan, WY 82801
307-672-7418

Region 7
3030 Energy Lane
Casper, WY 82604
307-473-3400

BLM Offices

Casper
1701 East E St.
Casper, WY 82601
307-261-7600

National Forests

Bridger-Teton National Forest
350 N. Cache St.
P.O. Box 1888
Jackson, WY 83001
307-733-2752

Bighorn National Forest
1969 S. Sheridan Ave.
Sheridan, WY 82801
307-672-0751

Shoshone National Forest
808 Meadow Ln.
Cody, WY 82414
307-527-6241

National Parks

Grand Teton National Park
P.O. Drawer 170
Moose, WY 83012
307-739-3300
307-739-3399 (Visitor Info)

Yellowstone National Park
P.O. Box 168
Yellowstone National Park, WY
82190-0168
307-344-7381; 307-344-2386

Indian Reservations

Shoshone-Arapahoe Game & Fish
Wind River Indian Reservation
P.O. 217
Fort Washakie, WY 82514
307-332-7207

Wyoming Tourism
1-800-225-5996

Wyoming Travel
1-800-225-5996

Wyoming Outfitters Association
Box 2284
Cody, WY 82414
307-527-7453

River Flow Data
www.waterdata.usgs.gov/wy

Wyoming Trout Unlimited
Kathy Buchner
P.O. Box 4069
Jackson, WY 83001
307-733-6991

Wyoming Fly Casters
P.O. Box 2881
Casper, WY 82602

Federal Agencies

US Forest Service
www.fs.fed.us

Bureau of Land Management
www.blm.gov

US Fish and Wildlife Service
www.fws.gov

US Fish and Wildlife-Pacific Region
www.r1.fws.gov

Chambers of Commerce

Idaho

Boise Metro
250 S 5th Street #800
P.O. Box 2368
Boise, ID 83701
208-472-5200

Salmon-Challis
P.O. Box 1130
7th & Main Street
Challis, ID 83226
208-879-2771

Coeur d'Alene Area
1621 N Third Street
P.O. Box 850
Coeur d'Alene, ID 83816
208-443-3191
888-774-3785

Hailey
157 W. Hayden Ave.
Suite 103
Hayden, Idaho 83835
208-762-1185

Greater Idaho Falls
505 Lindsay Blvd.
P.O. Box 50498
Idaho Falls, ID 83405
208-523-1010

Mountain Home
205 N. 3rd E.
Mountain Home, ID 83647
208-587-4334

Pierce
P.O. Box 416
Pierce, ID 83546
1-866-665-9736

Saint Maries
906 Main Ave.
P.O. Box 162
Saint Maries, ID 83861
208-245-3563

Salmon Valley
200 Main Street #1
Salmon, ID 83467
208-756-2100

Stanley-Sawtooth
21 Community Building
P.O. Box 8
Stanley, ID 83278
208-774-3411
1-800-878-7950

Montana

Anaconda
306 E. Park Street
Anaconda, MT 59711
406-563-2400

Big Timber
Exit 367
P.O. Box 1012
Big Timber, MT 59011
406-932-5131

Billings
815 S. 27th St.
Billings, MT 59101
406-245-4111

Bitterroot Valley
105 E. Main
Hamilton, MT 59840
406-363-2400

Bozeman
2000 Commerce Way
Bozeman, MT 59715
406-586-5421
1-800-228-4224

Butte
1000 George
Butte, MT 59701
406-723-3177
1-800-735-6814

Beaverhead County
125 S. Montana
P.O. Box 425
Dillon, MT 59725
406-683-5511

East Glacier
Hwy. 49 North
P.O. Box 260
East Glacier, MT 59434
406-226-4403

Ennis
P.O. Box 291
Ennis, MT 59729
406-682-4388

Eureka Area
P.O. Box 186
Eureka, MT 59917
406-297-7800

Gardiner
P.O. Box 81
Gardiner, MT 59030
406-848-7971

Glasgow
740 E. Hwy. 2
Glasgow, MT 59230
Phone 406-228-2222

Great Falls Area
P.O. Box 2127
Great Falls, MT 59403
406-761-4434

Hardin
21 E. 4th Street
Hardin, MT 59034
406-665-1672

Havre
518 1st Street
P.O. Box 308
Havre, MT 59501
406-265-4383

Helena
225 Cruse Ave
Helena, MT 59601
406-442-4120
1-800-743-5362

Kalispell
15 Depot Park
Kalispell, MT 59901
406-758-2800

Lewistown Area
408 N.E. Main
P.O. Box 818
Lewistown, MT 59457
406-538-5436

Kalispell
15 Depot Park
Kalispell, MT 59901
406-758-2800

Lewistown Area
408 N.E. Main
P.O. Box 818
Lewistown, MT 59457
406-538-5436

Libby
905 W 9th St.
P.O. Box 704
Libby, MT 59923
406-293-4167

Lincoln Valley
P.O. Box 985
Lincoln, MT 59639
406-362-4949

Livingston
303 E. Park Street
Livingston, MT 59047
406-222-0850

Malta
10½ S. 4E
Malta, MT 59538
406-654-1776

Missoula
P.O. Box 7577
Missoula, MT 59807
406-543-6623

Philipsburg
P.O. Box 661
Philipsburg, MT 59858
406-859-3388

Red Lodge
601 N. Broadway
Red Lodge, MT 59068
406-446-1718

Seeley Lake
P.O. Box 516
Seeley Lake, MT 59868
406-677-2880

Thompson Falls
P.O. Box 493
Thompson Falls, MT
406-827-4930

Three Forks
P.O. Box 1103
Three Forks, MT 59752
406-285-4880

Townsend
P.O. Box 947
Townsend, MT 59644
406-266-4101

Virginia City
P.O. Box 218
Virginia City, MT 59755

West Yellowstone
30 Yellowstone Ave.
P.O. Box 458
West Yellowstone, MT 59758
406-646-7701

Whitefish
6475 Hwy. 93 S.
P.O. Box 1120
Whitefish, MT 59937
406-862-3501

Wyoming

Casper
500 N. Center
P.O. Box 399
Casper, WY 82602
307-234-5311

Cody Country
836 Sheridan Ave.
Cody, WY 82414
307-587-2777

Jackson Hole
990 W. Broadway
P.O. Box 550
Jackson, WY 83001
307-733-3316

Lovell
287 E. Main
P.O. Box 295
Lovell, WY 82431
307-548-7552

Pinedale
32 E. Pine St.
P.O. Box 176
Pinedale, WY 82941

Sheridan
P.O. Box 707
Sheridan WY 82801
307-672-2485
1-800-453-3650

Thermopolis
119 S. 6th St.
Thermopolis, WY 82443
307-864-3192

Worland
120 N. 10th St.
Worland, WY 82401
307-347-3226

INDEX

FISHING DIARY

The next pages will provide a space

to collect your thoughts after a day on the

water. The "useful symbols" are meant to

aid in quickly logging key features and

events, while the "notes" section allows

ample room for any additional

information. Keeping an accurate diary

will take the guess work out of a repeat

visit and, in turn, make you a better angler.

Good Luck!

-Wilderness Adventures Press, Inc.

FLY FISHING DIARY

Date	Water Fished	Conditions		Fish Caught
		Weather	Water	
Useful Symbols	HD-Headwater CF-Confluence MO-Mouth ↑-Upstream ↓-Downstream	S-Sunny C-Cloudy R-Rain SN-Snow WY-Windy	CL-Clear OC-Off Color N-Normal (Flow) HI-High LO-Low	RB-Rainbow BN-Brown BT-Bull BR-Brook CT-Cutthroat ST-Steelhead MW-Mtn.Whitefish LB/SB- Large & Smallmouth Bass

Hatch Observed	Notes (i.e. time of day, flies used, fishing pressure)	Pg. #

BAT- Callibaetis spp BWO-Blue-winged Olive PMD-Pale Morning Dun MFY-Mayfly DF-Damselfly LC-Leech
CAD-Caddis TRC-Trico MDG-Midge STN-Stonefly HOP-Grasshopper SN-Sculpins EMG-Emerger SF-Spinner Fall
TW-Tailwater SC-Spring Creek FS-Freestone PW-Pocket Water CB-Cutbank

NOTES

NOTES

NOTES

FLY FISHING GUIDE SERIES

If you would like to order additional copies of this book or our other Wilderness Adventures Press guidebooks, please fill out the order form below or call **1-800-925-3339** or **fax 800-390-7558.** Visit our website for a listing of over 2000 sporting books — the largest online: **www.wildadv.com**   *Mail To:*

Wilderness Adventures Press, Inc., 45 Buckskin Road • Belgrade, MT 59714

☐ **Please send me your quarterly catalog on hunting and fishing books.**

Ship to:
Name _____

Address _____

City _____ State_____ Zip_____

Home Phone_____Work Phone_____
Payment: ☐ Check ☐ Visa ☐ Mastercard ☐ Discover ☐ America Express
Card Number _____Expiration Date_____

Signature_____

QTY.	*Tilte of Book*	*Price*	*Total*
	Flyfisher's Guide to Alaska	$32.95	
	Flyfisher's Guide to Chesapeake Bay	$28.95	
	Flyfisher's Guide to Colorado	$28.95	
	Flyfisher's Guide to Freshwater Florida	$28.95	
	Flyfisher's Guide to the Florida Keys	$28.95	
	Flyfisher's Guide to Idaho	$28.95	
	Flyfisher's Guide to Montana	$26.95	
	Flyfisher's Guide to Michigan	$26.95	
	Flyfisher's Guide to Minnesota	$26.95	
	Flyfisher's Guide to New York	$28.95	
	Flyfisher's Guide to Northern California	$26.95	
	Flyfisher's Guide to Northern New England	$28.95	
	Flyfisher's Guide to Oregon	$28.95	
	Flyfisher's Guide to Pennsylvania	$28.95	
	Flyfisher's Guide to Texas	$28.95	
	Flyfisher's Guide to Utah	$28.95	
	Flyfisher's Guide to the Virginias	$28.95	
	Flyfisher's Guide to Washington	$28.95	
	Flyfisher's Guide to Wisconsin	$28.95	
	Flyfisher's Guide to Wyoming	$28.95	
	Saltwater Angler's Guide to the Southeast	$26.95	
	Saltwater Angler's Guide to Southern California	$26.95	
	On the Fly Guide to the Northwest	$26.95	
	On the Fly Guide to the Northern Rockies	$26.95	
	Total Order + shipping & handling		

Shipping and handling: $4.99 for first book,
$3.00 per additional book, up to $13.99 maximum